being human

unofficial and unauthorised

joanne black

CLASSIC
TV PRESS

D0317882

First published in England in December 2010 by

Classic TV Press

103 High Street, Cherry Hinton, Cambridge, CB1 9LU, England

e: classictvpress@live.co.uk

w: http://www.classictvpress.co.uk/

ISBN: 978-0-9561000-3-0 (paperback)

being human: unofficial and unauthorised © 2010 Joanne Black

Illustrations © 2010 Chris Wreford

Internal design and layout by Classic TV Press

Printed and bound in Great Britain by
CPI Antony Rowe, Chippenham and Eastbourne

1 2 3 4 5 6 7 8 9 10 11 12 13 14 15

British Library Cataloguing in Publication Data

A catalogue record for this book is available from the British Library

being human

unofficial and unauthorised

Acknowledgements

Heartfelt thanks go to...

Mum and Suzanne – for thinking that what I do is mostly quite normal...

Nana – for passing on the writing bug

Andy and Marisa – for opportunity, encouragement and semicolons

Claire – for laughter and Lemon Fanta

Chris Wreford – for the drawings I had in my head but which were a million miles from my pen and paper

Contents

1

in the
beginning...

The birth of Being Human

"So... a werewolf, a ghost and a vampire decide to live as humans do. They get jobs, a house and a TV licence"

Herrick summed it up quite neatly in the last episode of series one, but what about the journey that took *Being Human* to that point? (And who actually went and bought that TV licence? I bet it was George!)

Being Human first existed as a non-supernatural drama. Developed by Toby Whithouse for Touchpaper (an independent production company founded in 2001 by Rob Pursey, the eventual Executive Producer on both series of *Being Human*), the original version was a flat-sharing drama about three university friends. Toby confided in the BBC's online *Writers Room* in March 2010 that it was one of the dullest ideas he'd ever heard! Despite this the three lead characters came to him fully formed, it all seemed to fall neatly into place and a year was spent getting absolutely nowhere.

At the last meeting before packing the idea away in the 'could have been good' box, Toby had a thought: "Well of course we could turn George into a werewolf," and so *Being Human* was conceived. After that, the notion of a vampire and a ghost made perfect sense. The first version of the show was a 'proper' sit-com where Mitchell worked in a call centre and George had his own company; even Annie had a job in an office.

Of course, the idea of making George into a werewolf had to have come from somewhere and Toby let slip a secret to Jason Arnopp's screenwriting blog *Bloggery Pokery* in May 2008. Apparently he'd been working on a rom-com about a werewolf, called (and he did say he cringed at this point) *Mild Thing...*

When the BBC asked if he wanted to be involved in a series of pilots for BBC Three he was initially reluctant, but it was an opportunity to actually get his idea made (*Being Human* that is, not *Mild Thing*). So a re-rewritten version of the show was submitted and *Being Human* as we know it was born.

So... who is Toby Whithouse?

Toby Whithouse, the creator and writer of *Being Human*, aside from being a writer is also an actor and a stand-up comedian – and has possibly worked out how to have more than 24 hours in a day! He started writing when 'resting' between acting jobs and partly as a reaction to the quality of scripts he was reading, convinced that he could do better.

As an actor he was a regular on TV in *The House of Eliott* between 1992-4, playing Norman Foss who married seamstress Tilly Watkins (Cathy Murphy). He also appeared in shows such as *Goodnight Mr Tom* (1998), *Goodnight Sweetheart* (in 1999), *The Last Musketeer* (2000) and *Holby City* (in 2000 and 2004), and in several films, including *Bridget Jones's Diary* (2001), *Breathtaking* (2000) and *Shadowlands* (1993).

His first play (what he wrote), *Jump Mr Malinoff, Jump*, won the 1998 Verity Bargate Award and, directed by Jonathan Lloyd, was the opening production for Soho Theatre's launch season in April 2000. The Soho Theatre also put on Toby's 2005 play *Blue Eyes and Heels*, which starred Martin

3

Freeman and John Stahl (Coroner Quinn in *Being Human*).

Toby's TV writing credits include: *Where the Heart Is: Letting Go* (1999); *Hotel Babylon: Episode 1.5* (2006), in which he also made a cameo appearance; *Torchwood: Greeks Bearing Gifts* (2006); and *Comedy Showcase: Other People* (2007), which again starred Martin Freeman. Channel 4 commissioned him to develop a new drama and Toby devised a tale of four nurses based in Leeds. *No Angels* ran for 26 episodes from 2004-6, eight of which were written by Toby, who also popped up as a waiter in the final episode.

He was invited to contribute to *Doctor Who* and wrote the episode *School Reunion* (2006), which reintroduced 1970s companions Sarah Jane Smith and K9. He talked about the challenges involved to the *Radio Times* in May 2006: "Until I started working on *Doctor Who*, I thought the fact that I could name the Doctors in order made me a sad anorak. But when I met [fellow writers] Matt Jones, Steven Moffat and Tom MacRae, I realised I was paddling in the shallow end." Despite this, the episode was a great success and Toby returned to *Doctor Who* in 2010, writing *The Vampires of Venice* which starred Alex Price (Gilbert in *Being Human*) as Francesco Calvierri.

Toby gave an extensive and fascinating interview to the BBC *Writers Room* in March 2010 in which he talked about how he writes, about *Being Human* – lots of really interesting material. One quote that still amuses me every time I see it is this one: "Occasionally I'll get a phone call from my Script Editor saying 'Such-and-such isn't sure about this line.' 'Isn't he? Oh. He's not sure if he'd say that? I think he does. It's in the script.'"

BBC Three Drama Pilots

Danny Cohen, the Controller of BBC Three, announced a new look to the channel to take effect in February 2008. He said that: "The channel should be obsessed with all things new – new talent, new programmes and a new relationship between television and the internet. So, in February, BBC Three will be transformed – and I hope will become known for being Britain's most ambitious attempt to combine television and the web."

Looking for a target audience in the age range 16-34, the week after the relaunch (and the week that saw the *Being Human* pilot aired) certainly delivered. BBC Three recorded its second highest weekly share of 4.5% and the highest ever weekly reach for the target 16-34 group of 4.7 million or 36.6%. Danny Cohen said: "I hope we will continue this excellent young audience growth over the next year or so, and take lots of risks along the way."

Part of the BBC Three relaunch was a series of six very different drama pilots, billed as youthful and fresh – a new generation of drama. The pilots were:

Phoo Action – a kitsch kung-fu drama co-written by *Spaced*'s Jessica Hynes, starring Ray Winstone's daughter, Jaime, as a high-kicking futuristic crime fighter

The Things I Haven't Told You – a mystery drama about a group of teenagers whose lives get extremely complicated when one is involved in a car crash. The cast included Lenora Crichlow (Annie in *Being Human*)

4

West 10 LDN – written by and starring Noel Clarke, delving into the intense and passionate lives of the teenagers who live on West London's Greenside estate

Dis/Connected – a group of disconnected teenagers from very different backgrounds are thrown together after the suicide of a mutual friend, forcing them to examine who they really are

Mrs In-Betweeny – a darkly comic look at modern British family life in all its guises. The Winslow kids' parents are dead; Uncle Brendan arrives to make it all better – but now he's 'Aunt' Emma...

And – of course – the pilot episode of Toby Whithouse's *Being Human*, described in the BBC Three press release as the story of a house share with a difference; a tale of three twenty-somethings, each of them outsiders with unusual afflictions: one is a vampire, one a werewolf and one a ghost.

> *Mitchell is a hospital cleaner. He's good-looking, laid-back and a hit with the ladies, but also something of a blood-sucker. George works in the same hospital as a porter. He's an awkward but loveable geek who, every full moon, sprouts a snout and grows a very hairy back.*

> *Having had enough of sleeping in hostels and temporary accommodation, Mitchell and George decide to get a house together. They just want to have a go at being normal; being human. But, as soon as they move in, they discover an unwanted lodger – Annie – a ghost with a distinct lack of self-esteem.*

Rob Pursey of Touchpaper described it as being "a warm, funny, aspirational drama with an irresistible twist. Mitchell, George and Annie are supernatural creatures but they are desperate to be a part of a life we all take for granted. It's an exciting and contemporary take on friendship and finding your way in the world. Toby Whithouse's witty, emotionally powerful script makes these three misfits come alive, even though they're far from human."

Of course we all know now how it turned out and *Being Human* was a huge success for BBC Three, but try and look at that list as if you've never seen it before. Which was the least likely to fit the new revamped 16- to 34-year-old BBC Three? Well, if I'm honest it would have to be *Being Human*... Where would you put your money? *Phoo Action* looks a decent bet – good cast, good writers and based on characters created by Jamie Hewlett (*Gorillaz, Tank Girl*) for the comic strip *Get the Freebies*, which first appeared in *The Face* magazine.

There was never any pretence that this was a publicity contest and there was no public vote. After all, the BBC have droves of very clever people who know about these things – or at any rate that's what they tell us! In fact, a full series of *Phoo Action* had already been commissioned before any of the pilots went out (although this wasn't widely advertised at the time). Despite this, all of the pilots were promoted reasonably equally by BBC Three.

The *Being Human* pilot was billed by BBC Three as a "witty, exciting, sexy and extraordinary look at the friendship between three, twenty-something outsiders." The comedy angle is well to the fore and the supernatural elements are presented in a humorous way – the press releases don't portray the darkness that is such an important counterpoint to the humour and the reality, and maybe that delayed the audience response, with many more viewers coming to the pilot after seeing the initial reaction.

It is interesting now to revisit the original interviews with Russell Tovey and the first incarnations of Mitchell and Annie – Guy Flanagan and Andrea Riseborough – about their characters and reactions to the show. Comparing what was said then to what we now know about the characters after two full series of *Being Human*, there are some differences and some constants – rather like life, it never goes quite as you planned...

As always, Russell was asked about the nudity and werewolf transformations, but in the *Being Human* Press Pack he talked about George's back-story:

> "George is around 26 years old; he is an academic; he's really bright with an IQ of 156. He was studying for his finals at university and was going to marry his fiancé. Everything was going well for him until he went on a recce to Mexico to find a wedding venue. Whilst he was there, he was attacked by a werewolf. When he came back, the transformations started to happen and he had no idea what was happening to him, so he had to get away. He slept rough on the streets and became suicidal. George was in a bar one night, about to be attacked by a group of vampires, when Mitchell stepped in and saved him. Ever since, George has been in debt to him."

The bones of George's story didn't change that much, just the details – the werewolf attack moved to Scotland (can't imagine Tully in a sombrero) and the vampire attack to a café where George was working. Russell seemed to have already 'found' George – the agony of the transformation, the curse, the sense of loss and the desperate, burning desire for normality.

As Guy Flanagan said at the time: "Who wouldn't want to be a vampire? I get to be invincible and bite beautiful people, what more could you want? It's a hard job, but someone has to do it!" The vampires in the pilot were much more gothic and Guy had taken this from the script, his research therefore went back to the films he had seen and the classic book Bram Stoker's *Dracula*. Some aspects of Mitchell were there from the beginning – he is described as laid-back, with an emotional coolness coming from his 120 years of existence. Despite this he has a respect for humans and a desire to be in their company. An interesting comment from Guy was that "He can't fall in love or experience the same love as normal people." In light of Mitchell's search for true love and his relationships with Josie and Lucy, this shows how the detachment, the languid watchfulness of Mitchell had to change after the pilot to make the character less of a spectator.

There's a nice remark about what was the standout scene for Guy – he chose the sex scene with Mitchell and Lauren, when Lauren is recruited. Not for any of the obvious reasons, but because it was filmed on the day of the Rugby World Cup Final – and they were running late! It was his first TV sex scene and he expected it to take some time, but "with 20 minutes to do the scene, I was thrown in at the deep end and all the electricians were threatening to pull the plugs if we didn't get it done because they didn't want to miss the final!"

In common with Russell and Guy, Andrea Riseborough was attracted to *Being Human* and the role of Annie by the quality of the writing, but for her it was also the opportunity to work with Russell who she had long admired. Her take on Annie was informed by the back-story she had been given – she saw her as "a young ghost-next-door. I decided that she might come from Barnsley – so I gave her that accent. She's a sweet, yet pushy, young woman who was engaged to be married." Andrea focused more on agoraphobia and self-esteem in her portrayal of Annie rather than just seeing her as a ghost. She could see the feelings of invisibility that are universal and human. Interestingly, Andrea saw an attraction between Mitchell and Annie: "Mitchell is so accommodating, wise and old; I think she becomes emotionally attached to him in a romantic way and starts to admire him."

In the pilot, Annie is played more for humour and there is less about the darkness that was to come for her as the series progressed. The pilot was portrayed more as a comedy-drama, but as the stories developed, the darkness and the drama became as important if not more so than the comedy – although it was still an essential component.

One lovely comment – when asked if she believes in ghosts, Andrea replied: "I believe in Annie."

So – let's go back to February 2008. It was a Monday, it was cold, and depending on where you lived it might have been raining. I think it's fair to say it was dark, and it was definitely three days from the full moon.

Are you sitting comfortably? Then we'll begin...

being human – the pilot episode

broadcast:	18 FEBRUARY 2008	director:	DECLAN O'DWYER
writer:	TOBY WHITHOUSE	producer:	MATTHEW BOUCH

cast:

Mitchell	GUY FLANAGAN	Seth	DYLAN BROWN
George	RUSSELL TOVEY	Mortuary Attendant	SAIKAT AHAMED
Annie	ANDREA RISEBOROUGH	Neeru	CHARMAINE HIBBERD
Julia	CLAIRE FOY	Cathy	ZARA RAMM
Herrick	ADRIAN LESTER	Rory	HUW DAVIES
Lauren	DOMINIQUE McELLIGOTT	Peter	WILL IRVINE
		Eleanor	NATHALIE ARMIN

"I've got this friend. He says the human condition, human nature, being human, is to be cold and alone"

A young man is in an isolated wood. He looks around and then takes off all of his clothes. Once he is naked he sits on a branch, he's waiting. This looks like a ritual – what is he waiting for?

Another young man, pale, languid, speaks of the human condition and the ancient machinery of the world. Is he alone? He could be talking to himself and he turns coins over and over in his fingers as he speaks.

He's not alone, a woman is there too. We can see the bottles of wine they have shared as she tells him how she and her friends have been talking about him. She tries to describe him, why they find him so intriguing, so very different, and it is as if she is trying to identify another species. He makes a visible effort to engage with her; she has not been listening to his treatise on humanity and she seems to rather bore him. She tells him he looks sad and that his eyes are old, her friends think he is dangerous. This amuses him and he's suddenly much more interested in her.

"Are you dangerous, Mitchell?"

She takes a phone call and as Mitchell watches her, he can hear a heartbeat, blood pumping, and his hands shake and his eyes flash black. He has to control himself, make himself concentrate on who he appears to be. Lauren looks at him but she sees nothing more than a fascinating, unusual man – she's going to bed and the invitation is clear.

In the woods, George is screaming in absolute agony, his body stretching and changing. We cut between Mitchell in bed with Lauren and George in the woods, howling with the pain as he transforms into a wolf – a werewolf. As Mitchell loses all control he too changes into what he truly is. He is a vampire and his fangs sink deep into Lauren's neck, but even as he drinks her blood his face is conflicted – agony or ecstasy?

George wakes up, human again, with the part-eaten carcass of a deer, perched on a rocky ridge with an amazing view of the Clifton Suspension Bridge in the background. Not that he's enjoying the view – he is miles from anywhere, stark naked and covered in blood. So, what now? In contrast,

Mitchell is hiding shamefully in Lauren's bathroom; her body is on the bed, what will he do? This is not the behaviour we would expect of a vampire, he seems regretful and ashamed.

"Stag party!"

George has found a house and conveniently there is a line of early morning washing out. He grabs what he can, to the perplexity of the householder, who can only watch as his grubby buttocks twinkle away. He's dressed in this odd assortment of flowered sheet, culottes and blouse when Mitchell drives up to collect him.

They obviously know each other well but Mitchell seems perennially and terminally sarcastic. "Nice blouse." He hands over a gold Star of David and George's glasses which he has been looking after. George is concerned, Mitchell looks weird, but he brushes away his concern. He's wearing all black, very covered up in sunglasses and hat, but this vampire seems to have no fear of sunlight. No love though... He asks George if it still hurts, obviously knowing exactly what he has been through. Of course it hurts. It's a curse, it's supposed to hurt.

"Come on, Lassie"

Mitchell and George work at the hospital – George as a porter, Mitchell a cleaner – and Mitchell is in the mortuary looking at Lauren's body. Her death has been signed off as a heart attack, tragically young but not suspicious. The coroner must be involved in a cover-up. Mitchell is still with Lauren when the undertakers arrive. When the assistant has left to collect the right paperwork, we see that Seth and Mitchell know each other and this is some sort of system. Mitchell has recruited Lauren, turned her into a vampire, but he's worried he may have been too late. She had to drink his blood but she may have been too close to death – it was not in his plans to drink from her so he wasn't prepared. Seth is a mixture of admiration and disgust. Mitchell clearly had a reputation but hasn't killed for some time, and now that he has, Seth finds the execution masterly. It's not what Mitchell wants to hear and he walks away as Seth asks him about his pet. Is this George, the werewolf? Oh, and Herrick is back – this is probably important!

George, meanwhile, sees a familiar name: his ex-girlfriend is in the hospital. He needs to talk to Mitchell about it and they choose a closed-off bathroom so George can have a very thorough wash. George's buttocks are obviously going to be two of the main stars of the show.

George wants to hide, change his shifts so that Julia won't see him; after all, she thinks he is dead. Well, she might think that, he doesn't really know as he left two years ago when he became a werewolf. Mitchell is concerned about him, how he is hiding from life so that the wolf can't become real. George asks him about Lauren but Mitchell quickly changes the subject.

"I was thinking maybe we could get somewhere, to live"

George is successfully distracted – he is in a hostel so this is a good move for him. Mitchell wants to go on the wagon, give up blood and he needs structure and organisation to do that, although it still won't be easy. Although keen to get a house with Mitchell, doing what everyone else does, George is concerned that by wanting to be normal they are asking for trouble. They aren't normal and don't deserve what other people have. He lost everything two years ago when he became a werewolf – if he opens up to Julia he could lose it all again. Mitchell tells George that the curse he has is not the transformation into the wolf but how it has made him live his life, how it makes him hide. Maybe he is thinking about himself as well.

"Your mum would go mental!"

George takes flowers for Julia's room, thinking he can sneak out again before she wakes up, but he can't. She sees him and knows him straightaway. There's a moment of horror and then she is thrilled – they all thought he had died. They grieved for him and here he is. He tells her he caught something, something old and that he had to leave – it's not much of an explanation but it'll do for now. He has to tell her he's a porter and she is amused and despairing – he has an IQ of 156, his mum will be so proud...

She has moved on, she's engaged but she confesses just how much she loved George, she adored him and missed him so much and the prospect of seeing him again is good. In contrast George has not moved on at all, he is hiding, static and by even starting to consider a life with Julia again he would be less moving on than moving back. His complete and total life change is underlined by Julia's assumption that he must be a doctor.

There's a shrine to Lauren in the hospital and Mitchell is looking at it. George finds him there to talk about the house they can get – or whatever they can afford. He is suddenly concerned about guests and Mitchell realises that he has spoken to Julia and that 'lady-shaped' guests are suddenly on George's mind. He is also very concerned about a cleaning rota and Mitchell promises to buy him highlighter pens.

They go to view a house – a quirky pink house on a corner. Mitchell only wants a sofa for watching TV with beer and pizza, but George is more randomly excited. The estate agent is excusing the "individual décor." The house was a sculptor's studio and the young couple who bought the house to refurbish it didn't get much done before she died. Mitchell tries to be quite downbeat with the agent but George is manically overexcited, running up and down stairs, enthusing about the kitchen and the garden – gorgeous, just gorgeous!!!

The agent assumes they are gay and Mitchell plays up to her, although George doesn't really get what she is on about. Still too busy running happily from room to room. What Mitchell can't understand is why it is empty – the rent is reasonable and they are near the college. The agent tries the "not much sunlight" defence but that's not much of an issue for Mitchell the vampire. OK, she has to admit that previous tenants found it creepy. This doesn't worry them – after all, it'll be creepier with them in it, as George realises!

"Shall I ring the landlord?" "What the hell"

So they move in. George is in his element – cleaning, mopping, hoovering, buying cushions. Mitchell hasn't learnt much mop technique at the hospital but he does make full use of the sofa.

But then odd things start to happen. A raw chicken is pinned on the cupboard and one day they come home to "Get Out" splashed in red paint on the walls. There's a noise upstairs and some genteel wrangling about who should go and investigate. George should, apparently – after all, he's... stocky.

"What could be scarier than one of us?" "A bigger one of us"

Upstairs a woman is sitting in an armchair, completely unconcerned as George approaches with a cricket bat. He speaks to her and she continues to ignore him – it's as if they aren't there. But suddenly she realises that he can see her! Annie is a ghost. She was the woman who died after buying the house with her fiancé. She stayed in the house after she died, although she didn't understand what was happening to her. She saw her grieving relatives go, her fiancé leave and then the tenants started to arrive. It's her house and so she has scared them all away. Mitchell knows what she is and is intrigued by Annie; he realises she is tied to the house, that something unresolved about her life or death is keeping her here and he wants her to stay. George is less keen. He and Annie don't get on, they are abrasive and they clash. He is really fed up; he wanted the house to be something normal and now they have a ghost. A ghost who moves things around and, annoyingly, rearranges his books. Actually, that was Mitchell – George's books are alphabetised, and he couldn't stand it!

"By normal I meant doesn't turn into The Littlest Hobo once a month"

Mitchell is at the hospital, cleaning, when he sees a bag of blood on a trolley. He can't resist picking it up, it calls to him and his eyes go black with longing. He's interrupted though and puts it back before anyone sees. One of the staff is telling him about the maze of old wards and rooms in the basement of the hospital, there's even an abandoned isolation room and Mitchell has an idea.

In the old isolation room, George and Mitchell look around. It would be perfect for the wolf – no one ever goes near it, it's soundproof and the door can only be opened from the outside. After the full moon is over and George has changed back, Mitchell can let him out. He'll be safe, contained and away from anyone he might hurt, it's perfect.

George can hear something, feel that something's wrong – his senses are enhanced by the wolf and he just has to track it down. He finds Julia and her fiancé outside. Peter is threatening her, hurting her and accusing her of being unfaithful, of flirting with every man she meets. George wants to help but Julia warns him off, she's scared for him. George can't walk away though and, without thinking, Julia uses his name and Peter now knows exactly who George is. He thinks he is there to get Julia back and he threatens George and goes to hit him, but George easily overpowers him and holds him down.

"The worst thing, the very worst thing is that it feels so good"

What a shame it is the night before the full moon, he tells him – that is when the monsters appear. He holds him down, talking to him, telling about the monsters and what they can do, about the violence and the death and how it would be so very easy for him to be like that. To kill and to relish the kill. He throws Peter down, warning him that if he touches Julia again then he really will kill him. Julia is terrified, this is a George she has never seen, never dreamed could exist. She remembers quiet and caring George, whatever could he have caught that could make him so savage?

At the house, Mitchell is ironing, pulling a black shirt over a pale and skinny torso. Annie has been making tea... and coffee... and hot chocolate. It makes her feel better – she can't drink it but it is her routine. It will drive George utterly, totally insane. As in all likelihood will Mitchell, as George puts away the iron and the ironing board that Mitchell has abandoned.

Mitchell can't convince either George or Annie to go out with him so he leaves them in the house. They are still uneasy with each other, but there is something that George has to ask her. He wants to know what happened, what she saw when she died. His existence has been so compromised by the werewolf that he has to believe that there is something more, that the life he has is not all there is. She doesn't know what to say and it is clear she can't tell him the truth. She tells him there was light and happiness just like all the films; it was a good place, she just hasn't reached it yet. He turns away and their faces both show how little they believe it can be that simple.

"I'm older than I look"

Mitchell is in a bar being chatted up by an older woman. She is happy to be with him, she doesn't even need him to buy her a drink. She's talking but he doesn't listen, he's concerned about George's view of life, that they are the unblessed. He thought that the house would make them normal but it won't, it can't, inevitably nature will out. He can hear the woman's heart, her blood, and his eyes are black – he forces himself back when she asks if he is dangerous. He's heard that before from Lauren and he tells her she should go. He can't risk what happened to Lauren happening again, it would just be too much for him to bear.

When Mitchell wakes up, Annie is sat on his bed watching him. He's slightly nonplussed – has she been there long? Over an hour is her less than informative answer when she asks how he defines 'long'. She must be bored! She tells Mitchell what she told George about death, how she thought it was best. He has a faith – he's Jewish – so it was the right answer. Mitchell agrees; no living person needs to or should know the truth about what is in store for them. He and Annie both saw the same thing: they saw the corridor and the men waiting for them, the men with sticks and rope. To know this when you are still alive would mean madness.

It's the full moon and George is heading through the hospital when Julia sees him and calls after him. He has headphones on and doesn't hear her, so she follows him. She tracks him through the basement until she finds him in the isolation room where he plans to transform. He's horrified to see her there. She needs to talk; she's finished with Peter but she needs to know what has happened to George, why he is so different. The moon is coming up and he desperately tries to fob her off. They should talk, of course, how about tomorrow? She won't be dissuaded and eventually she slams the door shut and they are trapped.

"We live on. We are our own monuments"

Mitchell has a vampire gathering to go to – it seems they are regular events. It's in rooms hidden behind a restaurant and he is greeted on arrival by Seth who tells him he is late. He wants to know about Lauren and Seth tells him not to worry about her. Seth is trying to show his dominance over Mitchell, but Mitchell neither notices nor cares. Seth isn't important enough for him to get territorial.

Herrick gets everyone's attention and starts to speak – normally he would not choose to impose formality on these occasions but he has been visiting other vampire communities and wants to share his thoughts and discoveries. What their culture, the vampire world means. He seems to be the natural leader of the vampires, but whether self-proclaimed or elected is less clear.

George is desperate. Julia has shut them in the room so that he would have no choice but to talk to her, but he knows what is coming. He knows that the wolf is not far away and once he has changed he will kill her. There is no way she can be safe. He phones Mitchell, desperate for help. Unfortunately Mitchell has left his phone at home, but Annie answers it when she sees it is George calling, offering to take a message. Getting more and more desperate he tells her she has to come to the hospital and help – he only has 20 minutes before he rips Julia to shreds. Annie is scared. She hasn't left the house since she died; she knows she can't, that something awful will happen if she tries. She's sorry, so sorry but she can't and she hangs up. Screaming vainly at her to answer, George falls as he feels the first agony of his transformation. Julia watches him; she's confused and now she's getting scared. This is not the George she knew and loved. This is something else entirely.

"I will kill her. I will tear her apart"

Herrick is talking about how they are hiding their true nature, keeping themselves away from society, hiding in the shadows, when in their day they used to walk with pharaohs. Why they are living with freaks, he says pointedly to Mitchell, showing the vampire hatred of werewolves.

As he talks we see Annie desperately trying to leave the house – she wants to help George but can't actually bring herself to open the door.

George is getting more and more desperate and Julia still doesn't understand. What does George think will happen? George finds a blunt, rusty knife – can he kill himself? Only as a last resort, he has to try everything else he can first. He uses the old tools to try and break open the door; his panic is starting to affect Julia too but she still doesn't know what is going on. How could she even begin to guess?

Herrick is talking about the humans, how they are in charge while the vampires hide and what a mess they have made of the world. Mitchell disagrees and stands up to him. They had their chance to evolve and they lost it, they killed and killed and could never be accepted. But Herrick has an answer for him. What about Lauren? Look at Mitchell's shame – it is not natural, not what they are. It is time for them to take on the world; time to rise, to feast and to live openly. He's talking about a revolution, a vampire uprising.

"Glory. Glory. And let the children of Darwin behold the final act of evolution"

George is still trying to break out of the room, terrified for Julia. The agony of transformation is almost too much to bear and the wolf is almost here. He has no choices left and he holds the blade to his chest, but he can't go through with it. But the door opens; Annie appears and pulls Julia out, shutting the wolf away again. She tries to keep Julia away from the door but she is transfixed. There is a spy hole and through it she watches George become the wolf, unable to look away, horrified and scared. This was the man she adored.

They have to leave him, and Annie and Julia are sitting together outside the hospital. Julia is deeply concerned, shaken and still scared – how can George bear it, the agony? At least she knows why he left her, that is all clear now. Annie can't answer her, what could she say? Julia wonders if Annie is a werewolf too, but she tells her she's something else.

"A ghost." "A ghost?" "I'm not a fan of the word"

Julia can see and hear Annie and she asks why, but Annie isn't sure. Since she met George and Mitchell she feels more confident, she is acknowledged and that seems to have made her visible. She isn't lonely anymore and she feels real. Julia wonders who Mitchell is, and when told that George's friend is a vampire she starts to become hysterical, and frankly, who can blame her?

They go back to George at daybreak – he's human again, naked in the middle of the wolf's devastation. Julia hardly knows what to say – she thought he was gay, she thought he was dead; she didn't know what to think. Anything would have been better than this. She can't be with George anymore, this is too much for her, she's only... human. She tells George he never did know how strong he is. He has survived this for two years but she can't, she doesn't know how. She leaves, telling Annie to look after him.

"I might start fading a bit. That might freak some people out"

Mitchell, George and Annie are in the pub taking nonsense like any other group of friends. After the dilemma of what house would you choose at Hogwarts (Mitchell thinks he'd be left in the canteen for five years), they wonder if George should eat bacon. He's Jewish, yes, but the werewolf thing rather wiped out any aspirations to orthodoxy. Annie does need to sit closest to the house so she stays visible, but she is fine, she can leave the house. She does need someone to drink her drink for her though – it just goes straight through her! The experience with Julia seems to have brought Annie and George closer; they may not be entirely comfortable together yet but they have definitely progressed. Is this normal, human? Have they escaped the monsters?

Mitchell heads to the bar but something distracts him. Something, someone is calling him. He goes outside to investigate and sees a transformed Lauren, glamorous and proud. He wants to apologise for what he did to her but she won't listen and she thanks him for the extraordinary gift he has bestowed on her. She is revelling in it, the power and the possibilities, but he wants to warn her. She must remember what she was. She doesn't care and can't see why he does. To her, humans are just sketches and Mitchell's desire to be like them is incomprehensible to her.

Herrick appears and Lauren goes to him. He is promising a new world. A world Mitchell cannot bear to think about, one where vampires hunt openly, kill without pause or consideration. He wants nothing to do with it – he is not with them anymore.

Herrick reminds him that things are changing; this is the world moving to accommodate them. It is beginning, here and now.

"You'll need to decide who your friends are"

He said, she said

When in Rome, stop killing the other Romans.

••••••

The back of the house doesn't get much sunlight.
I'm not mad about sunlight...

••••••

Ah well, you shouldn't be eating bacon anyway, should you? – you're Jewish.
Yeah, I gave up on the whole orthodoxy thing when I started turning into a wolf.
Do they have rules about being a werewolf as well?
I think you'd be hard-pressed to find a religion that doesn't frown on it.
What about the Moonies?

••••••

So, you've just arrived at Hogwarts, which house do they put you in?
I'd like to say Gryffindor, but they're supposed to be brave. What's the other one? Ravenclaw, does that have a characteristic?
I think they're brainy. You could be in Ravenclaw.
I quite fancy Hufflepuff actually. I've always thought in Hufflepuff they just spend the day making stuff with safety scissors and glitter.
What about you?
I think that they'd say, 'It's probably best if you just stay in the canteen for the next five years.'

Reactions and results

Although a full series of *Phoo Action* had already been commissioned before its pilot or any of the others in the series had aired on BBC Three, the viewing figures were disappointing at 232,000 and the series was eventually cancelled just before filming was due to begin.

Despite not being commissioned immediately, the BBC did keep *Being Human* in development. Once the pilot was broadcast, the viewing figures were good – 374,000 watched it on the night – but the audience reaction was something else and sent many more to BBC iPlayer and to watch the repeat showings, and viewing figures peaked at nearly 450,000. The day after the pilot aired, the show was the most requested on iPlayer. Message boards and forums were buzzing with excitement for the show and an online petition for a series was started by Narin Bahar of the *Reading Chronicle* and quickly gained several thousand signatures. Although the monolithic BBC cannot be that easy to influence, they would have been foolish to ignore this level of interest.

In March 2010, Toby Whithouse talked about the pilot process to the BBC's *Writers Room*, explaining that it was incredibly frustrating. Although the show had been kept 'in development' that really meant very little, especially as the decision had already been taken to make a series of *Phoo Action*. However, the response to *Being Human* took everyone by surprise and did manage to change the attitude of those who mattered at the BBC. Toby recalls that they started to take interest in his show again, "and bless their hearts, there's been a slight revision of history in that, like Trotsky, *Phoo Action*'s been kind of airbrushed out of the picture. And now it's all kind of 'Oh we always loved *Being Human*.' Apart, clearly, from the moment they turned it down."

Reviews of the pilot were largely online, in blogs and not in the mainstream press (that came with series one), but pretty much all were favourable. A few issues were raised about aspects of the show – the vampire plot was picked out by some as a little out of step. Positive reactions to the pilot came from some very varied sources, and *The Scotsman*'s Paul Whitelaw gave a particularly measured response: "Dare I say it, but BBC Three's recent relaunch has achieved the hitherto unimaginable feat of nearly justifying its existence. ... the surprisingly effective supernatural comedy/drama *Being Human* suggests that the cats in charge are actively trying to reverse the channel's deservedly tarnished reputation. *Being Human* is a fun confection thoroughly deserving of a series. BBC Three must recognise quality when they see it, surely?"

The *TV Scoop* website was much more effusive: "And that was it. But what an 'it' it was. I was a bit sceptical to begin with, but thanks to some intelligent writing, *Being Human* really worked. ... this odd couple (or trio) scenario gives *Being Human* an edge other vamp shows just do not have. In fact, even if you don't like this kind of thing, I'd recommend it – the fantasy stuff, in some ways, is just the top layer of the story. *Phoo Action* has been made into a series, but this was ten times better. More please."

In April 2008, only two months after the pilot was shown, the BBC announced that *Being Human* would be back for a six-part series. Danny Cohen, Controller of BBC Three, said: "Of all our recent drama experiments on BBC Three, *Being Human* struck the most powerful chord with the audience. At its heart is a bold and adventurous concept and I'm looking forward to seeing how this is realised across a series." BBC Wales Head of Drama Julie Gardner agreed: "BBC Drama is always looking for diverse and surprising pieces, and *Being Human* hit the spot with its irreverence and wit." On hearing the good news, Rob Pursey, Executive producer for Touchpaper Television, said: "The pilot of *Being Human* gave us the opportunity to try something really unusual, and we were quite overwhelmed by the positive public response. So we're delighted that the BBC has given us the go-ahead for a full series."

Moving on and into series one

Although the pilot doesn't contradict anything that happened later, it inevitably stands alone. After the show was commissioned, there was an opportunity to review how it worked and how all the various pieces fitted together. What had to be decided was how the story and the characters could best develop through the six episodes in series one.

Producer Matthew Bouch told *Digital Spy* in November 2008: "The pilot has been put on the shelf and won't be retransmitted. This is essentially a new show," adding: "We are reintroducing all of the characters and assuming that the audience have no knowledge at all of the pilot." I think that is a shame. Toby Whithouse considers the pilot canon and many people were disappointed that it wasn't included in the series one DVDs. Yes there are changes, recasting and the tone has been adjusted, but the pilot remains the root of the show and should be valued as such.

The most obvious change is the recasting of most of the main roles. The only actors to continue from the pilot are Russell Tovey as George and Dylan Brown as Seth.

In between the pilot and the commissioning of series one, Andrea Riseborough, who played Annie, moved on and the option on her services ran out. The casting of Lenora Crichlow to take over as Annie made the character very different. Aside from the change of accent and stature, Lenora played Annie as a more vivid character – her colouring, her smile, everything about her was sunshine and it made the character's invisibility heartbreaking. How could she possibly not be seen? Lenora's Annie is stronger, even when at her most defeated, and rarely seems to be in need of cosseting – maybe it would always have developed this way, but the original Annie seemed to be much more accepting of her limitations.

After the pilot, Toby Whithouse took the view that the vampire plot was out of place tonally with the rest of the show. The strength of *Being Human* is how it is firmly grounded in normal everyday life, but the pilot's vampires were out of step. It was just a touch too gothic, a shade frilly cuffed and rather Anne Rice-esque. Taking the opportunity to remedy this and make the vampires more everyday fits perfectly with the other characters. Adrian Lester's Herrick was smooth and polished, a leader and a showman, but hard to imagine out of the shadows and darkness. Turning Herrick into a policeman was an inspiration and Jason Watkins brings to the series a very middle-management style of evil that is truly chilling when combined with his purple prose and plans for world domination. Oh and lots of blood and death...

Lauren (Dominique McElligott) is also recast and the new version (Annabel Scholey) has a little less of the original's hair-flicking glamour but is still beautiful in a quirky way that is a perfect fit with the new Mitchell. This is a woman you know he would have singled out. She's younger, more innocent and yet more knowing at the same time, and the fact that she hadn't quite found her place in the earthly world makes her vampire struggles more realistic.

Guy Flanagan's Mitchell was etiolated, languid, drifting through the hospital, detached and sarcastic. The change to Aidan Turner made Mitchell more earthy and real and he has a look which could date from any time in the last century – his 116 years are more believable than they were for the indie-band styled Mitchell of the pilot. Aidan is conventionally better looking (which does no harm) but still has the 'otherness' that makes people wonder who or what he is. Guy's Mitchell would always stand out in a crowd; Aidan's Mitchell can blend in but probably doesn't and probably doesn't really care if he does or not.

On the recasting, Matthew Bouch explained "Having a new cast is mainly to do with the slight tonal shift in the show. We wanted to go slightly younger, mainly because [the pilot] skewed perhaps slightly too old for BBC Three's target audience." *The Guardian* also picked up on the age issue and the aiming at BBC Three's 16-34 demographic, and Daniel Matthew responded to the recasting news by saying: "Although all three leads were under 30, bosses were still not sure it fitted with the BBC Three demographic. Flanagan and Riseborough were out, replaced with the younger and more glamorous Aidan Turner and Lenora Crichlow in the same roles. And so the messageboards went wild again, with the same cries that greeted the news of Matt Smith's casting as the next Doctor: 'They're turning it into *Hollyoaks!*'"

I think that too much has been made of the age issue – Toby Whithouse maintains that the reasons were very simple. For the part of Annie, there was no choice but to recast as Andrea Riseborough was no longer available, while the recasting of Mitchell was to do with the switch in tone, to make the vampires less gothic and more grounded, more in keeping with the natural, everyday themes of the show. Toby said that Guy had played the part as he had been directed and played it well, but he wanted a different feel.

In the BBC Press Pack for series one, Matthew says "We had to reimagine how these supernatural creatures would be if they really did exist." Toby agrees and was particularly keen to humanise the vampires in the series: "The casting of Jason Watkins in the role of Herrick has helped with this, as he looks incredibly normal and human but as soon as he starts speaking he gives across this undercurrent of evil, ambition and cruelty. We wanted to give the vampires a much more convincing and realistic cover story."

Lenora Crichlow had not seen the pilot when she started filming as Annie, although she caught up with it later. She told *IFMagazine.com* in August 2009: "Andrea's portrayal of Annie is fantastic, but she couldn't be more different to me, which is great for me, because it doesn't put pressure on me to then try and imitate [her]. It was a completely different Annie, I think, than was [originally] written." In the same interview (for the launch of series one on BBC America), it was noted that the three leads finish each other's sentences and generally behave as if they are really as close in 'real life' as the friends they portray in the show. Aidan Turner first watched the pilot about six weeks into filming: "I didn't try and avoid it, [watching] it was just something that didn't really happen. I was just immersed in the work and busy working with these guys, so I didn't really feel compelled to watch it, but I

18

watched it and I loved it and I thought it was great. I think we've captured the essence of the pilot. It was good."

Lenora and Aidan are, perhaps, more classically good-looking, younger leading actors, but crucially – they are damned good. Demographics aside, the show works and much as I enjoyed the pilot I personally feel the new cast made the series really come together and the relationship they have with Russell Tovey is a joy to see. Russell said as much in the *IFMagazine.com* piece: "At the read-through, the first time I walked in there and they [Crichlow and Turner] both sat there, quite quiet and shy. And I walked in, quite quiet and shy. And then we read it, realised we liked what each other was doing and then we just bonded on set, and we realised that we just get on really well and really like each other. It's a nice balance." Aidan replied that "It's like a big family, isn't it?" and Lenora added: "It really is. It sounds so clichéd and cheesy, but it really is, and I do think it adds a lot to the show for everyone involved." This connection carries through to the characters themselves. The relationship between Mitchell and George was less equal in the pilot; George the puppy dog to Mitchell's pack leader. The sarcasm from Mitchell to George seems very pointed and in the pilot I'm not convinced that Mitchell cares for George at all. He seems to be a part of the construct of normality Mitchell is building for himself, whereas in the series there is a clear and deep affection between the pair.

Aside from the changes in casting, there are a few other points worthy of note. There are obvious limitations in a one-hour pilot compared to a six-part series, but the idea of Mitchell's struggle against his blood addiction is more implied in the pilot, not explicit. It would be quite easy to miss that he is on the wagon and how hard it is for him to stay clean. It could be interpreted as more of a lifestyle choice and less of the fight of an addict.

Russell Tovey plays George in both the pilot and the series and does such a good job of it that it seems effortless. He does change from the pilot to the series though. In the pilot George is manic, almost childish and frankly quite exhausting – all traits that stay with George throughout the series but in moderation, which is a very good thing!

It's nice to see the possibility of George having a cage mentioned and dismissed before it makes it onto his special 'to do' list in series two.

The scene where Julia watches George as the wolf through the spy hole in the isolation room door is very like Nina doing the same after George kills Herrick. The wolf didn't recognise Julia but he does Nina – maybe George and Julia were never kindred spirits after all.

Oh, and by the way, did the sarky estate agent in the pilot remind anyone else of Nina?!

Where have I seen...?

Andrea Riseborough (Annie)

Before *Being Human*, Andrea appeared on TV in an episode of *Doc Martin* (in 2005) and as Myra in *The Secret Life of Mrs Beeton* (2006). She was in the acclaimed series *Party Animals* (2007) as Kirsty MacKenzie.

Since then she has taken the title role in *Margaret Thatcher: The Long Walk to Finchley* (2008), and starred in *The Devil's Whore* (2008) as Angelica Fanshawe. In both cases she was nominated for or won awards.

Her film work includes Rose in *Brighton Rock* (2010), Brenda in *Made in Dagenham* (2010), Dawn in *Happy-Go-Lucky* (2008) and Dani in *Magicians* (2007).

In 2006 Andrea won the Ian Charleson Award for her performances as Isabella in *Measure For Measure* and the title character in *Miss Julie* for the Peter Hall Company.

Guy Flanagan (Mitchell)

Guy has appeared on TV in roles including Tim Evans in *Messiah: The Harrowing* (2005), Trev Stone in *Holby City* (in 2006), Felix Carerra in an episode of *Party Animals* (2007), Jason Devlin in *The Bill* (in 2009) and Raymundo in *Shameless* (in 2009).

His film work includes *Together* (2009), *A Bunch of Amateurs* (2008), *Stoned* (2005) and *Millions* (2004).

Stage roles include Oswald in an RSC Academy production of *King Lear* in 2002, Iachimo in *Cymbeline* for Cheek by Jowl in 2007 and Larson/Barnes in *Mimi and the Stalker* in 2008.

Adrian Lester (Herrick)

Adrian is a well-known TV face from playing Mickey Stone in 31 episodes of *Hustle* between 2004-10 and from *Bonekickers* in 2008 as Ben Ergha. He has also appeared as Myror in *Merlin* (in 2009), Mr Sholsky in *Ballet Shoes* (2007) and DI Felix George in *Afterlife* (in 2005), and he played Ellis Carter in eight episodes of US sitcom *Girlfriends* (in 2002-3)

Film roles include Henry Burton in *Primary Colours* (1998), George in *Maybe Baby* (2000), Oliver De Boys in *As You Like It* (2006), Pete in *Scenes of a Sexual Nature* (2006), Sgt. Norton in *Doomsday* (2008) and Wayne in *Case 39* (2009).

Adrian has had an extensive stage career which includes the Sondheim musical *Company* in 1996 for which he won an Olivier Award. He has also appeared as the eponymous *Hamlet* for Peter Brook in 2001, as Rosalind in Cheek by Jowl's all-male *As You Like It* (1991) for which he won a Time Out Award, and as the title character in Shakespeare's *Henry V* at the Royal National Theatre in 2003. In 2010, he played the part of Brick in an all-black version of Tennessee Williams's *Cat on a Hot Tin Roof* at the Novello Theatre.

In 2007 Adrian took part in Channel 4's documentary series *Empire's Children*, looking at the journey taken by the Windrush Generation to the United Kingdom. He also appeared in the documentary *When Romeo Met Juliet* in 2010 with his wife Lolita Chakrabarti. They were acting mentors to the pupils of two Coventry schools involved in a production of *Romeo and Juliet*.

2

vampires and werewolves and ghosts, oh my...

Writing about the supernatural has a weight of tradition and expectation to contend with. Anyone planning to tell tales of the undead, partly dead or just plain hairy has to start by taking a stroll down the pic 'n' mix aisle of the supernatural supermarket. Everyone knows what vampires are like and that werewolves just love the full moon, and we all have a dodgy ghost story to tell, but all that adds up to is a high level of expectation. After all, we already know how it works. Don't we?

So where do the *Being Human* supernaturals fit into the accepted mythology? Do they resemble the accepted lore and the much-loved fiction and, given all that, how can they be both mystical and still fit into Bristol society?

Let's face it, ghosts, vampires and werewolves – they're not actually real so every writer can use them in the way that best suits their needs. Toby Whithouse himself agreed that "the bottom line always had to be 'What gives us the best story?'" (BBC *Being Human* blog, February 2009.)

The Vampires

Let's talk vampires, because right now vampires are hot. Or cool. Either way, they're box office. We all know they died but are immortal, hate garlic, crucifixes and daylight, and can't be filmed or seen in mirrors – the perfect recipe for a series of very bad hair days.

The grand vampires of fiction vary enormously. Anne Rice's vampires can't eat or drink and – despite a series of erotic obsessions – don't or can't have sex. They can only come out after sunset and they fall into an irresistible unconsciousness at daybreak. In HBO's *True Blood* (2008-) there's no food, but sex seems rather more of a preoccupation and silver is toxic. Bram Stoker's Count Dracula (mistakenly thought to be the first fictional vampire) can go out in daylight but his powers are dramatically reduced if he does so. No shape-shifting for example – always a knotty problem, I find.

As in life, budget plays a part in setting the vampire rules for *Being Human*. They cannot be filmed, photographed or seen in mirrors, but the work involved in removing stray reflections in windows or shiny surfaces would have been prohibitive. So they do reflect but not through lenses or in silver-backed mirrors. This unsettling notion is used to full effect in the vampire snuff movie, and also when Fleur disbelieves and then rationalises what she sees when Mitchell is not beside her son in her hand mirror, and when Lauren first approaches George. It is also a serious moment of truth for Lucy when Mitchell is still in her bed but not visible to her in the mirror. When Lucy and Kemp consider the evidence on their giant whiteboard, it's interesting to compare WW1 photos of Mitchell with the drawings of his present-day look. There are photos of recently recruited Lauren and Cara, but only drawings of Herrick.

Of course vampires drink blood. That one is non-negotiable – or is it? The *Being Human* vampires can live without blood and Mitchell tries repeatedly to give it up, with the obvious parallel being that blood is an addiction. To other vampires a clean vampire looks pale and ill; most cannot understand why anyone would give up what is for them an immense pleasure. Some have tried but it all seems rather doomed. Carl stayed clean for 20 years before killing his lover in an action that seemed to be beyond his control, almost inevitable. The main reason most fail is that once they are free of the immediate desire for blood, the memory of every single one of their kills returns to them in excruciating detail and these memories torment them. The only way to stop it is to drink again. Mitchell told Josie that for him killing was cowardice because he couldn't face the pain of the memories. Mitchell tries to help them all stay clean with Vampires Anonymous, but what support group (however good the biscuits) has a chance against the strength and physicality of a vampire's nature? Maybe it would have worked, but thanks to Lucy and Kemp and their fun with nitro-glycerine we'll never know.

It is only when they are about to attack and drink that the *Being Human* vampires' fangs appear and their eyes go completely black. Their eyes can also darken when they are tempted or close to blood – Mitchell's do this when looking at blood bags in the hospital and when retrieving Lauren's vampire porn film from the bin. It also seems to be something that vampires can do consciously and Mitchell darkens his eyes to scare off the boys bullying Bernie in series one. There is a very good effect in series two after Mitchell has massacred 20 people on the train, when his eyes are not completely dark but the irises are black. It's extremely unsettling, a very effective touch of evil.

One very useful thing in the making of TV or films featuring vampires is that they don't age or change their appearance. It means they can be filmed in flashback entirely convincingly with just a change of costume and hair as we saw in the 1960s sequence with Herrick and Mitchell. I suppose the opposite of this is that, as they don't age, the prospect of a *Coronation Street*-length vampire saga would have to find a solution for the inevitably aging actors! *Doctor Who* did it with regeneration, so why not? I suppose employing real vampires is out of the question – photos for *Spotlight* would be a problem, as would be actually filming them in the first place. OK, so that was not one of my better ideas!

Daylight is OK for our vampires, although sunlight isn't great for them, meaning sunglasses and covering up are de rigueur and – of course – rather cool. Only being able to film most of the cast at night would have been unduly restrictive and a lower budget show can do without the expense of continual night shooting.

Vampires cannot cross the threshold unless they are invited in and as Lauren said in episode two: "That is such a mental rule. Who made that up?" It was used to great effect in *Buffy* and works well when Herrick almost manages to stake Mitchell, only to be foiled by the invisible barrier preventing him from entering the house. There's a slight addendum to this in series two, when Mitchell only needs to be invited to enter a block of flats, not each individual dwelling. This is how he gets into Josie's flat to hold her hostage. In series one, George and the very nervous vicar also repel vampires from the hospital by repeatedly telling them they are not welcome, and the chaplain uses the same ploy against Mitchell when he is looking for Lucy at the end of series two.

Classically, all vampires are repelled by religious symbols and *Being Human* is no exception, although, of course, there are variations. Mitchell can look after George's Star of David without harm because of the affection between him and George. Presumably this is why the preponderance of

24

crosses and other Christian paraphernalia in Lucy's flat doesn't seem to bother him in the slightest. George discovers his Star of David will repel one vampire but not many, as the effect is diluted.

Vampires, being dead, do not register on the hospital's monitoring equipment and Mitchell is a complete and utter mystery to the nursing staff after he is stabbed. He heals far too quickly and seems to need to be conscious to register any signs of life at all. He also tells us that vampires cannot make new blood, so if they bleed or are hurt then only drinking fresh blood will cure them. It's not clear what would happen if they didn't – maybe remain weak for ever, or just fade away.

There are some examples of the healing power of a fresh kill. Josie sacrifices herself to heal Mitchell, out of love, and so he can fight Herrick. When Daisy rescues Cara from the caves where Mitchell had left her after smashing her fangs, Daisy takes her a child to drink from and Cara is restored. Restored enough for her and Daisy to bleed all over Herrick's resting place and wake him up at the end of series two! No rest for the wicked...

Vampires are immortal but can be destroyed. In *Being Human,* the classic stake in the chest seems to be the foolproof method and we see Seth and Lauren go that way. Ivan and the other vampires are destroyed in the explosion set by Kemp at the funeral parlour and I suppose that the catastrophic damage to their physical bodies was what killed them, although it could have been the almost total blood loss. Herrick is dismembered by George as the werewolf in series one; George tells us he tore off his head. His remains are buried but he is not dead (or not entirely) and is resurrected by the blood of Daisy and Cara – presumably the older vampires get, the tougher they are. We have yet to see just how recovered Herrick is – maybe there are some consequences to being reanimated after being beheaded?

Being Human's vampires always seem to be cold. Mitchell is rarely out of his fingerless gloves, and layers of shirts and T-shirts and sleek black overcoats abound. However, there may be an exception to this rule in Daisy. She certainly doesn't seem to feel any drafts, unless she has a pair of substantial thermal knickers under her flimsy tea frock. Somehow, though, I doubt that! She doesn't look like a Damart girl...

John Mitchell

John Mitchell is a very modern vampire; 116 years old but he seems the perfect product of the early 21st century. A 20-something bloke, skinny jeans, Celtic rings and a good line of patter, you wouldn't look at him twice. Well, actually you might, but it wouldn't be to wonder if he was dead – although I'll admit this may well be a girl thing!

Mitchell eats, mainly cereal, pizza and beer – not a great diet but I suppose that getting your five-a-day become less important when you are dead. He is also – to quote Tully – "a serious poon hound." Nice. This reputation may be exaggerated. His exploits are legendary within the vampire community but are all in the past. He gets chatted up but he only has one serious liaison in series one – with Lauren, whom he recruited in the first episode and then destroys. He encounters Josie, an old flame from the 1960s, and the bitter sweetness of that story makes you question his outer skin.

Maybe the real romantic notion, hidden deep down in Mitchell, is that he believes that to be truly human you need to love and be loved. Of course there is also Lucy (a woman with one hell of an agenda) and, again, Mitchell is stricken with true love. Or the romantic idea that it would be the making of him. Bless. It's very sweet to see such optimism and romanticism surviving after 116 years...

What do we know of Mitchell? He lets slip very few hints about his past. We could assume he is from rural Ireland. He tells Bernie that his only career options were the army or the priesthood, which would fit. He lived blood-free for a while with Josie who he met in 1969, but we don't know how that ended. Probably not that badly, judging from their touching reunion. He was getting clean again in 1999 with Carl with the help of rope and a large plastic sheet. Lovely – vampire cold turkey is clearly rather messy... He must have then spent more time battling with his conscience but still killing and drinking until he met George, when he saved him from a beating.

He was recruited by Herrick in the mayhem of the First World War. He sacrificed himself so that Herrick would let his men go safe – although I do wonder if he really did. Is Herrick a vampire of his word? Hmmmm.

In *Being Human* it seems as though the vampires are fixed in some way at the time they are recruited. They live on, experience more, but their character development is largely unchanged. Mitchell was born as a vampire in the battles of WW1 and he has been fighting ever since. He fought to be the worst, the darkest and then he fought to be the one who got away. He fought the vampires and Herrick for his friends and for humanity and then he fought the humans for the vampires once Lucy got her claws into him. George has something when he calls Mitchell "deadly furniture" in the brief hiatus between battling Herrick and battling Kemp! He appears to be out of step with the modern world in many ways – his coffee mornings and expectations of community for example, and the laundered white handkerchief that he uses to clean up Bernie after he falls. Maybe his notions of the healing power of love stay untainted by contemporary cynicism.

Mitchell was – we are told – the darkest of the vampires and the murderous rampages of Mitchell and Herrick are legendary. It is only in series two that we start to see that this really was no exaggeration. The shock we feel in seeing that terrible, dark Mitchell is immense after the consciously human Mitchell we thought we knew. What did we expect? Vampires are beings of rage and fury, hunger and blood after all.

What next for Mitchell after finding his darkness once more? How can he retrieve the shattered threads of his hard-won humanity? Is there any way back?

Where have I seen... Aidan Turner (Mitchell)?

Aidan trained at Dublin's Gaiety School of Acting, graduating in 2004. He worked consistently on stage after graduation, making appearances in *The Plough and the Stars* (Corporal Stoddard) at the Barbican in 2005, *Titus Andronicus* (Demetrius) at the Project in 2005, *Drive-by* directed by Jo Mangan for the Dublin Fringe Festival 2006 and the Canterbury Arts

Festival 2007, and *Romeo and Juliet* (Paris) at the Abbey Theatre in 2008.

Aidan appeared in the first episode of *The Tudors* (in 2007) as Bedoli (although uncredited), and played the receptionist Ruairi in series 6 (2008) and 7 (2009) of *The Clinic* which showed on RTE in Ireland. He starred as poet and artist Dante Gabriel Rossetti in *Desperate Romantics* (2009) written by Peter Bowker. *Desperate Romantics* was quite a *Being Human* family affair – Rossetti's wife Lizzie was played by Amy Manson (Daisy) and her father by Ian Puleston-Davies (Chief Constable Wilson). Aidan will be seen in late 2010 as John Schofield in *Hattie*, playing Hattie Jacques's toy-boy lover, alongside Ruth Jones as Hattie.

Aidan is also working on *Resonance*, an innovative multi-platform drama series directed by Colin Teague. In this super-powered espionage tale of a group of people caught up in an epic struggle to control a mystical object, Aidan plays TT, who is described as a legend of the streets. While TV will be the main platform for the series, the pilot will get a theatrical release, there are games, online resources, graphic novels and an animated series.

Aidan appeared in two short films in 2007 – *Matterhorn* and *The Sound of People* – and in the thriller *Alarm* as Mal in 2008. He also starred as Kevin in the independent Irish film *Porcelain* in 2007 alongside Charlene McKenna (1960s Josie) and they dated for some time afterwards.

In March 2009 Aidan told the *Irish Sunday Tribune* how he got into acting: "I'd just finished my leaving cert and didn't know what I wanted to do," he said. "I've a cousin who's an actor so following that path wasn't as farfetched as it might have been for other people and it seemed like fun." There is a popular belief that this cousin is Ben Turner – seen most Saturday nights as Jay Faldren in *Casualty*. However in March 2010 Ben told *TV Choice*: "That's not true. The only link is we have dark hair and hairy arms! I know him; we've hung out a couple of times. My girlfriend Amy Manson is in *Being Human*, she plays the new vampire, Daisy."

William Herrick

Herrick is rather an enigma. Most likely he is one of the old ones, certainly he is older than Mitchell but we get no ideas or hints of where he came from. He is featured on Lucy and Kemp's board of images but only as a drawing – does he pre-date photography perhaps? Ivan knows him, although he's rather disparaging about him and his megalomania, and Carl spoke of him in the same dismissive way as a bit of an idiot. Cara claims he gave her the "blood of the ancestors." It could just be more of Herrick's sumptuous, purple prose, but might it be true? He could be very, very old. When he spoke of walking with pharaohs in the pilot, did he mean that *he* did? Of course, do bear in mind that Cara is (ever so slightly) mad...

The only time Herrick talks about his childhood is to remember his dream of being an architect and a picture book he had. He dreamt of building houses all over the mountainsides. Not much to get to grips with there except for childhood signs of a desire to build an empire.

He is leading the Bristol vampires – whether by general choice or self-appointed mission it is unclear, but he has a way of attracting people to his side. Even though Mitchell and he are locked in battle and hatred, it seems to take very little for them to slip back into the banter of long-time friends. He saw Mitchell as his vampire son, his protégé – the man who could eventually surpass anything he could do. The disappointment when Mitchell turned away was incalculable and his final act of allowing George to kill him was always intended to leave Mitchell in his place.

There's something oddly compelling about this kindly faced policeman with the open smile. Even the maddest speeches of his despotic devilry are somehow convincing. Maybe there is much more to come...

Where have I seen... Jason Watkins (Herrick)?

Jason Watkins has had a long and successful career in TV and film and on the stage. Trained at RADA, he is a member of the National Theatre Company and has also worked with the RSC. In 2001 he was nominated for a Laurence Olivier Theatre Award for Best Supporting Actor for his performance in *A Servant for Two Masters* at the Young Vic and New Ambassadors Theatres.

Well-known TV roles include Ed Croom in *Murderland* (2009), Plornish in *Little Dorrit* (2008), Colin Merrick, Gene Hunt's solicitor in *Life on Mars* (in 2007), Dr Jonathon Fowler in *The Life and Times of Vivienne Vyle* (2007), Dr Roger Brierley in *Housewife, 49* (2006), X-ray pioneer Ernest Wilson in *Casualty 1906* (2006), Bradley Stainer in *Funland* (2005) and Jason Buliegh in *Conviction* (2004). He will be appearing in the second series of *Pyschoville*, due to be shown in 2011.

In Victoria Wood's *Mid Life Christmas* (2009), Jason played Colin, who took on the unenviable task of trying to document the post-*Acorn Antiques* exploits of diva Bo Beaumont – the fabulous creation of Julie Walters. Watching her discuss her wonderful ways with a Ritz cracker with reporter Colin was Sinead Keenan (Nina) as Delia Smith's long-suffering assistant – complete with trademark tutting and eye rolling.

While we watched in grudging admiration as friendly, approachable Sergeant Herrick plotted to take over the world, we could also see Jason as a very different policeman in *Lark Rise to Candleford* – Constable 'Cabbage' Paterson (in 2008 and 2009). A glance down Jason's credits does throw up quite a few policemen – he must have a trustworthy face!

Ivan and Daisy

Ivan and Daisy are married vampires and for them it is all about sightseeing. They are war tourists, travelling together to trouble spots and looking for chaos, pain and terror. Then, they savour it.

Ivan is one of the old ones – he is 237 years old, 195 of them as a vampire. As with Herrick, we know very little of his past – I wonder if vampires do occasionally reminisce amongst themselves, but maybe they can't bear to. To live so many years, perhaps the memories disappear, otherwise it could become a torment. Ivan comes from an era when the Grand Tour was a rite of passage for young men and he seems to have continued in this tradition. For him, however, that tour is no longer about art, poetry and liberal education but about pain and death. He and Daisy are in Bristol because of the power vacuum left after the death of Herrick and to see what chaos ensues.

When Mitchell wonders if it could ever be possible for vampires to live openly, Ivan's answer sums up his character perfectly:

> "Good news for religion, mind, especially Christianity. There'd be standing room only in the churches all of a sudden. And as soon as they knew about vampires, they'd know about werewolves, they'd know about ghosts. They'd be next. And when humanity had finally finished with us, it would turn on itself. First the other religions, massively in the minority now, then the homosexuals, the disabled... Do you want to know what the future looks like? Enforced worship in churches a mile high and every country surrounded by a coral reef of bones. But fuck it, maybe it should happen. There's nothing on TV at the moment."

Ivan is so old he can no longer even imagine human emotion and he finds Mitchell's decision to go clean completely incomprehensible. He has drunk blood every day for the 195 years he's been a vampire and anything else is impossible. He becomes the poster boy for Mitchell's Vampires Anonymous group, showing the awe the old ones inspire, even though he is still secretly drinking blood from a store of emo-girls in the cellars. Like you do.

In one of the flashbacks we see how Ivan and Daisy met during a bombing raid in WW2. Daisy was a young widow with a baby that she could hardly believe was hers, a head full of dreams and a sense of non-fulfilment. Glamorous, seductive, hypnotic Ivan offered her eternity, the chance to screw her way around the world – how could she say no?

Their relationship in human terms is unconventional, but they love each other deeply. Ivan will watch Daisy have sex with George – it's an item on her 'must-see' list, something for her scrapbook, the killer of Herrick. I'm sure George would be thrilled to be an item on a tidy 'to do' list! Yet another soppy vampire, Ivan would only take over the vampire community when Mitchell told him he'd fallen in love – for that he would do anything. He saved Mitchell from Kemp and Lucy's explosion; he could have saved himself but saved his friend instead. Did he want him to have the happiness he had had with Daisy? Daisy is devastated when Ivan dies and her rampage with Mitchell is her memorial to him, the pile of bodies no less than he would expect and just what she thinks he deserves.

Daisy, like Mitchell, is a vampire forged in war, but she did not come from battle. She came from a time when a young widow like Daisy would have been desperate for freedom and fun – and she has been having exactly that with Ivan for the last 69 years.

Where have I seen... Paul Rhys (Ivan)?

While still training at RADA, Paul Rhys gained his first film role as Dean Sharp in Julien Temple's 1986 film *Absolute Beginners*. He followed this with other film roles, including two as the brothers of famous men – Theo Van Gogh in *Vincent and Theo* (1990) and Sydney Chaplin in *Chaplin* (1992). He also appeared in *Love Lies Bleeding* (1999), *From Hell* (2001) and *Food of Love* (2002). He will be seen as Archie Cookson in 2011 in the comedy thriller *ELIMINATE: Archie Cookson,* which follows the gradually unravelling life of the MI6 spy.

Paul has appeared regularly on TV in a variety of roles. Notable credits include: George in *My Family and Other Animals* (1987); Sandor in *Gallowglass* (1993); Dr John Lassiter in *The Healer* (1994), for which he received the 1996 BAFTA Cymru Award for Best Actor; Charles Stringham in *A Dance to the Music of Time* (1997); and Rupert Cazalet in *The Cazalets* (2001). More recently he has played Alexis Meynell in *Spooks* (in 2008), Prince Charles in *The Queen* (2009), Lucien Burgess in *Luther* (2010) and Sebastian Carter in *New Tricks* (in 2010).

On stage, Paul played *Hamlet* at the Young Vic in 1999, alongside Donald Sumpter (Kemp) as Claudius. Paul received an Olivier Award nomination for Best Supporting Actor for his performance as Edgar in Richard Eyre's production of *King Lear* in 1998. He won the Critics' Circle award for the best performance in a Shakespeare play for Angelo in *Measure for Measure* in 2004. In 2010, Paul appeared in National Theatre Wales's production of *The Persians* by Aeschylus, thought to be Europe's oldest recorded play.

Where have I seen... Amy Manson (Daisy)?

Amy Manson left her home in Scotland at 17 to study at the Central School of Speech and Drama. She left early when she won the part of Jodie Hatfield in the horror film *Pumpkinhead: Blood Feud* in 2007. She followed that up with another horror film in the same year, as Amy Armstrong in *BloodMonkey*.

On TV, Amy played Alice Guppy in *Torchwood: Fragments/Exit Wounds* (2008), Abby Evans in *Casualty* (in 2008-9), Lizzie Siddal, long-suffering wife of Aidan Turner's Rossetti, in *Desperate Romantics* (2009), and Ginger Corrigan in *Marple: The Pale Horse* (2010).

She will soon be seen in BBC drama *Outcasts* as young idealistic Fleur Morgan, part of a group of courageous pioneers facing a unique opportunity: the chance to build a new and better future on another planet.

In 2008 Amy won a Critics' Award for Theatre in Scotland for her performance as the Stepdaughter in *Six Characters in Search of an Author* for the National Theatre of Scotland.

The Werewolves

In contrast to the vampires, werewolves are just not sexy and the literature is much sparser. *An American Werewolf in London* (1981) tried to redress the balance, but however attractive the human version of the hero was, the transformations and the constant presence of the decaying yet animated corpse of his best friend didn't take them far into vampire territory. In complete contrast to Mitchell and Annie, George is only a werewolf – 'his thing' – for one night a month, 12 nights a year. This might seem a reasonable deal, but for a ghost or a vampire there is no time off and no respite.

Despite his lycanthropy, George is mortal and will age and die like all other humans. Perhaps as a consequence of this, his connection with the world is more grounded and considerably less rose-tinted than the cravings of

Mitchell and Annie to connect with those around them. In *Being Human*, vampires despise and hunt werewolves – they call them dogs, seeing them as inferior, dirty and crude, and George has been mistreated by them before coming under the protection of Mitchell. Despite their clear and deep affection for each other, the vampire still shows when Mitchell invites his friend to join him at the pub by saying "George – get your lead."

Vampires can smell werewolves. There is something about their odour, even when human, that is massively offensive to a vampire and they have hunted and tortured them through the ages. Maybe it is fear. For 27 days a month they can hurt, even kill a werewolf, although they would not drink from them, but on that one night, the full moon, the vampire is vulnerable. George dismembers Herrick when he is the wolf, so maybe the vampires are striking first – they don't want the werewolves to get the upper hand.

The origins of lycanthropy are rooted in folklore and confused with the lore of madness. There is also a mental illness known as lycanthropy where the sufferer believes they are an animal. Tully tells George that werewolves cannot cross water and that will restrict his wanderings – while not rooted in folklore, this may come from the historical practice of the mad being 'caged' on islands. Lycanthropy is also confused in stories with hydrophobia (fear of water) and rabies. This is probably due to rabies being a disease transmitted through the saliva of mammals, including dogs (or possibly the bite of a werewolf!), one of the main symptoms of which is hydrophobia. Nina threatens Annie with rabies if she lets her secret out after she becomes a werewolf herself. With no one else knowing what has happened to her, she has no one to ask and she would have to rely on half-remembered knowledge gained from old movies and folk tales.

In *Being Human*, the transformation into a werewolf is indescribable agony and tortures the man's (or woman's) body almost beyond belief. Mitchell's voiceover to episode two tells us about George's transformation: "It drags him through the fire and keeps him alive and even conscious to endure every second." Every month the human dies – the heart stops, organs fail and every part of the body breaks and stretches and reforms. The only reason the screaming stops is when the body is no longer capable of such sounds. Unlike Mitchell and Annie who died just once, George is still mortal and he dies every full moon. He goes through such agony every month that it is hard to see how he survives. Maybe the life span of a werewolf is not that of a human – how can anyone endure such torture for 70 or 80 years?

George already knows that he became a werewolf after being attacked and scratched by another werewolf – he still bears the scars on his left shoulder. Transmission of lycanthropy by scratching is rarely found in old tales but is an excellent device for *Being Human*. George is always so careful to quarantine the wolf and to keep it away from anyone, and his reaction to discovering he scratched Nina and gave her his curse is heartbreaking.

Traditionally there are a variety of ways to become a werewolf and the simplest is to put on a belt made of wolfskin while naked. Other methods, aside from the more well-known one of being bitten by a werewolf, include drinking rainwater out of the footprint of a wolf or sleeping outside on a summer night with the full moon shining directly on your face. The latter is a belief from Italy, France and Germany but it can only be done on a certain

Wednesday or Friday.

A distinction is often made between voluntary and involuntary werewolves, with the former generally thought to have made a pact with the Devil. Involuntary werewolves happen by an accident of birth or health, with some cultures believing that individuals born during a new moon or with epilepsy were likely to be werewolves.

There are myths of cures as well as of transmission – so Kemp has obviously been reading up! The Ancient Greeks and Romans believed in the power of exhaustion to cure lycanthropy. In medieval Europe there were three traditional cures for a werewolf: medicinally (usually using wolfsbane), surgically or by exorcism. Unfortunately most attempts at a cure killed the patient. Two other deceptively simple cures are to just address the wolf three times by its Christian name, or to give it a good scolding – of course, you have to get close enough first. Which may be a problem...

Werewolves like George have heightened senses just before and after the full moon. George notices a nurse has changed her shampoo ("You smell like a Polo") and he can tell Annie the milk is off without even opening the fridge – a supernatural trait she gets remarkably excited about! He also exhibits an enthusiastic and uninhibited sexual appetite around the time of the full moon, such as when he has his first 'encounter' with Nina in the hospital ("It's always the quiet ones") and his alfresco seduction by the vampire Daisy. Compared to George's usual awkward demeanour and his propensity to say the wrong thing – in fact to put both feet in it, pretty much up to the knee – this is striking. As Mitchell tells him, "I can actually speak to women without crying or setting fire to myself."

George Sands

George has a brain the size of a planet, an IQ of 156 and speaks German, Spanish, Italian, French and Croatian but only a smattering of Russian. He works as a hospital porter and he is a werewolf.

At the start of *Being Human*, George has been a werewolf for two years. He was infected on holiday in Scotland when talking a walk one night under the full moon. He and the man he was walking with were attacked; the other man died but George survived. He bears the scars of the encounter on his shoulder – deep scratches that will never heal and will always remind him of what he is.

Once he found out what that attack had done to him and realised that he would carry that burden forever, he walked away from his life. He left his family, his friends and his fiancée Julia – leaving them to assume he was dead. For two years he has drifted, trying to come to terms with his condition, until he meets Mitchell. Mitchell saves him from a beating by Seth and the other vampires; he is already becoming disillusioned by the vampire life (again) and takes George under his wing. George has not even accepted he is a werewolf, so to meet a vampire is both terrifying and comforting – he's not alone anymore.

George likes structure and order (just a bit!) and it would be hard to think of anything worse than the rage and chaos of a werewolf to someone like that. He overcompensates for the wolf by trying to impose order on everything else.

This is rather complicated by living with a vampire and a ghost...

All George wants is to be normal; he ignores the wolf, treating it as something separate to him. It is 'it', never 'him', and only after he attacks Herrick does he briefly acknowledge the wolf as 'him', although that doesn't last. There is a split in George's life – the craving for normality, the life he feels the wolf has stolen from him, and the friendship and support he has from Annie and particularly from Mitchell. How can he be normal with these supernatural beings as his friends?

George's biggest nightmare is that he will hurt someone and the climax of series one brings this into sharp relief. He kills Herrick – an action he has accepted is necessary and will not harm him, but it is the first time that the wolf has killed so he cannot know for sure what it will do to him. What he doesn't know until later is that he scratched Nina, gave her his curse, and that destroys them, leading Nina into Kemp's clutches in the hope of a cure.

George overreacts to the harm he has caused and leaps into a job and a new relationship plus a ready-made family. It ends in disaster – a terrified child, a close escape from a massacre in a primary school and a vicious beating that comes from the caged wolf bleeding through into George's normal gentle persona. It takes him too to Kemp and Lucy's Facility – whatever the cure is it can't possibly be any worse than the curse.

Werewolves seem to be solitary creatures, as opposed to vampires who congregate in communities. Tully, the werewolf who infected George, does come looking for him for company, but George can't accept him. Now that he is with Nina again we may see if a partnership of wolves can work. Can they transform safely together or would they tear each other apart? Just how separate are the wolves from their human alter egos?

Where have I seen... Russell Tovey (George)?

Russell Tovey began his career as a child actor in 1994 at the age of 13 when he was cast in *Mud*, a children's series broadcast on CBBC. In 2004 he took the life-changing role of Rudge in Alan Bennett's play *The History Boys* at the Royal National Theatre, which was followed by international appearances in Sydney, Wellington, Hong Kong and on Broadway, as well as playing the role in the radio and film adaptations in 2006.

He is a well-known face on TV, with roles including Midshipman Alonso Frame in *Doctor Who: Voyage of the Damned* (2007), a role he reprised in *Doctor Who: The End of Time: Part 2* (2010) when David Tennant's Doctor ("Allons-y, Alonso!") set him up with John Barrowman's Captain Jack as a farewell gift. He has recently (autumn 2010) been seen in *Him & Her* on BBC Three playing Steve, alongside Sarah Solemani as Becky.

He has also appeared as Budgie in *Gavin and Stacey* (in 2007-9), John Chivery in *Little Dorrit* (2008), Marcus Johnstone in *Ashes to Ashes* (in 2008), Ben in *Annually Retentive* (in 2007), and Leslie Durrell in *My Family and Other Animals* (2007). In 2009 he appeared in three short films: *Drop*, *Roar* and *In Passing*, and in 2001 he was seen in *The Emperor's New Clothes*.

Aside from *The History Boys*, his National Theatre credits include *Howard Katz* by Patrick Marber, Shakespeare's *Henry V*, Ralph in *His Girl Friday* and Roger in *His Dark Materials* based on the novels by Philip Pullman (all 2003). Elsewhere, he played Tintin in *Hergé's Adventures of Tintin* at the Barbican (2005-6), the Groom in Brecht's *A Respectable Wedding* at the Young Vic (2007), Hollarcut in *The Sea* by Edward Bond at Theatre Royal Haymarket (2007) and Gary in *A Miracle*, a new play by Molly Davies at the Royal Court as part of the 2009 Young Writers Festival.

Russell is also a playwright, and his play *Walls* was produced at Battersea Arts Centre in 2003. He has had readings at the National Theatre Studio of *In the Margins* (2007) and *A Rock and a Hard Place* (2005), and of *Hero* at the Soho Theatre in 2001.

Nina Pickering

Nina is a Senior Staff Nurse at the hospital which is where she meets George. With a distinctly fiery and rather stroppy manner she could not be more opposite to calm, gentle George, but there is an immediate attraction which she really doesn't quite understand. Why George? Eventually they get together after being set up by Mitchell – if he had left George to get on with it then they would never even have shared a lift!

Nina finds it difficult to cope with George as he obviously has secrets. He drops hints about how he is not the person he seems and in exasperation she finishes with him. He runs to her after Bernie is knocked down in the street and she takes him back. She shows him the extensive burn scars she has all over her abdomen but won't tell him what happened, only that "people are bastards." She recognises George as a man with secrets as she has secrets of her own to keep.

In the series one finale George transforms into a werewolf, intending to kill Herrick and having finished with Nina (again) first, as he thinks he may not survive. She tracks him down by following Mitchell and sees him as the wolf and what he does. He inadvertently scratches her during his transformation but she tells no one until the next full moon, when she confides in Annie. She is a werewolf.

It is impossible for them to deal with the fact that George gave her his curse and she cannot settle into the supernatural life she is living – a ghost and a vampire are a lot to cope with. Seeing George and Mitchell help Carl, an old vampire friend of Mitchell's, escape after he murdered his lover, is the last straw for her. She walks away, only to fall into the clutches of Kemp and Lucy. A serious case of frying pan versus fire.

They promise her a cure and she takes her place in the chamber, only for Lucy to save her – not from compassion but to keep her alive as bait to lure George to them. Her time in the Facility leaves her bitter and angry, desperate for revenge. Unlike George and Mitchell who have accepted – although not forgotten or forgiven – what happened, Nina is not going quietly. She blames herself for getting them all involved with Kemp. Can she and George find some sort of stability after all they have been through? Can two werewolves be happy and can Nina get over her anger and bitterness now that Lucy is dead?

Where have I seen... Sinead Keenan (Nina)?

Sinead Keenan is an Irish actor who has worked mostly in the UK. She is well known for playing Kelly Hawkins in *Moving Wallpaper* (2008-9) and for her appearance as Addams, the spiky green Vinvocci in David Tennants's final *Doctor Who: The End of Time* (2009-10). She has also appeared as Alice Martin in *Taggart* (in 2007), Elena in *Doctors* (in 2008), Nora Brent in *Agatha Christie's Poirot: The Clocks* (2009) and Delia Smith's secretary in Victoria Wood's *Mid Life Christmas* (2009).

Sinead has filmed two episodes of *Silent Witness*, playing Naomi Silverlake, which will be shown in 2011.

Her film appearances include Margaret in *Sunburn* (1999), Sinead Delany in *On the Nose* (2001), Majella in *Conspiracy of Silence* (2003) and Kathy in *Trouble with Sex* (2005).

Sinead has worked consistently on stage and was a member of the Royal Shakespeare Company. For the RSC, she played Hermia in *A Midsummer Night's Dream* and Luciana in *The Comedy of Errors*, both for the 2005-6 season, and was The Daughter in *American Pilot* by David Grieg in 2006. Other theatre roles include Adele in Gary Mitchell's play *Loyal Women* for the Royal Court Theatre in 2003 and Desdemona in *Othello* for the Salisbury Playhouse in 2007.

Lee Tully

Tully is the werewolf who attacked George and gave him the curse, made him into a werewolf. He has been trying to track him down and finally finds him in Bristol. He befriends him, tempting him with help on how to manage his condition. Eventually he tells George what he did to him, but when George learns the truth he rejects Tully and attacks him, leaving him scarred.

Tully is another enigma – we know he lost a wife and son when he became a werewolf but that's all. We have no idea who infected him or even how long he has been a werewolf, although he tells George he's been doing this "for years." He is lonely and looking for like-minded company, but does their doomed friendship give us a clue that werewolves make uneasy companions, even for each other?

Tully gains some redemption when he follows Craig and Amy into the chamber after leaving a message to warn George. He becomes one of the four ruined faces that Lucy sees every day in her nightmares: Craig Ford, Amy McBride, Lee Tully, Richard Galvin. The other werewolves.

Where have I seen... Dean Lennox Kelly (Tully)?

An extensive acting CV including playing Kev in *Shameless* (in 2004-7), Dickie in *Married Single Other* (2010), Hedley Huthwaite in *The Invisibles* (2008), Malcolm in *Robin Hood* (in 2009), Apostle James in *The Passion* (2008) and Job Gregson in *Cranford* (in 2007).

He will be providing the voice for John Lennon in the 3D remake of *Yellow Submarine* (but will not be singing!).

He played Shakespeare in *Doctor Who: The Shakespeare Code* in 2007 and tried out some similar charm to that which Tully used on Annie on Martha Jones – again not with great success but to a rather less tragic outcome.

He narrated nineteen episodes of *The Real Hustle* in 2006 – George and Mitchell's absolute favourite programme.

Dean starred with his brother Craig Kelly as Danny Rampton in *Collision* (2009), which also featured *Being Human*'s Lenora Crichlow, playing fictional as well as real-life siblings. Craig Kelly appeared in the 2009 series of *Strictly Come Dancing*. Partnered with Flavia Cacace his efforts were not, in all honesty, widely admired, but they survived until round eight – bowing out in Blackpool's Tower Ballroom. Dean appeared with them on one of the rehearsal shows and showed a lot more talent! Maybe they should have asked Aidan Turner for some tips. He told the *Irish Tribune* in March 2009, "I did Ballroom and Latin American dancing for about ten years; I even represented Ireland."

Despite some diligent online searching (and not just by me I would add), no photographic evidence of this fascinating tidbit appears to exist.

Unless – of course – you know differently...

The Ghosts

Ghosts, spirits and apparitions seem to have been subjected to fewer fictional rules than vampires and werewolves. Could this be because they may not actually be fictional? – a considerable debate to postpone to another time.

Sykes explains that the ghostly world in *Being Human* is very straightforward. There is death and the door and the ghosts are lingering somewhere in between. Trouble is, Annie is an exception, she is something different.

Most ghosts are still lingering due to something unresolved about their death or their life. Once that resolution is found then they can pass over to wherever it is they go next. Kathleen and baby ghost Rufus are waiting for their landlord to be prosecuted for the faulty heater that killed them; Gilbert passes on after he falls in love; while Jimmy's wife admitting her affair enables him to move on.

Ghosts are invisible to humans although they can be seen by supernatural beings such as vampires and werewolves. If they become angry or unsettled they may become poltergeists, and whether they can control this or not seems to depend on their inner strength. Annie becomes visible when her confidence is high early in series one but it doesn't last and it seems that no other ghosts can be seen, although there are psychics such as Hennessey and Alan Cortez who can hear them.

Ghosts are fixed in their appearance even more than vampires are; they cannot change their clothes, staying forever in the outfit they died in. Poor Annie – an eternity in Ugg boots. The clothes thing doesn't seem entirely odd but consider further. The ghosts gathering in the theatre waiting for Alan Cortez to help them make you think – the sensible smattering of nightwear and uniforms, but also a full diving suit, a dog costume and a bondage harness... Beware unusual and dangerous hobbies – you may have to wear the outfit for eternity!!

Ghosts cannot eat or drink and do not need to sleep. They can 'jump' from place to place instantly (useful trick) and Kathleen shows she can 'jump' her baby into her arms. That needs a genetic link though, and when Annie tries it she ends up embracing the toaster.

Ghosts have died and have seen the same dreadful things that the vampires have: "Men with ropes and men with sticks and men with black, black feathers on their black, black wings." Passing over for ghosts – a final death – is represented in *Being Human* as a door. While this may have been a decision originally driven by budget, it is neat and very clever. The doors are different for each person and as we see more we realise that what is inside the door varies too. In some cases there is light, in some there is darkness and through Saul's door is a red-carpeted corridor.

We don't really know what happens beyond the door – the bright light that welcomes Gilbert seems a far cry from the black void that took Annie. Annie rescues the boys by dragging Kemp through a door and manages to tell them about where she is. It's a Kafka-esque bureaucracy of numbers and forms, progressing through rooms while people whisper and others disappear – she's scared. Is there a way back from this limbo? Where are the other ghosts disappearing to?

Annie Sawyer

Annie Sawyer is a ghost. She has been haunting the house where she died at the age of 22 in what was apparently just a tragic accident. Tied to the house and unseen by the people around her, she has driven out all of the previous tenants – either deliberately or in a desperate attempt to make contact. When Mitchell and George arrive she finds that other supernatural beings can see her and talk to her. George, it has to be said, is initially unimpressed. Other people, he moans, get damp or woodlice, but they have to live with Casper.

Annie is a ghost due to something being unresolved in her death – Mitchell tries to explain but although he has come across ghosts before (he introduces Annie to Gilbert) he seems rather bemused by the whole deal. Annie's quest is to resolve her death and pass on, but the story turns darker after we find out that her fiancé killed her in a row over her alleged infidelity. The more we see about their relationship and learn about Annie and Owen, the more we can see how Annie was abused and her self-esteem destroyed. Her powers as a ghost are linked to that self-esteem – the more confident she is, the more visible to humans and the further she can move. After rediscovering the memory that Owen killed her, she becomes an angry poltergeist – although her powers are initially a little unruly and not great for the kitchen supplies.

Annie has a huge setback after she tries to haunt Owen having become visible enough for him to see her – and she tries to warn his new girlfriend Janey that she is in danger. Owen couldn't be less scared, in fact he is cruel, killing Annie again and again with his vicious words until she is completely lost. It is a valuable insight into what made Annie who she is. That casual but utter cruelty, the calculated confession of the affair he had shows us just how miserable Annie must have been when she was still alive.

Annie resolves her state of limbo by revenging herself on Owen – maybe not the most PC action in the world but we were all cheering her on. She uses her new confidence and the help of George and Mitchell to scare Owen with the unknown and she tells him the worst thing in the world. What this is we have no idea, but it must be much more than the men with sticks and ropes that await the dead. After sending Owen through the streets – driven quite mad – to the police station to seek sanctuary, Annie's door appears, the means by which she can pass over. She is torn, clearly finding it hard to leave, and by delaying is interrupted by Herrick's attempts to kill Mitchell and so chooses to help her friends rather than go through the door.

No one turns down death and initially this brings a new confidence for Annie. At the start of series two she can be seen by all and even has the confidence to get a job (despite still being a bit squishy). The Gatekeepers won't let her go – no one escapes their door, it just isn't done. They use any means they can to get her, including Terry Wogan instructing potential boyfriend Saul to drag her through his own door! She manages to escape after Saul realises he can't take her with him, can't destroy her, but the Gatekeepers will have their revenge and Annie is invisible again.

She learns more about her situation, helped by older ghost Sykes. He teaches her to read auras and how to close the doors and defeat the Gatekeepers. He knows these skills as he is avoiding his own door, mainly due to the fear of meeting the colleagues who died because of him.

Even Annie isn't perfectly safe – eventually a combination of exorcism, an available door and the power of the Gatekeepers drag her screaming through. Mitchell and George can't save her but they are determined to get her back.

Where have I seen... Lenora Crichlow (Annie)?

Lenora Crichlow trained as an actor with the YoungBlood Theatre Company in London. At just 19 Lenora made her first TV appearance as Stacy in *Bella & the Boys* (2004), followed by a recurring role in *The Bill* as Shirley Moss (in 2004).

She starred as Sugar in the ground-breaking Channel 4 drama *Sugar Rush* from 2005-6, followed by roles including Cheen in *Doctor Who: Gridlock* (2007), Jude Whiley in *Kiss of Death* (2008), Miss Baker in *The Things I Haven't Told You* (2008) and two appearances in *Casualty* (as Linda Surrey in 2005 and Michelle in 2008). She played Alice Jackson in *Collision* (2009) and starred as Ali Redcliffe in BBC One's *Material Girl* (2010).

Her first film appearance came in 2006 in the small-budget UK horror film *Wilderness* as Mandy, after which she played Maureen in *The Beloved Ones* in 2007.

On stage, Lenora has played Claudine in *Big White Fog* at the Almeida Theatre in 2008, as well as touring with Levi David Addai's play *93.2 FM* in 2006.

Gilbert

Gilbert died in 1985 and remained that quintessential 80s kid for ever – or at least until he met Annie. The height of 80s angst and cool, he drifted into her life on a wave of Euro Goth Chanson and discovered that he could – after all – fall in love.

In a continuing theme, we know nothing of how Gilbert died or where he came from, but he showed Annie something so important – a peaceful passing. He is a ghost who is happy to be so. He carried on doing what he's always done, invisible and yet content, not seeing any need to move on while the world moved on around him. However, when his door comes it opens to let out a clear bright white light and he smiles as he goes.

Where have I seen… Alex Price (Gilbert)?

Alex Price shows huge promise as an actor – I know that the point of acting is to be different in different roles but not everyone manages it. Alex Price certainly does – well worth looking out for!

He has the obligatory appearances in *Casualty* (in 2008) and *Doctors* (in 2010) on the CV, nicely seasoned with guest appearances in *Lewis: Falling Darkness* (2010) as Victor Clerval and as William in *Merlin: The Once and Future Queen* (2009). His film work includes *Fervour* in 2007 and *Clubbed* in 2008.

In 2010, he appeared in series five of *Doctor Who* in the episode *Vampires of Venice*, penned by *Being Human* creator Toby Whithouse, as Francesco Calvierri, an alien masquerading as a vampire in sixteenth-century Venice.

He is also finding a niche in narration and he narrated the *Being Human Unearthed* documentary for BBC Three, as well as thirteen editions of *Doctor Who Confidential*.

In 2007, Alex went to America to make the film *A Horse with No Name* with filmmakers Matthew and Barnaby O'Connor. What he didn't know – in fact, no one knew – was that they only had $10,000 and no script. They intended to literally make it all up as they went along. Alongside this was to be a 'making of' documentary, which turned out to be a brutally honest account of filmmaking in the raw. Against all the odds they did make a film, in which English DJ Vince Vinyl (Alex Price) meets American society girl Sophie (Molly Ryan) and they embark on a quirky voyage of romance and discovery.

Sykes

Sykes meets Annie when he closes a door that she is being dragged through. Did he search her out or just happen by? I'd like to think he was looking out for her. He's been a ghost since WW2, when he died with his men after a bad decision in the heat of battle. He doesn't want his door as he's scared of what he will find there and he has learnt to fight back. He teaches Annie to read auras, to fight the powers of the Gatekeepers and to close doors for herself.

We don't see Sykes pass over so maybe we'll see him again one day. He seems to be known amongst the ghost community – perhaps now he has helped Annie he can help others and so make up for the deaths on his conscience. Kathleen lets slip that there is a ghostly community that he tells all about Annie, a community where Annie is famous.

He also warns Annie – one day she may want to pass over, she may choose to. Life moves on around her and eventually it will become painful to see others live, love and die, knowing she can't ever participate. Maybe Annie's friendship with Mitchell negates this slightly, as she has another unchanging immortal around her to make it seem less frightening. Mitchell has survived 100 years – she can surely manage to do so too?

Where have I seen... Bryan Dick (Sykes)?

Bryan Dick trained as a classical dancer but worked professionally as a child actor; his first major role was in *The Life and Times of Henry Pratt* in 1992. After deciding that dancing wasn't how he wanted to spend the rest of his life, he studied at LAMDA and has worked extensively in TV since he graduated.

His TV roles include D.C. Blythe in *Blackpool* (2004), Prince Turveydrop in *Bleak House* (2005), Danny in *Sold* (2007), Jake Barton in *All the Small Things* (2009), Daniel Stafford in *Ashes to Ashes* (in 2010) and Ian Bately in *Excluded* (2010).

In 2008 he appeared in the *Torchwood* episode *Adam,* playing the eponymous character. It has to be said that there is a touch of Captain Jack about Sykes's outfit – although their characters could not be further apart!

In autumn 2010 Bryan is filming *When Eric Met Ernie*, a TV drama about the early lives of Eric Morecambe and Ernie Wise. Bryan plays the adult Ernie alongside Daniel Rigby as Eric and Vic Reeves as Eric's father. The drama is produced by Victoria Wood, who also appears as Eric's redoubtable mother Sadie.

Bryan's film work includes playing Joseph Nagle in *Master and Commander: The Far Side of the World* (2003), and he was also in *Brothers of the Head* (2005) and *Colour Me Kubrick* (2006). In 2007 he played the werewolf Rafe in *Blood and Chocolate*.

On stage, he played Mozart in *Amadeus* in 2007 at the Sheffield Crucible Theatre and has appeared at the National Theatre in *The Alchemist* and *The Life of Galileo*, both in 2006.

The Humans

Professor Lucy Jaggat and Kemp

In series two of *Being Human*, the threat comes from humanity rather than from the supernatural world. That threat is personified in the neat pairing of Kemp and Lucy – opposites in pretty much every way.

Their threat to the supernatural world is very real – Kemp hates vampires for what they did to his family, although the source of his contempt for were-wolves is less clear. He believes they are possessed and claims that their souls can be freed, but does he really believe this? As we see more and more of this man of faith, it seems that he just wants to destroy. His faith is absolute. The supernatural are evil, there can be no shades of grey and if they die then he won't mourn. Why would he – they weren't human after all?

Lucy is less absolute but is deeply influenced by Kemp. A scientist researching what she calls the genetics of evil, she always had a belief, a faith, but kept it as a guilty secret. When she published her hypothesis on intelligent design, her secret was out and her colleagues ridiculed and ostracised her. When Kemp searched her out she was initially wary but soon realised that this was someone she could work with. Her faith and her science could finally be aligned.

The control of the partnership switches back and forth throughout the series – sometimes it looks as though Lucy is redeemable and sometimes it looks as if she is more absolute about their aims than Kemp. That is something that is never fully resolved – for all her penitence at the end of series two, does she really mean it? She has been less than truthful throughout and her apologies, her reparations, may be just another item on her agenda. Can we believe any of it?

Kemp's role as her mentor takes a rather dark turn when we see he has been stealing her belongings and that maybe he is insane. Does Lucy ever see that? We don't know what happened after George and Mitchell left the Facility – were Lucy and Kemp continuing to plot or did she really walk away? She told George she loved Mitchell – that was what he wanted to hear but she never said this to Mitchell. Maybe that's what he needed all along, a woman who loved him and could save him. It would seem to be exactly what Lucy would want and her rebuttal makes me more convinced that she never intended to care. She slept with Mitchell as a part of her plan and then headed straight to church for some cleansing and forgiveness. Surely a bit of (hopefully) decent sex with a pretty vampire shouldn't have sent her so far into guilt that she felt blowing up 30 others would ease her conscience?

After Lucy allowed herself to be seduced by evil (as Kemp would have it), the balance of power shifted and Kemp was firmly in charge. Lucy had let him down. (Although – you have a choice: Mitchell or Kemp? What would you do?!) Kemp's desire to avenge his wife and child, the absolute truth of his belief and Lucy's betrayal add up to a madness that he can't control and which eventually leads him to kill Lucy.

A spirit Annie (if a ghost can have a spirit) then drags him through Lucy's door, saving Nina, George and Mitchell. This leaves us with a selection of interesting questions. What about Lucy's ghost? That was her door but her ghost did not appear. Maybe she felt she had resolved her life already, although I think that could be as deluded as the rest of her science/faith/nonsense! And what about Kemp? He has passed through a door but he isn't dead and it wasn't his door. As Annie says – there is no form for that.

Where have I seen... Lyndsey Marshal (Lucy)?

Lyndsey Marshal trained at the Royal Welsh College of Music and Drama and had appeared at the Royal Court Theatre in *Fireface* before graduation. She won the Critics' Circle Theatre Award for the best newcomer in 2001 for playing Lucy in *Redundant* at the Royal Court and Catherine in *Boston Marriage* at the Donmar Warehouse. She won a TMA Theatre Award for best supporting actress as Hermia in *A Midsummer Night's Dream* at the Bristol Old Vic in 2003. She has also appeared in *A Matter of Life and Death* for the National Theatre in 2007, as Sylvia in *The Pride* at the Royal Court in 2008 and as Nan/Lida in *Three Days of Rain* at the Apollo Theatre in 2009.

She is a familiar TV face from her role as Cleopatra in the lavish HBO series *Rome* in 2005, a role she reprised for the second series in 2007. Among her many other TV appearances are Lady Sarah Hill in *Garrow's Law* (2009), Jessica in *A Short Stay in Switzerland* (2009), Amy Gibbs in *Marple: Murder is Easy* (2008), Isabel Meredith in *The Shadow in the North* (2007) and Ethel Monticue in *The Young Visiters* (2003).

She is also known for the film *The Hours* (2002) in which she played Lottie Hope. Other film work includes Emily in *1234* (2008), Faith Myers in *Festival* (2005), Tracey in *Frozen* (2005) and Simon's Girlfriend in the segment *Standing Room Only* in the film *Stories of Lost Souls* (2005).

43

Where have I seen... Donald Sumpter (Kemp)?

Donald Sumpter has had a long and illustrious career spanning more than four decades. Picking out roles will inevitably leave more out that are just as good but I will try and give a taste of his TV and film work.

One of his early television appearances was the 1968 *Doctor Who* story *The Wheel in Space* with Patrick Troughton as the Doctor. He appeared in *Doctor Who* again in the 1972 story *The Sea Devils* with Jon Pertwee. A recent related role was with *Doctor Who* spin-off *The Sarah Jane Adventures* playing Erasmus Darkening in 2009.

Between 1995 and 2000 he had the recurring role of Uncle Ginger in children's series *The Queen's Nose* and has appeared as Matthew Pyke in *The Buddha of Suburbia* (1993), Commander Harold Chapple in *Our Friends in the North* (1996), Mr Brooker in *The Life and Adventures of Nicholas Nickleby* (2001) and Mr Gerald Gardiner in *The Chatterley Affair* (2006).

More recently he has been seen as Stephen Kirby in *Spooks* (in 2010), Lord Halifax in *Into the Storm* (2009), Max Planck in *Einstein and Eddington* (2008), Parson Tringham in *Tess of the D'Urbervilles* (2008) and King Edward in *Heist* (2008).

In the theatre he played Claudius to Paul Rhys's Hamlet in the play of the same name at the Young Vic in 1999.

Film work includes playing Tim Donohue in *The Constant Gardener* (2005), Dr Gennadi Savran in *K19: The Widowmaker* (2002), Leveret in *Enigma* (2001), Claudius in *Rosencrantz & Guildenstern Are Dead* (1990) and Donald Neilson in *The Black Panther* (1977).

In an interesting coincidence of titles, he appeared in the 1993 Bill Forsyth film *Being Human* as Salgedo, as well as a 2009 short film called *God & Lucy* in which he played God.

3

quote, unquote

Russell Tovey on...

... his first impression

"I thought it sounded like a kids' show. It didn't seem like it would ever work. Then, I read it and realised it was just so much more than that. That's why it's great. The levels in this show are so much more human than they are supernatural. That's what its selling point is, and that's why so many people connect with it." [Collider.com]

... George

"He's always had a slight neurosis... I'd say verging on OCD." [BBC Being Human blog]

"He hates, hates, hates what he is. He completely battles against it the whole time. It's exhausting for him. He's exhausted by it." [BBC Being Human blog]

"George is weird to normal people, George is very weird, George is weird to himself and he hates that but it suddenly becomes endearing to Nina which is a novelty to George." [BBC Being Human blog]

... Annie

"She loved life and it's been taken away from her." [BBC Being Human blog]

... Mitchell

"He's just cool. Mitchell is just cool, annoyingly. Yeah, really annoyingly. He's cool." [BBC Being Human blog]

... Nina

"Nina's horrible to begin with; Nina's a right mardy mare!" [BBC Being Human blog]

... Tully

"Tully is uber-confident, very charming. Tully has the same sort of quality that Mitchell has, which is what George thinks he will never be but in Tully, he believes suddenly that, you know, if he can do it, I can do it." [BBC Being Human blog]

... getting naked

"For some reason George always gets naked before he transforms and you see my bum all the time. If that's what people want to see! No, I go to the gym quite regularly anyway. I keep myself physical. I don't think George would be a superhunk at all. He's a fairly average man." [The Guardian]

... Toby Whithouse

"You are guided by the master. The Jedi, Toby Whithouse, through the show.

I'm his Luke Skywalker." [Digital Spy]

... what makes Being Human so good

"It's the writing, without a doubt. It's kind of *This Life*, *Buffy*, *Cold Feet*... all the good shows you like, it's got those qualities. And it's got a warm, human element; people just trying to get on in life and be accepted." [The Guardian]

... the American remake

"I think it means people will be more interested in our show. They've probably got a much bigger budget, but I think that part of why our show is a success is that it's low key. We're on BBC America so we hopefully won't be forgotten – people will make comparisons like with *The Office* and *Queer As Folk*. In the end it can only be beneficial, but it's nothing to do with us. I hope it's successful, but a part of me hopes they fluff it up and it's not as good as our show!" [Sky.com]

... working with Lenora and Aidan

"I think the fact [is] that this is, for us personally, so well written and the characters are so brilliant. And I think the fear we had right when we shot it, right at the beginning – if people don't like George, Annie and Mitchell, then they're not going to go in there with us. But people really love them.

"We're like the Spice Girls. There's one of you for everyone. Whatever Spice Girl you're into, we can cover those bases. So people get into the show and we can take them anywhere. And that's really rewarding." [Lifeofwylie.com]

Lenora Crichlow on...

... her first impression

"I remember going in for the audition and I thought it was such a stupid idea when I was told about it. I was like, 'Give me a break!' And then, I read the script and I laughed out loud, and I thought, 'Either this is really clever, because I drew the parallels from what was there on the page, or maybe I've read too much into it.' I thought it was such an interesting, different way of approaching all the relationships and dynamics of a flat-share. So, I went into my audition saying, 'Is this where you're going with it?' and when they said yes, I was like, 'My god, that's really interesting.'" [Collider.com]

... Annie

"Love-struck Annie – she's definitely still in love with Owen and in love with the life they had planned. Her idea of love is to be needed and to be doing something for someone." [BBC Being Human blog]

"The character itself, I think, had she not died, would probably have its tragic side, but I think the Annie that we see grow and develop is someone that is incredibly passionate and giving and loving and emotional, and those are good traits to set someone on the right road, so I don't know how tragic she'd be without her situation, but her situation just makes your heart bleed." [Bullz-eye.com]

... George

"George is just so lovely." [BBC Being Human blog]

... Mitchell

"He's more of a fatherly figure in the house or big brother role. He's definitely the alpha-male type character, and Annie and George look to him to just be solid as a rock." [BBC Being Human blog]

... Sykes

"He's got unresolved issues and fears that he clearly hasn't looked at and he finally tells Annie them. We don't see him pass over but we get the sense that just in sharing that with Annie there's some kind of resolution for him." [BBC Being Human blog]

... what makes Being Human so good

"There's a comedy aspect and a drama aspect so you don't need to be a hard-core sci-fi fan to like it. It's a mixture of genres – it's funny but dark and a bit unique." [Metro.co.uk]

... other supernatural shows

"What sets the show apart is that we're not very good at being supernatural. I think our characters have a different angst to these other shows." [The Guardian]

... the American remake

"I can't wait to see it. I'm very intrigued. It seems a testament to the British version of the show and I'm just very excited to see it really. It has nothing to do with me on a personal level. I don't have any input or anything like that. It will just be like watching a brand new show, which I think will be very interesting." [Craveonline.com]

... working with Russell and Aidan

"I think we push each other as actors, which is rare. Honestly, I'm inspired by watching these guys, and it's lovely to have people your age group, who are your peers, that you can vibe with and chill with, but then also, creatively and professionally, go to for advice and be inspired by and admire. And, we're all so different as well. None of us are going to be head-to-head for parts, so there's no competition. There's just complete love and support for each other, as actors." [Collider.com]

Aidan Turner on...

... his first impression

"The concept of a vampire, werewolf and ghost living together is so wacky and so wrong in so many ways." [TV Choice Magazine]

"For such an obvious idea, it just came out original, which is weird. It seems as though it's the most basic supernatural idea possible, in some ways, but Toby has created this show that stands on its own, which is really cool. We're all very happy it worked out." [Collider.com]

... Mitchell

"The funny thing is, when the idea was conceived, Toby Whithouse thought of the character as Irish for no other reason than he wanted to have an Irish vampire. Maybe subconsciously when I went into the meeting it triggered something in his head and worked in my favour." [Sunday Tribune]

"He struggles with it an awful lot... whether he should just give in to being a vampire and just going with what that's about because that is what he is and why deny that?" [BBC Being Human blog]

"I mean there's only so much of killing and rampaging you can do before you get a pain in your ass about it." [BBC Being Human blog]

... George

"I think Mitchell would and does trust him with his life and vice versa." [BBC Being Human blog]

... Annie

"Annie unknowingly gives a sort of essence to the whole, the trio, the whole friendship, that without her, I think we'd really miss, Mitchell and George would really miss." [BBC Being Human blog]

... Herrick

"Mitchell is a valuable commodity for Herrick." [BBC Being Human blog]

... Lauren

"Guess he feels really sorry for her. She's not a bad person. She certainly wasn't before she met him, I don't think." [BBC Being Human blog]

... what makes Being Human so good

"It works really well and that's what's the important thing about the show is, you have to absolutely believe that these guys are what they are and doing what they're doing. They're flatmates working through the hard times. If it was glamorised and more sci-fi you'd just lose that element. We're doing something that actually I think is quite original and kind of rare." [Pinkpaper.com]

... the American remake

"It's going to be a very different show, I would imagine, 'cause they have money and we didn't have any of that, really. They have a budget, those lucky swines. But, it will be a very different show. There will be tons more episodes. It's a huge testament to the brand that is Being Human, and to Toby Whithouse and his amazing, creative mind. But, there's no fear. People know that we exist. Budget doesn't mean better." [Collider.com]

"The Mitchell character has a new, sexy name as well, which is really cool. He's going to be called Aidan, in the new series. That's the truth." [Collider.com]

... working with Lenora and Russell

"We're so different, all of us, quite different people. Russell can be quite extroverted sometimes, and I'm quite the opposite in weird ways. [Our tight friendship] just happened. It's a funny thing. I did another series after this one where it's about a brotherhood in Victorian London, and we knew we had to get along, and we did [but it wasn't the same]. I don't know why it works, why you get on with some people, and sometimes you don't." [Thetorchonline.com]

Sinead Keenan on...

... her first impression

"Before I got the script, I was told it was called Being Human and was about a werewolf, vampire and ghost, and I went, 'Oh dear, is it for CBBC?' But it's so well written by Toby [Whithouse], it was a no brainer to say yes to it. The whole ghost, vampire and werewolf thing is almost incidental – it is about being human. They are doing their best to live like human beings." [Angel.greatbritishlife.co.uk]

... Nina

"I think I'm a lot warmer person than Nina. Because of her past (Nina's had quite a tough life) she's built up this wall and is now a bit of a hard nut to crack, though she does have a soft centre underneath, but on the outside she appears very tough and abrasive that you have to work to get past." [Company]

... George

"Nina's intrigued by him initially because she really wipes the floor with him the first time she's had any contact with him and then apologises and in her apologising he then becomes very cocky and asks her out." [BBC Being Human blog]

... getting naked

"When I was reading the scripts and I found out that I was going to be a werewolf, I thought, 'Oh, sweet Jesus.' Russell does his transformations fantastically and is very willing and able to take his clothes off, at a moment's

51

notice. And then, I read the first episode where Nina transforms and it said, 'And, in the morning, she wakes up and there's a coat covering her.' I went, 'Now, you're doing that because I'm a girl. Thank you for that, but it should be equal opportunity.' So, at the very end of the day, poor Lenora got an eyeful. There was a coat covering my derriere, but it was shimmied down a lot more. But, yeah, I do get a little bit naked, just not as much." [Collider.com]

... working with Russell, Lenora and Aidan

"I think we're all very aware that this is a very special project. It's not like a job. It's very rare that you go to work every day, wanting to go to work every day, and getting on with everyone, for the most part. We have fun." [Collider.com]

Toby Whithouse on...

... the reaction to the pilot

"It was getting this extraordinary response. And somebody said on the message forums at one point 'Does anyone believe this? This is clearly an orchestrated campaign by the producers.' I thought, well, you haven't met the producers - we had absolutely nothing to do with it. But it was wonderful to watch it." [BBC Writers Room]

... George

"George is a very punctilious, house-proud, fussy – some might say anal – type of guy who struggles to keep the wilder side of his nature at bay." [BBC Being Human blog]

"He likes to impose order and structure on his life in order to keep his wild side in check." [BBC Being Human blog]

... Annie

"For Annie, her life, as far as she was concerned, was just starting when she died." [BBC Being Human blog]

"Frozen in time, like Miss Havisham in *Great Expectations*. The clock stopped the moment Annie died, and her clothes always remaining the same is a good way of dramatising that." [BBC Being Human blog]

... Mitchell

"In a way George's humanity, in a sense of his kindness and his gentility and honour as a person – it's that humanity that roots Mitchell and keeps him anchored and is his rock." [BBC Being Human blog]

"When it comes to sunlight imagine that Mitchell is... ginger, I guess." [BBC Being Human blog]

... Annie and Mitchell

"Both of them are going to exist forever, in the state that they are. The notion of this screaming eternity in front of them is a terrifying prospect. There's something about that that unites them. Perhaps tragically, there is also an element of Mitchell that would fit into Annie's relationship history. She's not exactly made good choices, so why not go for a 120-year-old mass murderer? It's the next logical step, after dating the guy that killed you. Annie is a character who always looks for the good in another person. Whatever Mitchell has done, there is still an enormous vein of decency, kindness, compassion and humanity within him and Annie responds to that very well." [Collider.com]

... Herrick

"I was always adamant that Herrick should die at the end of the first series and it absolutely broke my heart because Jason Watkins's performance as Herrick was absolutely out of this world." [BBC Being Human blog]

"One of the best screen performances... the best villain I think I've ever seen on television. Absolutely fantastic. Everything I wanted that character to be." [BBC Being Human blog]

... are any of the characters based on him

"I think it's inevitable. Somebody pointed out to me that actually George and Mitchell are basically two halves of my personality. That there's half of me that's very kind of punctilious and house-proud and romantic and wussy. And there's another half that isn't. And kills people." [BBC Writers Room]

... the American remake

"At the moment, I'm a happy bystander because, to be honest, we're in production on series three and I'm still writing the last episode. So my priority is to the UK version. And I'm more than happy for the people of the American marketplace to be handling the American version while I handle the UK version." [Ugo.com]

"I trust that the audience is savvy enough to be able to tell the difference. Though I imagine that the weather in the American version will be much better." [Ugo.com]

... working with the cast

"I don't know specifically how, but the four cast we've got are four of the best actors working on television. It's impossible now to separate them from the characters, in my mind. I try to write every line within the specific voice of the actor. For example, Annie's death doesn't have a drop of blood in it, but it's one of the most horrific scenes in the history of Being Human. There's something about it. And, the performances of everyone in that scene, including Donald Sumpter who played Kemp, and Adrian Schiller who played Hennessey, were just absolutely terrific." [Collider.com]

... comics

"I'd love to [make a Being Human comic]. There was actually discussion of it. Whether that is going to happen or not I don't know, but it's been mentioned. We have Being Human novels already, so I'd love a comic book to follow it. My life would have gone full circle then." [Digital Spy]

... other supernatural characters

"Over the years, people have said to me, 'Oh, god, you know what you need to put in your show? You need to put in a witch. Do a witch. Do a zombie. Do a fairy.' They can move in next door. And, I must admit, there was never a policy decision that we wouldn't have any other creatures. We just couldn't really think of one. And then, we'd say, 'Why don't we do a leprechaun?' The thing is, if you're going to do that, you have to do it in a Being Human way. You can't have a guy with a ginger beard and a hat. You have to find a way of doing it where it fits in with the story, and we've never found a way of doing it. In Season 3, for one night only, there is another creature, but it's not a leprechaun. The reason we decided that we could do it was because we thought of the Being Human way of doing it." [Collider.com]

Jason Watkins on Herrick...

"My take on it was that he is quite a nice guy. Quite a happy, quite funny guy. He is very relaxed in his own company and very relaxed in his positions and in his opinions." [BBC Being Human blog]

"He's got all that appetite and that absolute pure evil." [BBC Being Human blog]

"He demolishes people and he wants slaves. He wants people to adore and worship him." [BBC Being Human blog]

Annabel Scholey on Lauren...

"In one episode she seems to be on top of the world, really confident and sexy and knows exactly what she wants. And then the next minute she's completely out of control and she's like a little child, an addict." [BBC Being Human blog]

"She does very unexpected things, appalling things." [BBC Being Human blog]

Alex Price on Gilbert...

"You could play a character who came from a period such as 1985 when it was OK to read Nietzsche and Shakespeare and be intelligent and be articulate. But I think nowadays it's so uncool, you almost have to hide your intelligence if you're 18, 19 nowadays. It's considered uncool." [BBC Being Human blog]

"He thinks he's God's gift but of course he doesn't really. He's extremely, extremely insecure so it comes out as this monosyllabic – all right, yeah, great, is it? whatever, dead..." [BBC Being Human blog]

Paul Rhys on Ivan...

"I don't think it's at all strange that Ivan sacrifices his own life to save Mitchell. Never occurred to me for a second that it was something that he wouldn't do." [BBC Being Human blog]

"I think Ivan would have liked to have gone in a more globally important situation... Kemp's motives are personal and real but they're finally domestic and minute in the scheme of things globally. They're pathetic and Ivan's not pathetic." [BBC Being Human blog]

Bryan Dick on Sykes...

"Sykes isn't really a hero. He performs heroic acts but he's not really willing to help Annie at first." [BBC Being Human blog]

"We never really find out what Sykes's story is but it's not a pleasant one." [BBC Being Human blog]

4

series one

The essence of being human is that one does not seek perfection, that one is sometimes willing to commit sins for the sake of loyalty, that one does not push asceticism to the point where it makes friendly intercourse impossible, and that one is prepared in the end to be defeated and broken up by life, which is the inevitable price of fastening one's love upon other human individuals.

George Orwell
1903-1950

episode one

George has nowhere to transform safely but he shouldn't go down to the woods today.

Mitchell avoids a memorial, has a date and almost falls off the wagon.

Annie has a setback when her former fiancé visits the house and reminisces.

It starts here – and Herrick wants to know which side Mitchell is on.

broadcast:	25 JANUARY 2009	director:	TOBY HAYNES
writer:	TOBY WHITHOUSE	producer:	MATTHEW BOUCH

cast:

Annie	LENORA CRICHLOW	Tully	DEAN LENNOX KELLY
Mitchell	AIDAN TURNER	Janey	SAMA GOLDIE
George	RUSSELL TOVEY	Maintenance Man	HOWARD COGGINS
Lauren	ANNABEL SCHOLEY	Canteen Girl	REBECCA COOPER
Herrick	JASON WATKINS	HCA Nurse	SARAH COUNSELL
Owen	GREGG CHILLIN	Werewolf	PAUL KASEY
Seth	DYLAN BROWN	Pizza Delivery Boy	GEORGE OLIVER
Becca	JESSICA HARRIS		

"Everyone deserves a death…"

It's an interesting challenge – episode one. Not only does it have to provide a fresh start for the many new viewers, it also has to follow on from a pilot that gained a cult following. A following that was considered vociferous enough to help to reverse the initial BBC decision and get *Being Human* made into a full series. While coping with recasting two out of the three leads as well as two of the main recurring characters, there is also a distinct change of tone and I think that the series is much better for the change. The vampires are less gothic, they owe a great deal less to Anne Rice and fit better with the other characters. It is more everyday and much more grounded. These are real people, they just happen to have some odd supernatural secrets. It is also funnier and the light and dark contrast beautifully due to some clever writing and neat delivery.

The pre-title sequence rattles us neatly through the introductions and definitions while Annie's matter-of-fact voiceover contrasts with the visions of death and despair. Mitchell's mortal World War One self was looking for glory but found a terrifying reality culminating in his conversion to vampirism "to save his men". Maybe that moment of sacrifice was his true glory. Cut to present-day Mitchell at the Bristol war memorial and introducing Aidan Turner. He's a less ethereal vampire than Guy Flanagan in the pilot, less gothic. He's pretty much a normal bloke (apart from being dead, of course) and rather more earthily good-looking than the pale and languid Guy.

In a remake of a scene from the pilot we see the new Mitchell and Lauren and the frantic sex that caused Mitchell to lose all control and kill Lauren. In comparison to Guy Flanagan's retreat from the situation – hiding regretfully in the bathroom – here Mitchell's furious physical punishment of himself is painfully real.

61

Life as a ghost is lonely. Invisible and alone, Annie desperately attempts to make contact at her own wake, trying fruitlessly to be seen. At least her family were all around her she concedes, even though she died before her specified ripe old age. Lenora Crichlow replaces Andrea Riseborough as Annie and gets a whole new costume to (knitted Ugg) boot! There's a glimpse of Owen, Annie's grieving fiancé, being comforted in his loss. Not to mention the considered but invisible one-fingered salute offered by Annie to the potential tenants of what was to be her and Owen's forever home. A tracking shot across the cracked tile where Annie fell reminds us that she is tied forever in death to the house where she lived and dreamed.

Then there are the ones who should never have survived. We see George being attacked and in hospital, scarred and in despair. Interestingly, it is only George's condition that isn't identified. Mitchell and Annie are named as vampire and ghost but for George the truth is not explicit. We see his scars, his transformation (and the first of many lingering shots of Russell Tovey's bum) and know that he is the "big bad wolf". A sign to us that while Annie and Mitchell are dead and there is a constancy and finality about their situation, George is still human (well, except for 12 nights a year). He alone has the chance of the normal human life that Annie and Mitchell can only dream of.

The pre-title sequence ends in the mundane. Mitchell and George are sharing a packet of Jammie Dodgers in companionable silence in the hospital cafeteria. We see them moving into Windsor Terrace with an assortment of black bags and a telly while Annie watches, thinking she is unseen. This grounds the episode in the everyday – the real business of being human despite the trio's supernatural reality.

"Maybe... we find each other"

Compared to the pilot the series has a much more domestic feel. Most of the scenes are interiors of the house or the hospital while the pilot had a more open, exterior sense. There is certainly nothing to compare to the amazing long shot in the pilot of George, post transformation, with the uneaten parts of a dead animal against the backdrop of the Clifton Suspension Bridge. This isn't to say that this is a change for the worse. The cramped and cluttered interiors better represent the restrictions and intensity of the lives of our trio. It also gives the opportunity to manipulate the interiors to aid the storytelling and this attention to the details of the settings makes the house in particular an additional character. In keeping with current BBC Three style there is a great soundtrack and the lighting is just gorgeous. The warmth of the house, the cold blue of the external scenes – it adds so much without cluttering the dialogue. You can almost hear the flickering and buzzing of the fluorescent tubes in the hospital.

"He could *so* see you!"

Lenora Crichlow makes a kooky, endearing Annie, excited by the changes that her new friends can bring to her previously bleak ghostly existence. While George is initially wary ("Other people get damp and woodlice – why do we get Casper the friendly ghost?"), Mitchell is already obviously very fond of Annie. It is one of the ways in which the hundred-years-plus age of the vampire shows. Where it could easily look as if Mitchell just fancies Annie, his attitude towards her is protective – not exactly fatherly but more that of a big brother.

There are few women who would be quite so thrilled to be called 'slag' in the street. For Annie, the previously invisible ghost, it is a cause for excited celebration. Since living with George and Mitchell her confidence has increased and she can be seen by people. Other *people* she specifies – supernatural beings like George and Mitchell can always see her. This link of confidence and self-esteem to visibility is a lovely parallel to the normal life of many young women. While they may not actually be invisible, low self-esteem can certainly make you feel that way. The pizza delivery boy seems rather taken aback to be engaged in conversation by an overexcited Annie!

While Mitchell seems to take everything in his stride there is still some distance between George and Annie. Annie likes her routine but her constant tea and coffee making is driving George mad. He can't see why a ghost needs to be busy or to feel normal. It is George's time of the month. "Won't miss that," laughs Annie, although in George's case biting someone's head off could be taken rather more literally. Given George's fear of hurting someone, this throwaway remark does little to diminish the distance between them. Unlike Mitchell, George does not find this at all funny. Annie infuriates George as much as she amuses Mitchell.

"A-positive? A bit Jacobs Creek-y for me"

At the hospital George is preparing for the full moon. He has a safe place in the bowels of the building where he can lock the wolf away until Mitchell lets him out the next morning. As George goes off to work for a while before making his excuses we know we are seeing an established routine and a rather inhibited blokey hug wishes George luck.

Tipped off by an anomaly on the CCTV, Mitchell finds Seth in the hospital. If Mitchell as a vampire doesn't show up on CCTV has no one ever wondered about the magical mop bucket which must seem to be self-operating all over the hospital? Not to mention where he got his photo ID from. After the perennial visitors' complaint that it is impossible to find anything in a hospital, Seth assesses an unconscious patient. "Something in the council," he thinks. Herrick, he tells Mitchell, feels that "recruitment should be more tactical." It's the first sign of a new level of organisation in the vampire ranks. Mitchell is outraged and sends Seth away and the alacrity with which Seth obeys gives us an insight into Mitchell's reputation among the vampires. In fact, he seems more upset at the allusions to his former vampire exploits and Seth's ridicule of him being on the wagon than at the prospect of the vampires feeding on the patients, even those with a frightfully common blood type.

We're not beaten around the head with Mitchell's attempts at abstinence. We are perfectly capable of working this out for ourselves and the parallels to addiction are clear. On the DVD, there's an extended version of Mitchell's pizza eating scene at the beginning of the episode, where Mitchell talks about carbohydrate as a blood substitute. Maybe I should be a vampire – it appears he can live on cereal, pizza and beer and stay healthy! Although I suppose it helps if you are already dead, the need for five a day being rather superfluous. Keeping this scene in the finished version would have made it nice and easy for everyone to figure out Mitchell's status as an on-the-wagon vampire, but quite rightly we don't take the easy route.

George is with Becca, a young nurse, and they are passing a shrine to Lauren, the nurse who died tragically young. Becca didn't know her but George did. "She was beautiful," he remembers, quite oblivious to her true relationship with Mitchell. Mitchell reminds George that it's time he left, it's almost the full moon and George makes a run for it, he's cutting it a bit fine tonight. Mitchell is left with Becca who is dropping some very heavy hints that she has a break due. It's not hard to see she fancies Mitchell.

In the canteen Mitchell is transfixed by the sound of Becca's blood – which is undoubtedly preferable to her rather inane conversation. Hands shaking and distracted, he excuses himself by saying he's given up smoking. She's trying to be all sophisticated to impress Mitchell to no avail. His philosophical treatise on the way his relationships end and his need for something normal goes right over her head. To a vampire who has lived for over a hundred years Becca's small talk must be painfully trite. Escape comes when George appears in a panic. He can't use the isolation room that has been the wolf's safe haven. Mitchell drives him into the countryside against his better judgement. George isn't really the outdoor type.

Mitchell tries to convince him to come back to the house to change but George doesn't want the wolf in the house. He runs through the dark woods seeking a quiet place, finding a family camping holiday, disturbing lovers and dog walkers, until he finds what looks like a likely spot. Starting to strip off, he jumps when a dark figure speaks to him.

"Hello mate. What are you running from?"

Mitchell is concerned for George but he can't hang around all night. Luckily (for George) his car won't start. Must be an occupational hazard of driving a rather stylish 1964 Volvo – just the one careful owner? George has time to catch him up and get into the car, suggesting they head home as if it was all his idea.

They prepare for George to transform in the house – Annie is not happy, she's just hoovered. They cover the windows to avoid reflections and put on loud music. If anyone asks they are having a party. Mitchell is really shaken and is genuinely scared of the arrival of the wolf. Presumably a werewolf could kill a vampire – assuming that tearing them apart kills them. It would be a little uncomfortable to be dismembered and still conscious. Is this why vampires attack werewolves whenever they find them? Get them first to leave them so frightened that they don't even think about what they could do to the vampires come the full moon.

Mitchell heads outside with the TV but Annie wants to watch George change. After all, she's already dead so the werewolf can't hurt her. It's too intrusive for George but Mitchell persuades him. It's part of him, however reluctant he is to acknowledge it. The weekly shot of a nude George, clutching his modesty, and we're away. His torment and agony are reflected in the horror and sympathy in Annie's face. Mitchell finds the screams of George's pain unbearable to hear, even from outside. Annie sticks with George until the transformation is complete, but when the wolf looks into her eyes with no sign of recognition she jumps outside to Mitchell. The George they know and love has gone. They huddle together on the doorstep – two unnatural creatures comforting each other while the crashing and howling of the creature that used to be their friend continues inside.

Dawn breaks to utter devastation – the house is a disaster zone. Furniture smashed, everything broken and the sofa shredded. George, unconscious or asleep, lies peacefully in the centre.

"I'm sensing a trip to IKEA – you know my feelings about that"

Mitchell and Annie clear up – George is horrified, clearly he has no idea what the wolf did. He sees it as an entirely separate entity to his human self. Despite the devastation Annie is excited as Owen, their landlord and her ex-fiancé, is coming to visit. After all, Mitchell and George are his prize tenants – no one else would stay in the house, presumably due to Annie's previous hobby of haunting the tenants. George thinks they are unhinged, his disbelief growing as they work through a list of questions Annie has for Owen. ("Has my sister had a baby?" "Is Owen seeing Janey Harris?") What would happen if Owen saw Annie – after all he buried her! They manage a compromise and Annie hides upstairs. George is adamant that he and Mitchell act perfectly normally; it's a normal situation, completely normal, the most normal thing in the world. "Good luck with that," says Mitchell dryly.

In his self-conscious attempts to act properly, 'normal' George ties himself up in knots and it is a relief to all when he goes upstairs to investigate a mysterious noise. It's Annie, who can't quite contain herself in her desire to see Owen. While they are alone Mitchell offers Owen a beer and takes the opportunity to ask him about her. He remembers how they moved in to the house and how she fell – it was dark – and how he hasn't really been back since. "She was lovely, cleverer than she thought," he continues – the perfect picture of a grieving fiancé who is reluctantly moving on. Although the last line – "and she was mine" – bears closer inspection. Annie was supposed to be the love of his life, not one of the boxes of possessions they were moving into the home they planned to raise their family in.

The reappearance of George and his desperate assertion that the noise had been a pigeon which he had killed (with a shoe) sends Owen on his way. Mitchell's teasing about just how normal George managed to act and George's worry about the clanky tap all fade as Annie puts Owen's discarded beer bottle to her lips, her face a study of loss and grief.

"We left humans to tend this paradise and look what they did to it"

Of course the vampires have a plot – don't they always? Herrick (now played by Jason Watkins) is an unthreatening person, a policeman whose uniform just seems to emphasise his approachability. You really would choose Herrick if you needed to ask the time. He is also in the hospital, doing magic tricks with coins to a fascinated group of staff in the canteen.

Although Herrick seems quite everyday, his speech with Mitchell is complex and distinctive, almost florid and a complete contrast to his open-faced appearance. It all adds towards Herrick's dissatisfaction with his lot. Vampires are all-powerful, immortal and charismatic – however much they try to hide in low-key jobs or in plain sight it can't last. These people could rule the world and one of them must regularly decide that that is their right. Running a funeral parlour, cleaning a hospital or working shifts as a copper is never going to provide an immortal with decent job satisfaction.

Herrick and Mitchell obviously know each other well – we already know that Herrick was the vampire who created Mitchell, although Mitchell insists it was only to save the lives of his men. Herrick is more cynical – of course he would accept immortality instead of old age, death and decay. He too is curtly dismissive of Mitchell's attempts to stay clean. "It's mental." He tempts Mitchell with the prospect of change, something to ponder on. He has to decide whose side he is on.

"You're a shark – be a shark"

George is planning on attending Lauren's memorial – they are planting a tree for her – but Mitchell is evasive, claiming that he didn't really know her. Becca arrives to collect some fresh linen and George surprises her by knowing she has changed her shampoo, just from the smell – followed up by the most excruciating attempt at a chat-up line! Sometimes you need to know when to stop... Mitchell offers to put in a good word for George if he fancies Becca but George finds it all just a little too juvenile. Probably this is just George – I can't see him as a lady-killer even pre-werewolf attack. Mitchell claims to have no interest in Becca but he is shaking – something about her blood is calling to him. Do vampires have a type? A blood type? Or is it the unexplainable call of the addiction to the addict?

After the memorial George is in the loo and Lauren is behind him, not reflecting in the mirror. She approaches him, banking on his terror to make him an easy target but – strangely – he isn't as scared as he should be. Even to a novice vampire this is odd, especially as George immediately makes the link that Mitchell did this to her. Lauren looks again, smells George and is horrified – a werewolf. They must have an odour that is only detectable to vampires or maybe to other supernatural beings. It's only episode one and it is already a normal assumption that there are definitely other supernatural beings!

A furious George finds Mitchell and punches him. How can they ever be human if he is turning their friends into the living dead, into monsters? Mitchell tries to explain. This is how he has survived for a hundred years, this is what a vampire does, but George's fury is unabated. He resents that he has to hide every month to become the wolf to keep away from people while Mitchell flaunts himself.

"Why are we even trying?"

George's anger and condemnation of what and who Mitchell is really hits home. George's disdain has hurt him deeply and when Becca finds him again he is on edge. She's been practicing her chat-up lines in the toilets and Mitchell sees no point in resisting. After all he is only doing what George expects him to; he might as well be the monster George sees. So what the hell?

Annie, meanwhile, having 'borrowed' George's phone, has sent Owen a message about the clanky tap that George finds so offensive. Waiting for Owen to arrive she practices how she will appear to him. She tries some classic ghostly whooooooooo-ing, a reassuring "be not afraid," a casual welcome from the kitchen or jumping out of hiding. Deep down though, she knows he won't be able to see her – but she has to try, she has to be really sure.

66

Owen arrives with company – the very Janey Harris that Annie knew would be after him the moment her head hit the tiles. It seems for a moment that Owen can sense something – he is standing right in front of her – but no, it's just a feeling and he shrugs it off. DIY is not Owen's forte. He has a look at the tap but doesn't have a clue what to do, apart from that man thing of tapping the pipes that achieves nothing but looks vaguely technical.

George arrives home, totally mystified about Owen having received his text until some frantic sign language from Annie helps him out. Owen introduces his partner Janey and promises to come back to sort out the tap.

Annie is desperate. She was so sure that he would be able to see her and she knew how he would react. He would... well, actually she doesn't know. She knows that she has lost him but seeing him with Janey turns the grief to fury. Janey gets to be with Owen while Annie has gone so far beyond him, she cannot even change her clothes.

George calms her, telling her about when he too lost everything. After he was attacked by the werewolf he had started to come to terms with his loss when he saw his ex. She had moved on and had someone new and the violence of that discovery was like losing everything all over again. He can empathise with Annie and they start to find some common ground.

He tells her about the night he was attacked, how when he saw the wolf he knew even then that it was somehow wrong. That thing had no place in the world and now he is the same and could cause the same appalling damage. In flashback we see him and the man he was with on the ground, George injured and the body beside him savaged and pouring blood. But – he survived, as did Annie in her way. She is so much prettier and nicer than Janey he reassures her, although it is scant comfort. He holds her and the ghost and the werewolf have become friends.

"You know. Him with the face"

Unknown to George, Mitchell is on a date with Becca, a fact dropped innocently into the conversation by another nurse. If she had been able to read Becca's handwriting would we be seeing a totally different story? She can't tell him where they went – it would have looked as if she cared – so he begins a frantic search. Is he really convinced that Becca is in danger? He trusted Mitchell before he met Lauren and it is some time since her death so was that trust so fragile? Maybe his concern is actually for Mitchell. A worry that his friend is about to plummet from the wagon and part of the fault may be his after he confronted him with his frailties. It's now we wonder just how much Mitchell has told George about himself. His vampire exploits are legendary – is this why George is worried, that he fears he's reverted to type?

Mitchell and Becca are doing the whole first date thing – telling each other embarrassing stories in a nice bar. He's given up giving up smoking ("once a smoker always a smoker") and he can still hear her blood. Is he really going to take her or is he testing himself against the ever-present temptation. You may admit you are a smoker but it doesn't mean you have to have a cigarette. Becca is just inviting him back to her place when Lauren joins them. Becca knows she's seen her before somewhere but can't quite work it out. Helpfully Lauren suggests that it might have been in a newspaper photograph and the memory of seeing that photo starts to surface. Mitchell hauls Lauren

67

out of the bar. People are looking, and having your last kill comparing first date stories with the latest conquest is never going to go well.

Lauren is furious with Mitchell. The vampire society has their ways of doing things and he did not play the game. She woke up as a vampire with strangers but Mitchell, as her creator, should have been there to help and to guide her. In his shame and disgust about what he had done he abandoned her to Herrick, Seth and the others. Mitchell tells her how he can make it up to her. He'll take her away, save her, there are places they can be safe. But that's wrong too. Lauren wants to kill, she relishes the blood. This may be the normal appetite of a new vampire or her anger with Mitchell and his abandonment of her to her fate that is making her that way but it revolts him. He walks away. His choice is made.

He also walks away from Becca although he's keen to see her safely home. She is so disappointed, even with the 'it's not you it's me' speech. Never a convincing one. Before Mitchell can get her to safety, Lauren finds her – and George finds Lauren. She shows off her vampiric strength and throws him away from her, dropping him beside the bleeding body of Becca. The scene with Becca in the alley mirrors the attack on George by the werewolf. A bleeding and helpless George lying beside the dead body of his companion, covered in blood, throat torn away. Maybe if he can save Becca he can redeem himself for not saving his friend. Mitchell finds George cradling Becca in his arms, both covered in blood. Lauren watches them, taunting Mitchell with the knowledge that only he could save her. If he lets Becca drink his blood she will become a vampire, if he leaves her she will die. It's a choice of death or everlasting death and one that terrifies Mitchell. He refuses to create another monster, the horrified condemnation from George just hours ago still fresh in his mind. George wants him to save her. He hears only the word 'save', not realising the consequences or what it would do to his friend.

"Not another one. I can't... I can't..."

Lauren walks away, absolved of responsibility – after all, it was Mitchell who made her what she is. She leaves Mitchell and George weeping over Becca's bloodied body. She doesn't survive. It's not really clear why Lauren kills Becca – maybe just because she can. Was she jealous, seeing her with Mitchell, the same Mitchell who left her? She wants to punish him and push him into making a choice. Unfortunately for Lauren when he makes that choice it isn't her.

Bloodstained and silent, George is waiting for the axe to fall. Is this how it ends, when all the connections are made? Mitchell explains – and Herrick and Seth are among the people gathered to deal with the aftermath. This is how it works, the vampires look after their own, there is a system and this is how they have survived undiscovered for so many centuries.

Herrick tells Mitchell that this is the beginning and now he must decide which side he is on. Having made the hardest of decisions in not saving Becca, especially after he had chosen to walk away from her, leaves him in no doubt. He chooses humanity. Herrick appears quite unconcerned. He knows Mitchell and he can bide his time. He cannot understand how he could ever choose to deny what he is and he knows the nature of the reformed addict. Mitchell is repulsed by the blood thirst of Lauren and the knowledge that he created her.

The influence of George is powerful as, for all his problems, George has a strong and calm moral centre. Maybe this time with the support of George and Annie it will work and he will be able to stay away, to stay clean.

"I choose them"

George has to rethink his friendship with Mitchell in light of the revelations about Lauren and Becca. His best friend is a monster, just like Lauren, just like Herrick. Are his dreams of normality, of being human, lying bleeding to death beside him as Becca has just done? Mitchell's matter-of-fact explanation of how vampires have survived for centuries ("branches everywhere") allows him time to reflect. After all, a vampire is always a vampire, they don't get days off. However much George may hate the system, he can see that which is good and clean in Mitchell and that must surely mean he is redeemable.

The house as a sanctuary becomes ever more important to them all. Mitchell has the support to stay clean and to suppress the bloodlust and fury. George can be himself but with people who also know the wolf. And Annie? Her confidence has been shredded by Owen's presence and she needs the house more than ever. The thought of leaving it, even for a moment, is too scary. In the house they are safe and she is sure that it will protect them from the horrors outside.

In the sanctuary of the house with Annie, George can see that Mitchell's desperate decision not to 'save' Becca by making her a vampire was brave and right. His encounters with vampires have made him wary, but Lauren has reminded him of the absolute rage and fury that makes up a vampire and the equivalent energy and control it must take Mitchell not to be that way. When Annie asks if Mitchell should have let Becca drink, creating another vampire rather than letting her die, George is sure. He knows that in truth Mitchell did save her.

As the trio battle with their demons, across the street outside there is a figure watching them from the shadows. The distinctive silhouette that we saw in the woods when George was changing – what does he want with George?

"There are monsters out there"

Musings on episode one...

There are several possible initial responses to episode one depending on whether you saw the pilot or not and if you were a fan of it. Newbies will see the start of a story and will either like it or not. Pilot fans will either love it more or just hate it, depending on their views on the recasting and the change of tone. Me? Yes, I enjoyed the pilot but this episode was a huge step forward. The recasting is spot on and the more grounded, less ethereal vampires are right up my street – or is that just wishful thinking?!

The settings work – the hospital is drab, the house is down at heel and these people have real lives. Not the shiny, glamorous existence found in many TV series – completely unattainable on the income the characters are supposed to have. Who lives in a house like this? Well, it really could be two low-paid hospital workers.

The characters' relationships are clear. We see straight away that Mitchell is very fond of Annie and George is not. Well, not yet. Herrick and Mitchell's comfortable antagonism speaks of long estrangement but with the deep-seated knowledge of those who were once the very best of friends. The new cast speak volumes with few words. Annie's despair after seeing Owen would melt the hardest heart.

We're straight into the series arc – no faffing about with lengthy introductions. The vampires are plotting and there are signs of a new level of organisation. Can Herrick pull Mitchell back to the fold? George and the wolf have a hate/hate relationship and the transformation contrasts beautifully with George's general awkwardness and overwhelming need to put his foot in his mouth. Meanwhile, Mitchell's last kill is stalking him for revenge, blood, sex – or even just acceptance. Annie is more tied to the house than ever before. The shock of seeing Owen and his new girlfriend has lost her both her confidence and her new found visibility.

The greatest thing about this episode – and in fact the whole series – is that not everything is spelt out. You actually have to have your brain switched on and it leaves you thinking and wondering. Dumbed down TV this is not and it's all the better for it.

Bum notes...

Not everyone agreed with the recasting although I think it's fair to say the new cast all grew on the sceptics. Most of them anyway.

Slight divergence from the plot of the pilot. Although Toby Whithouse says that the pilot is canon, there are arguments that pick fault in the details. There is nothing major that contradicts and the slight disconnect felt by some is an inevitable consequence of the change of tone. The only area I would pick out is George telling Annie about when he met his ex again. In the pilot, Annie was there!

... and the bottom line

Sightings of Russell Tovey's bare backside – three.

He said, she said...

It was a pigeon. I killed it. With a shoe.

......

How noble of you to take on the curse of immortality so that your friends could wither and decay in hospitals and old people's homes.

......

How did you do that, stay so calm?

OK shut up.

You're a spy, aren't you? You've clearly had training, because the way you held it together, it was chilling.

••••••

Before I died I had this one odd last thought, and now I'm going to make it yours. You know all the things you were scared of as a kid, all the monsters under the bed? They're all real.

Okay, I'm new to this, but aren't you supposed to weep or scream or wee yourself?

Where have I seen... Dylan Brown (Seth)?

After stage work including Puck in *A Midsummer Night's Dream* for Sheffield Theatres in 2003, Dylan Brown's sit up and notice TV role came in 2005. Playing gay serial killer Michael Keenan over four episodes of *The Bill*, he got terrific reviews for his portrayal of utter evil.

His films include: *Tu£sday* in 2008 with Philip Glenister and John Simm; enigmatic stranger Dante in *Devilwood* in 2006, again with John Simm; and Lefty in *Unleashed* in 2005.

He has a neat clutch of medical drama on his CV, with appearances in *Doctors*, *Holby City*, *Casualty* and *Peak Practice*.

In 2009 he directed the play *Nevermind* starring Chris Coghill and Daniela Denby-Ashe at the Red Lion Theatre in London.

His previous association with John Simm's work seems to have paid off nicely with the role of Rosencrantz in *Hamlet*, opening at the Sheffield Crucible in September 2010, with John Simm in the eponymous role.

Music in episode one

The Prodigy	*Smack My Bitch Up*
Arctic Monkeys	*When the Sun Goes Down*
Supergrass	*St Petersburg*
Dirty Pretty Things	*Wondering*
Maximo Park	*Books from Boxes*
The Pigeon Detectives	*Take Her Back*
Eels	*Friendly Ghost*
Johnny Cash	*Hurt*

episode two

George meets another werewolf – one who relishes his condition and gives him advice on lycanthropy, life and love.

Mitchell befriends the neighbours, talks Vin Diesel and receives a mystery DVD.

Annie is charmed and then scared out of the house by the sofa surfer from hell.

broadcast:	1 FEBRUARY 2009	director:	TOBY HAYNES
writer:	TOBY WHITHOUSE	producer:	MATTHEW BOUCH

cast:

Annie	LENORA CRICHLOW	Tully	DEAN LENNOX KELLY
Mitchell	AIDAN TURNER	Hannah	KERRY GIBSON
George	RUSSELL TOVEY	Maggie	LIZZIE ROPER
Lauren	ANNABEL SCHOLEY	Neighbour	JOE HALL
Herrick	JASON WATKINS	Werewolf	PAUL KASEY
Nina	SINEAD KEENAN		

"He should be dead within 30 seconds…"

The second pre-title sequence features the voice of Mitchell over the transformation of George into the werewolf. Starting with the already customary rear view of 'nude Tovey in wood', Mitchell talks us through the excruciating pain of the transformation. How George dies every single month to become the wolf. His heart stops, his organs fail – he only stops screaming when he can no longer physically make a sound. What George calls his curse, vile and inhuman, Mitchell sees as some sort of miracle. George is conscious through the transformation and forced to experience pain that would kill a normal man. It is cruel but perfect, Mitchell concedes. He sees the fingerprint of God – this could not possibly have evolved. His phrasing "victim begat victim" shows the view that Toby Whithouse's vampires have of werewolves. Victims of circumstance, somehow inferior to vampires with their choices and immortality.

Strangely, in two series of *Being Human* we never see the transformation in reverse. We see a sleeping human in the dawn light of the morning after, usually rather grubby and often with the remains of a half-eaten animal. Does the pain happen again? We know from series two that the transformation can happen when the human is asleep or unconscious. Is that how they change back and recover? There must be limits to what any body can endure.

On this particular morning after, George does not wake alone. He is being watched. The figure is instantly recognisable as the shadow under the street lamp at the end of episode one or at least it seems to be a distinctive hat (always a useful trick!). Rather too close for comfort, he's musing on how George (he already knows his name) gets home. He has no clothes and no money (unless he has a novel place to stash a small change purse). George takes the sensible route for once and tries to run, but the stranger calls after him: "I know what you are." There's a half-hearted attempt to prevaricate but George already suspects what is to come next.

"Because I'm one too"

Luckily, the mysterious stranger has a bag of clothes for George. There is something inherently comical about a grown man running through the woods clutching his penis and it is difficult to take poor George seriously until he gets dressed. He reluctantly takes the clothes offered but he's not convinced. How does he know that he really has met another werewolf? "One of *them*," as he puts it, not even wanting to give his alter ego the dignity of a name. Tully explains about the heightened senses around the time of the full moon and that George's senses will be telling him what his brain is refusing to accept. He tempts George – he can teach him the tricks of the werewolf trade. He lets him know that he knows all about him, that he's a hospital porter, and tells him that there is safety in numbers. He needs George to need him and so his clever psychological manipulation begins. Not only do the vampires keep beating him up, they have let slip that something is beginning and George will be safer with him. But making his other life easy is wrong for George. It's a curse and a curse should not be eased and so he walks away from Tully, telling him not to follow him. Surely hyper-intelligent George, wolf sense still on full alert, should have realised that if Tully knows his name and where he works, he will already have his address, postcode and probably his inside leg measurement?

"Doesn't he understand these people are British?"

Nattily attired in his borrowed shorts, socks and crocs ensemble, George strides back to the house and straight into a surreal situation. Mitchell has invited the neighbours in for coffee.

A very hyper and overexcited Mitchell drags George into the house to meet "everyone!" making sure he adds those useful snippets of biographical information we can't possible make friends without:

... a keen gardener...
... only has one kidney...
... knows all there is to know about Vin Diesel...
... former Miss Isle of Wight...
... has been 'working away'...

Plus the inevitable group of Meeeja Studies students who always seem to pop up at the mere whiff of a free Hobnob.

They all look slightly too keen, rather uncomfortable and definitely too far into each other's personal space, but in the centre of them all is the most bizarre sight of all. Considering we are suspending our disbelief to watch a trio of supernatural house sharers this is quite an achievement. I'm talking about the tea trolley. Note the floral cloth, the proper teapot – even flowers. Not to mention that the biscuits are actually on plates! Now Mitchell may think that this is what it takes to be human, to dive in and participate in the community, but I can't help thinking he is utterly misguided. In the vampire world of arrested development is he thinking back to his Irish childhood at the dawn of the twentieth century? Proper tea (with a cloth) and interacting with the neighbours would then have been essential and unremarked. In twenty-first century Bristol? Maybe not. It may be uncharitable but I would consider a tablecloth and biscuits not in the packet served up by a youngish bloke very odd indeed! A century of trying really hasn't quite got Mitchell to the blending-in point yet.

Speaking of blending in – why do none of them wonder about George's conversation in the kitchen with Annie? Perfectly sensible to him but Annie is invisible to them. Maybe Mitchell has already explained that George is just a little... odd. Although hearing Annie's pygmy goat/blow on the head explanation for Mitchell's mania probably wouldn't be a great help.

"Tully is as Tully does"

Without us seeing him arrive, Tully is suddenly in the house, mug of tea in hand, charming the room and joining in the Vin Diesel chat. That is until a horrified George hauls him out into the street. Having Tully in the house, wanting to meet Mitchell and Annie, brings his curse too close to home. Transforming in the house the previous month left him more determined than ever to separate the two parts of himself. The house is where George is just George, human George. The thing? Well, it's the thing. Tully is still tempting George, he can help him with his deepest fear that he will hurt or kill someone. George is wavering and the appearance of Mitchell (eating biscuits – don't vampires get fat? Or high cholesterol?) closes the situation. Tully is in.

Tully proceeds to charm the pants off Annie and Mitchell. Romantic tales of sleeping in the arms of Mother Nature, calling Annie an angel and producing appropriate bible quotes. George's discomfort begins to turn to jealousy, after all they were his friends first, and the plan begins to work. The signs are all there if they care to look. When Tully says he was scouring the local papers to trace animal attacks after finding evidence of a local werewolf, he claims he just happened across the 2007 Stirling Gazette with the report of George's attack. Even with utter dumb luck that is a leap too far. Stirling and Bristol are a long way apart and if it wasn't a lucky guess then Tully must have known more than he is letting on. The cracks start to show between Mitchell and George after Mitchell offers Tully the use of the sofa for a couple of nights. We need to engage with humanity, he reminds a furious George. George is determined to claim Tully as not human – apparently oblivious of applying that same status to himself. Mitchell thinks he is unhinged to refuse help. While George can ignore his condition for 27 days out of 28, Mitchell cannot – he is a vampire 24/7 and would welcome the help and support that Tully seems to be offering with open arms. Although he won't admit it, he misses the vampire community – even Herrick – and he is disappointed that Lauren, his last unwilling protégée, is not prepared to be with him on his terms.

"I am house trained you know!"

Annie comes down to Tully cooking her breakfast. Only slightly embarrassed that he had no idea she cannot eat, he helpfully polishes it off himself. For a werewolf who claims to have known ghosts before it seems he doesn't know a great deal about them – although the food issue is a clever way of getting a decent breakfast! Annie seems attracted to Tully. He is a charmer and a flirt and has the perception to identify and then play on people's needs. For Annie it is not only the joy of being visible to someone else but the confirmation that she is still attractive. She seems to be pasting aspects of her relationship with Owen onto Tully. Obviously there are similarities, both are charming, dominant and manipulative. Is this telling us there is more to Owen than meets the eye? And to Tully?

"And you can stop right there"

A brief diversion into the hospital and a potentially important figure storms into George's life. Nina, Acting Ward Sister, is in a monumental strop which she takes out on poor porter George who, after all, was only following orders. Sinead Keenan does play a great mardy woman but I have to admit I find her first appearance overly manic. Too much mugging contrasts badly with the naturalistic acting of the others. This may well just be me though as Toby Whithouse was so pleased with Sinead's performance that he made Nina a recurring character and a lead in series two. Once that was settled it all calmed down. The acting style that would have made a great impact in just an episode or two adapted to the overall feel of the show as soon as the character had a story and a history (and a future).

"Double bagging – you always double bag, George"

Tully begins to teach George the lore of the werewolf. Are we ever sure if this is actually werewolf lore rather than the law according to Tully? It's all common sense and nothing that George wouldn't have figured out for himself. All he needs to do is accept the wolf and live with it in some sort of truce if not in harmony. First a checklist – and I bet George loves a list. Spare clothes, wet wipes, money for the phone, bananas and water, all bagged and then double bagged. We're also let into a gruesome secret. The werewolf stomach copes with the raw meat of the animals it hunts under the full moon and the human one has to digest what is left on waking. Lovely. A seriously hard-core version of the Atkins diet! The *pièce de résistance* however is a classic – it's a chicken on a string. Dragging a raw chicken in a circle around the place where the wolf transforms will give it a trail to follow to stop it roaming. I'm not entirely convinced about this one. The prospect of a deer or rabbit, meat literally on the hoof, has to be more appealing than the distant prospect of a Co-op oven ready. It does reassure George though and gives Tully some stature. He has solved one of George's problems, the fear of running amok and killing or hurting someone, at the small price of looking just slightly ridiculous. Walkies?

Tully continues to undermine Mitchell – why hasn't he taught George these simple things? He picks away at the support and friendship Mitchell has shown George, dripping in the distrust and the doubt. Divide and conquer. While George accepts Tully, seeing that he could really make his wolf nights more bearable, Tully continues to charm Annie. Although he uses up all the tea, he leaves her a cute origami swan. The swan is a symbol of elegance and beauty and they also mate for life. Is Annie that single lonely swan or is it Tully's mating call? It is Mitchell, though, who gets the brunt of Tully's – let's say unfortunate – personal traits. Finding him on the sofa, feet up, very short dressing gown allowing for some thorough ball scratching, is not conducive to happy cohabitation and Tully's bathroom habits are probably best not described. For Mitchell, Tully is the friend of a friend who you help out with a temporary sofa to kip on who then stays on, hanging around forever. Emptying the fridge, stinking out the bathroom and sitting in your favourite chair. There is no gain for Tully in charming Mitchell. He needs to wind him

75

up, to get him really, really annoyed so he can get between him and George.

"That is such a mental rule. Who made that up?"

Mitchell doesn't want Lauren in the house, but when she turns up at the door he has no choice but to ask her in or risk her letting out his secrets in the street. Vampire mythology states that a vampire cannot cross a threshold uninvited – bonkers, but a fabulous plot device!

He is still furious about Lauren's attack on Becca and tries to throttle her. She jokes it all off, he's already killed her so what more can he do? She also reminds him that if Becca was too young to die then so was she. They were the same age, both nurses, both involved with Mitchell. Lauren thinks Mitchell owes her. He refuses to participate in the life he forced her into and by rejecting her lifestyle as well as her she feels let down. She misses him, she flirts with him, and she tries to tempt him – ostensibly with sex but really with blood. She can't even imagine how he can stay clean; it's totally alien to her thirst for blood and death. Mitchell is all virtuously evangelical. He made a total commitment to humanity and won't be tempted although it is still a struggle. There is no one more earnest than a reformed smoker and all that newspaper waving and stage coughing can get very dull, very quickly.

Lauren has already noticed the strained relationship between Herrick and Mitchell but denies he has sent her. Maybe she truly misses Mitchell or, more likely, she's being set up by Herrick to try and pull Mitchell back into the vampire world. "You can't ever check out," is Lauren's final sally, delivered through the letterbox. Or is it? What else is to follow?

"When did you last get it wet?"

George and Tully are in a café when Tully turns his mentor's eye to George's love life in his inimitable and sensitive fashion. He claims that the wolves have a huge advantage. In his view, women love a bit of rough, the scent of the wolf and the predators always come out on top. Of course we may just be hearing romance according to Tully here, but George has been swept along with Tully's wisdom so far that this to him is just one more useful hint. Tully chats up the waitress to prove a point, although we'll never know if that phone number was real. It could be a well-used technique to get rid of the letch!

"Well, I feel totally reassured"

Mitchell continues to have the neighbours in for a bite, to the despair of George. Mitchell inadvertently lets slip a little more information than he intended when he says it's best for them to be open, "especially now." Tully has told George about being beaten up by vampires and how it is happening more often and more openly, as if they no longer feel any need to hide. It is as if something big is happening. Mitchell is dismissive. There's always a vampire trying to take over the world, the time of the vampires has been almost here for centuries but Annie and George remain unconvinced.

If they could see Mitchell in the bathroom they would be even more concerned. He finds Hannah, who was here for coffee and has lost all track of time. She has cut her finger and is washing it clean, letting the blood fall into the water in the basin. She flirts with Mitchell, not realising he is transfixed by the blood still dripping from her finger. He shakes himself out of it with a visible effort and whisks her off downstairs so that George can find her a plaster. Hannah asks if George is the one who was "putting coasters under everything." It's a perfect image – maybe the floral tray cloth is the wolf's feminine side?

"George is as George does"

George is off to work when Mitchell calls him back to let him know that he can go back to transforming in the secure isolation room he used to use. Not impressed, George muses on the joys of being in the cradle of Mother Nature, leaving Mitchell and Annie puzzled. He also declines the chance to watch *Casablanca* with them – despite Mitchell being in it! Although his image doesn't resolve on film, he does knock over a chair which can be seen. George is singularly unimpressed. Suddenly light dawns on Annie – he's turned into Tully's mini-me!

Tully's mini-me then has a go at winning friends and influencing people at the hospital. Why a hospital when he has "a brain the size of a planet" wonders Tully, although he knows very well why. George thinks it is easier to hide and it is certainly the best place for Mitchell to avoid natural light, hospitals not being renowned for the amounts of sunlight streaming through them. It's always about Mitchell; Tully is much more overt in his criticisms of Mitchell now. He feels secure that George is so strongly linked to him that he doesn't need Mitchell anymore. Unfortunately this confidence is rocked a touch when George tries out Tully's chat-up technique on Nina after she tracks him down to offer a reluctant apology for her treatment of him. Her reply has to be the best put-down of an unfortunate propositioner ever, bar none! That went well...

"You have to get away from here"

Tully finds Annie in the kitchen. His growing confidence of his place in the household gives his charm a harder edge. He's still flirting but is more predatory, more forceful, taking the part of the alpha male. He grabs at Annie's arm – squeezing it, looking for a reaction, gauging her response. Annie is scared, tries to pull away and unconsciously calls him Owen. Another clue to her relationship with Owen. Was it as forceful and controlling as Tully is becoming? Did he hurt her? Tully continues to push, getting more direct, cruder – surely calling a ghost a corpse is pretty close to the bone. He goes in for a kiss (and probably a lot more) but Annie jumps away, leaving him in a passionate clinch with the refrigerator.

Has Annie ever jumped that far before? She ends up in the street outside the house and across the road. She's terrified, far more than her run-in with Tully should cause. Is the terror that she is out of the house, away from her safe haven? Far from the safety she feels with Mitchell and George, Tully has violated her sanctuary and pushed her away from the home she is tied to. Calling for help from people who have no idea she is there, she runs through the streets thinking only of finding her friends.

Following an ambulance – the best way to get to the hospital – she comes across a hectic scene. There are ambulances, police, and Lauren laughing hysterically, high on blood as they bring out a body. Herrick drags her away.

He has 'things to do'. The vampires have a system and he needs to make sure she is not found out, but this is too public, too obvious, a beginner's error. He is clearly furious with her.

How does Herrick know who Annie is? He obviously knows that Mitchell is living with a werewolf but has a ghost ever been mentioned? As a vampire he can see that Annie is a ghost, but maybe he knows far more about Mitchell's domestic arrangements than Mitchell realises. Can Annie tell he is a vampire? Has Mitchell even mentioned Herrick and the threat he poses? "Tick tock, tick tock," he says to Annie and it is amazing how much menace can come from such a cheerful and approachable face. Time is running out.

Meanwhile, George is visiting a lonely patient in the hospital, to the complete puzzlement of Nina who assumes he is skiving. "It's my day off," George says, "can I go now?" He is more confident, maybe this is Tully's influence, but he does not attempt another chat up. He leaves Nina thinking that maybe – just maybe – she has underestimated him. Is that a flicker of interest?

"He's a twat." "Well he's my twat"

Annie doesn't get to the hospital. It seems she is still limited in how far she can get from the house as well as having been scared by Herrick. She waits outside the house for Mitchell, who promptly tries to throw Tully out. Confident in George's support, Tully waits for the inevitable confrontation. It's exactly what he has been building up to for weeks. George is determined that he stays and challenges Mitchell about why he hasn't helped him manage his condition as Tully has done. He even turns on Annie, and Tully watches and laughs as they fight. George stands his ground, only wavering a touch, but Tully can't resist gloating. That is the final straw for Annie.

Annie retreats to her room. It's an empty space; a ghost has no need of a change of clothes or even a bed. She does have a nice comfy armchair though. Mitchell tries to reassure her and it's one of the times when his age is clear. The century he has lived through has shown him how time gets shaken up and then settles, over and over again – like a snow globe. He's sure that George will come back to them. They kiss – rather accidentally – and Annie admits that she feels something. Is a ghost/vampire relationship possible? Vampires revel in their physicality and thirst for blood, so can a ghost – however squidgy – ever fulfil that need? They are cute together but there is no passion, just the closest of friendship.

Tully is still imparting his wisdom to George, telling him that the wolf cannot cross water. This isn't strictly true according to most werewolf mythology. It's confused with madness, rabies and hydrophobia, but has been a useful device in some fiction. Obviously Tully is a fan of horror films! Tully never tells George how he became a werewolf and if he ever met another before George, and his wisdom may be a collection of learned tricks and ideas picked up from our shared cultural history. All of this George could have managed himself with just a little more acceptance and self-confidence.

George is worried about the fight with Mitchell and Annie but Tully is so proud of him for standing up to them. He feels that his sundering of George and Mitchell's friendship has reached the crucial point and he can finally tell George the secret he has kept from him. He thinks it will reassure George, convince him that he will never leave him.

Tully was the werewolf who attacked George. He was the one who gave him this gift.

It's a huge misjudgement. George is revolted and betrayed. Suddenly he can see what Tully has been doing, how much of his support and teaching was a lie. Tully pleads with him; he needed George to need him. He's lonely and wanted what George has. He too lost everything, including his wife and son, and George was his last hope, but George can't bear to be near him any longer and leaves Tully devastated at his total rejection. He has already lost one son and now the son of the wolf is walking away from him too.

Tully's envy of his situation makes George realise that, however much he has lost, he has gained friends. While having a house share with a vampire and a ghost is not quite a family, it is more – much more – than Tully has. Returning to the house he once again faces the wreckage and says sorry. Mitchell and Annie welcome him back unconditionally and for the first time he says it: "My name's George and I am a werewolf."

"Brown duvet – it's a cry for help"

Someone has posted a DVD through the letterbox. Assuming it is the promised loan of *Casablanca* from Carol at number 12 complete with Mitchell's invisible furniture shuffling, they all settle down to watch. This is certainly not a classic movie but a vampire snuff film and Annie is utterly horrified at the thought of watching someone have sex! Although she is definitely looking through her fingers. The vampire cannot be seen on film, but the victim dies and is drained of blood. Mitchell has seen vampire porn before but this is somehow different. It's Lauren. Showing him what he is missing, trying to bring him back.

I can't help wondering what an actor thinks when his agent rings. You've been offered a part in a new BBC drama. No, you don't actually speak, but you do get to strip off, have simulated sex with an invisible person and then die. It's not a BAFTA-winning role and doesn't even merit a credit – although maybe that's preferable!

"We'll tear each other apart"

George heads off to the shed that Tully showed him, complete with his (double bagged) kit of essential supplies, only to find Tully already there. He has his head in a noose, waiting for George to arrive before he kicks away the chair. George's instinct to help takes him to Tully but then he has second thoughts. Why should he help? Tully betrayed him, lied to him and gave him the curse. He walks away. But Tully is clever and he knows that George's biggest fear is that he will kill someone. Although it's a question of semantics, is walking away from Tully, leaving him hanging, killing him or not? It doesn't matter, as George won't be able to live with the knowledge that he let him die. He gets him down, but they are on the verge of transforming and in such a small space they will surely kill each other. Tully won't let George go and, claws erupting, George slashes him across the face until Tully runs. George has become the stronger one – he has evolved into the alpha wolf.

The morning after and the roles have reversed. This time it is George watching Tully, naked and dirty on the ground. He can't quite forgive him but understands that when he attacked him he didn't know what he was doing. That knowledge was gained at the expense of the deep scars across Tully's face. They won't meet again.

George walks away but Tully has the final word. There is no way out, no cure. One day, he claims, George will be forced into using the wolf and in doing so he will lose his conscience, his final human trait.

In contrast to George's new-found confidence, back at the house Mitchell is struggling. He's sitting on the floor, physical shorthand for his conflicted soul coming to the fore. He watches the neighbours he has tried so hard to befriend, wondering if he could ever be like them?

Finally he retrieves Lauren's DVD from the bin, his eyes black with longing.

"You can check out but you can never leave"

Musings on episode two...

Episode two and it's all about George. By pairing George with his polar opposite we learn so much more about him. When he first meets Tully he's sceptical and wary, but it isn't long before deviously clever Tully gets under his guard. It seems that George is rather easily influenced. With Tully's own agenda this is not good for our favourite wolf. Was George the same when he first met Mitchell? Mitchell rescued him and probably has influenced him but for the good, the sign of a true friend.

There is a pivotal moment for George: he meets Nina. Her stroppiness and his misguided chat-up attempt can't mask the attraction. George has no idea just what this woman will come to be to him. Nina couldn't even begin to imagine where George will take her.

Tully runs through this episode like a dose of salts. He flirts with Annie, charms and pursues her and gives us a glimpse of her abusive relationship with Owen. He plays up to Mitchell just enough to get into the house and then neatly and unobtrusively undermines him, goading him until he lashes out. Dean Lennox Kelly plays Tully brilliantly. You like him. You hate him. You quite possibly fancy him a bit. Clever writing brought to life by a talented chameleon of an actor.

The reversal of the opening scene of Tully watching George to see George watching Tully awake after the full moon bookends the episode beautifully and shows the transference of power. It reveals the vulnerability that Tully has so carefully hidden, and the amateur tattoos that cover his body just emphasise his self-hatred. Far from his breezy confidence, he hates the wolf as much, or maybe even more than George does.

On the BBC *Being Human* blog (18 May 2009), Toby Whithouse posted his original draft of the pre-title sequence for this episode. George talks about the history of werewolves – in the bible, in sixteenth-century France and in Hollywood. Using Cecil B. DeMille film footage (*The Ten Commandments* is suggested), paintings by Blake, and shots of ancient Greek vases, it would have been exotic and gothic. A wonderful sequence in the style of the pilot, but as Toby Whithouse admits it is wrong for the tone finally settled on for the series. Mitchell's voiceover describing George's physical transformation works far better, but it is interesting to see the roots of his description of werewolfism as a biblical curse.

Not much of Herrick this episode, but what he does is effortlessly menacing. He calmly threatens Annie in the street with the ticking of time running out. The vampire plot is coming and there are more hints that something is brewing, they are getting bolder.

Mitchell is lower key in this episode. He provides the comic relief with his cheerfully twee coffee mornings, but that all changes. After George's victory over Tully, the trio settle down to watch Mitchell invisibly messing with the props in *Casablanca*, only to see Lauren's vampire porn. The reactions of the trio take us forward in the story and we see just how much Mitchell's determination to stay clean is wavering. Lauren is calling him back.

Bum notes...

A minor quibble about Nina's first appearance. I find Sinead Keenan's acting a touch over the top in this episode, although I have to say she calms down and fits in much better in future. It looks as though she was trying very hard to make an impression – and it worked! Not planned as a recurring character, she played a major role in series two and continues into series three.

When Herrick and Annie see each other across a crowded kill, I appreciate that Herrick will know Annie; after all, it's in his interests to know all about Mitchell. What I can't work out is how does Annie know Herrick?

... and the bottom line

Sightings of Russell Tovey's bare backside – two.

He said, she said...

Maybe he's had a blow to the head.

I'm sorry?

Happened to my Nan. She got hit in the head by a radio-controlled plane at a county fair. From that moment - obsessed with pygmy goats.

······

The Earth my pillow, my canopy the stars.

Oh, I'd like to see George living like that. He had a panic attack in the Eden Project.

······

We have to put a stop to this. Doesn't he understand, these people are British? You're not allowed to talk to your neighbours until you've nodded at them for fifteen years.

······

81

He's a twat!

He's *my* twat!

You know, I'm sure that sounded much better in your head.

Where have I seen... Paul Kasey (Werewolf)?

Paul Kasey works as a choreographer, movement director, contortionist, dancer and model, and as an actor, playing costumed characters. As well as playing the fully transformed werewolf in *Being Human*, he has appeared in *Doctor Who* as a variety of creatures including Judoon, Slitheen, Ood Sigma, Hath Peck and the Cyber-Leader (in 2005-10). He has played Blowfish and Weevils in *Torchwood* (2006-8), and Kudlak as well as more Slitheen and Judoon in *The Sarah Jane Adventures* (in 2007-9).

After playing an infected victim in the film *28 Days Later* (2002), Paul went on to be the Movement Advisor on *28 Weeks Later (2007)*, choreographing the infected scenes and playing the lead infected victim. His other film appearances include *Blade II* (2002), *Finding Neverland* (2004), *Pride and Prejudice* (2005) and *Inkheart* (2008).

He appeared in the Arlene Phillips-choreographed production of *Grease* for two years and was also in the original West End run of *Fosse* in 2000.

Music in episode two

The Coral	*Something Inside of Me*
The Coral	*Shadows Fall*
Muse	*Showbiz*
Supergrass	*St Petersburg*
Roachford	*Cuddly Toy*
The Futureheads	*The Hounds of Love*
The Coral	*Secret Kiss*

episode three

Annie tries to resolve her death with the help of 80s ghost Gilbert.

George has an admirer, a dinner date and an almost-full-moon encounter.

Mitchell tries to resist Lauren but his resolve is tested when she shows her vulnerability.

broadcast:	8 FEBRUARY 2009	director:	ALEX PILLAI
writer:	TOBY WHITHOUSE	producer:	MATTHEW BOUCH

cast:

Annie	LENORA CRICHLOW	Seth	DYLAN BROWN
Mitchell	AIDAN TURNER	Owen	GREGG CHILLIN
George	RUSSELL TOVEY	Janey	SAMA GOLDIE
Lauren	ANNABEL SCHOLEY	Nina	SINEAD KEENAN
Herrick	JASON WATKINS	Gilbert	ALEX PRICE

"Love should be the opposite of death"

It's George's turn to provide the voiceover this week for a shorter pre-title sequence that is, nonetheless, still chock-full of back-story and pointers to the future. An episode about love. It sounds simple, but it can't be when love isn't the pure emotion that our trio crave. Can their love ever be simple or is it inevitable that it will be confused by death, lust and addiction, all the complications of their supernatural condition. Maybe the pure love they crave as a part of being truly human is only found in their friendship?

Annie is looking through her memory box – full of photos of her and Owen in happier times, or at least in times when Annie was alive. George catches sight of Nina at work and promptly wheels his patient into a bin! They are so attracted to each other but completely confused about why, especially Nina. Maybe Tully really has something in his "scent of the wolf" theory...

Mitchell, having retrieved Lauren's vampire kill movie from the rubbish is watching it again, alone in the house, eyes inky black with desire. For Mitchell, love and lust and blood are mixed into an addiction that he is finding harder and harder to fight.

"What else do we have? Football? Shoes?"

Resplendent in bright yellow rubber gloves, Annie is frantically cleaning out the kitchen, utensils flying. Even the still-clanky tap gets a good beating with a tea towel, so obviously something's up. PMT advises Mitchell sagely – as he and George keep to a safe distance. George is a little more rational, particularly as he has a steak in the fridge. After all, Annie is a ghost and is cheerfully free of all those monthly disadvantages (she tells us that in episode one). Mitchell is very reluctant to get close. Let's see, is the lady-killing vampire actually scared of a potentially hormonal female? It's up to George to enter the fray which he does, bravely asking Annie what's wrong. She brandishes a rather dangerous-looking implement at him; it was an engagement present and is now unused and unloved, rather how Annie feels.

It's a Mouli grater. Owen's favourite meal was (and probably still is) boiled ham and parsley sauce and the Mouli grater shreds the parsley for the sauce. Toby Whithouse, you are spoiling us – cooking tips as well!

Annie finally tells them what has upset her so much. Thursday is the day she and Owen were to have been married and now she is dead and he will spend the day with Janey 'Tango-faced' Harris instead of her. The Mouli grater is flourished wildly and using the physical comedy at which Russell Tovey is so skilled he avoids it neatly without acknowledgement.

Annie's tears have sent rivers of black mascara down her face. We know she doesn't sleep and cannot change her clothes and I would have assumed she never has to renew her lippie either. Apparently mascara still runs when you cry, even when you're dead. What a pain!

George and Mitchell really don't know how to deal with a grieving, crying ghost. "You still have so much to offer," Mitchell starts before realising that statement has nowhere to go, tailing off with "to the right... person." In a sudden inspiration he decides they need to go out. Annie needs to meet some kindred spirits, quite literally kindred spirits. Trouble is there are still all the cupboards to do, a woman's work is never done etc. etc. but OK, maybe they could go out, but just for a while.

"George - get your lead"

A nightclub. It's 80s night and Soft Cell's *Tainted Love* is the start of a fantastic 80s soundtrack that gives this episode a very distinct feel. There's a sly humour in the music choices, including The Smiths' *Girlfriend in a Coma* and *Ghost Town* by The Specials. Absolute classics.

Mitchell introduces Annie to Gilbert. She's slightly distracted by being out of the house and probably by the seriously naff club so initially she doesn't question that he can see her. When she realises, Gilbert confirms he's been dead since 1985. The personification of 80s angst and misery, Gilbert's reply to Annie's polite "Nice to meet you" – "Is it?" – gives us his character in just two words (helped by a good serving of very long overcoat, 80s quiff and some proper Walkman headphones).

While Annie and Gilbert get acquainted Mitchell and George hit the bar – and prepare to be hit on. Hang on, are they being checked out? Initially flattered, George is then horrified – he just can't, he doesn't trust himself. Is it werewolf guilt or Jewish guilt teases Mitchell, but George is right back at him. Go for it he says or is Mitchell not actually as controlled as he claims and scared that he too might just kill his conquest? So, it's George's time of the month and Mitchell is not in the mood – just a drink then boys?

"… and I get tempted to smash the granny out of it?!"

Lauren finds Mitchell in the hospital. She looks scared and tearful but still manages to stay defiant. Herrick and the vampires forced her to make the film and chose the victim for her. He was cruel, he hurt her, but the thought of Mitchell watching got her through the pain. Herrick is powerful and strong; he can control Lauren and is using her to tempt Mitchell back to the vampire world. Herrick the pusher sending the reformed addict the very thing he craves so much – a willing participant. Mitchell claims to have been so disgusted with the film that he threw up watching it (although we know different), but he seems to be wavering on seeing Lauren so desolate. Only her previous behaviour and the thought that this remorse may not be for real gives him the strength to walk away from her. This time.

"Are there two e's in fiancee?"

Annie is off to meet Gilbert, going all the way on her own on the number 17 bus. Although Annie managed to jump out of the house when threatened by Tully, her powers are limited and she can't get far without help (or public transport). Gilbert has a surprise for her. He's taking her to see her own grave. Annie has never seen it before; it would mean she was admitting that this existence is real, that this is really all she has. Annie is listing what she has lost – the man she loved, the children she never had – a poetic tribute suddenly interrupted by wondering if her gravestone has a spelling mistake! She can still be happy though, as Gilbert claims he is. Free from the normal cares and problems of human life, he sees the world as a beautiful place and Annie needs to see that too. After all, this is forever – unless she can resolve whatever it is that is keeping her here.

As Gilbert walks Annie home to the house, Mitchell and George are spying through the net curtains like two stern dads checking her curfew. Trying far too hard to look casual when she comes in, they end up entangled on the sofa before rearranging themselves!

Annie admits that her trip to the cemetery with Gilbert was "nice" and that it had made her realise something. There is unfinished business, something that she needs to resolve from her life so that she can move on. As if answering her, the plumbing gurgles and clanks – the tap is still not fixed. George is pleased for Annie, he sees it as a positive step, but Mitchell is less so. He could have told her this about resolution but was concerned about what she might find. George has a very different theory. Mitchell is attached to Annie and if she moves on he will lose her. By not telling her about her options he can keep her close, keep her in the house.

"… it'll involve some highlighter pens and a pad of paper"

Gilbert is rather keen on Annie and arrives clutching a mix tape to impress her in true 80s fashion. Unfortunately it is not really her style, "… a mix of Euro Goth and French chanson." Right. She switches it off to have a serious conversation about her new project. When she asks Gilbert to help her to resolve whatever issue is keeping her from passing over, his face is a picture. He loses all his apparent disdain and lets that so very, very cool look drop for a moment. He is thrilled that someone wants his help, and it's not just anyone, it's Annie. It will mean spending lots of time together, he checks, looking like the young man he would have been in life before twenty-five years as a dead 80s poseur took hold.

George and Mitchell are off to work and exchanging greetings with everyone they pass in the street. George still thinks this is odd but Mitchell clings to his idea of community. All very well but what happens if they accidentally kill one of them, muses George. Or maybe something just as bad could happen…

At the hospital, Nina is coping with an influx of victims of a fire at the language school, made worse as most of the students were asleep! The many nationalities are a problem; multiple translators are on order but not here yet. George is working and offers Nina his help – he speaks German, Spanish, Italian, French and Croatian. He has some Russian but it is quite basic he apologises and leaves Nina open-mouthed in astonishment! Yet another facet of George has been revealed for her to process and ponder.

There is a deleted scene on the series DVD that takes this setup a stage further. George is chatting to the patients – obviously after the crisis has passed – in a variety of languages. Dying of curiosity, Nina is watching him and can't resist stopping him to ask what he was talking about. She then just goes for it, blurting out an invitation for a drink. George has just had a break, he's fine, so she has to clarify – she means actually with her. Some typical George squeaking and stuttering and he leaves, highly amused. He thinks this is just one more Nina putdown, while she's wondering how she could possibly have been clearer. It's a neat, amusing scene and fits in but it isn't really needed.

"I'm talking about Gilbert fun"

The 'resolve Annie's death' project is underway and Gilbert has a pen poised to write down every detail about Annie's life in search of the answer. The trouble is that her life story is about Owen, how they met, fell in love and moved to Bristol away from her friends and family. On the surface a romantic love story, but dig deeper – it's all about Owen. No mention of Annie and who she is or even that she existed before Owen. He took her away. It may not have been his original intention, but isolating her in a strange, new city, in their house, kept Annie all his.

Dull, dull, dull. It's time for some fun, declares Gilbert, and Gilbert fun is to commence!

Gilbert fun consists of reading Nietzsche ("Human, all too Human" – nice touch!), some Morrissey-esque dancing accompanied by leafy branch, sharing a Walkman with the required stumbling and invisibly shouting "Fascist!" at policemen. It's a good job they didn't try this one with Herrick!

Annie doesn't quite get Gilbert fun, much to Gilbert's disgust. This isn't surprising – Annie is nowhere near old enough to have been steeped in that brief deep, dark time of 80s angst at an impressionable age.

"But... I can't let him go"

Owen is still trying to fix the tap in the house, watched in disbelief by his new girlfriend Janey. This obsession with DIY is so out of character for him and she cannot understand why he doesn't just get a plumber. She thinks Owen likes hanging out with Mitchell and George, reliving his youth and behaving badly. Little does she know that behaving badly with Mitchell and George is a whole new ball game and the smell of beer would be the least of her problems. Does Owen have something to hide? He does seem to be constantly drawn back to the house. When he leaves he looks around and it seems as if he almost sees Annie. Almost, but not quite, and that brief moment of hope leaves her desolate all over again.

Annie knows she still loves Owen even though there is little hope for any kind of life with him. She is still his fiancée and that is validation for her continued existence. This, she explains to a sceptical Gilbert, is going to be her resolution. She is going to be Owen's wife as she was always intended to be. She will care for him and cherish him and that will make sense of her lingering on in the house they shared. Despite his cynicism, Gilbert is upset that he is losing Annie to her past life; she is creeping under his protective veneer. Life as a ghost is lonely, as Annie told us in episode one, and for all his sharp responses and claims of being happy, Gilbert is lonely too.

They head to Owen's new house. It's a neat suburban semi-detached with a conventional interior and a far cry from the quirkiness of Annie's house. Annie has been planning and she starts by placing a special dish in the hallway for Owen's keys which he was always losing. Gilbert is not impressed by the house and you can feel the contempt oozing out of him, especially when he finds Michael Bublé on Owen's iPod. Annie is planning on playing guardian angel for Owen. She's even thinking about moving in, to Gilbert's surprise and disapproval. Given Annie's ties to the house where she died, is this a serious prospect; she can obviously visit but can she really up sticks and move?

"Just don't kill anyone"

Lauren is waiting for Mitchell at the hospital again. She looks distraught but claims to be clean, to be sick of killing but still desperate for blood. Again she blames Mitchell as it was he who made her what she is, absolving herself and making him responsible for the death she brings. Her withdrawal from blood is agony and Mitchell, despite his reservations, can empathise and is touched. There's a flash of something in Lauren's eyes as he holds her – is this another trick or does Lauren really want his help? Mitchell cuts his own wrist so that Lauren can drink his blood, but when she kisses him in frantic gratitude he tastes the blood from her lips and his eyes darken. He'll help her. The addict leading the addicted...

Taking a fag break, Mitchell finds Nina and takes the opportunity to approach her, asking her for a light. She is curious about the friendship between George and Mitchell and Mitchell just can't help playing Cupid. Nina is quite clear that Mitchell is not her type ("anymore" – there's clearly more to come here), but she is intrigued by George. Mitchell invites her to dinner, the invitation being really on George's behalf, of course. Nina is pleased but George less so! He's horrified and scared but comes around to the idea of just a meal between co-workers, starting a detailed shopping list on a handy poster. He is more concerned that there is "none of that". Far too risky, despite Mitchell suggesting he let go and live a little.

"I just want everything to be normal for one night"

George arrives home with bags of ingredients to find Gilbert has commandeered the stereo and Annie the cooker. She is making boiled ham and parsley sauce for Owen, intending to put it in a dish and take it round to him. George is flustered; he is intending to cook a nice meal and wants Annie out of the kitchen. Unusually determined and feisty, Annie doesn't want to give in. What is George getting his leg over compared to her acting the wife to Owen and resolving her death? After all, Nina won't even be able to hear or see her or Gilbert. Anyway, ghosts are quite normal, or at least that's what they say on *Loose Women*!

Annie and Gilbert allow themselves to be herded into the living room to watch Nina and George getting to know each other. George's first date nerves must be shredded by having such a keen but invisible audience. He finally snaps when Gilbert, bored with the lack of romantic action, puts on his 80s tunes. This dour accompaniment combined with Annie mutely cheering him on and the inevitable clanky tap makes him desperately grateful when Nina suggests they head upstairs.

Nina is looking out of the window at the moon and observes that it is full. Actually, it's isn't until tomorrow corrects George pedantically, being rather more closely attuned to the lunar schedule. Nina has to make the first move; she would probably die of old age waiting for George. George's enthusiasm increases until he realises he is growling – the wolf is just that bit too close. Horrified, he pushes Nina away, but he can't explain and she has to assume he has a problem. She does need to quickly ascertain that he is – and has always been – a man! Searching for words, all that George can come up with is "I have trouble containing myself."

In contrast, Mitchell and Lauren are not containing themselves in the least. They are having frantic sex, biting each other and tasting each other's blood, in an anonymous hotel bathroom. It satisfies Lauren for a while but she still wants and needs real human blood. Can she get it from the hospital? Seems a simple solution but no, Mitchell says it will not work. She has to go clean, there is no other option.

It is at times like these I am very pleased I am not a chambermaid! How on earth does anyone explain a blood-smeared bathroom on checkout? I'm sure there is a vampire way...

Gilbert is also musing on love. He has never been in love, always assuming it was a lie, possibly the consequence of listening to too much of The Smiths. Maybe this is part of his resolution and he is on the verge of telling Annie he loves her when he realises she is not listening. She's miles away thinking about Owen and how she needs to be with him. Clutching her dish of ham and parsley sauce, Gilbert alongside to make sure she gets there safely, Annie heads back to Owen's house.

Owen is home, opening wine as Annie puts the dish in the oven, whispering Happy Anniversary. Today is their wedding day. Trouble is that Janey is there and Owen is thanking her for all the lovely little things she has been doing for him. Things she completely denies – she hates the shirt that Annie had chosen and ironed for him. Annie flees to the bathroom and downstairs Owen hears the door slam. Going upstairs to investigate the noise, he finds a message written in toothpaste on the bathroom mirror – "Happy Wedding Day Tiger". Recognising Annie's writing and somewhere between angry and scared he smears it across the mirror before Janey can see, turning on her, shouting violently at her when she appears. She apologises and backs away, her reaction watched by an unmoving Gilbert. Was this how he treated Annie?

"What are you doing, Owen?"

Annie is alone in the house drawing hearts around a photo of her and Owen when the man himself arrives. For once he is without Janey but with a serious-looking tool box and a DIY guide to plumbing. Heading straight for the bathroom, he dismantles some sections of pipework and clears the blockage. It's a lacy thong, stained and tattered. He laughs, but Annie is scared, she's remembering what happened and starts to flash back to the night she died. She watches herself arguing with Owen – him waving the thong, pristine and white, in her face, accusing her of sleeping around. She tries to defend herself but whatever she says it makes him worse. He has her up against the wall, hands at her throat. He's hurting her and she has no choice but to push him away, but she knows this is going to provoke him further and cowers away apologising. It is the final straw and the violence in Owen takes complete control. He throws her down the stairs and we hear her bones break. Ghostly Annie is left looking down at her mortal body, broken and bloodstained, at the foot of the stairs.

Annie is devastated; all those suppressed memories now teeming through her head. Owen, the man she loved more than life itself, abused her, hurt her and then killed her.

Owen must have always suspected what was wrong. For all his clumsy pipe–tapping, the moment he knew (or thought) he was alone in the house he went straight for the blockage. His laughter on finding the thong, the source of all the problems, was partly in celebration that he got away with it, that he was right to do what he did. After all, Annie was his.

He is about to go, leaving Annie utterly bereft in her new-found knowledge. As he is standing in the hall, almost on the tile cracked by Annie's fall, someone knocks at the door. His guilt gets the better of him and he escapes the house by the back door. No one will even know he was there. Except Annie.

"You can't do this on your own"

Earlier at the hospital, Mitchell was sorting though a fridge of bagged, donated blood. There is obviously a choice to be made but how do vampires select? By type? Is the vampire world equivalent of ABC (anything but Chardonnay) something like ABO?

He takes a bag and despite having told Lauren that this kind of blood is not the same he is still tempted. Being so close to blood, even lifeless blood, is too much and he longs for it, for the high he is missing. He meets Lauren again in the hotel and can barely get in the room before she snatches the bag from him. She's desperate but it does not work, it's really not the same and she spits it out. "It's not fresh from the kill," explains Mitchell, the life has gone. It would be far too simple if it worked, but all it can do is dull the pain for a while. Lauren wants to drink from Mitchell again. She seems to see that as a way to stay clean (the delusion of the addict) but he insists she has to stop. He won't give her what she wants, won't help her – won't do what she says – so she leaves him. Outside the hotel, Seth is waiting for her to take her to feed, back to the vampires and to Herrick. As if they had ever let her go.

"Oh, you're a dead man"

George has been avoiding Nina, but as he is trying to get away from the hospital before the rising of the full moon she corners him. Nurse Nina has been reading up and without much to go on she has concluded that George is a premature ejaculator. She takes him to a consulting room, sits him down and gives him a very serious lecture on how he can still find many ways of giving a woman pleasure. She even has leaflets. So close to the full moon, George's senses are in overdrive and it is all too much. He leaps on her and with accompanying growling gives her what could be described as the 'seeing to' of her life. As she slides to the floor in blissful exhaustion he runs – the wolf is almost here!

Back at the house, Gilbert is doing his best to comfort Annie; it was Gilbert at the door when Owen left. Annie is trying to make sense of her tangled recollections. Owen wasn't really like that, although she concedes reluctantly that he was moody and sometimes he… She stops short, unable to say the words, to admit that he hurt her and she let him, but we know. The classic abused defence. Maybe it was her, after all she is so hard to live with, but all she wanted to do was love and be loved. How difficult could that be? Gilbert reassures her that it wasn't her fault and that she is wonderful and loved. He loves her; he finally has the strength to say it. "I really love you." As soon as the words are out he looks relieved, as if a weight has lifted. Suddenly Annie becomes aware of something odd. There is a door in the living room, a door that shouldn't be there. Gilbert knows it is for him. It is death, his time is here and all he had to do to get here was to fall in love. In fact, all he had to do was meet Annie. He has unknowingly been waiting all of Annie's life to meet her – she was born in the year he died.

He wants Annie to go with him, to take the door to the next stage together. She knows somehow that this is impossible, that door is for Gilbert and she cannot go through. It is not her time yet – she still has things to do.

He opens the door. Bathed in an eerie blue light he sparks up a final cigarette, smiling in anticipation. Then he is gone, leaving Annie smiling through her tears. She doesn't watch him go; either she is concerned about what lies ahead and would rather not see or more likely she knows this is a deeply intimate moment. How can another ghost share in that passing? Gilbert's resolution and her part in it has calmed her, she really does have a reason to be here. She was the one who helped Gilbert, even more than he helped her.

"Could I have not just had just five minutes with the biggest news?"

Did Mitchell know that Owen killed Annie? He never says as much but he must have suspected. He was never keen on Annie exploring why she had not passed on, and now that she knows, he seems to understand without an explanation. He just holds her, his fatherly role in the house showing in the tenderness with which he does so.

It is the morning after the night before and George is heading home. He's clean and fully dressed in his own clothes so he did learn something from Tully. Remembering his exploits with Nina with a hop and a skip up to the front door, he bursts in to announce his sexual successes at the top of his voice. Only to be trumped by Annie's rather darker news.

Mitchell thinks the house was telling them something was wrong, the clanky tap and the moaning pipes. Given Annie's ties to the building, it isn't unlikely. Of course, there may have been the fact that none of the other tenants survived Annie's haunting long enough to really test the plumbing!

Annie can't understand why she hasn't gone. She's tried being with Owen, the man she admits she felt owned her, but that wasn't it. She now knows he killed her and yet she is still here. What more does she have to do?

"What now? What's left?"

Musings on episode three...

The series is now firmly into its stride and while this is Annie's episode there are also strong developments for both George and Mitchell. Meanwhile it is the ghosts that take centre stage.

The attempt to distract Annie from her pending wedding day by introducing her to another ghost is inspired. It isn't just any old ghost but the ghost of the 80s. Gilbert is wonderful – a true 80s icon, right down to his high-waisted Levi jeans. A picture of studied misery and angst, he is the perfect foil for bright, bubbly twenty-first century Annie.

Alex Price talks about the details that created Gilbert on the *Being Human* blog. Having been given the Walkman headphones and Casio watch, he was also presented with proper Y-fronts! Apart from genuine period detail, they were the only undies that were going to fit under those tight 80s jeans. He fades out talking about VPL...

In the documentary *Being Human Unearthed*, Toby Whithouse talks about being a teenager in the 80s and that brief era of "professional, full-time misery." I confess that I too experienced the 80s and was well acquainted with the Gilbert type. To achieve that absolutely pitch perfect portrayal of Gilbert I do wonder if what we are really seeing is the young Toby Whithouse personified.

It is brave to bring in great guest stars like Dean Lennox Kelly and strong characters like Tully and Gilbert and then let them go all within a single episode. It must be tempting to do more with them, but our main trio are all on journeys (hackneyed *X-Factor*-y phrase that that is) and people will inevitably pass through their lives. The transient friendships add to the reality of the situations they are in.

Now we know the truth – Owen killed Annie. Toby Whithouse was surprised that not everyone had already worked that one out for themselves and he generously credits Gregg Chillin's performance for much of that. There were those who suspected already – the hints of abuse were all there. Owen thinks that he got away with it and there are also signs that he is starting to replicate his behaviour to Annie with Janey. However much Annie resents orange-hued tanning-queen Janey, she surely can't stand by and see that happen?

George is still using the wolf, his curse, as an excuse not to participate in life, but gradually he is being pushed out of his comfort zone. He has met Nina and there is such a spark there that even he can feel it. Mitchell engineers him a dinner date but he is still pushing Nina away. That is until the full moon approaches, along with Nina's very earnest lecture on sexual techniques. The wolf grabs George by the scruff of the neck and he follows suit with Nina! Bad dog! It's a huge turning point for George. Not just that he has had sex (although he's rather pleased with that), but that he can date and be with a woman like a normal man.

Mitchell on the other hand is a step behind George. He is still avoiding women except for the increasingly desperate Lauren. She is stalking Mitchell; he got her hooked on blood and she wants payback. He lets her have his blood – a deluded act that he seems to think is keeping them both clean – but eventually his rejection of her life and her sends her back to the vampires.

His 'know thy neighbour' programme is going well. He and George can't walk down the street without exchanging greetings with everyone they pass, from the Vin Diesel fanatic to the nice old dears. Mitchell is pleased but George is still convinced it is dangerous. What could possibly go wrong...?

Online review site *Den of Geek* voted this episode one of its fifteen best pieces of television of 2009 due to the realistic portrayal of an abusive situation that is sadly all too common. The truth shines through, even though *Being Human* adds the twist of the abused being a ghost after the abuse reached the furthest point – murder.

Bum notes...

Annie is not from Bristol so wouldn't it have been more likely that her family would have taken her home to bury her? Or did Owen overrule them to keep her away from them even in death. Even her gravestone proclaims his possession by branding her forever the "Beloved fiancée of Owen."

Mitchell finds Nina smoking – a fortuitous encounter that let him set her up on a date with George. Very fortuitous as we never see Nina smoke again! A useful trick or a slight mistake?

Even with suspension of disbelief, it does seem unlikely that a hospital cleaner could access the blood stocks so easily – even with vampire trickery.

... and the bottom line

Sightings of Russell Tovey's bare backside – only one. But there is a sighting of Mitchell in his pants as some compensation.

He said, she said...

I never know with you if it's Jewish guilt or werewolf guilt.

They're pretty much the same thing.

......

I'd like to be like his guardian angel and stop anything bad from happening to him.

Can you stop him from listening to Michael Buble?

......

Thank God you met me. It's time you had some fun, girl.

I thought fun was a bourgeois concept.

Oh no. I'm talking about Gilbert fun.

......

Loads of people have had an experience with a ghost, and if they haven't they know someone who has. It is a lot more socially acceptable than you may think. They talk about it on Loose Women all the time.

Where have I seen... Sama Goldie (Janey)?

Sama Goldie appeared as Jude in children's TV series *My Parents are Aliens* (in 1999) before training at the Royal Welsh College of Music and Drama, where she had stage roles including Nora in *A Doll's House* (2006), Isabella in *Women Beware Women* (2007) and Helen/Dor in *Road* (2007). She played Michelle in *My Friend Alan* in 2009 at the Lost Theatre Festival at the New End Theatre, Hampstead.

On television, she played Maz in the TV pilot *Foreign Bodies* (2008), appeared in *EastEnders* as Lindsey (in 2008) and in *Doctors* as Jemima Richards (in 2009), and played Alison Double in Sky's *Thorne: Sleepyhead* (2010). Also in 2010, Sama appeared in the short film *Interval* as Lucy.

Music in episode three

Soft Cell	*Tainted Love*
The Fall	*High Tension Line*
Echo & the Bunnymen	*A Promise*
The Smiths	*Girlfriend in a Coma*
The Specials	*Ghost Town*
Marc and the Mambas	*In My Room*
Fun Boy Three	*The Tunnel of Love*
Born Ruffians	*Little Garcon*
Joy Division	*Love Will Tear Us Apart*
Soft Cell	*Torch*
The Teardrop Explodes	*Reward*

episode four

Mitchell befriends a neighbour's young boy, Bernie, but things turn nasty after a serious misunderstanding.

The trio and the house are targeted in a witch hunt.

Annie is still traumatised after the revelations about her life and death with Owen.

broadcast:	15 FEBRUARY 2009	director:	ALEX PILLAI
writer:	TOBY WHITHOUSE	producer:	MATTHEW BOUCH

cast:

Annie	LENORA CRICHLOW	Janey	SAMA GOLDIE
Mitchell	AIDAN TURNER	Fleur	JULIA FORD
George	RUSSELL TOVEY	Bernie	MYKOLA ALLEN
Lauren	ANNABEL SCHOLEY	Jim	BARRIE AIRD
Herrick	JASON WATKINS	Shop owner	MARK FLITON
Seth	DYLAN BROWN	Old lady	WENDY BRIERLEY
Nina	SINEAD KEENAN	Ahmed	LEWIS RHOMES
Owen	GREGG CHILLIN	Stevo	MASON BEAUMONT

"Where do I belong? Where do I fit?"

Mitchell's voiceover for this episode is all about fitting in, belonging, about finding your tribe. Being human. Mitchell stands in the street, introspective, smoking and people-watching. Where does he fit? Are any of these people like him? Having rejected the vampires, Mitchell has lost his family, his culture and has effectively wiped out his century of existence. What now? Can he really be one of the humans he watches, have the life he thinks he wants? Mitchell believes that we choose our tribe, where we feel we belong, partly because being outside the lines, outside the tribe, is so painful. He is now choosing humanity after having chosen vampirism so many years ago, but surely it can't be that easy.

A shot of George from the pilot – walking home, grubby and wearing some very odd clothes obviously acquired after waking up post-wolf (and pre-Tully). Annie sits on the stairs where she fell and died, as Mitchell talks about drifting through life like a ghost. Rather uncharitable to Annie. Are the labels we carry forced on us as they were on George and Annie, are they with us forever or can we fight them, subvert and change them? Mitchell's label was acquired through choice, Hobson's choice maybe, but with free will and after a century in that tribe he wants to choose again.

There's a sequence of Mitchell walking through the dark streets, his appearance changing. Showing how he has been attired through his century of immortal existence, the personas he has tried out. A soldier, a natty dinner suit, a smart business suit, a punk and a new romantic – the uniforms of the tribes we choose. Ending with his current look, he knows that you only truly live when you work out who you really are. Mitchell thinks he has done this. He is going to be like the humans; maybe he can actually be human but is that really achievable after a century of blood and death? After all, Herrick tells us he "had the blackest heart of us all."

"Where do my loyalties lie?"

Mitchell is looking for Lauren at the vampires' HQ, the funeral parlour, and he has Seth by the throat. The effortless way he lifts and holds Seth off the ground gives us a rare hint of Mitchell's true nature, the strength and power he has as a vampire. He really hurts Seth, a vampire who is older but not stronger than him.

He intends to take Lauren back but it is all a bit 'dog in the manger'. He didn't really want her stalking him and her constant desire for blood was a nuisance, especially as she was not prepared to conform to his lifestyle. Now she has made her choice and he is still not happy. She has a home with the vampires – what had Mitchell offered her? Certainly not that, as there was never any prospect of her joining George and Annie in the house. When they met by arrangement it was in a hotel.

Herrick is frighteningly matter-of-fact as he tells Mitchell a few home truths. Whoever's side you are on you can't really argue with his logic and this is one of Herrick's greatest strengths, his reasonableness. He reminds Mitchell that he made Lauren and then abandoned her, tried to fit her into his bloodless lifestyle but kept pushing her away. Herrick recruited Mitchell and he took responsibility for him – it is how it is done – but Mitchell left Lauren and she had nowhere to go except back to the vampires.

Herrick accuses him of cruelty – he took away Lauren's humanity and then tried to help her by keeping her away from the people she had joined. The evangelical zeal of the reformed addict. But is Mitchell wavering? He can't deny Herrick's accusations and he is still lying to himself about the film. Yes, he watched it, but unknowingly – he won't admit to Herrick that he played it again and again. Let Lauren be what she is, Herrick tells him so reasonably, so sensibly that it's hard to disagree.

Mitchell is not as controlled and as far from the vampires as he thinks he is, and Herrick knows it. He sends Mitchell away like a naughty schoolboy to "get it out of your system." There will always be a place for him with the vampires, with Herrick. It's only a matter of time.

"Raiding the dressing-up box, pretending to be human. It's a game!"

George meanwhile has his own dressing-up box and is preparing for a not-a-date with Nina. He parades some outfits for Mitchell and Annie's approval and they prove helpful although rather short of Gok Wan.

Black shirt? "You look like bar staff."
Floral orange – well, let's just call it an item? "It's hideous."
Casual T-shirt? "That just looks like you can't be arsed."

Despite all the not-a-date stuff, George is smitten – sex with Nina was "poetic" and he's keen to create a good impression, despite Mitchell and Annie's teasing. His only concern is that last time he was with Nina it was almost the full moon and he was on the verge of changing. What if it is only the wolf that she wants? Annie and Mitchell are not quite quick enough to contradict him and he flounces off – presumably to try on some more shirts. Let's hope he kept all the receipts.

Mitchell has concerns other than George's wardrobe. Annie is clearing up a broken plate and a mug has just slid along the shelf into his hand. Annie prevaricates but it is her – she's a poltergeist. It's been happening ever since she found out that Owen killed her and she can't control it. As if to prove this the drawers open and close and the lights flicker. Annie is convincing herself this is normal and is maybe one of the classic stages of grief – she is getting angry. Annie wants to channel it as she is keen to move the fridge so she can clean behind it, but Mitchell is worried. Never mind cleaning the kitchen, she needs to come to terms with Owen killing her, but just this tiny contradiction of her intentions and the coffee jar explodes. You really won't like her when she's angry!

"I was the dorkiest of dorks"

Mitchell heads out with customary dark glasses in place, but he suddenly has second thoughts. Taking them off, he stands on the doorstep looking up at the blue sky. The sunlight obviously hurts his eyes, but what's a bit of squinting if you want to look human (allowing for the fact that humans do tend to wear sunglasses in bright daylight!)?

There are a couple of kids bullying another boy and while Mitchell tries to ignore it, he just can't. Mitchell can't help getting involved – all part of the 'engagement with the community' project he holds so dear. Showing his distance from the real human world, he is genuinely startled when the two bullies are quite prepared to take him on despite only being kids, and resorts to showing them his black vampire eyes to scare them away. The other boy is relieved but really could have taken them on, he claims. Mitchell is surprised – he certainly couldn't have at his age and confesses that he was a total dork. A glimpse of Mitchell's long-past childhood, he certainly wouldn't ever have been permitted to have stood up to adults as he has just experienced.

Bernie's mother Fleur arrives, obviously concerned, although it's not clear whether it is finding her son with Mitchell or the bullying that worries her most. She seems very welcoming, thanking Mitchell for his help and inviting him in for a cup of tea. She echoes George in saying that modern living means she doesn't know her neighbours, so she obviously missed Mitchell's coffee mornings! He's thrilled to be invited into a neighbour's house, to see a bit of the family life he's been denied. Fleur is a single mum, rather harassed and outwardly a bit of a hippy. She's pleased Bernie is different, he's sensitive, and she can't understand why people pick on those who are different. All good stuff to Mitchell, except for the chamomile tea she serves which is totally unwelcome. She gets a bit carried away and makes the sign of the cross, causing Mitchell to flinch in traditional vampire fashion.

"And you're one of the good guys"

George has chosen the black shirt. Standing awkwardly in Nina's sitting room clutching a bunch of flowers, he looks less like bar staff and more like a cloakroom attendant. Nina is annoyed as she has to work and can't make their not-a-date. They do have some time to get, well, close and sort out a few assumptions. Nibbling rather enthusiastically on George's ear, Nina makes him squeak in pain. She thought he liked it rough but that's what the wolf likes and it left her rather stunned. They sort themselves out and agree to take things slowly, to step back to "flowers and... romance." So George and Nina manage to get over one more hurdle in their – frankly quite exhausting –

relationship. Where next?

Mitchell is still forcing himself to 'enjoy' the sun and blue sky but it is becoming easier. He bumps into Fleur and Bernie – she's off to Tesco's and he offers to take Bernie out. Now I know that all women go a bit gaga when Mitchell is around and let's face it he's a good-looking man (although not in that hat), but there must be something of the vampire here. An unconscious charisma that makes grown women daft – after all, why else would she let her twelve-year-old son go off with someone who, as Mitchell himself reminds her, she has only just met?

Fleur doesn't believe in "wrapping kids up in cotton wool," so off they go. Her ex-husband sees Bernie as a playmate and maybe that makes her less likely to question why a grown man is happy in the company of a child. She checks her makeup in her handbag mirror as they walk off. That's odd. She sees Bernie behind her but where is Mitchell? Vampires do not reflect but she consciously rationalises why she didn't see him – an odd angle perhaps – but maybe a lingering doubt remains.

They go bowling and Mitchell is rubbish. Maybe he's letting Bernie win, suppressing his strength and agility, but maybe he's just rubbish. Vampires and bowling? Just can't see them in the shoes...

Mitchell has not thought this through; Bernie is a curious child and is asking him lots of questions. What did he want to be when he was Bernie's age? Mitchell tells him about way back when people didn't have careers; it was the church or the army, and he went into the army. Bernie is impressed and Mitchell has to admit that he did fight (and sometimes ran away), but what war could he have been in at his apparent age? This story won't stand up to many questions and it's probably a good job that Lauren appears to give him a break.

"Could you just cut to the bit when you make me feel guilty...?"

Lauren has come to say goodbye. The vampires have got the message and they will leave him be. Mitchell is astonished and almost scared; he can deny and reject the vampires, but them rejecting him? That's something he never anticipated. He's expecting Lauren's usual pleas to help her, the tantrums and scenes, and he is disappointed. He can tell that Lauren has been taking blood, he can see it and smell it, but she denies she has been killing. She's completely in control, embracing the vampire world. She's a functioning addict, as are all the vampires, and Mitchell is weakened by her strength. Lauren being the strong one is wrong and he can no longer control her, his last hope to get her off blood has gone. She absolves him of responsibility for her condition, it's OK, she is happy. A last embrace and she leaves, head held high, at ease with who she is and leaving Mitchell alone.

Bernie slips and hits his head, he gets a strike and in his excitement doesn't notice that he has cut himself, but Mitchell is horrified. He picks him up and produces a hankie to clean his forehead. Worried about being so close to Bernie's blood, he is relieved to realise that actually it is fine! There's another Mitchell out-of-time anomaly – how many young men carry even a cleanish tissue, never mind a well-laundered, ironed white handkerchief?

Back to the house with several carrier bags of E-numbers and additives masquerading as party food, and Mitchell invites George to join him and

Bernie for a party. They even have balloons. There's a sticky moment when George and Mitchell respond to Annie who Bernie can't see, but some quick pre-biscuit neck exercises cover that up. George is initially wary – treating Bernie as if he is four and then twenty-four – but they soon settle down to eat themselves stupid.

Annie stays with them, criticising the catering – "is any of this actually real food?" – but her musings about the children she wanted lead to her angrily sending a plate flying across the room. Mitchell distracts Bernie by sending him to get a DVD from his room – Bernie has never heard of Laurel and Hardy, the duo that Mitchell thinks are the funniest ever. Just pick any of their DVDs, he instructs Bernie and watch it as soon as you can.

George is concerned about Bernie's safety but Mitchell is convinced his human side is taking over. When Bernie cut his head he felt no thirst for the blood. George notes his very well-hidden soppy streak, which Mitchell shrugs off. Is the vampire finally becoming human?

"And that's another fine mess you got me into"

Next morning and Fleur is a little the worse for wear, as is George after far too many Party Rings. While his mum rests her head on the table, Bernie takes the chance to watch Mitchell's DVD. It looks familiar. It's a very long way from Laurel and Hardy – it's actually Lauren's vampire snuff film. (There are many puns available here but I'm resisting!)

Bernie is transfixed, he knows it isn't right but keeps watching, checking that Fleur still has her eyes shut. The DVD plays on and eventually – inevitably – Fleur sees it.

She's straight across the road to Mitchell, screaming at him, attracting an audience who are all keen to hear just what he's been up to. Fleur's allegations are loud, explicit and cutting – and maybe just a little guilt driven, should she have been more careful? She throws the DVD back at him and Mitchell realises what has happened and that now everyone in the street knows he has given Bernie gay porn to watch; there is no way he can explain.

George and Annie are just as horrified as they had no idea he had kept the DVD. He had convinced them that he had left that life behind and he still can't admit to watching it. He wants to put it right but Fleur won't listen and the other neighbours are already on the bandwagon – they want him out.

The house is covered in graffiti, rubbish thrown at it and surrounded by the neighbours. They throw eggs and rotten food, the little kids have placards and Fleur is winding up the tension – it could have been any of the kids. Mob rule, is this what being human really is?

Mitchell thinks it will all blow over but he's wrong. The kids who started everything by bullying Bernie are thrilled to have a new target. A brick through the window shows how the situation is escalating. There is no way they can explain now.

"We are monsters Mitchell. We deserve to be cast out"

George can't take any more – he always knew this would happen, that they couldn't live like normal humans. He wants to get away, but Mitchell reminds him that they can't leave Annie. She can't go with them and they are all she has, he explains, unaware she is listening.

Determined not to drag Nina into the situation, George finishes with her. He tries the 'it's not you it's me' speech but Nina is made of sterner stuff and she won't accept it. He tries to convince her that he has dark secrets, his determination is clear and he is close to tears. She stops arguing but he hasn't won this round.

"I will bring this house down!"

Annie's new powers become quite clear when Mitchell tells them that Owen is coming over. At the mention of his name the light bulbs start to explode, ornaments fly around and smash and – worst of all – the radio starts playing *Barbie Girl* at top volume. She can't control her power but Mitchell does his best to calm her down and hides her upstairs.

Owen arrives hand in hand with Janey and they come in, Janey with a brown envelope that was on the doorstep. George opens it to find human excrement which is not a great start to the meeting. Janey needs to wash her hands, while Owen is impressed at the aim!

Mitchell explains to Owen what has happened, it's all a misunderstanding. The kid should never have seen the DVD and yes, it was a man – he has "eclectic tastes." Owen is quite amused but nevertheless he has no choice, he can't afford to upset the neighbours and he has an investment to protect, so he gives them notice to move. It's Janey that lets slip that they will want to live in the house themselves and she heads upstairs to do some measuring. Annie is up there and just about everything Janey says adds fuel to her fury – culminating in the light fitting almost dropping on their heads. Janey is quite unperturbed but Owen is bothered. He grabs Janey and hustles her roughly out of the house and away. What has he seen?

"And there you are. There's the Owen I remember"

Hot on the heels of Owen and Janey leaving, Nina turns up. Fleur is outside, warning her off, still shouting at the top of her voice. Knocking at the door, which is emblazoned with a spray-painted 'peedos', Nina wants to know if that is George's secret. Of course it isn't – and anyway, he shouts to the world, it's spelt wrong!

He tries to reassure her that his secret isn't kids or anything else the neighbours have thought of, but won't – can't – tell her any more and he won't even ask her in. She's convinced it was a woman who has left him in such a mess and warns him that he will push everyone away. She can't imagine what could be so bad that thinking he was a paedophile could be any better and she walks away exasperated.

"I would have listened"

Herrick wants to take a statement from Mitchell. Fleur's allegations have been reported to the police. It is now official and child protection is involved. Mitchell doesn't take it seriously and doesn't seem to see Herrick as a real policeman, which I suppose he isn't. Herrick wonders if he thought he was a kissogram... He can make all of this go away but it could be very awkward for Mitchell. Despite Mitchell's rejection of him he is still protecting one of his kind, those are the rules.

Herrick draws Mitchell into reminiscing about 'back in the day', when things would have been very different. They talk about kills from the past with the shared memories of good friends. Herrick knows he'll get him back, he can wait, and he leaves Mitchell both confused and relieved.

In the freezing house, the wind whistling through the broken window, George and Mitchell are watching an old film. An outcast chased by the mob, it seems almost like a documentary to George. Mitchell is either despairing or sulking – all his dreams of being human, of how he thinks humans are, have been smashed, the mob outside will never accept him. Suddenly George shrieks. He can see flames; someone has set fire to the house! Luckily they haven't, as he only has a kettle of water to throw on it. Annie is burning all her photos of her and Owen in the yard and she's strangely calm. She realises that she had no life but Owen and that was wasted. Now she has a reason to be here – she will not allow Owen to take anything else away from her, not the house and certainly not George and Mitchell.

"Oi, Gary Glitter! You're just takin' the piss now!"

Bernie is at the door – he's managed to sneak out and he wants to explain. He knew it was not the DVD he should have had and knows he shouldn't have kept watching. He is convinced that everything is his fault and he is sorry, desperate for Mitchell to understand. Mitchell reassures him that it is not his fault, he has nothing to apologise for, but inevitably someone sees him and instantly there is a crowd.

Bernie is pushed away as they surround Mitchell, threatening him, and this time he fights back. It isn't physical, no one has lashed out yet, but it is only a matter of time. Fleur shouts for Bernie, he wants to sort things out but she is furious he has disobeyed her. He runs back but a car is approaching and it is only Mitchell who can see or hear it coming. It is only Mitchell who is fast enough to try and help. He's just too late and the car hits them both. Immortal Mitchell gets up but Bernie is lying motionless in the road.

Mitchell turns on the watching neighbours, furious that the situation has reached this point, that Bernie is hurt, maybe dying. George grabs him, tries to stop him saying something that he can never take back, as after all they are only...

"Human!? Then it's our mistake wanting to be like them!"

Annie hears the sirens and comes out to see what has happened. A neighbour tells her and she is astonished to realise she is visible. Someone pushes past her and apologises. Her decision to move on from Owen, seeing him for what he really is, has increased her confidence, she is calm but determined. She can be seen.

George has to get away after seeing Bernie hurt and he instinctively goes to Nina for comfort. Despite all he has said, she lets him in. He asks her if she can live with knowing he has secrets that he can't share with her. She doesn't answer but shows him her stomach – the skin is badly scarred, probably from burns, and she tells him that she too has secrets. Here are more hints of abuse, "people can be bastards" is all she will say, she doesn't want to remember. George puts his hand over her scars; he never wants her to be hurt again, two damaged people together.

Bernie is dying, Fleur at his bedside. Mitchell is there too and she almost apologises – Bernie tried to explain but she wouldn't listen. Mitchell wants to help – he feels responsible and he tells Fleur the truth, that he's a vampire. He points out that she saw the car hit them both and he walked away. She thinks he's deluded, but he shows her he doesn't reflect in a mirror and she remembers that she saw (or didn't see) that before. Maybe what he says is true. He offers to make Bernie a vampire so he will live forever. She has to choose but she turns it back on him – is Mitchell happy? She thinks not. In her place would he chose that life for his son?

Weeping, Fleur kisses Bernie for the last time before the nurse pulls the sheet over his face and she runs out, passing Mitchell slumped in a chair, waiting. The next we see of her is at the station saying goodbye to Mitchell. She has explained her mistake to the neighbours she says, told them that Mitchell tried to save Bernie, but nothing matters to Mitchell now.

Suddenly Fleur sees Bernie coming towards her – he looks pale and somehow changed. Fleur's love for her son is mixed with horror at what he has become and she is panicking. Should she change too she asks Mitchell, but he wants her to stay human, she has to keep Bernie good. Bernie tries to thank Mitchell but he'll have none of it and walks away, leaving mother and son to a new life.

"Mum... I'm hungry"

Mitchell goes straight to the funeral parlour where Herrick is waiting for him. He knew Mitchell was coming, this is no surprise to him and he needs say nothing. It was only a matter of time. Once again, Mitchell has made his choice.

"I'm in"

Musings on episode four...

This is a brave episode. It takes on some very dark subject matter and not the least of this is child abuse. Of course it is all a terrible mistake, but it's a topic that could have gone so very wrong and been extremely uncomfortable to watch. While its execution may not be quite perfect, it is pretty close. The humour is still there – only one 'e' in paedo – and the speed and ferocity with which the mob gathers is genuinely scary, not to mention very real.

One theme of the episode is all about labels, those we assign to ourselves and those pasted on us by others. Mitchell wants to be human but is labelled vampire. George and Annie have labels they didn't ask for. Mitchell's musing on tribes is telling – he is choosing to be human but uncertain about whether it is possible. Despite all, he's going to try.

His 'meeting the neighbours' programme has only extended so far, and this week he meets Fleur and Bernie. Just across the road, they've slipped through the coffee morning net. Mitchell befriends Bernie and there is just a touch of hero worship on both sides. Bernie asks Mitchell questions about his childhood; the answers could sound a little odd unless you know that that childhood was in the very early years of the twentieth century. Mitchell is just

101

happy to be accepted as human; his determined innocence about humans and their behaviour means he doesn't ever question spending time with a child or consider how it may look. He's just happy to be accepted.

Inevitably, it all goes very wrong and Bernie gets to watch the vampire snuff film. Does Fleur overreact? Of course she is protecting her child, but is there a slight guilt that she 'handed' him to Mitchell? Most twelve-year-old boys would be curious about the DVD and she may not want to think about her boy growing up. She likes it that Bernie is different to the other kids, that he is sensitive, but would being gay just be too different for her to accept?

Ostensibly about 'paedos' and children, the episode is more about mob rule – the unpleasant aspects of human nature, collective hysteria and the singling out of anyone different – paedophilia is a handy hook to hang this on.

When Mitchell takes the hard decision to make Bernie a vampire rather than to let him die, it is with the collusion and probably the blessing of Fleur after he has explained what he is. We recall the conversation between Herrick and Mitchell in episode one, when Herrick is talking about openly offering the chance of immortality and how he feels there would be queues stretching a thousand miles. He suggests they visit the children's ward, where the worried parents of ill children are. "Would a single one of those turn us away?"

George's relationship with Nina gets going, falters and stops, and then slowly picks up again. She reveals that she too is damaged and they agree to keep their own secrets. George's fear of being unmasked is so close to being realised in this episode. It is Mitchell that is reviled but there is guilt by association and under that scrutiny can he keep the wolf away?

Annie has become a poltergeist – an uncontrollable one! This is a natural stage in her grief after finding out what Owen did to her. She has hit rage, will acceptance soon follow? Annie is the one who listens and watches and she knows all about Mitchell and George, more so than either of them realise. She is the one who challenges Mitchell about keeping the DVD after all he said about moving on, rejecting Lauren and the vampires and all that that stood for. He has no answer – he can't even admit he'd been watching it – especially as he is the one urging Annie to move on from Owen.

Annie's anger peaks when Owen is in the house, especially when Janey is planning to finish the decorating, to live the exact life that Annie had planned. Strangely, Owen giving Mitchell and George notice to move calms her. She knows that she cannot let this happen and that determination not to let Owen take any more away from her lets her move forward. She burns their photos and the boost to her confidence in rejecting her life with Owen as a lie makes her visible again.

It's interesting to watch the house developing as the series moves on. From the stark emptiness after the wolf wrecked the ground floor in the first episode, to the homely clutter we see this week. It's realistic – cast-offs, curios and odd bits of furniture, a stack of old board games and a selection of curious lamps – or at least there were before Annie the poltergeist got to work! The state of the house is a good barometer of the state of the trio. As their lives get more complex and entangled so the house gets cluttered and cosy. It's now a home not just a house.

A dark episode such as this needs humour to lighten it and the balance is just right. George's fashion parade is a highlight – mainly for Mitchell and

Annie's expressions. George's observation on keeping rotten tomatoes just on the off chance that you may need to throw them at a house is so surreal in that situation, that it's perfect.

So what next? George has found some peace with Nina. Knowing that they both have secrets soothes him a little although it isn't a great basis for a lasting relationship. Annie is visible and ready to make Owen see what he has done. And Mitchell is back with the vampires – will we see now just why Herrick is so keen to have him there?

Bum notes...

Would Fleur really have allowed Bernie to spend the day with Mitchell on such short acquaintance? He may have proved a godsend – babysitting while she shopped, cooked, hosted a dinner party and rather overdid the gin, but didn't she ever wonder why Mitchell might be so keen to befriend a twelve-year-old?

Mitchell's return to the vampires is very sudden. The behaviour of the mob and Fleur is awful but he's a 100-odd-year-old vampire – he must have seen worse. Maybe the swiftness with which he goes back is a true measure of how human he had become. His rose-coloured view of humanity felt more real than the dark vampire world and sweeping it away so horrifically was such a blow that he can't see any other way forward than going back.

Although we don't know yet, we do not return to Nina's secret at all throughout series one and two. Hopefully we'll find out more in series three. There's a story there that we need to hear.

... and the bottom line

Sightings of Russell Tovey's bare backside – none I'm afraid, and quite frankly Mitchell's dodgy tracky pants are in no way making up for that!

He said, she said...

Who keeps their rotten tomatoes? Who looks in their salad cooler, sees their tomatoes are on the turn and thinks 'oh no, no I'll hang on to those in case some paedos move in opposite'?

•••••

There's a whole dark and beautiful world, and you're obsessing about what we eat.

•••••

For all I know this could be perfectly normal. You find out your fiance killed you, you become a 'throwing things about' ghost.
Poltergeist.
See, you know the terms, you know how this works. I mean, do you know if I can channel it because I have been dying to pull that fridge out and

clean behind it.

......

I'm not the pervert, that's my housemate. And actually, he's not a pervert either.

......

Do I look like a paedo?

If paedos looked like paedos they'd never to do any paedo-ing.

Where have I seen... Annabel Scholey (Lauren)?

Annabel graduated from the Oxford School of Drama in 2005.

Her stage work is extensive and includes *The Cherry Orchard*, *Hobson's Choice*, *Hamlet* and *The Taming of the Shrew*.

At the time of writing in 2010, she has already appeared this year as Hermia in *A Midsummer Night's Dream* and as Julia Melville in *The Rivals*, both for director Peter Hall, as well as playing Kitty Verdun in *Charley's Aunt*.

On TV, Annabel played a lead role in *Personal Affairs* (2009) as Michelle 'Midge' Lerner. She also appeared in *Eastenders* in 2007 as Maddy, as Diana Rivers in *Jane Eyre* in 2006, and had roles in *Holby City*, *Doctors*, and *Poirot: After the Funeral* (all in 2006).

She has also lent her voice to radio drama including *All Passion Spent*, *A Harlot's Progress* and *Under Milk Wood*. She was runner-up in the BBC Carleton Hobbs Radio Competition 2005.

Music in episode four

Alabama 3	*Don't Call the Doctor*
Alabama 3	*Sad Eyed Lady of the Lowlife*
Aqua	*Barbie Girl*
Hans J. Salter	*Dr Kettering's Death*

episode five

After the neighbourhood witch hunt, Mitchell turns away from humanity and back to Herrick and the vampires.

Annie plots her revenge.

Mitchell meets an old flame and Herrick makes his move.

broadcast:	22 FEBRUARY 2009	director:	COLIN TEAGUE
writer:	TOBY WHITHOUSE	producer:	MATTHEW BOUCH

cast:

Annie	LENORA CRICHLOW	Owen	GREGG CHILLIN
Mitchell	AIDAN TURNER	Janey	SAMA GOLDIE
George	RUSSELL TOVEY	Josie	CLARE HIGGINS
Lauren	ANNABEL SCHOLEY	Duncan	GLENN DOHERTY
Herrick	JASON WATKINS	Policeman	MORGAN WALTERS
Seth	DYLAN BROWN	Billy	JOSEF ALTIN
Nina	SINEAD KEENAN		

"Our lovers sculpt us. They define us, for better or worse"

The penultimate episode of series one and George's voiceover tells us of the marks that are left by those whom we love. Some good, some bad. We see the funeral parlour vampire HQ, and Lauren outside. Is she waiting for someone? Mitchell is there and she stops him, tries to hold him and kiss him. Now he has returned to the vampires she knows they can have the life together she always wanted. It's not what Mitchell wants, it never was and he pushes her away. It's written all over his face that he thinks she is deluded, how can she possibly think they were ever meant to be together?

A flashback to Owen viewing Annie's lifeless body, his last chance to say goodbye to the woman he loved. The tears of the loving fiancé turn into something else as soon as he is alone. There's a calculating look, a look of triumph. No one else can have her now.

George is watching Nina dress, she is rattling on about everything and nothing but he is not listening to her. He is looking at her scars. The marks of another life, her dark secret. He promised her he wouldn't let anyone hurt her but is wondering how he can keep her safe from the monsters and the wolf.

Owen is in the house. He sees Annie reflected in a CD, he really sees her and he spins round horrified but there is nothing there. He knows though, he knows she is waiting. Annie watches him go, not with the doe-eyed devotion we are used to, but something harder.

"Our lovers linger inside us like ghosts..."

George comes in with a jar of homemade jam and puts it in the cupboard with the other ten. It's another gesture of apology by the neighbours after the 'trouble' as they don't know what else to do. Homemade jam is always welcome though; baked goods would be overdoing it. It would be painful to keep lingering on the 'peedo' incident, but this is the only acknowledgement

105

that it is over, surely it can't have been forgotten by their neighbours so quickly?

Annie has made a big decision. She is going to haunt Owen. She sees this as the next stage, this is how she is going to resolve her death and pass over. There's another big change for Annie as she is no longer wearing her engagement ring. While George is happy to help her figure out what to do, he wants her to note that he really doesn't want her to go. Very direct for the normally tongue-tied George and a measure of just how much he feels for Annie. They usually discuss their supernatural problems with Mitchell but they haven't seen much of him since Bernie's accident. They don't know that he is back with the vampires.

"... this is where I belong. I'm home now"

Herrick is telling tall tales, past exploits from the glory days when he and Mitchell would stop at nothing. The vampires are enthralled but Mitchell still looks out of place among the smart suits and neat dresses. Herrick is delighted to have his prodigal son back in the family but Seth is less pleased as Mitchell has stolen his place. While Seth knew he could never replace Mitchell at Herrick's side, he revelled in Herrick's 'friendship', his closeness to the throne. Mitchell tells them he is home, he has seen what humans really are and he knows he isn't one of them. The words are all in place but there is no great emotion behind them, who is he trying to convince? The vampires or himself?

Lauren is also watching, the ghost at the feast. She looks the part but there is always a space around her. The vampires don't get close to her; they can all sense that she isn't really one of them. Poor Lauren – she never seems to fit anywhere. She is the only one who challenges Herrick, making him explain why they gravitate to funeral parlours. They are attracted to places where death and life are close as that is the basic fact of their being. They feel at home in places where life and death cross. Hospitals, cemeteries – these are the churches of the vampires. There is also a very practical reason – the newly dead are brought to the parlour to wait for their reawakening as a vampire.

"Plus there's plenty of room for storage"

George and Annie are rehearsing haunting with the help of a few DVDs. "What would Patrick Swayze do?" Annie is trying and failing to be really scary. George does a bit better (not much) but they manage to come up with a basic routine for Annie to use. Annie wants to terrify Owen, get her revenge. This is no longer about getting him to confess, she wants to hurt him, make him suffer.

Her powers are more controllable now. She can go from standing in front of George to sitting beside him in an instant but she can't quite get the hang of being frightening. She's concerned that wanting to scare Owen so much, to have her revenge, is wrong, but George is reassuring.

"It's human. Not everything about being human is nice"

Accompanied by some slightly cheesy suspenseful music, Mitchell is sneaking Herrick into the hospital. Quite why he has to do that is a mystery. As a policeman Herrick could walk straight in the front door, but I guess that just isn't as much fun. They're going to see a terminal patient, a new candidate for Herrick's ambitious recruitment plans.

In the lift there's a rather surreal reverie from Herrick about his childhood dream of being an architect. He had a picture book and imagined building houses all over the mountainsides. Even back then (and we have no idea how old Herrick is) he was dreaming of building an empire. Herrick knows he was chosen to lead the vampires. It's been a long time coming but it's his calling, his vocation – just like all the best dictators.

Mitchell takes him up to the ward. He is picking out likely candidates for Herrick to recruit, patients with terminal conditions – and no one has even questioned why a cleaner is walking about with patients' notes. It does look as though Mitchell is not actually recruiting – killing – yet. There may be some humanity left in him.

In the canteen he sees a familiar face. Surely it can't be...? He takes her a coffee, exactly as she always liked it and Josie is astonished. Mitchell hasn't changed and she can hardly believe it is him. He tells her that she, too, hasn't changed, but she calls him a liar. It's obvious that it's a long time since they met and that they were close. Can the vampire see the person beneath the years or is there something in the substance of the person that they recognise? They reminisce about the weekend they once spent in Bristol, mostly in bed. They signed into the hotel as Mr and Mrs McCartney – well, it was the 60s! In just a couple of sentences we see their shared history and they laugh together at the memories.

Josie is concerned that Mitchell is alone but he reassures her he lives with friends. She knows what he is and he tells her they are not vampires, but something else. At that moment George arrives needing to speak to Mitchell, but Mitchell says he can speak in front of Josie. George is one of the "something elses," he explains. George really isn't sure what to make of this and his face is a picture when Mitchell explains that he and Josie dated in the 60s. Knowing your friend hasn't aged for over a hundred years is one thing – seeing the evidence is another! Mitchell sees Josie as just Josie, the woman he knows, but all George can see is the older woman. Josie chides Mitchell but gently – he outed George, it was mean – and you can see how much they must have meant to each other.

Josie tells Mitchell she is ill. Lung cancer. Terminal. Faced with her own mortality, all she can see is the immortal Mitchell, unchanging and young while she grew old. She reaches out to him and he takes her hand.

"Look at you. Frozen... like a photograph"

George has lured Owen to the house with a spurious excuse about the tap not working. Again. Owen arrives, tool box in hand, to a dark, empty house – why not turn on the light? In all the classic horror films why does no one ever turn on the light?! The tap works, to his annoyance, and he is leaving when he's faced with... Annie.

He falls in shock. Scared, cringing away from her on the floor. She goes into her haunting routine. It goes well, until "sapphire and... steel" anyway. She finishes on "confesssss" and leaves him on the floor. Heading upstairs after a job well done, Annie hears him call her back.

"Hey Annie. That the best you've got?"

He's regaining his bravado; he confronts her – now it all makes sense. The mysterious things he thought were happening, he thought it was guilt but now he knows it wasn't. He starts to dominate her again. Accuses her of sulking, taunts her, laughs at her – just as he did in life. And just as he did in life he leaves her alone and downtrodden.

Herrick's recruitment went to plan and the man from the hospital is on the slab, Mitchell waiting for him to reawaken. Herrick brings him takeaway, tells him to take a break, but Mitchell is glad of the solitude. The others won't leave him alone – they all want a piece of the mythical Mitchell. We also learn that even male vampires find farting funny – is there no escape?

Lauren appears and Herrick is distinctly uncomfortable around her. Does he see a true rival for Mitchell's affections? Lauren has the potential to be a true rebel and if she had Mitchell by her side who knows what she could achieve? When Mitchell abandoned her it seemed to set the tone among the vampires and, while she is tolerated, she is treated with suspicion. It must be galling for her to watch Mitchell waiting patiently for the latest recruit to wake when he couldn't do the same for her. She also hears him ask Herrick to talk to Josie – yet one more person he cares about that isn't her.

With a jerk and a gasp the new recruit awakes and Mitchell rushes to him, he will have seen awful things. He comforts and reassures him, telling him that he's home now.

"Men. There were men there"

Annie tells George how Owen reacted to her haunting – or more correctly how he didn't react at all. She's worked out why. What did she expect from a man who killed his fiancée and then rented out the house where it happened? It's hardly indicative of sanity and normality. There are no other options left to her, she is going to have to talk to Janey. She can't risk Owen doing the same to her.

Mitchell comes in and he's uncomfortable that George and Annie are in the kitchen, he doesn't want to have to talk to them. He has secrets from them now. They try to engage him in conversation about Annie's haunting of Owen but he is evasive. George realises he is back with the vampires and they are so disappointed but characteristically they won't push him away. Mitchell reacts angrily – he doesn't want to be human, it was all a lie. Humans are cruel and brutal and there is no way any of them should ever aspire to that. Anyway, the vampire thing is different now – it's all voluntary, they are giving people hope. Again, he's not convincing, he's still angry and lashing out. He knows that Annie and George care and will worry about him and while he has rejected humanity he isn't prepared to reject them too.

"Humanity? Most of humanity still point at planes"

As requested Herrick is talking to Josie, Mitchell watching from a distance. Herrick is laughing, open-faced and confident but Josie is wary. She doesn't meet his eyes and looks doubtful. She is starting from a different position to the other recruits. She knows Mitchell, what he is and what it means. She's had more time to consider what it means to be immortal, a vampire, and

Herrick is going to have to work a lot harder with her.

Mitchell tries to help convince her – she will recover from her illness immediately. Everyone will always be healthy and hospitals will become museums. He goes on and we hear echoes of Herrick – florid claims of the perfect world – and Josie has heard enough. It's all spin and this isn't the Mitchell she knew. He tries to tell her that she will come round to it, everyone finds it hard, even him at first, but she knows his story and he can't fool her. His situation was different and Mitchell's claim that they can be together forever rings false. Josie doesn't know how many other people he has made this offer to – she can't be the only one. He calls it evolution; she calls it a full stop. Everyone lives forever, no one dies and no one is born – it's a con. She is adamant, you have to die to be human and the vampires are stealing that basic right from humans and they have no right to. Mitchell thinks that he is being altruistic; all he wants to do is save Josie's life. She is dying and that is the only reason he asked Herrick to recruit her, but Josie knows him far too well. She knows that he really wanted her to know what was going on, he trusted her to stop him. She is the one who can tell him it is all wrong. He already knows that this is not the answer, that Herrick's scheme is unattainable, but he needed someone he trusts to make it clear to him. Josie has no axe to grind, she has much to gain but she tells Mitchell that dying is her right.

"Being human means being mortal"

Annie is waiting for Janey, wandering in Owen's house, looking around. She picks up a white lace thong from the washing. Ironically it's just like the one that started all the trouble and she flings it down quickly as Janey gets home. "Hello. It's me," and Janey faints.

Annie makes her comfortable, cushion under head, lifts up her feet and takes off her shoes – nice shoes by the way – and waits for her to come round. Unlike Owen, Janey is completely hysterical and runs away from Annie, locking herself in the bathroom. Annie tries to talk to her and – after some confusion about removing feet – finally manages to tell her that Owen killed her. Janey doesn't want to believe it but you can see in her eyes that she can't be sure. If Janey can tell Annie that Owen has never hurt her, never scared her, then she'll go. Janey can't. She starts off "sometimes he gets..." It's just what Annie used to say.

Before Annie can convince Janey that she has to be careful, that Owen really did kill her, Owen is home. Janey flings herself into his arms; she thinks she is going mad. He holds her, keeping her from seeing Annie while he convinces Janey she is seeing things. Looking straight into Annie's eyes, he tells Janey there is nothing there. He knows what buttons to press with Janey, he can manipulate her. He convinces her that she only thinks she can see Annie because she feels guilty. Why does she feel guilty? Janey and Owen started their affair before Annie died. This is news to Annie and Owen carries on, piling on the misery – they even had sex at her and Owen's engagement party. In the toilets. Classy. He carries on undermining Annie, how she was bitter and stupid and he looks her right in the eyes as he beats her with his words. He smiles at her tears.

"She lived her life in the periphery. Like a ghost"

George and Nina are having one of those slightly too sugary conversations that we all wish loved-up couples wouldn't have at work. They have graduated to calling each other "my boyfriend" and "my girlfriend" and are in the process of discussing Nina's breasts when Josie interrupts. She needs to speak to George.

"They're making it sound all New Labour, but this is an invasion"

Mitchell is in trouble and Josie cares enough to want to help. She knows George is Mitchell's friend and tells him about Herrick's plan, the recruiting and Mitchell's role in it. Josie is desperate for help – she tries to tactfully ask exactly what George is. He won't tell her, still unable to name his curse, but does say that his is just a part-time thing. She is disappointed, hoping he was a wizard or something useful, which George finds amusing. Josie is more grounded – dating a vampire rather expands your boundaries and wizards don't seem that unlikely. George wants to know just how bad this is and Josie remembers what Herrick said to her.

"No one gets left behind"

At the funeral parlour, Seth is staffing the front office. He wants to know why they have ended up in Bristol and Mitchell gives him a quick history lesson. The first vampire who lived a double life did so in Bristol – he can't believe Seth doesn't know this stuff, what sort of vampire does he think he is? Seth still resents Mitchell for usurping him with Herrick, even though he was only ever keeping the seat warm for him. Despite that, he wants Mitchell to be his friend, but Mitchell doesn't care, he has no time for Seth. All in all he's not finding any kindred spirits with the vampires, all his friends are elsewhere.

There's no one around but Mitchell can hear something. The sound of muffled screams and there's a door with bloody fingerprints on the frame. He finds a cellar full of runaways, all desperately scrabbling away from him. They have clearly been there for some time, there are beds and belongings, but they all look scared and unhealthy. One comes forward, trying to help the group and tells him they are coming too often. None of them have time to recover and they are starting to die. He has bloodletting tubes in his neck and there are bloodstained bowls and cloths strewn about. Mitchell realises that he is in the vampires' pantry.

Herrick appears – Seth has tipped him off that Mitchell is around. He really was going to tell him when the time was right but he knew Mitchell would disapprove. It seems that Mitchell is still off blood (except for Bernie) and farming humans was never going to go down well with him, however much he professes to despise humanity.

"Stereotypes clearly hold no fear for these people"

George has rushed home to see how he can help Mitchell and expects Annie to join him. He rattles around in the kitchen looking for appropriate implements and ends up with the prospect of defending himself with an egg whisk and a phone charger.

Annie hasn't moved. She's given in. She can't touch Owen and every time she tries he just kills her over and over and over again. She's done.

George is quietly furious. If she gives in now, when Mitchell needs their help, then Owen will really have won. He'll have killed her for the final time – by taking away her love for her friends.

Annie and George arrive together at the funeral parlour. Standing just inside the door they look the least likely SWAT team ever. Thinking they are proper customers Seth politely turns them away, until he gets close enough to smell the werewolf and realises that these must be Mitchell's housemates. He hasn't seen a ghost before – "What the cock is that?" Poor Seth, he really doesn't get out much. Annie and George demand to see Mitchell and the only way to do that is to get past Seth. Bravely they move on Seth, but the vampire strength is no match for George and he is soon held aloft. Annie is panicking and she throws the telephone, unfortunately it is still plugged in and doesn't stretch far enough. Last resort and she picks up a chair and hits Seth with it, but she has to apologise straight away. It doesn't do a great deal of damage but it does get Seth off George long enough for them to regroup. Seth goes for the old-fashioned solution. Fangs bared, he heads for George's neck, only to be repelled by his Star of David. It weakens him just enough for George to knock him out. It's odd as it doesn't affect Mitchell, he even looks after it when George transforms. This was Annie's first ever fight, but George's bravado at having knocked Seth out makes him bluster that this is going to be their life and they have to toughen up – even though he has actually really, really hurt his hand!

"We were like the world's gayest ninjas"

Herrick can't believe that Mitchell thought everything would be painless and bloodless, although perhaps he was just waiting for this moment. Maybe Herrick never really wanted Mitchell back in the fold but it was safer than him being outside. Mitchell has the reputation and the charisma to wrest control of the vampires from Herrick if he'd wanted to. Herrick could see the potential of Mitchell and Lauren – King and Queen of the Vampires – and he couldn't risk them getting the opportunity. He destroyed Lauren to keep her away from Mitchell.

Herrick lectures Mitchell on the Romans, the Ottoman Empire – he can already see his place in that history. Evolution is not painless; inevitably there will have to be casualties. It was always the intention to keep some of the humans, keep them pure so the vampires would have something to feed on. The runaways in the cellar were just a small part of that – a trial run of a human farm.

That is the bottom line. It's all about the blood. Mitchell sees it now – it's just a new way to feed and kill.

"But it feels so nice"

Mitchell is revolted. His abstinence from blood has reached a point where he can no longer see the pleasure, the needs of the addict. The balance has tipped and he is closer to human than vampire and he cannot stand by and watch them. Herrick won't let him go; he was never going to let him go. He can't be allowed to pop in and out when he pleases, he will need to be made an example of. But it's OK, Herrick will do it himself, it will be quite painless. Mitchell, resigned to his fate, just asks that they stop boasting about his exploits, he'd rather be forgotten.

The tension has reached a height when the 'gayest ninjas' arrive and, taking advantage of the element of surprise, George hits a henchman with a chair! Annie is there too – she just hasn't prepared anything to shout. Despite the ludicrousness of their rescue attempt, the vampires are distracted and they have the chance to run. Annie jumps ahead to check out their escape route but they are soon cornered.

Seth is blocking the exit and Herrick's heavies are behind them. George tries the Star of David again but there are too many of them and the effect is too diluted. Mitchell wants Annie to go but she won't leave them. He offers himself as a sacrifice if they let George and Annie go, but before anyone can move something happens to Seth. A look of almost comical surprise in his face, he falls forward, a stake thrusting through his chest. Lauren is behind him.

"Well, he won't be staring at my tits when he speaks to me anymore"

It's their chance to get away and they run, taking Lauren with them. For the first time Herrick is really angry. Eyes black, fangs bared, he howls in frustration and rage that Mitchell has got away from him. For the first time the plan is faltering.

They are outside heading for home, but Lauren can't run anymore. She wants Mitchell to kill her as she did Seth; she even has a spare stake. He created her and she wants it to be him that completes the cycle. She can't go on any longer, the human Lauren has almost completely gone – soon she will be just a distant memory. She enjoyed the blood too much and the people in the cellar were the final straw. She went to them and she hated it and loved it and it is enough. She can't go back and doesn't want to go forward. Mitchell instinctively backs away. He's never done this before although he has killed many times, but she convinces him that he'll be saving her. Saving the human Lauren, the girl who got hay fever, the girl who fancied Mitchell and thought her luck was in, not knowing where it would take her. He steels himself, the stake goes into her heart and he sets her free.

"But you saved us." "So save me"

Owen is back at the house. Arrogant and cocky as ever, he doesn't even bother knocking. This time though, it's different. All three are waiting for him. They stand silent and let Owen rattle on. He's still finding this funny, are they all ghosts? He doesn't feel guilty, if that's what this is all about. He's killed and he knows that he got away with it. That makes him untouchable.

This time Annie is calm. Coolly and deliberately she tells him what George is, what Mitchell is and Owen sees his eyes go black. In the world of evil, Owen is small fry, a mere beginner. He's not like them and wherever he goes, however he hides, they can always find him. It is Annie's strength that is the worst thing for Owen. He can deal with anything except Annie turning on him, finally proving that she doesn't need him.

"... and now I'm going to tell you the very worst thing in the world"

She whispers in his ear and his face crumples, it can't be true. Annie has told him what only the dead know and it has broken the barrier to the living. He runs, but even in the street he can't escape. He knows there are ghosts and werewolves and vampires – what else is waiting for him in the shadows?

George wants to know what she told him but she can't say. Only the dead know; Mitchell knows too, but to know when he is still alive would drive George mad, just as it has done to Owen.

Annie wonders what happens now. She wanted fireworks and Elvis at the very least but they just have to wait. After all, what is closure? Owen turning himself in maybe? In the meantime, *The Real Hustle* is on at 8.30.

Owen is a broken man and can only think of going to the police. They can keep him safe and all he has to do is confess. He gives them what he thinks is a sensible and comprehensive explanation. He killed Annie and she's now living with a vampire and a werewolf who are going to pursue him to the ends of the earth. Can they keep him safe?

"Well, in that case, we're going to need a different form"

Back at the house all is calm until Mitchell realises that Annie's door has arrived, Owen must have made his move. It is different to the door that appeared for Gilbert – more substantial with a letterbox and proper handles. It is labelled 1 High Street for reasons never explained.

Annie isn't sure what to do – should she pack? George is worried that she should be going somewhere good, if not then she should stay, but Mitchell knows it's an end and that is right. They'll be alright without her – "I'll look after him," they say in chorus. She hugs them and says goodbye. "Don't kill anyone," she tells Mitchell. Even then she is apprehensive and is finding it so hard to tear herself away – even with the chance to say goodbye to them properly. She knows it is important that George should not see inside the door. He is the only living member of the trio and she doesn't want him to know what is coming for him one day.

She takes the handle – it's cold – and there is a loud knock. They all jump but it's the front door and whoever it is they're not going to go away. Mitchell goes to get rid of them so they can concentrate on Annie.

He opens the door and Herrick stabs him. He can't enter the house, but as Herrick demands to be asked in he manages to get close enough to drive a stake into Mitchell's chest. George pushes him away and shuts him out but it's too late. Mitchell is bleeding, dying, and Annie is torn. George wants her to go – this may be her only chance – but she can't leave Mitchell. George calls for an ambulance while Annie goes back to the door. What will they do?

"I can deal with this. Annie, just go"

Musings on episode five...

For me this is the best episode in series one. It's got it all – humour, horror, pathos, death, despair and redemption. I'm not sure I breathed at all in the last ten minutes.

Mitchell is back on the dark side, although it's not clear if his heart is really in it. He has no real friends among the vampires but George and Annie love him and will forgive him (almost) anything. Although it's not explicit, it seems that Mitchell has not yet gone back to killing and had no idea there was a blood farm in the cellar. This is how he retains some humanity, that side of himself that shows such revulsion when he realises exactly what Herrick had planned all along. He can't see a way out – he can't subscribe to the vampire plot and he can't leave, so he accepts that his end at Herrick's hand is inevitable.

It could be seen as a giant fit of pique that sent Mitchell back to the vampires. The behaviour of the humans over the DVD affair sickened him, especially after all that coffee and biscuits. Even chocolate ones! He claims to have turned his back but his essential trace of humanity has been nurtured by George and Annie to be stronger and eventually he does the right thing.

The appearance of Josie is beautifully played by Clare Higgins and in this outwardly odd couple we can see the genuine fondness and the echoes of a grand passion for them both. However it ended, there is a deep and enduring affection and it is Josie who helps Mitchell to see Herrick for the ego-driven megalomaniac he is. I love Josie's scene with George when she hopes – quite seriously – that he might be a wizard, or at least something of some use. George's amusement shows he still really isn't a part of the supernatural world and his denial may be slightly tinged with the irritating knowledge that this woman knows Mitchell as well as or maybe better than he does.

Just when we think Annie is getting somewhere, Owen throws her right back down the stairs again. Rather than Annie haunting him, it is truly he that haunts her – over and over until she is comatose in despair. It is only some straight talking from George, and Mitchell needing help that can only come from her and George, that pulls her out of her despair.

Showing the strength of the trio working together, they break Owen, telling him the secret that crosses the boundary between life and death. It drives him mad and in that madness comes Annie's resolution. Her door is here.

Annie's door looks nothing like Gilbert's. Only having seen two it's hard to draw conclusions and I am desperate to know what the sign saying '1 High Street' means. I have never been able to find out. Her door is substantial – does it signify the stature of the journey she has taken or the journey that is still to come?

As well as Annie's resolution, Lauren also finds redemption in this episode. She never found her place among the vampires – rejected by all she stayed a rebel and Herrick saw her potential. She and Mitchell could have made a formidable team, but her stalking and his evangelical abstention never let him see that. She knows she has lost her human self, and after she kills Seth to let our trio escape, she can't go back. She begs Mitchell to kill her and in a moving and beautiful scene, wonderfully complemented by the music, she finds her peace. It's hard to portray the death of a vampire – the body has to go but how do you do it? This worked well, not too much detail, just a hint of dust and sadness and relief. I'm not sure it was wise to leave her clothes on the ground though – it does look a little like Guy Fawkes Night.

It's a grand achievement to give Lauren a good end. She was stroppy, soppy and annoying at times, strong and determined at others. This young woman who had never found her place in the mortal world left immortality having done the right thing and before the 'evil Lauren' completely took her over.

The look and feel of this episode are spot on. The pace varies and the last ten minutes are non-stop amazing. There are also some changes of scene – the location outside the hospital under the sun and blue sky works so well. What better place to discuss the vampire revolution and the eradication of humanity than by the river in the sun?

For an episode full of action and drama there is also a huge amount of humour. All of it works; there is a neat balance between light and dark. The practice haunting, the world's gayest ninjas and "a little bit of wee" are only some that come to mind. Some of the lines I so wish I'd said myself – although, in truth, I probably will...

Bum notes...

I can find very little to quibble about in one of the best episodes but here are a couple of minor issues in the interests of balance.

Herrick is taking medication in the vampires' HQ. What could it be? I'm sure running a revolution is a headache but can the immortal be ill? Maybe it is just a little boost, in between the blood.

When Lauren died – a beautiful, moving scene – I couldn't help noticing that her tights changed from burgundy when she was running to black when they are on the ground after her body goes to dust. (I did say these were minor!!)

... and the bottom line

Sightings of Russell Tovey's bare backside – none, but plenty of bared souls.

He said, she said...

It's like what happened to my Auntie Linda.
She kept seeing the Bronte sisters in her en-suite.

......

My thing is a part-time thing.
Oh right, I thought perhaps you were a wizard or something.
A wizard? That's ridiculous.
Trust me. Once you've dated a vampire you tend to have different criteria for what's ridiculous.

......

What the cock is that?
I'm a ghost, actually.
Get out. Can you, like, move things about and walk from one room to another?

Yeah, I'm pretty sure everyone can do that...

......

I killed my girlfriend. And now she lives with what I think is a werewolf and a vampire and they're going to torture me. So I need to find somewhere safe.

I see. Well in that case, we're going to need a different form.

Where have I seen... Gregg Chillin (Owen)?

Gregg Chillin's TV roles include Ash Chopra in *Nearly Famous* in 2007 and Jack in *The Queen's Nose* in 2002. He has also appeared twice in *The Bill* (in 2004 and 2006), as well as in *Jackanory* (in 2006), *Holby City* (in 2007) and *Waking the Dead* (in 2008).

He played Raffee Hussein in the one-off drama, *Pulse*, which was part of BBC Three's pilot season in June 2010.

His film work includes playing Manuel in *4.3.2.1*, which was directed by Noel Clarke and Mark Davis, and Kayvan in *Huge*, directed by Ben Miller, both in 2010.

Gregg made his stage debut in 2008 at the Royal National Theatre playing Mark in *DNA* and Trousers in *The Miracle*.

He has provided the voice of Ron Weasley in several of the *Harry Potter* video games.

Music in episode five

Aaliyah	*More Than a Woman*
Franz Ferdinand	*Take Me Out*
Ivor Novello	*Love is My Reason*
Kings of Leon	*Use Somebody*
Michael Crawford	*Spirit of the Living God*
Scissor Sisters	*Comfortably Numb*
Bombay Bicycle Club	*Open House*

episode six

Josie helps Mitchell recover so he can set up a showdown with Herrick.

Annie is stronger than ever having rejected death to help her friends.

Decision time for George – fight or flight?

Can Nina ever go back to her normal life?

What happened to Owen after he turned himself in for murder?

broadcast:	1 MARCH 2009	director:	COLIN TEAGUE
writer:	TOBY WHITHOUSE	producer:	MATTHEW BOUCH

cast:

Annie	LENORA CRICHLOW	Billy	JOSEF ALTIN
Mitchell	AIDAN TURNER	Turlow	JOHN HOLLINGWORTH
George	RUSSELL TOVEY	Marco	ADAM DEACON
Lauren	ANNABEL SCHOLEY	Chaplain	MICHAEL BEGLEY
Herrick	JASON WATKINS	Kemp	DONALD SUMPTER
Nina	SINEAD KEENAN	Dr Newell	RICH BACON
Seth	DYLAN BROWN	Paramedic	ABIGAIL DAVIES
Owen	GREGG CHILLIN	Nurse	RHIANNON
Josie	CLARE HIGGINS		HARPER-RAFFERTY
Canteen Girl	REBECCA COOPER	Werewolf	PAUL KASEY

"Just a small good deed in the darkness"

Two years ago, a small backstreet cafe. There's the usual motley collection of nighttime customers and one noisier group. It's only when the camera pans around and we see Seth that we realise these are vampires. And they're discussing *10 Years Younger*... Their empty mugs are collected and for some reason that *really* gets their attention, and in fascination they all watch the kitchen hand walk away. It's George. "I haven't seen one of them in years," one says in anticipation.

"Let's have some fun"

George is taking out the rubbish and the vampires surround him in the dark alley. He has no idea who or what they are – he thinks it's a mugging, not getting the doggie references. They beat him savagely, laughing, until George is on the floor. They are kicking him viciously when Mitchell arrives.

He stops them by pointing out the obvious. How many people saw them, can identify them, what sort of trail have they left? He's spoiling their fun but they realise the truth in his words. In fact, one of them left a business card for the undertakers with the café manager – nice move!

Mitchell shows his authority over them and they reluctantly leave; they don't like it, but won't disobey him. He had a reputation and status but is the power and blood already starting to pall? He tells George that they would have killed him, they just don't like werewolves. George is so startled – how can he possibly know?

Mitchell explains that vampires know werewolves and George is even

117

more horrified. He has been a werewolf for six months and hadn't even begun to come to terms with it and now he discovers there are vampires as well. What sort of a world has he been thrown into?

George pleads with Mitchell – now what? He's already lost everything, how can he keep moving on forever? His fear and his loneliness strike a chord with Mitchell. He is already tiring of the vampire life and maybe, just maybe, fate has given him an alternative. Is this the start of the truly odd couple?

"Fate pushed them together. And now they were going to find out why"

Mitchell is being rushed through the hospital, surrounded by staff. They all know him and will pull out all the stops for one of their own. George and Annie are with him – so Annie is still here – and they make sure he knows they are there. He wants to struggle, to get away, but he's too weak.

Medical instructions are flying around and he's connected up to machines to be monitored but there's no reading. How can that be? The real diagnosis, that he's already dead, is never going to occur to the team and they assume the machine is faulty. When will they realise that it just doesn't add up?

"Just get me another machine"

Nina has found out that there is something strange about Mitchell's condition. His body is just somehow not... right. She challenges George, there is something odd about George and Mitchell and she is getting increasingly frustrated by the secrets and the mystery. George tries to fob her off but his vague explanation – "it's a family thing" – isn't convincing anyone. Nina is concerned; she knows that her relationship with George involves her in whatever vague "family thing" is going on. What could be going through her mind – genetic oddities, a Bristol mafia? Luckily her pager goes off before she can push George any harder, but she's starting to wonder if her relationship with George is ever going to work.

Mitchell is stable – or as stable as a crack medical team can make a dead but immortal person. They'll just have to wait and see what happens, but it is all rather peculiar. He is healing far too quickly and they still can't find his heartbeat. Surely not all the machines can be faulty?

George knows they have to get him away before anyone works it all out, but what can they do? Neither he nor Annie is an expert on vampire physiology and they can hardly call Herrick for help. Annie knows they are filling him full of blood and is sure it's what he needs, but we already know that donated blood is dead to a vampire so it won't help Mitchell recover, although it may dull his pain.

"He's too impossible"

George wants to know why Annie would not go through her door. She refuses to go anywhere until Mitchell is better, but having refused her door, her death, will she ever get another chance? It will change things – in fact it already has. Annie has a nice new top and she can transport herself much further than ever before. When George and she decide to take turns watching over Mitchell, she is home before she can even question how.

She is back in the house, standing over the cracked tile where she died, which is now stained with Mitchell's blood. Her door has gone. Not a trace remains and Annie is left wondering what next? She can hear voices, crying, calling for help, but there is no one there. Where are they? Who are they? Is this what happens next?

The hospital staff have called the chaplain in to see Mitchell, they don't think he'll last the night. George is not welcoming, it all seems a bit pointless. After all, he's Jewish and Mitchell is, well, he's complicated. The chaplain is making some misguided attempts to lighten the atmosphere when Mitchell starts to stir. Is it the representation of religion standing by his bed that is rousing him? Suddenly he is wide awake, sitting bolt upright in the same way the new recruit awoke in the funeral parlour. He knows the vampires are coming; they're already in the hospital.

George goes into panic mode. He attempts to move the bed but that really isn't going to work. Accepting the reluctant offer of help from the chaplain, they head out into the corridor. Two of Herrick's henchmen are approaching. "Say something religious!" demands George as they see flashes of the true vampires. Between his Star of David and the chaplain's bible quotes, they ward off the threat and the vampires leave. Although they had not needed to be invited across the threshold of the hospital as it is a public space, George repeatedly telling them they were not welcome seemed to have an effect.

The chaplain has no idea what he has seen but he knows it was very wrong. George can't even begin to explain, but does stand by sympathetically while the chaplain has a good vomit.

"Think of it like organ donation"

George has told Josie what happened to Mitchell and leaves her with him while he gets coffee. He still isn't entirely comfortable with her. Mitchell is conscious and has somehow managed to register on the monitors. Maybe that is something that vampires can only do consciously? He hates being hooked up to the machines, trapped and knowing that sooner or later someone will figure him out. Josie is distraught at how ill he is. The last she knew was that he was in high favour with the vampires. When he tells her of his change of heart they both know it was mostly her doing. Her determination to make Mitchell see what Herrick really is was the catalyst that led to him standing up to Herrick – and to the SAS-style rescue by George and Annie!

The vampire body cannot make new blood and Mitchell knows that there is only one way for him to recover but he can't bear it. Every time he feeds it takes him further away from humanity and he won't hunt, not even to save himself. Josie has another option. Her illness is worse and it is only a matter of time... Mitchell can't take in what she is offering to sacrifice for him but Josie is adamant. Someone needs to stop Herrick and if Mitchell doesn't do it then who will? She is ready to go, she's weary and she wants nothing back from him. She has already saved him once – a story we will hear one day – and he wants to make her immortal, to save her too, but she doesn't want it. It is her choice to be human, to be mortal; for her, death is not unwelcome. She will do anything to save Mitchell – he was her grand passion, her true love and maybe she was his.

"How do you think this ends?" "We kiss?"

119

George heads to the canteen for his coffee only to find that the slightly unhinged assistant is now a vampire and Herrick is there. He just wants to talk to George, he's not after Mitchell. Not yet anyway – Herrick knows they will get him and he can wait. Herrick wants to hear where George thinks this will all end. George admits he knows something about Herrick's plans and Herrick overreacts. He denies that his schemes are an ego trip. This is nature, Darwinism, and we can see the first signs of madness creeping in to that matter-of-fact persona.

Herrick threatens George and the others with the usual dire fates and walks away. George has never hinted to Herrick that he might fight back, but for once he retaliates. He's seen Owen routed and mad, Annie turn down death and Mitchell stabbed and dying. Right now Herrick is just one more monster to deal with. He and Annie – Casper and Digby – walked into the vampires' lair and took Mitchell from them. Didn't that make Herrick sit up and think? Herrick is goaded, just a little, and starts pushing George, taunting him until George snaps and hits back. For a moment we see shock on Herrick's face. Partly that George has reacted at all, but also that he doesn't know yet just how strong George is. He soon recovers, pushing George further and further until his hands are on Herrick's throat and the maniacal canteen assistant runs over with a knife to rescue him. Herrick could have got away at any time and his laughter takes the last of the fight out of George. He's just too human to beat Herrick and leaves him passionately kissing his obsessively devoted new recruit. Not the behaviour of an entirely sane man.

"It's like Top Trumps! Werewolf versus Vampires"

Josie is sitting in a chair in her hospital room, a shaft of sunlight shining on her. The nurse checks her pulse but she's gone. She looks calm, at peace.

Mitchell looks stronger but is sobbing, a trace of blood at the corner of his mouth. He's lost Josie forever and the weight of her sacrifice is hard to bear. One more death on his conscience, one more reason he can never be human, and a promise he has to fulfil.

The hospital is quite glad to get rid of the mystery that is Mitchell and he is home, being 'nursed' rather vigorously by Annie. He wants to know what Herrick said and George relates the curses and threats. Annie, though, is hugely confident. Whether it was turning down death or fighting the vampires, something has given her a whole new positive outlook. She feels changed – the person she was, her life and her death are all overlapping into a single whole. George cannot relate to that at all. He is still insisting that the wolf is separate, nothing whatsoever to do with him. Annie is adamant that they can fight Herrick, she knows they can. After all, he can't hurt her, she's already dead.

Mitchell is less sure. It is only Mitchell and George and her ties to the house that keep Annie safe. If Herrick took all that away – and he would burn the house to the ground if he had to – Annie would drift away on the wind.

Nothing daunts the new improved Annie. It won't come to that, they will be fine. Mitchell will get better and they will fight together and care for each other and it is because they care for each other that they will endure. She's oblivious to George and Mitchell's worried looks.

"We'll look after each other. That's why he can't win"

Nina is still saying she doesn't want to know what George's secrets are, but is that true? She can't cope with the life he has and her only wish is to be happy, to have something that is normal and kind. The implication is that it is her or Mitchell, and George starts to think that he is going to have to choose. Nina has always been wary of Mitchell – there's nothing she can quite put her finger on but something isn't right. She resents the depth of their friendship and the claims he has on George. She wants George, but not his world.

Herrick knows that the only way Mitchell can have recovered so quickly is by feeding and he makes sure he knows it. Mitchell challenges Herrick to meet him, to finish it once and for all. Just the two of them.

Herrick is cocky, arrogant – he'll beat Mitchell, it's a foregone conclusion. He can't see why Mitchell is doing this, but Mitchell has to stop him, it was his last promise to Josie. He tempts Herrick – when he wins just look at the message he'll be sending about those who go against him. Mitchell sets the date – it has to be tomorrow and he wants the vampires to let Annie and George go. Herrick gives them 24 hours to get away and hide – after that, they'll be hunted. There is still a lingering disappointment for Herrick that Mitchell, his protégée, the best ever, is not by his side.

"And I was going to give you South America"

Mitchell tells the others of his plans. They think he is deranged. Annie wants to help, but George transforms tomorrow so he can't be there. Mitchell wants to, has to, do this alone. Annie knows he'll lose – Herrick is the older vampire and somehow I doubt he'd fight fair. Mitchell thinks he is sacrificing himself to keep George and Annie safe, but Annie disagrees. She thinks Mitchell is looking to be punished for going to the vampires; he intends to make himself a martyr. Maybe she's right, Mitchell has more to atone for than they know – there was Bernie and Josie, maybe more. Is he repenting for a lifetime, a century, of killing?

George has no idea what to do next. Mitchell's suggestion that he takes Nina and starts a new life has added to Nina's almost-ultimatum about choosing. Should he go? Can he leave Mitchell?

He needs to talk and searches out the sarcastic hospital chaplain in his church. He asks what George believes. It's all changed since he became a werewolf, become a little more flexible. We have never heard George talk about being Jewish, but he admits now how much it still matters to him. He doesn't feel he deserves to participate – or maybe the wolf doesn't – but the belief is still there along with the Star of David he always wears.

George has been thinking about the bible quote the chaplain used when he faced the vampires with him. "*When I was a child, I spake as a child, I understood as a child, I thought as a child: but when I became a man, I put away childish things*" (from 1 Corinthians 13:11). He asks what it means. For the chaplain it's about belief and in particular that the vampires (although he doesn't know that's what they are) have altered his understanding of what is possible. He asks George what they were, but George tells him they were only men – evil men, but men. He mustn't lose the faith he has. Is George reluctant to undermine the chaplain's belief, or is he trying to convince himself that the vampires are not all-conquering, that they are just men? For George, the meaning of the quote has becomes straightforward, for him it means...

"... that it's time to grow up"

An ominous rumble of thunder outside and in the kitchen Annie is laying out the battle plan, still trying to convince them she's right. Mitchell is determined – he will meet Herrick alone and he will end it. George backs him up, to Annie's disgust, and they argue over Mitchell's head. George wants a future – he alone of the trio is still alive. His life is finite, unlike Annie's and Mitchell's, and he wants that time to count. He wants to think about Nina. They are scared and Mitchell is in quiet but determined despair – he knows he can't come back from this. George is fighting tears but Mitchell supports him – he wants him to have the life he deserves. George only asks that he lets him talk to Herrick, one more chance to get him to see reason and if not, then he'll tell him where to meet Mitchell. Mitchell reluctantly agrees and George leaves.

In utter frustration, Annie sweeps all the crockery off the counter – physically, not with her telekinetic powers. She is seeing her family fall apart. Without Mitchell, and if George is with Nina, what is there for her? Nina can't see her and she'll be lonelier than she was before.

Mitchell tries to explain to her the torment of his memories. He knows that other vampires have given up blood and he thought that the lust for blood, the addiction was what beat them. He didn't know what would be the worst thing. When the craving recedes, the memories take its place. He can remember every kill, all their names, who fought and who didn't and it's killing him. Going against Herrick is a form of suicide for Mitchell. He doesn't want to feed and kill again but he can't bear not to and he can't see any other way.

Annie finally sees his utter desolation. She understands and she cries for him.

"We are all scared"

George is meeting Herrick. An old lady is reading the brochures and George is confused for a moment – he didn't think the funeral parlour was real. "Oh, that's Nanna," confirms Herrick; she makes the place look genuine. George is surprised at the recruitment of an old woman but, as Herrick says, when you're out and about and you get hungry you have to take what you can get!

George makes one last appeal – particularly as he doesn't get quite why Mitchell is so important. Herrick tries to explain, he was the most evil of the evil and he is dangerous. Not even Mitchell knows just how dangerous he could be. The very fact that the darkest vampire could find something strong enough to make him repent and give up his addiction could cause a revolution among the vampires. Herrick is bringing them out of the shadows, changing a thousand years of hiding and if Mitchell has found an alternative then he could lose them. He has to kill Mitchell, he has no choice. Symbolism matters and if Herrick lets his long association and deep friendship with Mitchell deter him then he doesn't deserve to own the world he has planned.

"He had the blackest heart of us all... and he repented"

Preparations.

Mitchell is psyching himself up, preparing to accept his end. He wants to be sure George will look after Annie. It's important to him that she will be cared for. George is packed, but first he will transform in the woods tonight.

Herrick is dressing – his latest recruit helping him while the others look on. It's reminiscent of a knight preparing his armour for battle. In contrast, Mitchell hasn't made much of an effort, but at least he isn't wearing those dodgy tracky trousers, going instead for a reasonable selection of basic black.

Herrick never intended to let George and Annie go. Once Mitchell is dealt with, they will track down George in the woods and then burn Annie's house and watch her float into the clouds. They'll make a night of it.

George is ready to go; he will meet Annie at the station after the full moon. "Maybe," she says, "maybe I'll stay and fight." He wants to hold her, make her understand, but she won't touch him, she is so disappointed in him. He and Mitchell embrace, both fighting back tears, and George reminds him of when they met, when Mitchell saved him. Is he trying to tell him something? Mitchell remembers that George expected nothing of his life back then but they have had the house, much more than he thought he could have, even though it could never have been as human as they hoped. Maybe it was something that was much more than human. Knowing the worst of humanity did they avoid it themselves?

George leaves, the tears finally spilling over, and Annie really wishes she'd hugged him but it's too late, he's gone. Outside, George has changed; clear-eyed he heads off, he has a purpose. There's a half-smile of anticipation.

Herrick and Mitchell leave. Herrick has the vampires cheering him on; it's already a triumphal progress. There is no doubt among them who'll be the victor. Mitchell leaves alone. Herrick is ready. He has cleared away his memories and whatever small part of him that still felt for Mitchell. His brave new world is waiting for him, just one more obstacle to clear.

"They kept coming"

Annie is hearing the voices again, howling and screaming in her head until she can bear it no longer. They stop when a figure appears in her room. It's Billy, the leader of the humans being farmed for blood by the vampires. He tells her that the vampires kept coming, they were angry, and Annie realises he is dead. He takes her with him back to the funeral parlour.

Annie is powerful now. She rages through the headquarters using just gestures to throw the vampires out of her way. She's also got a new cardigan and a neat wind machine for some great hair effects. She forces her way to the cellar without having to lay a ghostly hand on anyone – not only is she powerful, she can control it. She frees the captives and they escape onto the street.

Mitchell is on the hospital roof waiting for Herrick. He sees him come through the gates and starts to prepare. His eyes are black; he knows Herrick will be here in a moment.

"Congratulations on mastering the whole 'speaking like a twat' thing"

Annie finds the Canteen girl under a table, still giggling, still slightly mad. Herrick took her and she seems to have become his confidante. She rattles on about Mitchell's death and Herrick's splendour but when she mentions dungeons Annie realises exactly what is going on.

Annie jumps to the roof where Mitchell is waiting. She's worked it out –

Herrick is going to the isolation room and George will be waiting for him. George has fooled them all.

Herrick is in the isolation room as Mitchell runs through the hospital. The door closes and George is there. Nina stops Mitchell as she's looking for George; he has written her a letter. He has dumped her and Mitchell is now sure that Annie is right. George is going to take on Herrick. He's desperate to get to George but Nina wants to have her say. She's furious about being chucked by letter and gives Mitchell a lengthy and contradictory list of instructions for George. Eventually Mitchell tells her to shut up and stay away, where she'll be safe.

George is on the verge of changing, the moon is coming up and he strips off his shirt. Herrick flinches away from his Star of David. He manages to explain that it won't affect Mitchell due to their affection for each other and George thanks him. So far it's all very polite, almost civilised. Herrick is getting his confidence back – after all he can't be killed. George begs to differ; this is not about knives or guns, it's about him.

"I... am... the weapon"

Mitchell and Annie have arrived at last and are watching through the spy hole, frantically shouting at George to get out, but he ignores them. Herrick doesn't think George can cross the line; if he kills him that means he will be different – he doesn't think George can do it. But George has thought this through, this is payback. Mitchell saved him and he will save Mitchell. He knows the wolf is almost here and he's feeling the first pains of his transformation.

Annie jumps into the room and opens the door and she and Mitchell are beside George and all three face Herrick together. Herrick is still full of bravado – he talks to them about their experiment, their attempts to be human. He trivialises it and laughs at the improbability and the inevitable failure. The only aspects of humanity they managed were the dark parts – deception and destruction – but he can't hurt them now. The three of them have been through too much, this is an end. Whatever happens, they know that they did achieve something quite precious. Something that Herrick will never understand and he can't sully it with words.

Reluctantly they leave George to face Herrick alone. Mitchell is still concerned about what this will do to George, but he can't be stopped. Annie whispers "thank you" as she leaves him.

"You can't come back from this"

They watch from outside as George screams in the agony of his transformation. Between spasms he and Herrick still talk and George cannot understand why Herrick is not scared. Instead he is eerily, icily calm, he has accepted his fate and he realises that he was never meant to lead but to be the key to whoever comes after. His place in history is assured, he has fulfilled his role. He quotes from Bertolt Brecht:

> *"The world was almost won by such an ape!*
> *The nations put him where his kind belong.*
> *But do not rejoice too soon at your escape*
> *The womb he crawled from is still going strong."*

He knows that someone else will rise, either now or in years to come. The strength of the vampires is that they have all the time in the world. At last he is starting to look scared – unlike Mitchell he never considered this might be his end and he suddenly has to face that. George is part-wolf now, his teeth and eyes have changed and his claws are erupting. If Herrick goes to hell tonight he will drag George there with him.

Nina has followed them. It was inevitable, I doubt many men tell her to shut up and get away with it. She hears George scream and they can't keep her from seeing. Through the spy hole she can see him in agony, changing, and she can't understand what is happening. Before anyone can stop her she is in the room and a horrified George flings out his arm to push her away. Falling into Mitchell's arms, she is paralysed with fear – partly for herself, but more for George – but they pull her away.

"Humanity... is about love and sacrifice. This doesn't rob me of my humanity. It proves it"

The wolf is almost here. The transformation is happening and Nina cannot look away, watching transfixed at George's pain. There is nothing that Mitchell and Annie can say and they can't watch. They know they can't help, this is what George wants. What George planned all along. Herrick too is fixated on the wolf – has he ever seen the transformation before? I can't imagine he has and like Nina he can't look away. He's revolted and scared but he won't run, won't try and hide. He stands his ground and taunts the wolf until it strikes.

We hear Herrick scream, the crunching of bones and the tearing of flesh, and we watch Nina watch it all. Then the wolf comes at the door, flinging aside what's left of Herrick. Even with his vampire strength Mitchell can't hold back the wolf. He wants Annie and Nina to go, to evacuate the hospital, to get away while he holds it for as long as he can. Nina is not hearing him, she's still staring through the door at what was George, the man she loves, and the wolf is staring back.

The wolf is still, it becomes calm and holds her gaze. What does it see?

"I thought the two things could exist side by side. Something I hated and something I loved"

Back at the house it's the morning after. George is back and he and Nina are trying to reconnect. She knows his secret now and knows he was trying to protect her. She can't imagine the pain of the change and George has no words to describe it. She wants to know how he got it and he explains that the scars she has seen and thought were from an accident were actually the scratches of a werewolf. She's very calm, probably shocked, and wants to be on her own – she'll be down in a while and George leaves her alone.

Mitchell and Annie are discussing George. Mitchell is worried that he is not reacting, he has killed and it must be having an effect on him so they need to watch him and care for him. Annie is also confused, why can she hear the voices, the sound of the dead? It's new. Mitchell can't explain but it must be because she didn't go through her door. She refused death and that is something no one does. Who knows what powers she has now?

George joins them – Nina is a bit shocked but OK. The wolf stared at her for a long time – maybe I recognised her, George wonders, and maybe there was a connection. As he says this we see Nina in the bathroom pulling up her sleeve. Across her arm are deep raw scratches. The scratches of a werewolf.

All of them are changed. Annie turned down death. Mitchell faced his end and was saved by the love and sacrifice of friends. George has accepted the werewolf; he talks about it as himself and no longer as 'it'. He has killed and even having done so with the best of intentions this has changed him deep down. Can he accept that part of himself; can he live with that morality?

They may never be out of danger. There will be other threats and someone will inevitably take Herrick's place. For now they are home, they are together and this could be safety.

"Maybe that's it. Maybe nothing happens now"

"Did she actually say the word 'vampire'?" A distinguished elderly man is talking to Owen. He is twitchy, manic, trying desperately to make him understand. Yes, his dead fiancée told him these things and yes, it was a vampire and a werewolf. Isn't he making himself clear?

As the camera pulls back, we see they are in a cell or a secure room and a guard is behind Owen watching him. The interview is obviously winding up – the visitor asks if there is anything Owen wants, maybe some "yummy snacks," but all he wants is reassurance. Is this place safe? There hasn't been an escape for seven years but that is not what worries him. What Owen needs to know is can anyone, anything, get in?

Owen is led away and the man watches him go, smoothing back his grey hair with an expression of quiet triumph. He returns to his car – a nice car – which along with the expensive suit gives a look of money, of opulence. Who is this?

He takes out a phone and dials.

"Professor Jaggat. We've found them"

Musings on episode six...

This time it's all about fate. Karma. What goes around comes around. It's the end of series one and it's payback time. How many loose ends can be tied up in neat bows and how many ends will be left frayed for the next series? How many new threads?

After a flashback to George and Mitchell's first meeting, we pick up straight from the end of episode five. Annie has not gone through the door and Mitchell is in hospital. A slight problem as he's dead and they can't find a heartbeat – damn these machines! Somehow the hospital staff avoid the conclusion that we think is just so obvious and treat him as best they can, but he's not going to recover. Not without help anyway and it is Josie who saves him – for the second time, Mitchell admits. She's quite practical about her sacrifice, and the scene of them reminiscing, cuddled up on Mitchell's hospital bed, is so wonderfully bittersweet. Beautiful performances from both Clare Higgins and Aidan Turner. In the last episode, Josie claimed that dying is what makes us human. It is ironic that she knowingly sacrifices her life to save someone who is beyond that, who is immortal. It only underscores the love between her and Mitchell which, for her, was never over.

Annie is changed. She is stronger, her clothes have changed and she is powerful. It's all due to turning down death. Karma again – she refuses to pass over because Mitchell is dying, only to gain the power that ultimately helps the trio survive Herrick. There is much more to explore here. If no one has refused death before then this is all new and there are no limits to where Annie can go in the future.

The geeky sarcastic chaplain could have been an awful cliché but the character is written well enough for that to not matter and it is nicely understated. He has the same foot-in-mouth tendencies as George, but in reassuring the chaplain George finds a strength he didn't know he had. He puts away childish things with a vengeance. His assertion to the chaplain that the vampires are "just men" is so measured that we really believe him – for a moment.

Herrick's plan is reaching fruition; there is just the small issue of Mitchell to sort out. He knows that Mitchell could usurp him; he has the reputation and the charisma to steal all of Herrick's followers if he wanted to. Herrick sees this strength in Mitchell but Mitchell doesn't. He's turned his back and I don't think he knows yet how powerful he could be. His focus is on trying to be human but what might happen if this starts to get dull? Will he miss the joy of the chase? The unearthly power of being a vampire? Mitchell has already hinted that none of the vampires before him have stayed off blood for long.

Herrick never considers that he might lose. He knows Mitchell is weakened after the stabbing and this is going to be a walkover, a statement. Herrick is rather pleased with the knowledge that he will be the one who finished the mythical Mitchell, the darkest of the dark world. But it is not going to be that easy and he's just a little too complacent and has seriously misjudged Annie and George and the strength of the trio when they are together.

Two years ago Mitchell saved George's life. Now it is time for George to pay that back and he will take on Herrick to save Mitchell. Open, honest George – who would have thought he could put together such a clever plan? No one suspected – not Herrick, not Nina and certainly not Mitchell and Annie.

It is the full moon and George knows that Herrick is going to have to face the wolf. Does he think he will kill Herrick? It seems that he has thought it all through and found no other solution. The end justifies the means and he has accepted that to be truly human he has to remove the threat to humanity, however he can. He is quietly sure he will win, but does he know enough about vampires? We saw Seth and Lauren die from a stake in the heart. Mitchell too was stabbed, but as Herrick couldn't cross the threshold he missed his heart and he didn't die. Although, without fresh human blood, without a kill, would he have lingered in weakness forever? Can a werewolf really kill a vampire?

Herrick's messianic tendencies have started to slide into madness and Jason Watkins's performance is mesmerising. He really shouldn't be that scary but somehow that look of menace and those calm, understated but deadly threats are just terrifying. He's ready to tear Mitchell apart, to hunt down George and Annie and then take over the world.

When he realises what George has done he is unworried. He faces him, he knows the wolf is coming but he can't die. Or can he? His realisation of the savagery of the wolf finally cracks his bravado and he screams for George to finish it.

In the end, Herrick let George kill him because he knew what it would do. George has crossed a line; he has killed for the very first time. He can never step back from this and the effect it has on him is yet to be measured. It was an act of humanity but still a murder; even the death of a monster will hurt George deeply. It will also impact on Mitchell and George's relationship. It may be what George sees as payback but Mitchell has always been George and Annie's protector. He's failed them and George felt he had to take his place. The guilt of what his friend chose to do will stop Mitchell ever considering taking Herrick's place. Maybe this is the way Herrick sees his plans surviving.

Is Herrick dead? He is certainly in bits. We didn't see what the wolf did but there were some very meaty sound effects and the ferocity of the attack was clear. Is a dismembered vampire dead or do shreds of consciousness still survive?

Nina couldn't stay away and gets very much more than she bargained for. She wanted a showdown with George – how *dare* he dump her in a letter! What she gets is the truth, everything he was hiding from her. She not only has to accept what George is and see the pain of his transformation, she also watches him kill, tearing a man apart. And she hasn't even been introduced to vampires and ghosts yet... On top of all that, George has inadvertently scratched her and she knows she has his curse. She can't tell him. Yet more secrets.

Herrick quotes from Bertolt Brecht's *The Resistible Rise of Arturo Ui* in the isolation room. It's a great choice and very appropriate. The play reminds us that greed and complacency are all it takes for evil to thrive. What will happen to the vampires now they have been deprived of their leader?

The end of the series leaves the trio much changed. Mitchell has explored his dark side and knows that humanity is the right choice, but can he stay away from blood? Annie is strong, just how strong we don't yet know, and her living and dead selves have fused into a powerful whole. George has killed. He has accepted the werewolf and seems to have survived unscathed. Outwardly he seems the least changed of the three, but he doesn't know what he has done to Nina.

As they consider their future, wondering if this is what safety feels like, we see a sinister scene. An insane Owen is talking to someone about his dead fiancée and how she lives with a vampire and a werewolf. Just who are these people who knew about them and what will they do now they have found them?

In series one, the trio have dealt with the threat from the supernatural, but in series two the threat will come from humanity...

Bum notes...

In the flashback to when George and Mitchell first met, Duffy's *Mercy* is playing in the background but it hadn't been released then. It's still a good track for the scene though.

For a vampire on the wagon Mitchell gets his fair share of blood – Lauren (although as a vampire did that count?), Bernie and now Josie. Wouldn't that stop the memories that he describes to Annie? If they are the result of staying clean, off blood, why is he still having them?

In episode one, the isolation room where George transforms can't be opened from the inside. This keeps the wolf secure and Mitchell has to let him out in the morning. Now it can *only* be opened from the inside and Annie has to jump in to open it. I suppose this odd but convenient alteration might have happened during the abandoned renovations, but...

... and the bottom line

Sightings of Russell Tovey's bare backside – none, but a topless transformation for a change. Not to mention some lingering shots of a bare-chested Mitchell in hospital.

He said, she said...

If you're non-believers that's fine, we can just sit together for a few moments of quiet contemplation.

Contemplation about what?

The fiery oblivion that awaits all atheists?

......

Jewish people pray, I've seen Yentl.

You're very sarcastic for a vicar.

Yeah, so people tell me and I feel really bad about it and then I forgive myself.

......

Say something religious.

Christ!

......

That's Nanna, she's one of us. She sits there, reads the brochures. Good for appearances...

Someone actually recruited an old woman?

Well, you know how it is. You're out and about, you get the munchies, you'll eat anything.

......

So, a werewolf, a ghost and a vampire decide to live like humans do. They get jobs, a house and a TV license. They make friends they will lie to, take lovers they will infect. In fact, the only part of humanity they successfully adopt is its ability to deceive and destroy. All in all I'd say your scheme has been something of a failure.

Where have I seen... Clare Higgins (Josie)?

Clare Higgins is often recognised for her role as Julia in *Hellraiser* (1987) and *Hellbound: Hellraiser II* (1988), performances that gave her a cult status that quite suits *Being Human* with its themes of morality in fear and under duress and resurrection using blood.

However, this credit gives no hint of Clare Higgins's extensive, award-winning stage career spanning thirty years, which includes three Laurence Olivier Awards. It's hard to pick a selection of roles, but hopefully this gives a flavour of an enviable career:

She has worked extensively with the Royal Shakespeare Company and the National Theatre. Her many roles have included some of Shakespeare's greatest women – Titania in *A Midsummer Night's Dream* (in 1989), Gertrude in *Hamlet* (in 2010) and Cleopatra in *Antony and Cleopatra* (in 1992), and modern classics including Madame Arkadina in Chekov's *The Seagull* (in 1998) and Stella in *The Walls* by Colin Teevan (in 2001). In 2003, she starred on Broadway in an award-winning performance of *Vincent in Brixton*. She also has a trio of Greek tragedies under her belt – *Hecuba* in 2004 (for which she won one of her three Olivier awards), *Phaedra* in 2006 and *Oedipus* in 2008.

Clare has also worked on TV, but these roles have never been as high profile as her stage work. In the 1980s, she appeared in a number of classic mini-series: as Christine Barlow in *The Citadel* (1983), Kitty Bennet in *Pride and Prejudice* (1980) and Rachel Jordan in *After the War* (1989). More recently she has appeared in *The Curse of Steptoe* (2008), *Casualty* (in 2009), *Casanova* (2005) and *Murder in Suburbia* (in 2005).

Other big-screen roles include the Johnny Depp film *The Libertine* (2004) and the 2005 comedy/drama *Bigger than the Sky*. She also played Ma Costa in the 2007 film adaptation of Philip Pullman's novel *Northern Lights* (brought to the screen as *The Golden Compass*).

In 2009, Imogen Russell Williams of *The Guardian* asked Clare what was her favourite part of her job:

> "That moment when the house lights go down and you're waiting to go on. You think: 'There's nowhere else I'd rather be.' I don't care how many times I've done the play, each night is different. There's something wonderful about that. I've never really found television or film very fulfilling, for that reason. There's something slightly unnatural to me about acting at 8.30 in the morning. Acting is like sex – it's best done in the dark!"

Music in episode six

Duffy	*Mercy*
Bloc Party	*Where is Home*
Elvis Costello	*Baby Plays Around*
Johnny Cash	*The Man Comes Around*
Michael Crawford	*The Holy City*

5

and once more from the top, please

Almost as soon as series one got underway, people were already wondering if there would be a series two – and it's fair to say that most people were rather keen on the idea, if a little impatient.

In a post about *Costumes, iPods and Blood* on the BBC *Being Human* blog on 16 February (the day after episode four aired), one of the questions fired at Toby Whithouse was: "If *Being Human* is recommissioned, are you tempted to build in a hook for the next series?" His reply – and this was before the commissioning of eight episodes for series two was announced – was: "Well, the whole of series one has already been filmed, so it'd be too late to put in a hook for series two now. So it's just as well I wrote one! And I think you will all absolutely love it..."

Ten days later, series two was duly announced and the BBC Press Office noted the multi-platform success of the show. *Being Human* was the most watched programme on BBC iPlayer for its first two episodes, as well as having one of the best performing BBC websites.

Danny Cohen, Controller of BBC Three, said: "I'm thrilled that we are recommissioning *Being Human*. It's hugely popular with young viewers and earned great critical acclaim at the same time. It's also a very important staging-post in the successful development of home-grown young drama on BBC Three."

Ben Stephenson, Controller of BBC Drama Commissioning, added: "I am very excited *Being Human* is returning for a second series. It's a distinctive modern series that has captured the imagination of the BBC Three audience in terms of strong viewer loyalty and critical acclaim, signalling a real breakthrough for drama on the channel."

Rob Pursey, Executive Producer for Touchpaper Television, promised that there was much more to come: "We already have some very exciting, very dark new stories up our sleeves, so we're delighted to have the opportunity to make a second series of *Being Human*. BBC Three has been a brilliant platform for us to mount an unusual and ambitious drama."

As the first series ended on 1 March 2009, overnight figures indicated an impressive 822,000 tuned in for the final episode. This gave an average of 720,000 viewers for the six-episode series, not including those watching the repeats or catching up on the BBC iPlayer.

What the papers said...

"Being Human – a simply brilliant comedy drama... quirky, gruesome, sassy and poignant. Check it out."
Lorraine Kelly, *The Sun*

"Kinda *Buffy* meets *This Life*... it's sharp, dead funny and sexy"
The Guardian

"An engaging fusion of the very dark and the very funny"
The Daily Telegraph

"Gripping, funny and moving... BBC Three's best ever drama"
Heat

Being Human Unearthed

Celebrating the success of *Being Human*, BBC Three commissioned a one-hour special documentary to give fans another taste of all things human and otherwise, which was shown a month after the end of series one on Saturday 28 March 2009. It was followed by a re-run of episodes one to three, with episodes four to six following the next Saturday.

Unearthed gets up close and personal and right in behind the scenes of Bristol's oddest house share, meeting many of the actors including Aidan Turner (Mitchell), Russell Tovey (George), Lenora Crichlow (Annie), Jason Watkins (Herrick), Annabel Scholey (Lauren) and Sinead Keenan (Nina). As an added bonus, *Unearthed* is dryly (very dryly...) narrated by Alex Price – none other than Gilbert himself!

The documentary also features interviews with Toby Whithouse, who asked on the blog on 29 April 2009: "Oh did you like *Being Human: Unearthed*? I hope it answered some questions for you. I loved it. Though I did spend the whole hour thinking 'Couldn't someone have told me my glasses were on wonky?'"

There are some really interesting scenes in *Unearthed*, including 'the difficulty of running with a stake' (you could have someone's eye out), and especially when your costume lacks a useful stake-shaped pocket. We see the real logistical difficulties of filming Lauren's last moments in a cramped alleyway, and seeing those constraints it is even more amazing just how moving Lauren's death is. Sinead comments on the joy of her parents watching her have ferocious werewolf sex (on TV)! Aidan was working on *Desperate Romantics* when *Unearthed* was filmed, and the hair extensions and added sideburns sit rather uneasily without an appropriately sweeping brocade coat...

I was fascinated by Toby's detailed analysis of the professional misery and long-coated music fascism of the 1980s; it was all worryingly familiar to me too. Oh, and is it just me or is anyone else more and more convinced that Gilbert is actually Toby?

Toby says thanks (and quite possibly wipes away a small tear...)

On 2 March 2009, the day after the final episode of series one aired, Toby posted his final series one blog and teased us with a few hints about series two – or what he knew just at that moment, anyway. He also said some very gracious thank yous (which bear repeating in full) and which should undoubtedly be imagined with a poised hankie and a slight catch in the voice...

"I want to say thank you to all the fans for their feedback and enthusiasm. The response to series one has been amazing and I couldn't be happier.

"So, do you want to know something about series two?
Well, I'm not going to tell you too much. Partly because I don't want to ruin it for you, but mainly because we're still storylining so I, er, don't know much. I know about our new villain though. The

mysterious Professor Jaggat. But who was that sinister man interviewing Owen? And what is his connection to our heroes? All will be revealed in time, but I promise you Mitchell, Annie and George will be facing a threat even deadlier than Herrick.

"In one episode, Mitchell, George and Annie will be forced apart.
Someone will die.
Someone will kill.
Mwa ha ha ha ha ha haaaaa!

"This is probably the closest I'll get to an acceptance speech, so as well as our extraordinary cast and crew, I wanted to say thank you to Matt Bouch, Rob Pursey and Phil Trethowan. Without them, you'd have been looking at a picture of a basket of kittens for the last 6 weeks.

"In terms of the finished show, there are too many highlights to mention. But just off the top of my head... The transformation in episode one. Annie in episode three watching Gilbert go through the portal. Mitchell in the kitchen, turning on George and Annie in episode five, raging about the brutality and stupidity of humanity. George in episode four, promising he's going to protect Nina. Pretty much every time Jason Watkins opened his mouth. The last scene in episode five. Oh, and episode six, one word: Nanna.

"But once again, it's the fans that have made this show the success it is. You helped get the show commissioned in the first place, then tuned in every week.
It's your show as much as mine.

"Though obviously if it does ever win an award, I get to keep it."

Speaking of which...

"Awards are like haemorrhoids. Sooner or later every asshole gets one."

... or so said Sarah Morton (played by Charlotte Rampling) in the 2003 film *Swimming Pool*.

That opinion does seriously underrate the pride and recognition that awards bring to hard-working people and *Being Human* repaid the faith of the team behind it as well as the BBC when it was awarded the following prizes and nominations in 2009:

Broadcast Awards 2009

Best New Programme
The judges remarked that the series was "one of the boldest, most original and exciting new drama series for some time."

Best International Programme – Nominated

Best Multichannel Programme – Nominated

Writers' Guild Awards 2009

Tony Whithouse – Best Drama Series

RTS Craft & Design Awards 2009

Phil Hookway – Best Tape and Film Editing

The judges said: "Bold, ambitious and a very fresh piece of television... in which the editing treads the line brilliantly between drama, comedy and horror, allowing the show as a whole to be a terrific modern twist on genre television."

Millennium FX – Best Special Effects

"Working with small budgets and tight deadlines with no post-production enhancement, this work illustrates a real commitment to the profession and the genre. The effective transformations into a werewolf were a tour de force."

Broadcast Digital Awards 2009

Best Programme Launch

That difficult second album syndrome...

Being Human series one was a great success, so all Toby and the team had to do to follow it was to do it all over again! In an update on the writing of series two on the BBC *Being Human* blog in April 2009, Toby said: "The problem with having a successful series that gets recommissioned is, you have to do it again. If one more person says the words 'second album syndrome' to me, I'll punch them in the neck."

Oops! (Sorry...)

Toby was giving very little away:

"You want to know about series two. Well if I say it's difficult to tell you anything specific, that's not me being mysterious, it's because I keep changing my mind. Characters surprise you. I've talked before about how the line in the pilot about the men with sticks and ropes came out of nowhere. Similarly in episode five when Owen said 'Hey, Annie, is that the best you've got?' Well, things like that happen a lot. It makes writing exciting. So I'll come up with a new character and think 'Oh yeah, he'll be a major player' ... and then he just kind of withers on the page. Conversely a bit-part character suddenly expands and becomes the guest lead. That's pretty much what's happened on episode one actually. So if I say anything now, the chances are by the time you read it, I'll have changed my mind and it'll be a show about psychic firemen.

"Rest assured the next series will be bolder, darker, funnier and even creepier. Hopefully."

So what happened to the psychic firemen? I was really looking forward to them! All we got was an unseen date for Kathleen with a dead fireman... it was hardly Pugh, Pugh, Barney McGrew, Cuthbert, Dibble and Grubb (deceased)!

A few more hints were dropped in June 2009 when Toby updated the blog on the progress of series two and how the characters have developed:

> "The characters have evolved, so to an extent it's like writing a new show. They've been hardened by their experiences in series one, but at the same time their friendship has become firmer. In episode one of series two, one of the characters is very different to how they were in series one. And that was interesting to write. But before anyone panics, the character soon sees the error of his or her ways..."

So what happens next for our supernatural trio? At the end of series one, after Herrick is destroyed, they are feeling a sense of peace, of safety – is this it? Can they now just concentrate on being human?

Well, what do you think?

6

series two

Men never do evil so completely and cheerfully as when they do it from a religious conviction.

Blaise Pascal
1623-1662

episode one

George and Mitchell are confronted by a married pair of vampires.

Brimming with confidence and visibility, Annie lands a job in a pub and meets a man.

Nina finds George's double life difficult to cope with and faces her first full moon.

Mitchell meets an intriguing woman in a unisex loo.

broadcast:	10 JANUARY 2010	director:	COLIN TEAGUE
writer:	TOBY WHITHOUSE	producer:	MATTHEW BOUCH

cast:

Annie	LENORA CRICHLOW	Hugh	NATHAN WRIGHT
Mitchell	AIDAN TURNER	Technician	MARK FLEISCHMANN
George	RUSSELL TOVEY	Saul	ALEX LANIPEKUN
Nina	SINEAD KEENAN	Hennessey	ADRIAN SCHILLER
Kemp	DONALD SUMPTER	Galvin	JOEL GILMAN
Ivan	PAUL RHYS	Old lady	MARGARET JOHN
Daisy	AMY MANSON	Werewolf	PAUL KASEY
Lucy	LYNDSEY MARSHAL		

"Can I just state for the record, *huge* fan!"

No new pre-title sequence for this first episode in series two, just a quick romp through the events of the first series, culminating in the death of Herrick and the presumed safety of our trio. A presumption immediately countered by the mysterious Kemp telling the even more mysterious Professor Jaggat that "we've found them."

George and Mitchell are in the pub discussing Nina, or more accurately why George isn't enjoying living with Nina as he'd hoped he would. Tampons in the bathroom are not a reliable indicator of 'happy ever after'. Quite reasonably, Mitchell wonders if she is scared and having problems dealing with their supernatural household. George is not sympathetic – he's changed. He's more certain of himself, it's bordering on arrogance. His main concern with Nina is that they aren't having sex – what has happened to sweet and stuttering George? Apart from having torn the vampire leader limb from limb, of course, while his girlfriend watched.

There's a distance between Mitchell and George, both physically and within their friendship, which is new. Mitchell seems puzzled at George's lack of understanding of how Nina feels; he's looking at him as a parent might consider the horrors of their adolescent offspring's bad behaviour. Surely George can remember just how hard it is to adjust to their world, how frightening it is?

George is waiting outside for Mitchell when he hears some heart-rending sobbing. A flash of the old George and he goes looking for the crying girl, wanting to help. She's crumpled on the floor, terrified, not meeting George's eyes. She's been attacked, she whispers, there were three of them – and their eyes were black. George reaches for her hand but just before they touch she's up on her feet, all trace of tears gone, her own eyes black. A vampire... and she

143

knows exactly who George is. Her companion is behind George and they have him trapped. He too knows that George killed Herrick but finds him a rather unprepossessing specimen, not at all what he was expecting. The female vampire may well not agree, not with the ravenous way she is looking at George. Instead of walking away as he would have done in the past, George isn't having any of this and he attacks the vampire. He makes no impact, this vampire is too strong, but he won't give in. He runs at him again and again. He's going to get a beating, but Mitchell arrives and manages to separate them. He recognises the vampire couple, he's met them before. Ivan and Daisy run, laughing, not to get away but just for the thrill of the chase, and George – new George – can't let them go.

"I need to show you something"

While Mitchell and George have their inconclusive heart-to-heart in the pub, Annie and Nina are doing the same in the house. Nina is asking Annie about George, how he became a werewolf. She makes a conscious decision and shows Annie her arm, the scratches George gave her a month ago. Annie's face tells Nina all she needs to know, she is devastated for her but she tries to be positive. George hadn't completely changed, even though his transformation had started. That is bound to mean that Nina will be fine, even though Nina knows that he was already part wolf – the scratches attest to that. The supernatural world that Annie has learned to live in is not a logical one. She insists to Nina that it isn't worth trying to make assumptions about what will happen. Despite these brave words they both know the truth: George has given Nina his curse and nothing can make it any better.

George and Mitchell are still chasing the vampires, ending up in a multistorey car park. George will not be stopped, even though Mitchell tells him they should just walk away. George has been attacked three times, presumably since he killed Herrick, and he has finally had enough. He is not going to back down or run away anymore. George follows Daisy – he can smell her perfume – but Mitchell warns him to be careful, he knows her.

Daisy watches until she is sure George is alone. She apologises for her husband's behaviour. He was rude to George but that is really out of character, he should get to know them. She is tempting him, flirting with him in a way so obvious that even George can't fail to notice. He is hooked; there is something primeval attracting him to her. She explains that she and Ivan aren't interested in world domination, they are just tourists and seeing the werewolf killer of Herrick was on their to-do list. Daisy wants George for her collection and she'll have him too if the stunned expression on his face is anything to go by.

"I was in Baghdad. I saw Phnom Penh. Now I want to see what happens here"

Mitchell is not really looking for Ivan, instead Ivan finds him. There's a sound, a bat-like shriek on the soundtrack that alerts us to a vampire. Ivan wastes no time, he punches Mitchell and throws him down and it's a clear assertion of his strength and superiority over Mitchell. We are used to seeing Mitchell as the oldest and strongest vampire and it is odd to see him so easily dominated by Ivan. Ivan has the usual vampire attitude about Mitchell giving up blood –

he can see he is clean and to another vampire he just looks ill, aside from the punch in the mouth he's just given him. Ivan is curious about the power gap Herrick has left. No one is leading the vampires and the wound left by cutting out Herrick is bound to fester. There will be others looking to take over the power and control that Herrick has left behind. Ivan has no interest in taking over, chaos beckons and he is here to watch the show. He only attacked George because he felt it was his duty. However much he hated Herrick, he was a vampire and one of their own. He warns Mitchell that there will be many more hunting George down for what he did. Shaken out of his phlegmatic calm, Mitchell makes sure Ivan knows that he is protecting George, and that Ivan should let the vampires know that. It is time they were back in hiding, the revolution is off.

Daisy wants to know what it was like when George killed Herrick. She has hypnotised him and is now close, touching him and holding him – definitely provoking a reaction as he tells her how Herrick's blood was cold. Their frantic kissing and groping is only interrupted by Ivan calling Daisy to him. She leaves George without a qualm, flipping up her skirts in farewell, but he is rather less sanguine about being left high and dry.

While George grapples with Daisy, Nina has more pressing worries. Tomorrow is the full moon and she has been thinking of nothing else. She has been having trouble sleeping and when she does sleep, she dreams. Nightmares of changing and killing, and we can sympathise with why she has kept a distance from George. Without that space between them how could she not tell him what she suspects? She doesn't know what to expect if she transforms and she asks Annie to go with her to the isolation room, she doesn't want to be alone and Annie agrees. She is still trying to convince Nina that she will be fine, but they both know she is wrong.

Ivan and Daisy face George and Mitchell. Ivan is looking forward to watching the madness, while Daisy is still tempting George, gazing directly at him, pouting as she kisses and caresses her husband in front of him. They leave, intending to hunt, to pick up someone on the way home. Although are they really staying in a Travelodge? Surely not...

George tells Mitchell that Daisy attacked him but he managed to fight her off. Mitchell is less than convinced, pointing out the lipstick on George's face. As he wipes it away, annoyed at being caught out, we see a glimpse of old, uncertain George as he shakes off Daisy's spell.

"I didn't even believe in homeopathy before this"

George is keen to be with Nina and she is adroitly avoiding getting close to him. She wants to talk instead and this seems to have become the pattern of their relationship. She is having problems getting used to the supernatural world she is living in. After all, it has only been a month, it's not long to come to terms with your lover being a werewolf and a murderer and the fact that your housemates are both dead. George is totally unsympathetic and impatient with her; if it's so hard then she could just leave. Nina is dropping plenty of hints but he isn't listening. "I just need you to get me through this," leaves him even more exasperated. Nina is right when she tells George he has forgotten just how frightening finding this world can be.

Nina is off to work but Mitchell is looking at her strangely, he knows something is up. George, on the other hand, is more interested in Annie's new hobby of dunking biscuits in the multiple teas and coffees she is still making.

Annie can't contain herself any longer and tells Mitchell and George her news. She's applied for a job in the local pub! Something she always wanted to do. OK, so the ambition is low, but has Annie ever worked before? Maybe Owen preferred her safely in the house. Mitchell is less than impressed – she may be visible but she's squishy, not solid – but George is pleased that she is moving on. Irritated at their scepticism, Annie reminds them that while she may not have any experience, it's all about giving it 110% – she's seen *The Apprentice*! That told them...

New bumptious George is really getting on Mitchell's nerves, especially as he thinks he's got Mitchell all worked out. Mitchell has no purpose, that's why he's unsettled and can't bear to see Annie and George moving on. He really rubs it in – Mitchell has no girlfriend, no family, no career and nothing to do, even the craving for blood has gone. George and Annie are moving on, they don't need him to protect them anymore. All in all he's a bit pointless.

"Did you just call me deadly furniture?"

George may have a point. Mitchell the vampire was forged in the battles and chaos of the First World War and he has been fighting battles ever since. He fought to be the darkest and then the one who got away. He fought his cravings for blood and killing and he fought for George and Annie. Even conceding that George does have a valid argument, there are ways of telling a friend some home truths and this isn't one of them. He's lucky he didn't get a slap, instead Mitchell just tells him in disgust that lately he's been a prat.

Annie's interview is going well. Hugh, the landlord, is quite taken with her but is more than a little startled when she produces a business plan for the pub – he doubts the climbing wall is going to fit. It's a relief when he just gives her the job and it stops Annie re-creating the entire run of *The Apprentice*.

"If we're comparing isolation and disappointment, then I think I win"

Mitchell is cleaning when he comes across Lucy, a doctor, sneaking a cigarette in the loo – it's a unisex loo as well which she finds ludicrous. He's leaving her alone as requested when she manages a sob. He asks if she is OK, prompting a potted personal history of a boyfriend lost, a disastrous job change and ending with the mysterious disappearance of her goldfish. Mitchell is remarkably helpful – "Do you have a cat?" Of course none of us would have thought of that! Mitchell is attracted to Lucy but he is also confused by her. He's got the point though, she's single and vulnerable – after all, she did lay it on with a trowel. She also has rather low expectations – wine in mugs and Twix fingers were the very pinnacle of a good time. Yet another woman falling for Mitchell's charm – or is it? She tells him to go but doesn't lock the door and as she takes a deep breath, one, two, three and he's back. He's not happy; clearly not many women have sent Mitchell packing. He's far more rubbish at life than she is, he points out, although just what he thinks he is achieving here isn't clear. 'Hello, I'm a loser,' has never been high on the list of greatest ever chat-up lines.

Full moon tonight and George is packing his bag, complete with a chicken on a string – he's still using Tully's tricks. Nina watches and even as he kisses her goodbye she wants to tell him but she can't, not yet, she has to be sure first. George heads off and, compared to his previous terror of the wolf, he looks happy, anticipating his transformation with a relish we've never seen before. He hasn't just accepted the wolf, he has embraced it.

Once he's safely away, Annie and Nina leave too. Mitchell sees them go, Annie holding Nina close. Does he suspect?

A shot of the multicoloured houses of Totterdown in the sunshine as George walks along an old railway line contrasts with the claustrophobic darkness of the isolation room where Annie and Nina are locking themselves in.

"What happened to the other werewolves? Are they human now?"

Despite his earlier bravado George is still scared; naked in the woods singing *The Teddy Bears' Picnic* to himself, he is waiting for the agony to begin. In the isolation room, Annie realises that the remains of Herrick have gone. Nina is worried that she might hurt Annie, but Annie assures her she is totally and completely dead. Nina doesn't know what to do next – should she take her top off? Good idea, shame to spoil it, agrees Annie. A quick *Buffy* reference makes poor small talk – especially as it's wrong, Nina the werewolf was in *Angel*. All they can do is wait.

Kemp is in a control room with a technician, and in a chamber, a pressurised chamber, is Galvin. Wearing a gown, he's wired up to monitors and looking nervous. Kemp is reassuring and punctiliously polite; Professor Jaggat has explained what is going to happen so Galvin need not be scared. Some pseudo science about the tidal force of the moon that triggers the transformation and we realise that Galvin is a werewolf. The plan is that the pressure in the chamber will counteract this tidal force and so stop it having an effect on Galvin – he will not transform. Kemp is so calm and has such an air of authority that we really believe him, although the face of the technician shows more doubts.

The full moon approaches and they increase the pressure in the chamber; Galvin stays unchanged. He feels sick, and without thinking the technician replies, "Yeah, that happens," and Galvin suddenly realises he is not the first. He starts to get agitated, they told him this had never been done before. Does that mean the others were cured? He doesn't want to consider the alternative. Kemp distracts him with their success: the moon is now full and he is still Galvin, he hasn't changed.

We see George starting to change, screaming in agony. Nina too is transforming, Annie watching helplessly as she howls. We go back and forth between the two and then back to Kemp and Galvin. Nothing has happened and they laugh in relieved triumph. Too soon. Galvin starts to bleed, blood spurting from his arms and his whole body spasms. He's desperate to change, begging to be allowed to transform, but Kemp won't listen, demanding that the pressure be pushed higher. As he and the technician watch, Galvin's body tears itself apart inside, blood pouring out, his face distorted. He begs them to let him change until he can speak no longer. The technician is clearly bothered but Kemp is unemotional. He turns off the intercom to mute Galvin's screams but he shows no compassion, no remorse. As we see George and Nina fully transformed, Galvin lies dead, a ruined body in a spreading pool of blood, and

147

Kemp just walks away.

"That was the last type three"

Dawn, and an unconscious Nina starts to stir, a weeping Annie still watching over her. Nina's first thought is for George – she needs to get home or he'll wonder where she is. She's exhausted, totally drained. She is determined not to tell George that she too has his curse but Annie can't agree. She can't know about Nina and not tell George – he is her friend. Nina is too exhausted to argue but threatens to give Annie rabies if she tells him. Quite how she can do this to a ghost she may not have thought through. Nina knows that to tell George would mean telling him how she became a werewolf. He may still love her whatever she is, but to know he gave her his curse would destroy him.

George awakes cuddled up to the half-eaten remains of a large stag. He's more accustomed to the change so less tired and he can't resist just one last taste of the blood. He isn't alone either, but instead of Annie's supportive presence, a challenging Daisy is enjoying the view of a naked and grubby George. She chides him for being so close to houses but maybe he likes the risk. She has his bag and throws it down to him and he's suddenly very conscious of his nudity and her avid scrutiny of it. He is exasperated with her; he sees two types of supernatural creatures, those who love it and those who don't. Daisy wants him to enjoy what he is as she does and he refuses. Daisy can see through this – destroying Herrick changed something for George. If he hasn't fully accepted who he is yet then he is close, just one more step will do it. George can rationalise the wolf still and feels strongly that the life he should have had and the person he was before have been stolen from him. Maybe the relish for the change only happens just before it and the hangover and remorse are still as bad.

Daisy tells him why she went with Ivan – he offered her the chance to travel the world and have sex. What else could be so much fun? The prospect is too much for the lingering traces of the wolf and George gives in, after all Nina doesn't want him so why not? As they couple enthusiastically we see Ivan watching, face impassive.

"It's all wine and roses"

Mitchell is sitting by the front door, patiently waiting for Nina to come home. He doesn't say a word but she realises that he always knew. He wasn't sure though, not until now. He tries to reassure her that although her life will be different, it is still a life. A better life than he and George and Annie had when they were first changed.

Nina is still angry. Mitchell is just trying to ease his conscience. She blames him for pushing her and George together, for pushing him to have a life. It was inevitable that someone was going to get hurt. Poor Mitchell, women always want to blame him – Lauren blamed everything she did on him and now it's his fault that George made Nina a werewolf. Undoubtedly Lucy will find something that's his fault fairly soon. George arrives home, walking into a very awkward silence between Nina and Mitchell. It's nothing, they assure him.

In their room, Nina and George are trying to avoid each other in the confined space. They are going over familiar ground. Nina needs George;

George wants Nina – unfortunately in very different ways. Nina smells perfume on George. That's odd – she smelt the same thing last night after he and Mitchell had been out. Her senses are werewolf sharp and George's reaction comes from his guilty conscience – the perfume is Daisy's. Oh yes, he shouts, it's all about Mitchell – are he and Nina...? Maybe that is why she won't leave. Of course, he's just lashing out in self defence. He can't really believe that Mitchell would do that to him? Nina has never heard anything so ridiculous and it's the final straw. She can't hold it back any longer and she finally blurts out the truth, that George has made her a werewolf. She shows him the scratches he made and they silently face each other. George can't speak, there are no words; he can't even bear to look at what he's done and he walks away from her. Wracked with sobs, desperate for him to hold her, Nina is inconsolable.

"These things take time. And that's one thing I've got"

Mitchell has bought Lucy a new goldfish. Trevor has a smart jar, complete with gravel and a string handle – it's all very cute. In spite of her calm self-assurance Lucy is pleased and he's pleased she's pleased. Although – why Trevor? Might have been a nice touch to call him Herrick or William! Trevor is entirely Lucy's but Mitchell asks for visiting rights and for Lucy this is a step too far, too fast. Lucy explains she is fresh out of a relationship and she needs time to adjust. Mitchell's face as he turns away is perfect, it exactly catches the feeling we all have when we know we've said something very, very silly. Lucy on the other hand looks as though everything is going exactly to plan. Mitchell isn't very good at this – instead of women coming over all peculiar at the sight of him he's really having to work at Lucy and it looks as though he may have lost the knack!

Annie is in training at the pub and all she needs now is a customer. So far Hugh hasn't noticed that his first employee is actually dead, never changes her clothes and can't drink anything – but then he's a man so that's fair enough! Annie has had far too much time to watch TV since she died and when her first customer arrives she goes into a dodgy *EastEnders* routine, spilling his drink and making up the prices. It really can only get better.

Nina and George see each other at the hospital but neither can speak – they don't know what to say and, anyway, how will they ever be able to sort this out? George turns away and catches a glimpse of someone familiar. He finds Daisy in an elderly patient's room, on the bed with some scary-looking scissors held to the unconscious woman's neck. The woman is Daisy's daughter, abandoned as a baby when Daisy left with Ivan. She's the last link with Daisy's human self and Daisy had already tried to kill her but she survived to end up comatose in hospital. It hurts Daisy to see her still alive; it reminds her of who she was before she became a vampire and she doesn't want to remember. It still hurts and it is no fun.

She's still goading George though; she wants him to become cruel like her. She laughs at his morality and ridicules his attempts to retain his human self. This time he resists her touch, the memory of Nina's need still strong. He tells Daisy her daughter needed her, she wanted her and she was the last human being who did or ever would. Whether or not Daisy kills her she will not get rid of that knowledge. His words hit home and Daisy is torn. She can't be like

George, she doesn't want to be and she loves Ivan deeply in her way. Is there a deep buried envy of George's humanity? From trying to kill her we leave her kissing her daughter. There is something unhinged about Daisy, Ivan has spoilt her, let her run wild and she has no boundaries left. She weeps on her daughter's unconscious shoulder.

Released by his new clear-eyed assessment of Daisy, finally unclouded by her physicality, George can finally face Nina. Although he is totally, utterly devastated, it all makes sense now. He can't believe he has done this to her, can't take it in. He has given the woman he loves the thing he hates most in the world, his curse. He collapses, distraught and she can finally comfort him.

"Not you. Don't let me have done this to you. Not you"

Annie still has her customer, good-looking property developer Saul. They are laughing together while Hugh hovers over Annie protectively. Saul has left his jacket in a colleague's car and needs to give him a call as he can only afford one drink without his wallet. Annie invites him home to use her phone. Hugh is doubtful, "I might kill you," jokes Saul, but Annie can laugh it off – she's safer than they could ever know. Hugh is resigned but unimpressed as Annie and Saul leave together.

"Well... we all saw that coming!"

Saul is waiting for Annie to make him a cup of tea when Nina and George get home. They've been out drinking and seem to have reconnected; they are just a little tipsy. Nina is extremely curious about the very handsome man in the living room, although George begs to differ about his handsomeness. Mitchell gets in and joins them in the kitchen to continue discussing Saul. He agrees with George, "Nah, he's not handsome." Annie's two 'dads' are back and, while they don't actually warn Saul off, they are obviously checking him out – or are they just jealous? After all, Nina and Annie are both quite happy with Saul being there to gaze at! It's good to see Annie have some girl talk in the house for a change. Saul in the meantime is popping pills, a headache maybe – or something more serious?

Hopefully the handsome Saul is also hard of hearing, as Nina drunkenly announces that she is a werewolf. Actually, they all know, but it's a useful way to change the subject from the respective handsomeness of Saul and Mitchell. Oh, and George, who was a bit of an afterthought in the attractiveness stakes! Mitchell is still trying to reassure Nina that she is not alone. Annie was alone in the house for a year before he and George moved in; George was a werewolf for six months before he met Mitchell; but Nina has them.

"Whatever happens next, there's four of us now"

There's a knock at the door and a boiler-suited engineer tells them they are investigating a suspected gas leak. They need to clear the street, just to be safe; they're going to have to leave the house for a while. It's all very plausible but the man in the overalls is Kemp's technician. There's no reason for them to doubt him, so Mitchell, George and Nina, Annie and Saul head out bearing a huge tray of tea and coffee for the neighbours. (By the way – it was nice of one of the men to offer to carry the heavy tray for her!) Standing in the street talking to the neighbours, drinking tea, Mitchell realises that this is pretty close to the community he strove so hard to create before. All it took was the right circumstances; it just needs to happen, it can't be forced. For the moment, they are happy. Mitchell has his community, Nina and George are embracing and Annie is mothering the whole street with cups of tea and coffee, a smitten Saul by her side. The sun is even shining.

Back at the house there is frantic activity, equipment is being installed and Kemp is overseeing the work. A prisoner in handcuffs is brought in. He's some kind of psychic and after they hook him up to a lie detector Kemp asks him about the house. There is no one there now that they cannot see but there has been lots of activity. There is nothing happening now though, just a residue. The prisoner asks if this will help him, Professor Jaggat said it would, but for Kemp this is God's work and he tells him it needs no other reward.

Finally, Kemp walks through the upstairs rooms, looking in disdain at the contents of each room (they are pretty untidy!). He seems to sense no presence or echo in Annie's room, but in George's and Mitchell's he quotes from the Bible, the Book of Daniel. What do he and the mysterious Professor Jaggat have in store for our housemates? And who do they think has been thrown into the lion's den?

"Now the king spoke and said unto Daniel 'Thy God whom thou serveth continually he will deliver thee'"

Musings on episode one...

We pick up the story just a month after the death of Herrick. Almost to the day – tomorrow is the next full moon. In that month, Nina has moved in and got a new hairstyle, and Mitchell – or Aidan Turner to be more exact – has acquired a new tattoo. Annie is now consistently visible, and George? Well, frankly, George is an arse.

Our trio – or foursome if we include Nina – are all changed by the death of Herrick. Annie refused death after Herrick stabbed Mitchell and in doing so gained new powers. She is now visible, almost solid, and as cheerful as we've ever seen her, although bordering on slightly manic. She gets a job and there is some lovely comedy in the interview as well as her first day at work. Her new boss Hugh is beautifully underplayed by Nathan Wright and his wistful sweetness as he watches over Annie is touching. She's moving on; now she can be seen she is less reliant on George and Mitchell and they are nonplussed when she brings home Saul, they are used to having Annie all to themselves.

Nina has the greatest change and the acting honours in this episode are all for Sinead Keenan, with a beautiful performance of hurt and betrayal. You can see that Nina doesn't want any of this – she doesn't want to be a werewolf and she hates pushing George away. But it's the only way she can get through the month until she knows for sure. She can't leave without knowing but she can't stay either and she doesn't know what to do. They are trapped in a pattern of behaviour and until Nina tells George what has happened, what he did to her, they can never break out. I have said I found Nina's first appearances overdone – I still feel that – but Sinead Keenan has settled into the role and I can see perfectly well why Toby Whithouse was so keen to have her stay. I'm never going to be a big Nina fan, but not every character can – or should – be everyone's favourite.

Mitchell is low key in this first episode and George is on the right lines when he calls him "deadly furniture." It's snide and cruel – very much 'new George' – but Mitchell is treading water. If the essential nature of a vampire is formed when they are made, then Mitchell's nature is to fight, he needs a cause. His blood cravings are finally under control, he is essentially alone and George and Annie seem to be doing quite well without him. He doesn't even have Herrick and Seth to fight anymore. On top of that, Ivan has arrived, stronger and older than Mitchell, just to rub it all in. Mitchell also seems to have lost his allure – maybe that mysterious vampire charisma is linked to the blood, a way to make it easy to find prey. His attempts to charm Lucy aren't entirely successful, but then does this new doctor have her own agenda? She seems to be deliberately drawing Mitchell in and then pushing him away and he is totally on the back foot.

The biggest change of all is in George – he's arrogant, condescending and up for a fight. So far from the home life of our own dear George. Killing Herrick, putting himself in that position to stand up for his friends, has changed George. He has not only embraced the wolf but he welcomes it. He's unsympathetic to Nina; he really has no idea why she is finding their life difficult.

Killing Herrick could not have left George unaffected, but this complete change of character for George was a brave move. Watching him behave so badly – especially having sex with Daisy – feels very uncomfortable. He's pushing Mitchell and Nina away – where is this going to take him? Nina tells him he made her a werewolf and he walks away. It's only when he sees through Daisy's cynical façade to the confusion and loss underneath, the last link to humanity she feels for her abandoned daughter, that he can see what he is becoming. His humanity too is leaving him and he finally fights it, feeling the pain of what he has done to the woman he loves.

We get straight into the new threat to the friends, although they have no idea yet what is happening. In this series, the threat comes from humanity and we soon get the measure of Kemp. Far from being the psychiatrist or investigator we wondered about, it appears he is a religious zealot, or more likely maniac, who thinks he can cure werewolves. Presumably the mysterious Professor Jaggat is providing the 'science' – otherwise known as how to blow up a werewolf.

The new series has a different look; it still has the great interiors of the house and the hospital, but more locations. The chase in the car park is particularly effective, and Mitchell surveying the town laid out before him – almost tempting him – is a great image. There is also a lovely scene showing the pretty coloured houses of Totterdown in the distance as George heads off to transform in the lap of Mother Nature. The new locations fit well – there's no sudden shift to more glamorous parts and it is all still perfectly in keeping with the slightly run-down reality of series one.

The episode is paced nicely. In particular there is a very clever change of mood between Nina's heart-rending sobs after she tells George she's a werewolf and Mitchell presenting Lucy with Trevor the goldfish. It should jar (sorry Trevor!) but it doesn't.

Best bits? Glad to see the humour is still there and that, conversely, the tone seems to be getting darker. It's a very good move to have Nina's secret unveiled in this first episode – it might have been tempting to drag it out a bit but this keeps the story moving forward. Best of all – the bits of Herrick have disappeared...

Bum notes...

Even in a local pub I would think that Annie's lack of a valid NI number or any sort of up-to-date identification could be a problem. Do the dead pay tax?

Another plot-smoker (the dramatic equivalent of a social smoker!). After Nina's single cigarette so Mitchell could ask her to dinner in series one, now Lucy is sneaking a smoke in the loo – never to be seen with a cigarette again.

A rare continuity error – when I say rare I mean it's rare for me to spot one! When Mitchell puts Trevor in his jar down on Lucy's desk his sleeves are rolled down, when he straightens up they are pushed up to his elbows.

... and the bottom line

Sightings of Russell Tovey's bare backside – two, one a lengthy and lingering shot including some rampant alfresco sex with Daisy!

He said, she said...

The disembodied spirit of a dead woman is getting a job in the service industry. What could possibly go wrong?

......

It's a lot to take in. I mean werewolves, ghosts, vampires. I didn't even believe in homeopathy before this.

......

Black coffee...

Cheers.

... and weird camp herbal fusion thing.

Yep, that's me.

Where have I seen... Alex Lanipekun (Saul)?

Alex Lanipekun is best known on TV for playing Ben Kaplan in *Spooks*, a role he left RADA early to take. Appearing in two series, he came to the traditional *Spooks*-style sticky end in series seven in 2008.

He has also appeared as Ashley in *Apples and Oranges* for Channel 4 and as Tiger in *Beautiful People* for the BBC, both in 2008.

His theatre work includes Eric the Red in *Wig Out!* at the Royal Court Theatre in 2008 and Danilo in *Dimetos* at the Donmar Warehouse in 2009. In autumn 2010 Alex took on the character of Laertes in Nicholas Hytner's production of *Hamlet* at the National Theatre, alongside Clare Higgins (Josie).

After being turned down the first time he applied to RADA, Alex turned his hand to a number of things, including journalism and a degree in Anthropology. He also wrote and performed for hip hop collective One, and reached the finals of the 'MOBO Unsung' competition with their 2002 album *Onederful World*. His second application to RADA was successful.

Music in episode one

The Cure	*Lullaby*
Feist	*Mushaboom*
Willy Mason	*Simple Town*
The Frequency	*Sanity Overture*
The Accidental	*Time and Space*

episode two

A body arrives at the hospital drained of blood, for Mitchell it's the harbinger of an old friend in trouble.

Annie has a date but will Saul's past come back and bite them?

George and Nina's relationship is under increasing strain as Nina struggles with the supernatural life.

Not to mention the best guest star – ever!

broadcast:	17 JANUARY 2010	director:	COLIN TEAGUE
writer:	TOBY WHITHOUSE	producer:	MATTHEW BOUCH

cast:

Annie	LENORA CRICHLOW	Technician	MARK FLEISCHMANN
Mitchell	AIDAN TURNER	Saul	ALEX LANIPEKUN
George	RUSSELL TOVEY	Carl	STEVE
Nina	SINEAD KEENAN		JOHN SHEPHERD
Kemp	DONALD SUMPTER	Quinn	JOHN STAHL
Ivan	PAUL RHYS	Newsreader	JONATHON ARIS
Sir Terry Wogan	HIMSELF	Policeman	DAN MERSH
Lucy	LYNDSEY MARSHAL	Werewolf	PAUL KASEY
Hugh	NATHAN WRIGHT		

"Because it's what you'd do for me, Mitchell"

This series, the pre-title sequences take us into the past and this time it's to Vienna in 1999. An elegant room and by the window an elegant vampire is looking out over the fireworks of the New Year celebrations. The only incongruous element is Mitchell, wearing only jeans and tied to a chair. This is clearly an established procedure – there is thick old-fashioned rope around his wrists and ankles and the knots that hold him are complex and ornate. There's a large plastic sheet on the floor under the chair – this is vampire cold turkey.

With the deviousness of the addict, Mitchell is trying to trick Carl into letting him go – it's a new century, they should join the crowds, have a drink... Calmly Carl reminds him that he saw the last one, as did Mitchell in his long ago childhood. He's changed his mind, he's not ready – he's sweating and struggling, his hair falling over his face. He tries threats and cajoling but nothing flusters Carl. He's been there – he knows how it feels.

Carl's partner Dan comes in and Mitchell threatens him, calls him queer, demanding he sets him free, and Carl, quietly but firmly, makes him apologise. He does, he's genuinely contrite. Mitchell gets increasingly desperate, especially when he's told that it could take six months to get properly clean and he wants to know why Carl is doing this, tormenting him so. It's the right thing and Carl and Mitchell both know that. One day Mitchell will thank him.

"Two customers? We'll be talking about this for years"

Annie is in the pub talking to Saul – well, listening to Saul – as Hugh looks on. George arrives, he promised he'd visit and while he waits for Hugh to notice him he can watch Hugh watching Annie. It's clear to George just how fond he is of her already. He smiles and we can see the George we know and not the arrogant idiot of the last episode.

Mitchell and his faithful mop and bucket are in the lift when Lucy gets in. Trapped together, he has to make conversation. "Someone's been sick in the shop" is not a great opening gambit but it is best not to compound it by listing all the other waste products he has to deal with... He has no idea what to say to Lucy except for the wrong thing. The effect she has on him is very strange and he has a moment of horrified realisation. He's turning into George.

Lucy does try to reassure him. Buying Trevor for her was lovely, exactly the right gesture, but his suggestion of buying her another goldfish is – frankly – just weird. She keeps wrong-footing Mitchell and then giving him just enough encouragement so he keeps coming back for more. While he is properly smitten, she is playing him, and playing him beautifully. She suggests coffee and he looks like a kid at Christmas!

She's off to certify a dead body and Mitchell tags along. When she uncovers the corpse he's horrified to recognise Dan, partner of Carl, the vampire we saw in the flashback. He was found after an anonymous call, there are wounds on his neck and his body has been drained of blood. Lucy is rather enjoying the intrigue and she happily announces that the murderer has to be a gay vampire! The nurse and policeman find this highly amusing but Mitchell is horrified.

Meanwhile George and Nina are getting on better – at least on the surface. George has prepared the perfect breakfast for Nina after a night shift – eggs Benedict, ginger beer and a choc ice. Although they are talking they are still not comfortable together – George can't cope with Nina's sarcasm about being a werewolf and his part in it. He still feels too guilty to joke about it and has never found anything even faintly amusing in his own condition. She persuades him to stay while she eats and although it's not perfect they are starting to get somewhere.

"Your face. You look like you've seen a ghost"

Saul is home, keys on the table and Terry Wogan speaking to him from the television. Why does this feel strangely normal? Saul is still popping pills and thinks this is a joke but Terry gets his attention – he wants to talk to Saul about Annie. He reminds him about the corridor, about his accident. He wants Saul to tell Annie about it and especially about "all the interesting things" that he saw afterwards. She'll like that, girls like that sort of thing. He's very keen to get the two of them together.

Nina and Mitchell are having yet another conversation about what might help her. She is deflecting all his comments and questions with jokes – after all, it is getting a touch repetitive. She'll adjust. George, however, finds her apparent acceptance of her new circumstances rather scary.

As they talk, we focus in on a tiny microphone in the living room and know that someone is listening. Kemp's technician is in his control room, monitoring their conversation. Hearing Nina talk about being a werewolf certainly gets his attention.

156

Mitchell wants to talk to George about the body brought into the hospital. He tells George that Carl has been clean for around twenty years and that he tried to get Mitchell off blood when they lived together. Rather than worry about the situation, George is more than a little miffed that Mitchell has lived with other people before him – he really doesn't grasp the hundred-years-old thing!

"Do you think I've waited the last hundred years for you and your three different types of upholstery cleaner…?"

Carl and Dan were lovers, and Mitchell cannot image that Carl would have killed him, he was besotted with Dan. He's not worried about the body, after all there's a process, but if it was Carl that killed him then that does bother him. He has been clean for so long – if he has succumbed after all these years then what hope is there for Mitchell? Maybe it wasn't Carl, after all it could have been anyone, but these are empty hopes.

Annie is in the pub and in charge; Hugh is visiting his ill father. Saul is still a little perplexed about his instructions and Terry Wogan continues to encourage him from the pub TV. He dives straight in, no preamble, telling Annie he almost died. He had a bad car accident – no one else was hurt – but he technically died for six minutes. Annie isn't quite sure why he is telling her all this, it's all a little close to home. He continues, he saw a corridor, bright white but terrifying and there were men there, men with sticks and ropes. Annie can't help herself and she tells him she saw it too. She almost tells him she died but stops herself, but she saw exactly what he did and she has so wanted to talk to someone about it. She just doesn't understand why he told her. Intuition he says, Terry Wogan we think. Saul catches hold of her arm – he doesn't notice that she is squishy, or that she is cold, and Annie impulsively kisses his cheek.

Terry and his quiz contestants reward Saul with a round of applause, but what is Saul? Not exactly a ghost but definitely something odd, and something that wasn't sensed by Mitchell or George. Only the truly dead see the men with sticks and ropes but Saul came back. Somehow.

"You think you're free of it, but it finds you"

Mitchell answers the door and smiles in welcome – it's Carl, and Mitchell, despite the situation, is pleased to see him. He needs to know what happened and Carl tells him he had been dreaming about blood. All those years clean and there is still no escape. He sees it as a bill to pay for all the time he abstained. He seems puzzled about what happened as if it was totally out of his control. Dan, he says, wasn't frightened, he just looked disappointed in him. George overhears – he wants to know why Carl didn't recruit Dan. It was because he was kind, Carl explains, and if he had become a vampire he may not have been that same person anymore, not the person he loved.

George is adamant that Carl cannot stay but Mitchell overrules him, he wants to keep Carl safe until everything is sorted out. George would do the same for him. Carl doesn't help his case by reminding George that he is a celebrity.

"Beasts should be put in cages"

Kemp is at prayer, on his knees in front of an altar, when he is interrupted by the technician with the transcripts from the house. In his office he reads the passage pointed out to him where Nina confirms she is a werewolf. "The possession has spread," he growls. The technician can't understand why they have left them in the house and Kemp explains – Professor Jaggat wants to observe the three types interacting. We already know that 'type threes' are werewolves, so 'type one' is Mitchell, a vampire and a 'type two' must be a ghost. They have never known them live together before, let alone try and pretend to be human. Kemp is evidently less in favour of this course of action – he yearns for a harsher approach. The technician reminds him that in twenty-two days there will be a full moon and they are without a type three for the chamber. Kemp considers their options.

At the pub, George is listening to Annie recount every single detail of her last conversation with Saul. He's understandably not enthralled. He's worried about Annie, she has to be careful. Annie doesn't get what he means, she considers herself "a bit old and dead for the contraception conversation." This is so not what George was thinking! She's only been at the pub for a week and she has both Hugh and Saul chasing her, he just doesn't want her life to get too complicated. Annie is fine with Saul pursuing her, they have lots in common, although she is not going to tell George what. That Saul has quite possibly died probably comes under the heading of complications. She has to take a chance on Saul, otherwise she will be faced with spending the rest of eternity on the sidelines. What she can't understand is why George thinks Hugh fancies her – surely he must be wrong. Is George sure? He is – he recognises that look of unrequited yearning, he's been there himself. Annie is rather chuffed.

"Still got it!"

Nina gets home from a late shift to find Carl tucking into her shepherd's pie; George made it for her earlier. She knows about him, Mitchell has already explained. He wants her to know that although he is staying she isn't in any danger. She's dismissive, it's not her house. A telling remark – Nina isn't really at home here. Nina points out that he killed someone and he tells her not to be too hard on George. Nina is annoyed – he didn't need to point this out. She knows George killed but she seems to have rationalised it or blanked it out. After all, he didn't kill a human; Herrick was a vampire so maybe that's OK. She is echoing what George used to say, they shouldn't be living with normal people, near to children. She fears for what would happen if she loses control – exactly the same fears that George had. It's another indicator of how far apart she and George really are that they haven't been able to talk about this.

Carl wants her to feel secure, he tells her there are ways of keeping people safe, but Nina is dismissive. They are both proof of what can go wrong. They reach an uneasy truce over George's shepherd's pie.

"You've no idea how much a gay vampire would liven up my week"

Mitchell and Lucy are having coffee in the garden outside the hospital – and so far they are actually having a proper conversation. In a nice touch they are sitting on a bench in memory of Lauren and Mitchell is unconsciously stroking the plaque with her name on it.

Lucy is still fascinated by what she persists in calling gay vampire man. She knows the cause of death is likely to be disappointingly normal but as she has no social life at all this is keeping her entertained – yet another hint for Mitchell. However, she tells Mitchell that the coroner has agreed that another postmortem should be carried out. Mitchell is concerned – what about the system – and he finds out the coroner's name. "The plot thickens." Yes, it certainly does.

Saul is still getting odd messages, now they are in the local newspaper. An article proclaims that he and Annie are the perfect couple. Annie also thinks so and asks him out to the cinema. He could say no, of course, and they could just behave awkwardly for evermore, but he accepts. Hugh warns Saul, he's watching him, but when Saul finds another message in his paper – "Breaking news: Hugh is a dick" – he starts to get slightly hysterical. He tells Hugh he's too late, Annie and he are going out and Hugh's face falls.

"Herrick's gone. I'm handling this"

Mitchell confronts Quinn, the coroner. He has not made the death of Dan 'disappear' and Mitchell needs to be sure the deal is still on. Quinn didn't know that Herrick has gone – "politics" explains Mitchell – but he hasn't had his bribe, his payoff, for a few weeks. For the first time, Mitchell admits he is following in Herrick's footsteps and he tells Quinn that he is handling it, that he cannot walk away. It would be suicide.

Quinn has had enough; Herrick convinced him that the vampires were a natural force and the deaths inevitable, but he has come to see that they are just murderers. For all these years he has been an accessory to these killings and he can't do it anymore. He wants to be able to face his family with a clear conscience and he is prepared to take whatever consequences follow.

Has Mitchell found his cause? Is he stepping up to the role vacated by Herrick, however reluctantly?

George has finished work but there is a note from Ivan in his locker. He wants to meet George in the isolation room, where he killed Herrick. George is frustrated but he can't avoid the meeting. Is he feeling guilty about Daisy or is it just that he doesn't want to have another fight?

"What did you say, that made her feel again?"

Ivan tells George the rumours about him and Herrick: that George drugged him; that George begged to be recruited; even that Herrick survived. Ivan just wants to know what really happened. He doesn't threaten George, only in his very presence is he intimidating, but George tells him the truth. He tore off Herrick's head. Ivan doesn't really care about Herrick – he feels nothing anymore. He's 237 years old and the years have worn away all his compassion. It takes more and more to hold his interest but George is doing so; for now. He already knows that George and Daisy had sex – he watched – but what he can't understand is how George made Daisy feel again, to remember being human. George persuaded Daisy to let her daughter live, something Ivan can't understand. His humanity is so very far away now that it means nothing to him.

He asks if George has a girlfriend and if he loves her. "Very much," replies George and Ivan picks up his coat to leave. "That's nice," he says, but under that laconic façade is Ivan a bit of a romantic?

Annie and Saul have been to the cinema as planned; Annie is horrified at the price of the sweets! Back at Saul's flat, he puts on the TV and offers her wine, coffee, olives? A difficult question for a ghost but Annie has an answer prepared: she doesn't like eating in front of people. Slightly eccentric but just about understandable. Saul is still getting messages. The TV presenter is gesticulating, shouting and miming – increasingly crudely – exactly what he should be doing with Annie. Obediently listening to the voices, Saul asks Annie if he can kiss her. Once she establishes he means now and not at some indefinable point in the future, he does so with enthusiasm – rather too much enthusiasm. He scares Annie but she manages to get out from under him, shaken and angry. He looks at her, leering at her, and tells her to get undressed, she is locked in. He lunges and she jumps away, disappearing and leaving him sprawled on the sofa alone.

Back at the house, she's trying to explain to Mitchell and George what has happened. Mitchell is unsympathetic – that is all he needs right now. Annie is not happy with him, maybe he'd like to pick a better day for her to be attacked? Anyway, why is he being all holier than thou – surely Annie is owed a couple of mistakes, after all, when was Mitchell ever perfect? George tries to pacify them both. Annie is OK and if Saul tells anyone she vanished they'll just think he is barmy. So that's fine and Annie will just have to stay in the house for a bit. Mitchell doesn't want her to go back to work and Annie is furious with him again, she doesn't want to let Hugh down. Trying to stop them winding each other up anymore, George tells Mitchell to go away and he heads off, looking for Carl. He isn't in the house and George isn't interested in where he is.

"He's your murdering fugitive. If you want to keep him then you have to look after him"

Annie is thankful that George hasn't said he told her so about Saul, and she can see she has picked yet another unsuitable and potentially violent man. George mouths "I told you so" at her and they sit in a companionable silence. But however keen George is to see Saul off, I can't see the men behind the doors letting Annie out of his clutches this easily.

Mitchell finds Carl looking at the house he and Dan shared. The door is still covered in police tape but he has realised he has no photos of Dan and he can't leave without one. Mitchell has to tell Carl that Quinn won't honour the deal any longer, he won't lie. Once the truth gets out the police will come looking for Carl, everyone will be looking for Carl. Carl knows that if they can't find him they'll come for Mitchell. He has made himself known to Quinn, he is no longer in the shadows, but Mitchell doesn't seem unduly worried. He is already accepting that he has to do something; the system has to survive for him and for the others. He's even starting to sound like Herrick, although Carl points out to him that it is all rubbish – Herrick was an ego-driven maniac and they all talk like that. It's a warning for Mitchell but is he listening? Carl is tired, maybe it's time for him to end his existence, but Mitchell won't hear of it. He has a plan.

The camera pans over an amalgam of candlesticks, goblets, drug paraphernalia and a used syringe, a skull. In the middle of this is Carl's body, cold and dead.

Mitchell calls the police – an anonymous tip – so they know where to find the body. Wisely, he destroys the phone's SIM card, not knowing that Kemp's minions are listening to every word.

The police find Carl and he is taken to the morgue. So far so good – until Nina sees his body.

George sets off the fire alarm to clear the way and Mitchell finds Carl standing over Dan's body, weeping. Mitchell can see how much he loved Dan – will he ever have that with anyone?

"We were going to tell you about that"

Saul is still wondering how Annie could just disappear. He's switched to whisky and is well down the bottle. The TV is still talking to him – the announcer reassuring him that "all women are whores." Nice – hardly *The One Show*, is it?

The announcer decides it's time to level with Saul. The thing is, he tells him, Annie is actually dead. Saul is struggling to understand. In turning down death Annie has made enemies, she upset some "very important people," she's still around and she should be with them. Quite who 'they' are is unclear – maybe Terry Wogan is the King of the Underworld? He encourages Saul to keep drinking – a nice big drink – and then, maybe a drive?

Annie is hiding in the house in the dark when there's a knock at the door. Peeking through the letterbox is never going to convince anyone there's no one in, but luckily it's only Hugh. He was worried about her after she didn't turn up for work. Annie offers him tea – there are a few already made – and gives him her new line about not eating and drinking in front of people. She realises that she does, actually, sound mad, but Hugh is reassuring and shares some rather odd childhood information!

"Let's never discuss that"

Hugh knows it must have been Saul who has upset Annie. He has a conversation all about it with himself, concluding that he never liked him. When Annie can get a word in she explains that she just wanted to be like everyone else. She wanted to get away from herself – the Annie she is – and rediscover the Annie she might have been. Hugh can't understand this, he only sees how beautiful she is, he thinks she's perfect, and as they get closer she kisses him. Hugh pulls away – not because he doesn't want her, but because he wants her to want him. He'll do anything for her – "I'll move mountains. I'll kill bears." So what now, Annie wants to know, and his simple words mean so much to her: "I'll wait." Finally Annie has found someone who sees her and loves her for just what she is and not what they want her to be. Someone who'll cherish her and protect her. Who probably won't throw her down the stairs.

"It's you. This whole time, there you were"

Mitchell's plan to get Carl away is working. George and Carl are waiting in the shadows, while Mitchell greets Ivan, who is going to take Carl to meet the ship that will take him to South America. Carl still looks stunned, he thanks George for helping but George doesn't want to talk to him. He only did it for Mitchell – he doesn't think Carl should be escaping. Carl considers this – neither does he.

Ivan has a pristine sports car he has had for fifty years and it's much admired by Mitchell. He's amused to be a part of Mitchell's plot, but more so at his naivety. Mitchell thinks once Carl is safe it's over, but Ivan has no such illusions. They will never be safe. Once the vampires are hungry they will come out of hiding to feed. There will be headlines and panic and once the vampires have been eradicated then humanity will turn on the werewolves. Then the ghosts. And then on itself – the weakest first. Christianity will flourish in the horror and enforced worship is the future. He paints a vivid but gruesome picture and Mitchell can see the truth in his vision. This is the chaos that Ivan seeks and Mitchell realises he has some difficult choices to make.

"Maybe it should happen. There's nothing on TV at the moment"

Carl and Mitchell embrace and we can see the echoes of their deep friendship – different to the one that Mitchell had with Herrick. Their history is a positive one and maybe this is payback for Carl helping Mitchell in the past. Ivan leaves with Carl, to the strains of Kate Bush's *Wuthering Heights*.

Mitchell and George return to the hospital just in time to see Saul pulled out of an ambulance. There's been a car crash, he was drunk. He has serious head injuries and it doesn't look good. They let Annie know and she is in his room listening to George tell her that, this time, he's hurt other people as well.

Nina pulls George away – she's angry with him for getting involved, for helping Carl get away. She doesn't seem surprised to see Saul so badly hurt, is she beyond wondering what will happen next? She is angry with George however much he tries to explain. To her it's simple – he's let a murderer get away. For George nothing is that clear-cut any more – it's all tangled up with Mitchell and Herrick and the compromises and deals they have to make to stay safe. To Nina it's murder; for George sometimes it is the only way. She is losing patience with him – why can't he just behave how she thinks he should?

Lucy is desperate to update Mitchell on the new developments. Although she professes to be concerned that she has made a mistake, has declared a man dead in error, it's not convincing. Mitchell is tired, he can't really deal with her right now and he gives her the tale of the occult he had planned with Carl. Perhaps the gothic novel/heaving breasts section could have been left out though. Lucy sees she is losing him – he really doesn't care right now so she tempts him back. "Buy me a drink."

"If you see the guy I declared dead walking around... kill him"

In Saul's room the monitors go mad and there is no one to help however much Annie calls. The lights start to flicker and, as the machines flatline, Saul is there standing with her, looking at his own dead body. His door is there too and Annie realises she must have met Saul so she could help him move on, to accept death.

She's wrong – the radio stops playing cheesy lift-music and a voice tells Annie how they've missed her. She is trapped, she can't jump, can't disappear and Saul has to get her through the door. Looking at his own body, he obeys – they will let him live if he gives them Annie. He grabs her, dragging her towards the door as she begs and pleads with him to let her go, calling out for George, for help. The voice confirms what we suspected – Saul was a means to an end, he did die but they sent him back so that Annie and the door could be there together. The door opens and for the first time we see inside – an endless red-carpeted, wood-panelled corridor. It's very different to the bright white corridor that Saul and Annie have both seen – different destination? Saul continues to fight with Annie, dragging her towards the door while the voice eggs him on and on – they have tortures planned for Annie, she should never have turned them down.

George returns, puzzled to see the lights in the corridor flickering, then he hears Annie's cries but he can't get in. She is trapped. The voice continues, promising Saul he'll live again if he does what they say. He picks Annie up despite her fighting, biting him, screaming, while the voice goes on and on telling them what is waiting...

"Men with ropes and men with sticks and men with black, black feathers on their black, black wings"

Annie is still fighting desperately, she knows this is not her door but the voice continues, there is no reward for kindness and mercy. As they get to the threshold, Saul can't do it. Maybe the reminder of the men with sticks and ropes has made him think of the connection that he and Annie shared, her joy and her essential goodness. He can't do it and he pushes her away. The door slams on him – is he redeemed or damned?

Nina is walking out, leaving George asleep and trying to get away with no one knowing, but Mitchell is downstairs, in his jammies. He tries to get her to stay, she needs more time to adjust, but Nina is no longer prepared to give them that time. She's sickened by this new world of monsters and murderers and she can't bear to be with them knowing that they accept it. She tells Mitchell that his much vaunted humanity has long gone and he doesn't even know it.

She loves George, really loves him, but she can't bear to be with him anymore. She's left him a letter – exactly as he did to her before he went to meet Herrick – but now it's OK, although Mitchell thinks it's cold.

George wakes, looking for Nina. Instead he sees her letter and he knows without needing to open it.

Nina is outside the station, deep in despair – is she really leaving, leaving Bristol? As she considers her future, Kemp approaches her. "Hello Nina." Maybe he has an answer for her, some sort of solution.

After the voices, Annie is wary of the radio – switching the one in the house off from a safe distance. She heads off for work, looking forward to seeing Hugh, but he doesn't look at her. Has she upset him? Suddenly it's clear – Hugh is busy, setting up the pub, talking to himself. He has no idea that Annie is there.

She is no longer visible, is this the revenge of those behind the door? She's devastated, everything has been ripped away from her. Even Hugh, the man she hoped might have been her future. She sits in the middle of the pub, isolated, alone, while the world carries on around her.

"Oh, God. Not again. Please. Not this again"

Musings on episode two...

This week is all Annie's. She tends to get sidelined in the supernatural tales, an inevitable consequence of being invisible, untouchable and tied to the house. Now she is more powerful and confident, she can get out there and be like everyone else. Can't she?

Annie's job has brought her into contact with two contrasting men. Saul – arrogant, confident, but with secrets – remind you of anyone? Then there's Hugh – self-effacing, sweet and protective. Of course Annie chooses Saul, and their date culminates in his attempt to rape her – totally horrifying but this time Annie doesn't have to take the abuse. She can disappear. She gets no sympathy from Mitchell, he seems to think she's brought it on herself. It's jarring hearing this from the vampire who has always cared for the ghost with tenderness, but Mitchell is old, older than we tend to remember, and his attitudes don't entirely fit in the modern day. He also has the future of the vampire race on his mind and might be slightly distracted...

The scene where Saul tries to drag Annie through the door is true horror. The fight looks real and her despair is painfully clear. Juxtaposed with the voices from the radio, and the threats of just what Annie has waiting for her, it is a powerful sequence. We hear the next stage on from the men with sticks and the men with ropes. There are also men with black feathered wings – a classical gothic image, familiar enough to give a shiver of impending doom.

At the very last minute Saul is Annie's hero – their connection, her kindness, won't let him do it and he lets her go. They can take their revenge on Saul but the other side is never going to let Annie escape. Is it their way of saying that she is theirs when she loses her visibility? Seeing her sitting in the pub, invisible to Hugh, is heart-rending. What more can they take away from her?

The instructional voices from the radio and the TV are genius, such an everyday medium and so much more powerful than we realise. How else can 'they' get to talk to anyone they want to? Casting Sir Terry Wogan as the voice of the other side was inspired – so inspired that I really don't think there is anything else to say!

Lucy is still busy reeling Mitchell in. He's tongue-tied in her presence and is worried he's turning into George! His wretchedness is well done and even his words and phrasing change. His chatter about poo and sick are not how Mitchell speaks and in his discomfort Aidan Turner manages to make him look younger, as he might have done in more innocent times. I wonder if we are seeing a glimpse of human Mitchell. Perhaps in those far-off days he wasn't such a charmer, maybe he was George!

Ironically, as he gradually gets involved in the vampire affairs he also starts to get more confident with Lucy. It's a nice reminder of his past relationships that they sit and flirt on Lauren's memorial bench – and Mitchell caresses her name as they talk.

There has to be more to Lucy than meets the eye – she is too smooth. What does she really want with Mitchell – a doctor and a cleaner? Her obsession with "gay vampire man" is a little overdone. If she just needs amusing why not buy another box set?

Mitchell is at the top of a steep slope. So far he is keeping his footing, but you can see he is about to start sliding. Once that starts where will it stop? In order to save Carl, he has to get involved in the system that Herrick set up. In his innocence he thinks he can sort out Carl and then slip back into the shadows – or even bring the vampires into the open. Ivan's amusement at this and his speech about the chaos that that would bring is wonderful; a highlight of the episode. Mitchell is starting to realise that he may have to get involved, and there are some worrying echoes of Herrick's grandiose rhetoric. Knowing that Carl has killed – and killed the man he loves – has shaken Mitchell; will he ever be able to find peace and stay clean if Carl couldn't?

Steve John Shepherd gives us a different kind of vampire. Far from Herrick's mania, Mitchell's worldliness or Ivan's ennui, Carl is calm, centred and elegant. We know nothing about him – although I would assume he is old – except that he has been clean for twenty years and lives with and loves a human and that is where his tragedy begins. Externally Carl is serene, almost detached, but watching him weep over Dan's body just highlights his internal struggle. Beautifully done.

He and Mitchell have a history we can only guess at, all we really know is that Carl tried to get Mitchell clean and that they lived together. Maybe that ended when Mitchell lapsed, went back to blood. Maybe their relationship went deeper – vampires live long and the boundaries of love and sexuality must blur over time. They clearly care deeply for each other and the small smile of relief and welcome Mitchell gives when Carl arrives at the house is lovely.

Nina is still struggling, although on the surface she and George seem more content. The arrival of Carl is the final straw for her and she has to accept that she cannot live in George and Mitchell's world. To her it is wrong, it is just murder. She can't make the concessions to the supernatural world that George has learned to. She still does not understand Mitchell and George's relationship and their debts to each other. It's a little unreasonable of Nina – she claims to love George deeply, so much so it makes her stomach churn, so why can't she really talk to him. George loves Nina despite her secrets and the guilt he feels about making her a werewolf, but she wants George to give up all the ground he has reluctantly made and the acceptance he has finally achieved. Maybe the source of Nina's scars runs deeper than we yet know. She leaves George with a letter. She's changed – when George tried that she was furious.

Kemp's plans are moving forward. The listening devices are giving them more and more information and he now knows that Nina too is a werewolf. The mysterious Professor Jaggat is still mysterious and the contrast between the Professor's observation and Kemp's rather more 'fire and brimstone' approach is becoming clear. The level of menace Kemp put into "Hello Nina" was just fantastic acting by Donald Sumpter.

The humour was lower key this time but there was still enough to leaven the tragedy – "mince of darkness," George on unrequited love, and Ivan as a Kate Bush fan. Unusually it was an episode without effects – no werewolves, no transformations and no black vampire eyes. Just Annie disappearing and the electrical flickering indicating the other side.

Last thought – did anyone else want Scottish coroner Quinn to say, "There's been a muuurrrder," in true *Taggart* style? Just me then...

165

Bum notes...

Where did Carl come from? The assumption is that he and Dan lived in Bristol and Carl and Mitchell are close. Wouldn't he have been around before?

A short series has to keep some of the stories brief and means that everyone our trio meets inevitably has an importance to them. While Saul and particularly Hugh are well written and played, we know there has to be more to them than it might initially seem. Saul could have been a little more three-dimensional.

Where was Daisy?!

... and the bottom line

Sightings of Russell Tovey's bare backside – none, but there were plenty last episode! Instead we get a sweaty, bare-chested, tied-up Mitchell (calm down...) and a nude Carl, although in a very moving scene.

He said, she said...

Ladies and Gentlemen... somewhere in Bristol is a gay vampire. Count Spectacular! Mince of Darkness!

......

I don't know how to talk to you. I know I came on too strong the other day but now... Oh my God, I've become my flatmate.

......

I'm just going to go over there and sneak glances at you from behind my copy of Take a Break.

......

Okay, two rules for Ivan's car: no food or drink and I get to choose the music, and tonight we shall be listening to Miss Kate Bush.

......

Fifty years and still the same car?

Been keeping her in storage, you know what it's like. If it goes, has a good body and you like being inside it, why get rid of it? It's a recipe for a happy marriage, too.

Where have I seen... Sir Terry Wogan?

Are you kidding?!

Where have I seen... Steve John Shepherd (Carl)?

Steve John Shepherd is best known on TV for playing Jo, the law clerk, in the critically-acclaimed BBC drama *This Life*. He remained in the role for two series between 1996 and 1997.

Other TV credits include *Maisie Raine* (1998-9), *Dalziel and Pascoe: A Death in the Family* (2006), *The Bad Mother's Handbook* (2007), *Bonkers* (2007), *Plus One* (2009) and *Lunch Monkeys* (2009). He also appeared in an episode of *Material Girl* in 2010 with Lenora Crichlow.

He appeared in *EastEnders* in autumn 2010 as Michael Moon, Alfie Moon's cousin.

His film work includes *Too Much Too Young* (2007), *Layer Cake* (2004), *Star Wars II: Attack of the Clones* (2002) and *Forgive and Forget* (2000).

He appeared for the National Theatre in *The Five Wives of Maurice Pinder* (2007) and *Sing Yer Heart Out For the Lads* (2004), and has also been seen on stage in *Original Sin* (2002), *Dangerous Corner* (2001) and *Piaf* (2008).

In 2001, Steve dated the actress and singer Martine McCutcheon, who played his sister in an episode of TV drama *The Knock* (in 2000).

Music in episode two

Fatboy Slim	*Right Here, Right Now*
Kasabian	*Where Did All the Love Go*
Mumford & Sons	*Sign No More*
Kate Bush	*Wuthering Heights*
Benny Goodman	*Stars Fell on Alabama*
Al Bowly	*I Love You Truly*
Loner	*Farewell to My Friend*

episode three

The vampires are in chaos, the system has fallen apart and bodies are turning up – Mitchell is compelled to step in.

George is desperate after Nina's desertion.

Annie plays Cupid – one of the few occupations available to an invisible ghost.

Mitchell's love life suffers from time spent organising the vampires.

broadcast:	24 JANUARY 2010	director:	COLIN TEAGUE
writer:	LUCY CATHERINE	producer:	MATTHEW BOUCH

cast:

Annie	LENORA CRICHLOW	Hugh	NATHAN WRIGHT
Mitchell	AIDAN TURNER	Technician	MARK FLEISCHMANN
George	RUSSELL TOVEY	Quinn	JOHN STAHL
Nina	SINEAD KEENAN	Cara	REBECCA COOPER
Kemp	DONALD SUMPTER	Wilson	IAN PULESTON-DAVIES
Daisy	AMY MANSON	Kirsty	LAUREN O'NEIL
Lucy	LYNDSEY MARSHAL	Priest	PEARCE QUIGLEY

"Demons. Bloodsuckers. Incubi. Spreaders of the great pestilence"

This week's pre-title flashback goes way, way back – to Bristol in 1665. In the caves under the city, a procession of soldiers is lead by a priest with a scroll. The gathered families cower away in terror as he reads the proclamation. These are a persecuted people, thought to be spreading the plague and pestilence and they are to be punished. Their teeth will be smashed from their skulls and their heads cut off. There's a *Monty Python* moment over having enough light to complete the reading and a quick query on the best order of death, but nothing delays the inevitable. They hold down the first man, the first victim, and raise a stone to his face. His eyes change and we realise that these people are vampires.

What we don't know is if these vampire families are in hiding or in captivity. Maybe they thought they were safe. Perhaps all they wanted was to be left alone to live their lives. Sound familiar? After Ivan's forecast of the future in store for the vampires if they came out of hiding, can we be sure if anything has really changed since then?

"You are to be destroyed so that our kingdom might be cleansed of your devilry"

An early morning jogger running by the river curiously follows a trail of blood from an abandoned trainer and finds rather more than she bargained for. Two bodies are lying sprawled in pools of blood, their throats are torn apart but they are holding hands in death. Suddenly the eyes of the man spring open – one of them is still alive.

At the hospital, Mitchell is polishing floors when the first stretcher is rushed past him with Lucy leading the resuscitation attempts. He sees the wounds and the slower progress of the second trolley just confirms his fears.

168

On TV, Chief Constable Wilson is making a bland statement about the attacks. They need to wait and talk to the survivor before they will know anything. To the reporter who asks about the reports of vampires he recommends an early night, but despite this denial people are already speculating.

"I suppose the bad working conditions have driven you to believe in a monotheist deity"

Mitchell and his ever-present mop and bucket – his passport to anywhere in the hospital – finds the bed where the survivor is hooked up to machines, bandages hiding the wounds on his neck. He is imagining a quick fix. He could disconnect the breathing tube, turn off the monitors and the problem would just go away. Unfortunately Lucy finds him mid-fantasy and he needs a quick excuse. That he was praying is not entirely convincing, even if he only makes up the numbers from time to time. Lucy sees a lot of sudden religion in CTD patients – "Circling the drain," she cheerfully translates – but it's unusual in a cleaner. She blames Thatcher. Don't we all?

Lucy has been praying for Marcus in the hospital chapel and she is pretty confident he is going to pull through. She teases Mitchell about his usual roster of excuses; this is no ritualistic sex cult or occult fetish, this time it is murder. Mitchell is still staring intently at Marcus as she leaves. Perhaps he's hoping to make him die by force of will. Lucy calls him away – what about that drink he was supposed to buy her, how about tonight? Yet again her perfect timing leaves Mitchell stammering about having to "be somewhere" and she walks off without giving him a chance to rethink. He'll be back for more though, she's making quite sure of that.

"Being invisible makes purchasing pyramid teabags a touch awkward"

Devastated by Nina leaving, George has taken to his bed. With his socks on. A locked door is no barrier to Annie but her relentless attempts to get him up and showered are not working. George's normally orderly space is pretty messy, although nowhere near the normal state of chaos of Mitchell's room! Annie has brought him a mug of hot water. They have no tea, coffee or milk and it sounds as if Mitchell is thoroughly distracted. He hasn't washed up and has never, ever cleaned the bathroom. George really doesn't care and Annie's offer to hear him talk about "Nina dumping you" is less than encouraging. He retreats under the duvet, Annie can't possibly understand. She points out – quite rightly – that being killed by her fiancé and then nearly killed again by her latest beau will have given her just a touch of insight. But George is quite content to wallow in his misery. And his socks.

George is still in his pit of despond under the covers when Annie finds the poetry he has started to write to Nina and is less than complimentary about it. Annie always responds to setbacks with relentless over-cheerfulness but her determination to shake George out of his depression is not working. Her care and concern for him show as she reassures him that he really is very sweet.

Hugh is back and looking for Annie since she (literally) disappeared. With a little physical persuasion and forced removal of the duvet, Annie gets George to talk to him. The conversation between them is slightly stilted, mainly due to Annie prompting George unseen and unheard by Hugh. Hugh knows that

Annie leaving is his fault – exactly the same thing happened when he got serious about Kirsty, his ex-girlfriend. George does try to reassure him that it isn't his fault, as instructed by Annie, but he isn't really interested or very convincing. He isn't bothered about Annie and Hugh and even less so about Hugh and Kirsty. He has more pressing concerns. Now he's up he realises that he needs the traditional shower, shave and ... well, not a shoeshine!

"The killing has to stop"

Mitchell wants to know who attacked the young couple and he goes in search of the vampires. He finds Cara, Herrick's hospital canteen protégé, in an underpass, dirty and huddled in a sleeping bag but still defiant, still loyal to her brave recruiter. Mitchell sees her as rather pointless; he just ignores her threats and tells her to gather everyone together that night. He is taking steps to sort things out, slowly taking over the control that Herrick had, although he won't admit it to himself yet. The warnings of Carl and Ivan have had no effect on him and there is a stubborn blindness in Mitchell, an unwillingness to consider what might go wrong. He is clean after all and that is the only answer. The trouble is that, right now, he doesn't even know the right question.

Annie has a cunning plan. She is going to get Hugh and Kirsty back together so that Hugh can get over her. George is going to help, whether he wants to or not. Surprising him with her proposal when he is comfortably ensconced on the loo with a newspaper may not have been the ideal moment. Regardless of the timing, George is unconvinced about his usefulness but Annie is determined. George and Hugh have both been battered by heartbreak and abandoned by the women they love. Annie's vulnerability shows when she tells George that she knows that the "men from the other side" will try for her again and again. She doesn't know how long she can stay – or what is in store for her – and she wants to make every day she has count. She feels cursed, that everything around her goes wrong. It's a familiar story to George, and Annie has won him over. Maybe it will help him too.

"I'm glad my misery is proving useful"

Mitchell meets Chief Constable Wilson for a lesson on the realities of his situation. Wilson holds all the cards and he's not a bit worried. He assumes that Mitchell is the new Herrick. He didn't think much of the old one, the "despotic ginger arsehole," but they understood each other. Mitchell won't even commit to what he is trying to achieve. Being a representative says nothing – he needs to make up his mind. He offers Wilson whatever it takes to get him on side. It's good to know that the vampires have sufficient funds for bribery due to some sensible investments they made in the 1800s. Immortality obviously makes sound financial sense! Wilson takes what's on offer, but without Quinn the conversation has no point. Without Quinn there is no way the system can work. It's yet another wake up call for Mitchell – Wilson has nothing to lose and nothing to fear. Who would ever believe Mitchell over him? Mitchell needs to make some decisions – it's time to put up or shut up. This isn't going to be easy.

Cara has gathered the vampires in a disused church – dangerously close to a stereotype, as Lauren would have said. They're a disparate group, some old, some young, but all wary. There's no immediate respect for Mitchell. Maybe they don't know who he is or maybe his feud with Herrick altered their view. He tries reason but that is never going to work, and the idea of them going clean is greeted with derision. In a nice nod to the pilot, the vampires chorus "*Rehab*" at him. This is a group of killers, immoral and immortal, and he has to deal with them in the only way they will understand. That's it – the choice is made.

"My name is John Mitchell and I've killed more people than you've met"

He warns them. If they don't stop killing then they won't be able to hide any longer, the system that protected them is gone. They will be persecuted and all they will have to look forward to is funeral pyres and executions. Daisy comes out of the shadows to challenge Mitchell, to make him fight back, to make him really commit to what he is doing. Does she want him to do this or is she just stirring, preparing the show and the chaos that Ivan craves. She pushes him, he's unrealistic and she belittles his withdrawal from blood. He seems to have forgotten that it wasn't as simple as he'd like them to think. There were lapses and the system, the vampires, even Herrick kept him safe. He is asking them to change their essential nature but why would they, why should they? "A shark can only ever be a shark," insists Daisy, echoing Herrick, who said almost exactly the same thing when Mitchell told him he was clean. There has to be something in this for them and while Daisy is loving playing devil's advocate there is truth in her words. Mitchell has no right to turn up, order them to change and then walk away. He has to accept what they are. She might support Mitchell and want him to make this work but – more likely – she's probably just having fun.

Mitchell has to speak to people, put arrangements in place, but he threatens them as he leaves. If anyone feeds – anyone – he will kill them himself. Whatever happens now he has committed; will he be the new Herrick after all? Maybe he thinks it is possible to do it better, that he can lead the vampires into a blood-free paradise. It's a stupendous level of arrogance, especially when founded on a reputation that is thoroughly blood soaked.

Back to domesticity for Mitchell, but he's still on a high from his domination of the vampires and he might be a touch tetchy. Annie and George are having a house meeting and they want to talk, particularly as Mitchell hasn't been pulling his weight on the grocery front. Annie feels they need to reconnect, so Mitchell and George get on with some proper male bonding. They establish they have both been better and so they should go out sometime and get drunk. Annie's face is perfect – is that it?! No, actually it isn't, they can watch *The Real Hustle*, it's always on now. Except it isn't and from the reaction of the boys this is clearly the end of the world as they know it. Their disgusted rant about the TV schedulers and the impact they have on their lives culminates in George sobbing and Mitchell ostentatiously waving his yellow rubber gloves because he's DOING THE WASHING UP. Annie wonders if she has slipped into an alternate universe.

"We don't need to turn this into an episode of Oprah"

Cara hasn't exactly taken Mitchell's words to heart. Maybe she doesn't understand the risks of being caught or maybe Herrick left her feeling invincible. Perhaps she just doesn't care. She is watching three young girls in a shopping mall – two of them bullying the other – and she can't keep away. Could this be her revenge for those who bullied her and made her an outsider, or is it just the call of young, fresh blood? She doesn't rationalise it but catches them in broad daylight and she kills and drinks.

That alternate universe that Annie was in with Mitchell, George and *The Real Hustle*? It exists in the pub as well. Hugh is telling George about Kirsty while Annie provides an unseen and unheard – to Hugh at least – commentary. Hugh tells George that Kirsty even hated the way he washed up and George is in total agreement. They bond over the importance of coasters and not getting limescale on the draining board. They should go out sometime and get drunk. Annie is utterly exasperated but at least she has found out a bit more about Kirsty.

Mitchell meets Wilson and hands over the cash – a substantial amount of cash in the traditional plain brown wrap. Now that Mitchell has proved he is serious, Wilson is more upbeat. Marcus is now conscious and making a statement, to Mitchell's dismay, but Wilson is confident that it can be sorted. The only problem is the dead girlfriend and the lack of cooperation from Quinn. He and Herrick always had a plan up their sleeves for just this eventuality and he hands Mitchell an envelope.

"Give him this" "What is it?" "Leverage!"

Annie and George are watching Kirsty at her flower stall. Annie is excited about how they are going to sort out Hugh and Kirsty, George rather less so. There's a lovely line when Annie compares them to detectives Crockett and Tubbs and George ripostes that they are much closer to Randall and Hopkirk (deceased).

Kirsty is very down. Hugh has told them that she used to describe herself as an artist with flowers, but George's request for something wonderful (with roses) is met with a bunch of straggly carnations. She just can't be bothered anymore. Annie stays with her, watching her. She sees her wash a plate and then carefully dry it just as Hugh said she should, then she calls about her lonely hearts advert only to find that no one has replied. She is lonely and on the verge of tears, and Annie is desperate to comfort her but knows she can't.

Another telling moment sees Mitchell spying on Lucy. She is deep in conversation with Marcus, we can't hear every word but vampires are definitely mentioned. She gives him a small silver cross to protect him and even from a distance Mitchell flinches. When Lucy catches sight of him through the blinds, he pretends he was just passing and quickly walks away.

Mitchell is meeting Quinn, not because Quinn has changed his mind but because he has been thinking about Mitchell. He thinks he's different, that he has the morals that Herrick (and Wilson) lacked and Mitchell reluctantly agrees. He wants to believe so too. Quinn begs him to walk away but Mitchell can't bear the thought of the suffering that would follow. They disagree about whether the end justifies the means. Quinn can see no moral way to ever be involved in the concealment of murder and wants Mitchell to agree with him.

"I don't really have a choice now"

Mitchell is battling with the conscience he wants to cling to, the struggle evident on his face, but finally he makes his choice. He has come this far and he can no longer even consider walking away. He gives Quinn the envelope and he opens it to find photographs of his grandchildren. Mitchell assures him that they will be safe – as long as he does what Mitchell wants. Quinn is disgusted; he truly thought that Mitchell had the capability to be different to his race but he is just as bad as the others. Maybe worse; Herrick never involved the children.

He calls after Mitchell, telling him that the girls killed that day were only fifteen, that they were just children, but Mitchell has no idea what he means. He tells him of the attack, horrified to realise that Mitchell has no control over what is happening. That is three dead in one week – how many more?

Mitchell is back with the vampires, demanding to know who killed the girls, smelling out who has fed. He is coldly, clinically angry. Cara confesses, although confession is hardly the word. She is not sorry, they were delicious and the blood was everything she remembered it to be. Still cold, Mitchell knocks her down and challenges the rest to disobey him. They back away and they can see that right here, right now, he means every single word.

"Now, who here has a suit?"

It was inevitable, there are no new patterns in nature – the funeral parlour is reopening. The vampires are busy cleaning up, bringing in the cars while Nanna makes tea. Mitchell walks among them, master of all he surveys.

Meanwhile Wilson, as promised, is dealing with Marcus. Gloved hands open the drugs cabinet and a shadowy figure in a police uniform injects something into Marcus's intravenous line. He sets the scene – a spilled glass, scattered tablets, must be suicide – while Wilson chats on his mobile and waits.

In the morgue, Quinn is reluctantly signing off the report on the two girls killed by Cara. The system is back in place.

Wilson hands cash to a policeman as the hospital staff, including Lucy, fail to resuscitate Marcus. Wilson burns the statement and holds a news conference to announce that the deaths are now considered to be a suicide pact between the couple. No further action will be taken. The system is working.

Mitchell sees this on TV and knows that the vampires are safe for now but at the expense of the devastated and grieving parents. It has all been made to go away, but at what cost? One more level of Mitchell's humanity dissolves away.

He meets with Wilson, and Wilson's cynicism and feeling of superiority over Mitchell are clear. Marcus was just "collateral damage" and as the two girls in the shopping mall were repeat offenders he is actually quite pleased. In fact, he hoped they had been targeted. Using the vampires to clean the streets – surely that couldn't be his plan? He has no time or sympathy for Mitchell's distaste for the process, he wanted the system back in place and that is exactly what he got.

"What, did you expect it to be pretty?"

Operation Hugh and Kirsty is in full swing and as Hugh won't consider a blind date, Annie has another plan. Kirsty needs to have a date that is so bad, so

173

unbearable that it sends her back to Hugh. Who better to do this than George? Rather uncharitably, Annie cites his relationship with Nina as the perfect example of how to get it all wrong. George has the local listings and he finds the perfect bad date. A very, very long German subtitled art house film – and a George dressed in perfect geek style. Kirsty looks worryingly excited and to George and Annie's horror she adores German films and whisks George in before he can change his mind. A very long three and a half hours later he escapes and takes her for a kebab. Which she loves. There's nothing else for it – he tells her he's written a poem about her but he only manages to declaim two lines before she flings herself into his arms and kisses him passionately. This is the point when Annie admits defeat. Maybe they are actually the perfect couple and she should just forget about Hugh!

Mitchell is delivering supplies and finds Lucy in the morgue with Marcus's body. She is convinced that it couldn't have been suicide; apart from the logistical difficulties, she had been talking to him. Mitchell tries to parrot the police line but it all gets a little uncomfortable. He takes his chance and asks her out for a drink.

"Are you asking me out in a mortuary?"

Mitchell seems to have regretted asking Lucy out. Not exactly trying to impress, he takes her to a scruffy pub and buys her a two-for-one pint of scrumpy. Last of the big spenders. She asks him about himself, just trying to do what people do on a date, but he is evasive. She wonders if he is extraordinarily boring or has deep, dark secrets. Surely Mitchell usually has the chat; he doesn't normally have these problems with women. Is it Lucy or the vampires that have put him off his stroke? The band starts their sound check and that is the last straw for Lucy.

Mitchell walks her home. In truth he just follows Lucy as she stalks home ahead of him. She berates him for not treating her better, for not wanting to talk to her. Best they just forget it all. He's confused, a little disappointed and as he turns away there is that look on Lucy's face again. Self-satisfaction at a job well done. She's back in control.

"It's been a long day. Lots of dead people"

George has realised that the funeral parlour has reopened and suspects that Mitchell is involved. It's just a short-term measure, he claims, long term he's going to get them all off blood. George is disbelieving – that is so not going to happen. How could Mitchell possibly think he could do that?

Kemp is listening intently to their conversation, fascinated by the news of the undertaker's. As they talk George grabs his glasses, not realising he also has the tiny microphone caught up with them. As he cleans his specs he washes the bug down the drain, leaving Kemp incandescent with fury at the loss of such a valuable source of information.

Mitchell admits to George that it's a mess at the moment. The system is back but it is going to have to change. If he ignored the vampires there would be a bloodbath and he can't see any other option, but who is he trying to convince? It's all insane but George sees that he can't do anything to make Mitchell see sense, so he grudgingly accepts what his friend is trying to do. It's a relief for Mitchell – he had no one he could talk to about this.

George is pleased to have his friend back – he's missed him – but when he wants to talk to Mitchell about Nina he finds him entirely unsympathetic. George would have liked his support, but Mitchell can't and won't keep on holding his hand. Fair enough, he has things on his mind, but the way he dismisses George, telling him to grow up, is unfeeling and unlike the Mitchell that we thought we knew. This is a new Mitchell – or possibly an old Mitchell returning.

"Do it properly... you'll never have to do it again"

At the funeral parlour Mitchell gets Cara from the cellar where she is imprisoned. It's time. As he takes her through the building, the other vampires are gathered, Daisy to the fore. They want to see justice done; they want to see that Mitchell is not all talk. Daisy is watching him with a calculating look in her eyes. Does she think he can do it? Does she want him to?

Annie is dragging George back to Kirsty's flower stall to continue with her plan. He would quite like the ground to open and swallow him up. Ignoring Annie and her plan, he uses his instincts and tells Kirsty the truth. He can't keep leading her on, it's unfair and George is not a cruel person. He tells her he loves someone else, that he can't keep seeing her. He tells her how his loss feels and his words are raw and painful. She can feel it too; she knows exactly what he means. George has realised that fixing other people's lives does not heal their own and he makes sure Annie hears this. She can't cure her loss and anger this way. Maybe Mitchell needs to hear it too but he isn't ready to listen. He tells Kirsty of the most wonderful, valuable thing in the world – it's a second chance. They say goodbye and as George walks away, Annie hugging him, Kirsty is calling Hugh. A second chance.

Mitchell has taken Cara to the caves, the same caves we saw in the time of the plague. He tells her about this history, of how those suspected of being vampires were executed and how the vampires then adopted the same cruelties as a punishment for their own. She is utterly terrified, begging, pleading, promising never to be bad, to do anything. He holds a stone over her, he doesn't want to do this and yet again he says he has no choice. He smashes the stone into her face.

Back at the funeral parlour he throws Cara's teeth down, claiming that she has been executed. He is glaring, challenging them, any of them, to defy him and the chanting begins. "Long live the king." Daisy sits in the centre, not joining in the chant but just watching Mitchell and how he stands straighter and taller. Now, there really is no way back for him. But he has started his reign on a lie – Cara is not dead. As the vampires proclaim Mitchell their leader, she is in the caves, in the dark, waiting and hoping for rescue.

"The king is dead. Long live the king"

Hugh and Kirsty are back together, holding hands, watched by a smiling Annie. George is off the hook and he is in the house when the phone rings.

It's Nina. She wants to say goodbye properly and she has things she needs to say to George. She wants him to promise her that he will get on with his life, stop using the wolf as an excuse to hide from everything. He should be out in the world. He is wonderful and she loves him. He loves her too and wants to know if she will come back, but no. She's going to do something wonderful.

She leaves George in anguish, he's lost her all over again and this time there is no room for hope.

Nina is with Kemp. She is grateful that they have let her speak to George – to say the things that had to be said. Now she is ready. Kemp reminds her that God loves her and he turns to a formerly unseen figure, to Professor Jaggat.

It's Lucy.

"You know God loves you very much"

Musings on episode three ...

Mitchell and the vampires take centre stage this week and much is made of his lack of options. At every turn he is claiming that he has no choice. Why? He's chosen to leave the vampires before, to live quietly as a human, so why can't he walk away now? Maybe it's guilt. As Daisy points out to him, the system and even Herrick all colluded to help him get clean, they covered up after his little accidents. It was down to Mitchell that Herrick was deposed and decapitated and the vampires scattered. He was selfish at the beginning – he only wanted to protect his friend when Carl killed his lover. Adding all that together makes a pretty strong reason for him to play this role. The role that Herrick may have wanted for him, had planned for him, as soon as he faced George and knew his time was at an end.

Rampant, rapacious Daisy is underused in this episode (and there is no Ivan at all!). She is a useful device to challenge Mitchell and to push him further down the road he is tentatively taking. She is right that he has to commit, he can't play around with this. Daisy loves every part of what she is and she's reminding him that the vampire nature is an essential unchangeable force. The other warnings from Carl and Ivan and even from Annie and George also go unheard. After all – he has no choice...

While Mitchell's struggles and his reluctant descent into the vampire world are well played, the constant cutting between the meetings with Wilson and Quinn is a little disjointed. It's necessary to fill out the tale but has a workmanlike feel; it just needs to be got through.

We've never seen Mitchell as Herrick knew him, the vampire with the "darkest heart of us all," but that dark Mitchell is starting to break through the human façade he has so painstakingly constructed for himself. It shows in his increasing distance from George and Annie and his lack of understanding of their all-too-human problems. Does he really think he can get the vampires clean? It's the misplaced fervour of the recent convert, the evangelist – and a worrying reflection of what Kemp is up to.

The remains of Mitchell's humanity leave Cara alive in the caves – although just how human it is to leave her in the dark and cold is debatable. It could be a deliberate and cruel punishment. He lies to the vampires that she is dead to gain their respect and this lie will come back and haunt him one day. Daisy already suspects something is not quite as it seems.

So Lucy is Professor Jaggat and now it all starts to make sense. Her conversations with Mitchell take on a whole new meaning; her teasing about his claims of vampires and the occult and her tempting him into saying things he may regret. It's a lovely performance from Lyndsey Marshal, which is all the better once we know what she was doing. She really has been reeling Mitchell in like a fish on a hook. So, she knows he is a vampire, but when will he find out she knows? Is this the start of a love affair or an experiment? Will Lucy help and support him or is she only willing to bring him down?

George and Annie get the short straw this week and their comedy escapades are the necessary light relief from Mitchell's brow-furrowing angst. It does little to progress either of their stories, but George needs to move on from Nina and his taking to his bed, easy prey to Annie's plans, is realistically done. Despite himself he starts to accept his loss – until that final devastating phone call.

What can you do with an invisible ghost? Annie's stories are as limited as her interaction and while it seems sensible that she wants Hugh to be happy there is a sense of ticking off the next box. Here's the man who might have been my true love – made him happy. Tick. Moving on.

The comedy is nicely judged. It could have jarred very badly with the darker themes but the balance is finely held. I was worried at times that it would tip over and feel trite, especially as the cutting between scenes is quicker, but it never does. George's despairing "clowns... so many clowns!" is lovely. The worse date in the world is classic comedy and George's neat centre parting a particular highlight! The lightness was needed to lift the darkness of Mitchell's situation, although Mitchell's part in the *Real Hustle* rant deserves a mention and the Marigolds are perfect. A wonderful image.

The trio are very much divided – Mitchell is busy with his new world of bribery, corruption and covering up a few murders, so buying milk is low on his 'to do' list. Annie and George, meanwhile, are united in loss and their frustration with Mitchell. They don't know exactly what he is doing yet so their annoyance hadn't turned into concern.

Nina's final call to George is heart-rending and destroys him all over again – just as he seemed to be getting over her. Cruel to be kind. The music in this scene is gorgeous, and really adds to the emotional impact. However, Nina has changed her tune. She wants George to go and live his life, to get out there and stop hiding behind the wolf. It's a far cry from her condemnation of Mitchell who wanted George to do just that. Nina blamed Mitchell for her becoming a werewolf.

When Nina is talking to George, we can only guess that she is with Kemp. What we don't know is what she has been told or what her motives are. The way she is filmed suggests a lot. The lighting is glorious – she almost has a halo – and the heavy makeup makes her look beatified, saintly, and we can see she feels that she is sacrificing herself to a noble cause or greater good.

This isn't one of the best episodes. George and Annie are treading water: there are no great changes, no major resolutions, just consolidation of what has come before. It does reconnect them in a greater friendship, especially with Mitchell otherwise engaged. The vampire story and Mitchell's part in it is largely housekeeping. We do need to see the system back in place and the series of short meetings with Wilson and Quinn have to be dealt with so we can get on. Mitchell's interactions with the vampires are hasty, a lot is assumed from what we already know of that world and what we have heard of Mitchell's fearsome reputation. We get it – the system works, Mitchell is in charge (and in denial) – let's move on.

Having said all that, the reveal of Professor Jaggat is a beautiful conclusion to the episode. I had my suspicions all along, but there were many who didn't and it was a classic 'WTF' moment on Twitter and the forums.

Bum notes...

Only one issue in this episode and something that I feel was the only major mistake that *Being Human* made over series one and two. In the scenes after the killing of the girls in the shopping mall, there is an emphasis of their youth – they were fifteen, they were children. In light of that, the lingering full frontal nude shots in the mortuary are unnecessary and in poor taste. I'm not saying that everything should be clean and nice and tidy – I like dark and edgy, boundaries are there to be pushed. This, however, was a misjudgement – a rare one – but still a misjudgement.

... and the bottom line

Sightings of Russell Tovey's bare backside – none, and the 'depressed in pants and socks' look is not a good one!

He said, she said...

Your teeth will be smashed from your skull as a warning to other devils, then your head will be removed from your body and... [*turns over warrant*] no, that's it actually.

......

I suppose the bad working conditions have driven you to believe in a monotheist deity.
That's what happens when you haven't got a strong trade union.
I blame Thatcher.

......

We need to talk. So... George you start.
Are you OK?
I've been better. You?
Likewise.
We should go out one night and just get hammered.
Yeah, that's a good idea.

......

So, how do I look?
Like a Christian who's really let themselves go.

178

Where have I seen... Ian Puleston-Davies (Chief Constable Wilson)?

Ian Puleston-Davies has had an extensive TV career since graduating from the Guildhall School of Music and Drama.

He has played recurring characters in *Brookside* (Stephen Nolan in 1986), *Hollyoaks* (Terry Williams in 1995-6), *EastEnders* (Jimmy in 1998) and twice in *The Bill* (Mick Glover in 2000 and Alan Best in 2003). He had lead roles in *Conviction* (2004), *Funland* (2005) and as John Durbeyfield in *Tess of the D'Urbervilles* in 2008.

In 2009 he appeared with Aidan Turner in *Desperate Romantics* as Mr Siddal, father of Rossetti's wife Lizzie.

At the time of writing in autumn 2010, Ian is currently appearing as Owen Armstrong in *Coronation Street*, as well as in the role of Charlie Fisher in the sixth series of *Waterloo Road*.

Ian has talked openly about his struggles with obsessive compulsive disorder and in 2005 he co-wrote the drama *Dirty Filthy Love* based on his own experiences. Starring Michael Sheen, *Dirty Filthy Love* won a Royal Television Society Award for Best Single Drama and was nominated for a BAFTA Award.

Music in episode three

Aqualung	*Strange and Beautiful*
The Anomalies	*Employee of the Month*
Florence and the Machine	*Dog Days are Over*

episode four

George gets a new job, a new girlfriend and a new cage. A cunning plan, but will the wolf be locked up?

Annie meets an enigmatic ghost who reluctantly teaches her new powers – can she keep the other side at bay?

Mitchell is pulled further into the vampire world and further into the darkness.

broadcast:	31 JANUARY 2010	director:	KENNY GLENAAN
writer:	JAMIE MATHESON	producer:	MATTHEW BOUCH

cast:

Annie	LENORA CRICHLOW	Sykes	BRYAN DICK
Mitchell	AIDAN TURNER	Technician	MARK FLEISCHMANN
George	RUSSELL TOVEY	Sam	LUCY GASKELL
Nina	SINEAD KEENAN	Campbell	ALEX WARREN
Kemp	DONALD SUMPTER	Ross	VINCENT FRANKLIN
Lucy	LYNDSEY MARSHAL	Welder	DALE MEEKS
Ivan	PAUL RHYS	Pablo	FEDERICO ZANNI

"... a gene that could be the cause of all evil"

We go back a year and Professor Lucy Jaggat is working in a DNA laboratory, testing for disputed parenthood. Kemp arrives and initially she thinks he is there to work, but he quickly corrects her. His interest is in some scientific papers she published, papers that postulated that a single gene could be the source of all evil. Lucy looks uncomfortable, she is reluctant to discuss her theories and it sounds as if she has been thoroughly ridiculed by her colleagues. She suspects that Kemp may well be, well, another nutter.

He has to convince her that he means business. He reminds her of a blood sample she received that made no sense, even after repeated testing. He reminds her that she would have blamed the machines. She remembers it and wants to know more – what was it?

"Evil" is all he will say and he leaves her with his business card, she should call him when she wants to know more. She's intrigued but wary, looking around to see if anyone might have overheard. After all, this is science that most people would dismiss as fantasy.

"They told me to wait for you"

Annie is looking for new occupations, it must be very boring being invisible. This morning she's out with the postman, seeing what people have delivered, until she is distracted by a police car pulling up across the road. They are checking a dead body in the alleyway, it looks like an overdose. Annie can't resist having a look and finds the ghost of the body standing in the alley. She goes to ask if he is all right and takes his hands. It's a trick and he tries to pull her through the door that has appeared from nowhere. He was waiting for her, *they* told him that's what he had to do. He pulls her towards the door while she fights him. There's a confusion of voices and a glimpse of a strange man watching her struggle.

"You put the thing on a list, you do the thing and then you tick it off"

Mitchell wants to check that George is OK. Maybe he's feeling a little guilty about his former dismissal of his friend's problems. Despite Mitchell's concern, George has a whole new lease of life – it is all fine, he has had a revelation. He is making a list. Lists create order and order is what George wants to achieve.

Mitchell is dubious. From the look on his face, I doubt he's been sitting in the funeral parlour drawing up a neat 'to do' list of his own. He obviously doesn't believe that it is this simple for George to move on. Mitchell thinks that George's list is just as sensible a way forward as George thinks about Mitchell's 'drying out the vampires' plan!

Annie is helped up by the stranger. He is happy to confirm that she is safe, he closed the door – and yes, he's dead too. He introduces himself as Sykes, he's an older ghost than Annie and he's wearing a WW2 RAF uniform. He says "cheerio" and is keen to be away. After all, just because they are both ghosts they don't have to become instant bosom buddies. Annie doesn't want to let him go. He closed the door and she wants to know how to do that for herself.

She is determined not to let him get away. She follows him, threatening to haunt him and finally Sykes relents. He isn't promising to teach her about doors – that's complicated – but he might be able to show her how to read auras.

Mitchell and George are still discussing George's new list and the ramifications of his plans. He's been thinking about the werewolf, he earnestly lectures Mitchell, who is looking a little startled. This is likely to be due to hearing the word "exactamondo" used in normal conversation, but George presses on regardless. The wolf is just a big scary animal and he's going to put it in a cage. And buying a cage is on his list. After all, one night a month is all the wolf takes out of his life and this shouldn't stop him living normally, getting a decent job. All the things that the others have been telling him, he's finally worked out for himself.

At this point George's list is up to number six:

1. Buy a cage
2. Get a better job
3. Soundproof room
4. Eat a better diet
5. Get fit
6. Polish shoes

"Well, that's addicts for you. Always looking for little loopholes"

At the funeral parlour, the vampires have come up with a great new idea, and you have to admit it is quite ingenious. They have found a girl on an emo website. The theory is that she actually wants to be fed from – although the reality may not be quite what these young Goths have fantasised about. She's pretty keen, dressed in designer frills and fishnets, with a perfected pout and happy to offer her neck. Mitchell is despairing, no blood means no blood. How can he make himself any clearer? He wants her out and she goes; apart from getting her bus fare home, she didn't get anything else out of her day. Ivan watches the exchange and is amused, there's always a way around the rules. He remembers an alcoholic he knew who stayed dry and went conscientiously to meetings. He convinced himself that Advocaat didn't really count and died of cholesterol poisoning. Something that Ivan says makes Mitchell stop. You can see him thinking. He has had an idea.

George is ordering his cage, list in hand. He's trying to explain what he wants without actually explaining what he wants, but the welder soon realises. It's a sex cage; he gets loads of business from the S&M community and he knows exactly what George needs. He even throws in a free pair of handcuffs!

Next is soundproofing and yet again George is horrified to realise that the assumption is that it is all about sex. Lots of business in dungeons by all accounts and he wonders if there is anyone left who has normal sex!

Sykes is at the house – Annie persuaded him to come back with her – and he is now being quizzed by Mitchell. He's suspicious about his sudden arrival, but Annie is sure Sykes is OK; after all, he did save her from another door. Mitchell's overprotectiveness is perhaps another sign that he knows he has been neglecting his friends. George starts on Sykes as well; surely he is morally obliged to help Annie if he can? Sykes tries to explain his reluctance. If Annie doesn't get what he teaches her she will be lost, the men behind the door will get her and he doesn't want her on his conscience. Annie knows that if he doesn't teach her she stands no chance anyway, so why not? It's a fair argument and he concedes defeat.

"0900 tomorrow. That's if it's OK with your two dads"

Mitchell is still glowering, but George, in his role as house mother, cheerfully says "Well, I liked him." He also wants to ask Annie if they can swap rooms. He can't fit the cage into his room. She really can't see where this has suddenly come from – he is still obsessed with his list and his whole new life and she is worried about him. As Mitchell commented, "Hyper. Fixed grin." It's not altogether a good sign.

Back at the funeral parlour, Mitchell has put his new plan into action. Standing in the middle of a small group, Campbell announces "I am a blood addict." After Ivan's comments about AA, Mitchell has started a support group to keep the vampires clean. Ivan is absolutely horrified, and he's unhappy that Mitchell got the idea from him. What on earth is he trying to achieve?

Mitchell is sitting in his chair behind the desk – or should that be on his throne? The ornate carvings give him an air of power and command that he is starting to relish. He wants Ivan to sign up for the programme. He has almost mythological status among the vampires, he's one of the "old ones" and he would make the programme valid, give it kudos. It would give the others hope that they could stay off blood if Ivan can.

What's in it for Ivan? Why should he bother? But Mitchell reminds him of what is going to happen as the vampires dry out. They will be in pain, their memories will torment them, and their suffering will be exquisite. It may seem that he is going to ask Ivan to help, but it's clear that he is in fact tempting him with that pain, pain and torment that he can watch and savour, and Ivan licks his lips in anticipation of this heady pleasure.

"Each moment, a stab of pure undiluted sensation"

George has an interview at a language school – that was number two on the list. The Principal is bothered; he can't imagine why George would want to work there, not with his CV. For once, George has thought about this in advance and he has a story ready to explain his years as a hospital porter. He also meets Sam and they make some awkward conversation about children – she has a seven-year-old called Molly. It's awkward by most people's standards, but pretty successful by George's. He doesn't spill anything, break anything or set fire to himself! Well done.

Sykes is starting Annie's lessons. The men behind the doors use agents to get at those who are still in this world – usually someone who is weak or vulnerable, and that is what she can tell from their auras. Annie is trying, but she can't do 'magic eye' pictures either. She's impatient but finally manages to see something. It is also a lesson that what she sees isn't always going to be pleasant. She wants to read Sykes's aura but he recoils, absolutely not, and Annie wonders just what might be there that he is so keen to keep hidden.

"That's not so much a conversation, more like a job application"

Mitchell has a whole new approach to Lucy, inspired by his vampire AA group. He makes her an offer: twenty questions that he will answer completely truthfully, to finally bury his deep dark secrets image. Knowing what we now know about Lucy – Lucy Jaggat – this is not so much a remarkable offer as a stunningly dangerous one. When asked where he was when he told her he 'had a thing', he tells her he was at an AA meeting, but she challenges this, she's seen him drinking. OK, he concedes, it wasn't alcohol that was his addiction, but he's clean and has been so for a while. Lucy regroups – how to deal with this one – and shows that she is familiar with the rehabilitation programme, but lets Mitchell know he still has to make amends. They are both pleased with their progress although in very different ways.

George finally gets a look at Lucy and points out the utterly bleedin' obvious that no one else has said. She's way out of Mitchell's league – what on earth is a doctor doing with a cleaner?

George got the job at the Language School and as he and Mitchell look at his official letter they run the bed they are transporting into the wall. Luckily the patient is doped up to his eyeballs with tranquillisers – enough to knock out a horse. As George says this, he realises this could be a refinement to his plan that will need to be added to the list.

Mitchell manages to get his hands on some tranquillisers for George, although he can't guarantee that they will put the wolf to sleep. Strangely, the right dosage for werewolves isn't listed. George's list now has two new items:

7. Get tranquillisers
8. Knock out the wolf

As with most people's lists, George has crossed off most items but "Get fit" and "Eat a better diet" are destined to remain there forever!

"It's eight hours of a sleeping werewolf"

George is preparing to transform, but before he locks himself in his cage he sets up a camera. He takes the tranquillisers and as the agony begins he passes out.

Nina is in the compression chamber at Kemp's facility, wearing a gown, monitored and nervous. As the pressure rises, her head hurts and her nose bleeds. Professor Jaggat tries to reassure her but she is unsure. If the settings are the same as last time, then is Nina going to die? For a moment it looks like compassion, but she wants Nina alive as bait. They can use her to lure George to them. As Nina convulses in agony, Lucy demands they lower the pressure and she is allowed to transform. Lucy informs Kemp that they have learnt something – the wolf still arrives even when the human in unconscious. Kemp is not impressed. He was quite clearly prepared to watch Nina die.

George wants to show Annie and Mitchell something beautiful. He plays them his DVD showing the werewolf sleeping through the night. They watch it avidly and they are so pleased for him. He is free, he has put the wolf to sleep and none of them can see how this isn't the very best thing for George.

"I am going to teach you about swearing"

It's George's first day as a teacher of English and he is very neatly turned out – we know his shoes are shined as it was crossed off on his list! His students though are not keen on sticking to the lesson plan. They want to know about the 'F' word. It's not a new-boy tease and George considers the request and realises that it is a valid part of language, so he takes a small part of the lesson to deal with swearing. What could possibly go wrong?

Sykes is explaining how the men come through the TV. Annie will know when they are there as there is a distinctive low hum. She needs to learn to switch the TV off without touching the set. She manages it once but they get slightly distracted by Sykes stopping her so that he can watch the weather girl! While Annie tries to tell him about *Sex in the City*, they hear the hum and the weather girl starts to beckon. Annie switches it off successfully, but that is enough for one day.

George is running through the meaning of the abbreviation 'STFU' for his students and they are happily repeating the phrase together as the Principal comes in. He is not happy, not at all, how dare George, a mere hospital porter, defy him? He takes George into the corridor and thoroughly patronises him. He makes George repeat apologies verbatim back to him, leaving him annoyed and frustrated – but he needs this job.

"The thought of life without it seemed absurd; it's futile to even try"

It's the next Vampires Anonymous meeting and Ivan gets up to speak. His eloquent speech about the hunger for blood and his desire to try to be free of it is inspiring to the younger vampires, in awe of his 195 years of blood drinking.

George is taking Sam out for lunch, and for him lunch is a whole roast chicken which he tackles with his hands. Nothing wrong with that – he's hungry. Sam is convinced he'll be gone in six months, but he convinces her that he had a dangerous and hair-raising life and so the boredom of his job is welcome. They joke – she suggests he's a spy; he was going for superhero, with excessive hairiness as his special power. They laugh together but George realises his hand is shaking; something is not right. Another indicator – standing at the urinals, he compulsively shouts "cocks" at the top of his voice. Unfortunately he is not alone and gets a very odd look. Something is going on.

What is happening to George?

Sykes has a test for Annie, with George's help. She is going to see if she can taste. She puts her hands on George's head and as he eats she tries to feel what he tastes. She manages to identify the cold, bright lemon of lemon sorbet and it is thrilling for her to realise she can do this. When George bites into a rib with obvious enjoyment, Annie knows he is eating meat and lots of it, but, as he bites again, she feels and sees the werewolf and recoils, scared and shocked. That is enough – she really can't take any more, but she can't tell them what happened. She doesn't want George to know he scared her so much. They call a halt to the test and George bellows at them, furious about the waste of food and all his efforts. More out-of-character behaviour. Maybe Annie would have taken more notice if she wasn't distracted by the werewolf and Sykes or her first taste of food since she died.

The next VA meeting goes well and more of them are signing up. It's all down to Ivan; they want to follow his example. Ivan likes the adulation and adoration. It's rather like being in a boy band, an image Mitchell feels is somewhat disturbing, giving him a whole new understanding of Take That... Ivan elaborates: it's all about image, what people see. It has nothing to do with reality; it's just smoke and mirrors. He's leading up to a confession. He can't do it. He reassures Mitchell that he will go to meetings, he will encourage and support, he'll do everything that he promised, but after 195 years he cannot give up blood. Mitchell is upset, why can't Ivan do it, why is it so hard? He has to accept his decision as there are too many people who are only following the programme because of Ivan. Yet another lie to undermine Mitchell's reign.

Sam is re-entering George's details on her computer. She checks that Mitchell is just a housemate and goes to get a file from behind George's head. Misinterpreting, he goes in for a kiss – a bold move for George – but she backs away. She confesses that she did actually put that file there on purpose and his details weren't so much lost as deleted. (Although who trusts a grown woman with a menagerie of soft toys on her desk?) Despite the cuddly audience, they kiss.

That night, George is watching the sleeping werewolf film again – is it really this simple? Is this the start of his normal life? Or is it that has he never seen the wolf before and this is the first chance he has ever had to get acquainted with his alter ego. The wolf has always been a stranger and a mystery to him.

"Fuck! Balls! Shit! Shit! Shit! Shit! Shit! Fuck! Shit! Shit! Parking Ticket. Shit! P-P-Piss off!"

George is meeting Sam again when the overwhelming compulsion to ejaculate crude words becomes too much. He manages to hide from her but he can't stop and he is getting scared. He tries to explain it to Mitchell and Annie and they can't help but find it seriously funny. He had an attack in class and his students faithfully repeated every single word back to him, "effing and jeffing." Mitchell can't resist teasing George and is shocked when he explodes into violence. It is only Mitchell's vampire speed and strength that stop George knocking him through the window. Now they know it's serious, they have never seen George like this.

They sit on the floor together – the usual place for anguish and troubled souls – and George tries to analyse what is happening to him. He thought he could make the wolf sleep, thought it would go away, but it refuses to be caged. It is punishing him for not letting it have its rage, its one night of freedom a month. The wolf needs to have that rage. George can't be comforted – the wolf is not going to let him rest until it has had its turn.

George is scared that he is going to hurt someone. Annie tries to reassure him but George cannot be consoled. Considering how the essential nature of the werewolf cannot be caged, is Mitchell wondering about himself, about the vampires? Can he really cage the blood lust? After all, Carl managed to stay clean for many years until the craving overwhelmed him.

"You know, Mitchell, eventually it just makes children of us all"

Mitchell's confidence in his plan is further shaken when he meets Ivan. Ivan tries to make a joke but Mitchell is not in a mood to be amused. He thinks Ivan has been messing him around, he never really thought he could give up. Ivan admits that he did think he could do it, that he was strong enough, powerful enough, but he was wrong, he was arrogant. Another warning bell for Mitchell – how strong does he think he is?

He lets Ivan into a locked room. In it, gagged and chained to the wall, is the emo-girl, who must still have her bus fare in her stocking top. She is terrified by the sight of Ivan. Is he the first or have others been there before him?

To Ivan, like Wilson, the end justifies the means – with his support, more vampires are not drinking. There could be something more disturbing though. "How many do you have now?" he asks Mitchell. He could well mean how many dry vampires, but are there other innocents locked in the cellars? – it's Herrick's human farm all over again. Mitchell is resigned – he doesn't like it but yet again he feels he has no choice.

"I'm a fucking hero. Enjoy your meal"

Sykes knows that Annie is strong enough to be tested. Back at the house – close to where she died – they turn on all the radios and the TV, creating a deafening confusion of noise. And then they wait, Sykes standing at ease, watchful but ready. The noise dies out, leaving the hum we recognise, and there's a thumping and Annie sees her own body fall to the hallway floor and lie, dead, in a spreading pool of blood. A door appears – the same door that came for Annie in series one, right down to the sign. It swings open, letting a bright white light spill through. The body speaks to Annie in her own voice, trying to make her despair, but now Annie resists its lures. Now she has the answers, she knows Owen didn't love her – so what? Going on another tack, the body pulls in Sykes, telling Annie he was a coward and men died because of him. He cowers at the sound of gunfire and planes and it is Annie's strength that pulls him back, calms him.

Annie realises how far she has come, and her determination is clear. She challenges the image of her own death; she knows it is a mask, a trick and the voice changes, becoming deeper and more resonant. She is sure now that they can't do anything to her. They are keeping her scared because they know that is all that they are capable of.

She walks to the door and puts her hands on it. She slams it shut. The image of her body is gone and the door disappears. She's done it.

"You've lost your audience"

Lucy and Kemp are in front of a huge board covered in pictures and cuttings. They have photos of George and Nina, and of Annie and Mitchell when they were alive, Mitchell in his WW1 uniform. There are photos of the house, inside and out, drawings of Herrick and even pictures of Cara and Lauren. There are newspaper cuttings of the attack on George and Annie's tragic death. This is extensive and detailed research, not some tinpot fantasy land. Lucy is fascinated by the idea of a clean vampire sect – a nest – led by one who is clean. Kemp is less accepting and certainly less curious. He tells her of the reopening of the funeral parlour and how convenient it has been for twenty-seven years, a discrete way to dispose of the bodies. He thinks Lucy is distracted and maybe she is, maybe she can see past Mitchell's tortuous conversations with her. Kemp is stern, he cannot forget that vampires are pure unredeemable evil and he doesn't want Lucy to get sidetracked from their aim of finding a way to free the soul trapped by the werewolf. Lucy, however, is definitely taken with Mitchell, although she is still covering up that fancy with scientific curiosity.

"He is capable of change. And I will prove it"

George's werewolf Tourette's is not easing up. In fact it is getting worse and is now completely out of his control. He overhears the School Principal with Sam. He is joking with her, heavy on the innuendo, sleaze personified, and George has to leave before he erupts, smashing his hand into the blackboard in his classroom. Sam comes after him and tells him she doesn't mind his swearing, she knows it isn't really George. He is the nicest person she knows – maybe she doesn't get out much – and she finds it quite amusing, leaving George with a kiss.

Washing the blood off his hand in the toilets, George despairs at the standard of grammar in the graffiti, has nothing he has said in his lessons sunk in? "Mr Sands suck cocks" is emblazoned across the mirror. Horrified, George finds a marker pen and corrects it, it's "Mr Sands *sucks* cocks." Of course this is the perfect moment for his boss to walk in.

He looks very pleased to have caught George out. Again. He is so condescending and patronising and George just grits his teeth and takes it. He apologises, as instructed, but it still isn't enough. Now we find out what he has really done wrong: Sam likes him and how dare he have designs on her, on the Principal's own property.

George can feel the wolf's violence getting close; he wanted to walk away and he wasn't allowed to and now it is too late. He viciously beats the Principal, leaving him whimpering on the floor. George threatens to kill him if he tells anyone what he has done. It's a cold and nasty attack and thoroughly alien to George.

"But you… You were something different"

Annie can't understand why she is still invisible; surely closing the door herself should have changed something. Sykes can't really explain it either;

Annie is something else, and something that isn't in the natural, or supernatural, order. For most the door comes sooner, there's an implication that old ghosts are rare. Sykes is still here because he can't bear the thought of what is through his door. He made the wrong choice in the heat of battle and men died. They died because of him and he has spent seventy years with the guilt. He knows he's a coward, however much Annie disagrees.

At least she is safe for the moment, she has vanquished the Gatekeepers. The door is now a matter of choice, when she is ready. Annie can't see that ever happening, but Sykes cautions her. She'll never change and she can only watch, seeing people live the lives she can't have and that cannot be borne forever. Maybe one day she will need to go.

However, Sykes leaves her with a mystery. She'll move onto another new adventure, but he won't even give her a clue. Does he know what is in store or does he just assume that Annie, being something new, is not destined for quiet haunting. A crisp salute and he is gone, leaving Annie stronger, resolute, but also somehow sadder.

Mitchell watches Ivan at the support group – shaking hands, hugging and kissing the vampires. Encouraging and praising. Only the two of them know it is a lie. How much longer can Mitchell hide it? His doubts are written all over his face, inscrutability is not one of his strengths.

The moon is up. It's only a quarter moon and a long time until George's next transformation, when he can let the wolf out to rage and free himself from its malign influence. Scared at what he has become and at the failure of his plans, he lies curled in a foetal position in his cage, sobbing as his heart breaks. His list shredded, his dreams ended.

"Dismissed"

Musings on episode four...

It's all about George. We follow him on a rollercoaster journey from excited optimism to the deepest despair. It's a tribute to Russell Tovey's acting that we are with him every step of the way and, even on a second watch, are really hoping that this time it will all work out. The beating of the Principal is savage, cold and calculating and totally over the top, and for George to retain our sympathy despite that is an achievement. Of course it helps that Ross was a malicious, condescending sleazebag, but then no one's perfect.

George may be convinced that he has the solution, but his manic push to get on with his life is less getting over Nina and moving on as following her instructions to the letter. It seems too obvious that the wolf could be shut away or doped, but it can't possibly be that easy. Working through the list is classic George – the sex cage and the dungeon comments really bother him, and even when Sykes suggests "better they think you're a nonce than a werewolf," he still isn't convinced!

The wolf is denied its one night of freedom and it will have its revenge. George's werewolf Tourette's is inspired and what starts as hugely funny random inappropriate swearing becomes desperately sad and harder to watch. The portrayal of another identity leaking through George's normal behaviour is very clever. George has to realise that the bedrock of his beliefs about his condition is wrong. The wolf is with him all day, every day and it is only that one night of rage that keeps it quiet. He is a werewolf – always. Such a devastating revelation for a man on the verge of a new life, a new relationship and more than likely a new list. Will he persevere – can he get the wolf back in its cage by not caging it at all? His utter heart-rending devastation at the end of the episode leaves that open – what next for poor George?

While George has tranquillised his wolf, Nina also transforms while unconscious but for a very different reason. She's in the tank at the Facility. Kemp would happily watch her explode (if Kemp is ever happy) and it is only Lucy that stops him. It's not sympathy – she wants George, and Nina is the way in.

As Nina was unconscious when she transformed, did she also have wolf-Tourette's and anger issues for the rest of the month? Her wolf had no chance to rage either. Or did the genuine near-death experience act differently to George's forced unconsciousness via drugs?

What to do with Annie? She's sorted out Hugh, so she's left with not much to amuse her except following the postman until she meets a new friend. The enigmatic Sykes is another ghost with lessons to learn and teach. Gilbert showed Annie resolution and a happy, peaceful passing; what can Sykes give her? He's not keen to have anything to do with her at all – he thinks she'll be through the door whatever, but he comes to see she is stronger than she seems. Like Gilbert, he falls under Annie's sunny spell, and Mitchell and George are right back in their 'two dads' role.

There is a feeling that this is the next logical step for Annie – she learns to read auras and close doors, and gets a bit of a life-lesson (death-lesson?) from Sykes. She may want to pass on one day, he warns her – she is trapped, she'll always be just as she is now and can never have love and children, only watch others. It's a warning, and something for Annie to consider.

Annie passes the test and she shuts the door. Sykes can leave her, safe in the knowledge that the men behind the door are vanquished – for the moment, at least. A snappy salute and he's away, but unlike Gilbert, Sykes hasn't passed over. Maybe we will see him again, there is much more to learn from and about him. Did he just make a genuine mistake in the bedlam of war or did he misjudge and cause people to die? Did he die with them or sacrifice himself in horror or survive in guilt for a while? So many questions!

In an interesting parallel, both Mitchell and Sykes are war casualties. Sykes made the wrong decisions and his men died. Even though he died too he still feels guilty, and has done for seventy years. Mitchell also had to make a decision in the heat of battle, but his men survived at the cost of Mitchell's humanity. Does he feel guilty? Actually, I don't think he does, he may have regretted what he became but never the reason why. Two different wars; two different outcomes – but two very different men? They both care for Annie and there is a touch of the dog in the manger about Mitchell's 'welcome' of Sykes.

It was left to George to say what I had been screaming at the TV since episode one – what is Lucy doing with Mitchell?! Yes, of course he's quite decorative, but she only ever hears him talk drivel and anyway, he's a cleaner. However egalitarian Lucy is, cleaners and doctors are not a natural pairing. Now she has been unveiled as Professor Jaggat, we know exactly what she sees in Mitchell. He's a curiosity, a contradiction, evil personified but a dry vampire – not to mention a bit of a challenge. Sad stereotyping but yes, some of us do always go for the bad boys...

In revealing Lucy as Professor Jaggat at the end of the previous episode, the implication was that she's the 'big bad', but this episode shuffles that around. Kemp approached her in the flashback and it's still unclear who is really in charge. She keeps Nina alive – compassion or cunning? – and we still can't tell just what she has in store for Mitchell – steak or stake? The genetics of evil? Yeah, right.

For comic relief this week we have Vampires Anonymous, the twelve-neck programme, insert your own joke here! Mitchell is convinced this is the way forward, but it is pretty bonkers. I'm rather enjoying the idea of Ivan in a boy band though, just not entirely sure about what he's up to with the swans... No Daisy this week. Ivan and Daisy are such a great pairing it seems a shame to only see them separately – is she avoiding the support group? I can't see Daisy dry any more than Ivan.

However, the most memorable moment for me is when Mitchell and Annie are teasing George about teaching his students to swear, laughing as they always do at George's little foibles. George's explosion into violence and Mitchell's equal swiftness in stopping his fist makes a striking scene that says a lot about both of them.

Bum notes...

We've seen Mitchell smelling out vampires who have fed – he did it to Cara and to Lauren. Can all vampires do this or only when they get to a certain age? I suspect it's a special skill otherwise Ivan would soon be unmasked as having lapsed by the support group – all those hugs!

A quibble only – if I were Annie and had learnt to read auras I'd be hard pressed to resist reading everyone I went near!

Oh, and the mysterious blood sample that Lucy had in her lab? Tell us more...!

... and the bottom line

Sightings of Russell Tovey's bare backside – two, but the final shots felt so intrusive into George's grief... (back to gratuitous listing next time).

He said, she said...

No, this isn't the other side. Yes, I did save you from the door. And yes, I'm dead too.

••••••

There must be some other reason for chatting you up, like access to drugs.

She's a doctor! She can steal her own drugs.

Ah, so she's on drugs. That makes perfect sense.

······

This can't be happening to me! This can't, I teach language!
You could teach bad language.

Where have I seen... Vincent Franklin (Ross)?

Vincent Franklin has appeared in a wide range of TV shows including playing Stewart Pearson in *The Thick of It* (in 2007-9). He has also appeared as Chris Parsons in *Doc Martin* (in 2004 and 2009), Barry in *Lead Balloon* (in 2007), Rawdon Hull in *Five Days* (2007) and Rowan in an episode of *The Office* (in 2001).

Film roles include Dr Bree in *British Star* (2009), Loschek in *The Illusionist* (2006), Mr Lewis in *Vera Drake* (2004), Rawlins in *The Bourne Identity* (2002) and George Lusk in *From Hell* (2001).

In 2006 he played Archie in *Confetti* alongside Jason Watkins (Herrick) as his partner Gregory. They are the fluffily camp but rather caring wedding planners who assist three couples in their quest to win the title of most original wedding of the year...

Music in episode four

The Pretty Things	*Rosalyn*
George Thorogood and the Destroyers	*Bad to the Bone*

episode five

Annie babysits a ghost baby and wonders what life she might have had.

Mitchell starts to think that Lucy could be the woman who could save him.

Does history repeat itself? We meet Josie again and see the dark-hearted Mitchell of the past.

George and Sam's relationship races ahead of itself.

broadcast:	7 FEBRUARY 2010	director:	KENNY GLENAAN
writer:	TONY BASGALLOP	producer:	MATTHEW BOUCH

cast:

Annie	LENORA CRICHLOW	Douglas	JOHN PAUL HURLEY
Mitchell	AIDAN TURNER	Sam	LUCY GASKELL
George	RUSSELL TOVEY	Campbell	ALEX WARREN
Kemp	DONALD SUMPTER	Kathleen	SARA PASCOE
Lucy	LYNDSEY MARSHAL	Molly	MOLLY JONES
Wilson	IAN PULESTON-DAVIES	Policeman	GLYN GRIMSTEAD
Josie	CHARLENE MCKENNA		

"I sort of killed his Mum"

Mitchell wakes, dazed and bloodstained – and unusually bouffant of hair. He tumbles off the bed to find a dead girl beside him on the floor and another in the hall. The caption tells us we're in London, in 1969. So that explains the hair – and the pants – and the wonderful Velvet Underground on the soundtrack!

Herrick is there too, looking rather chipper (and also with remarkable amounts of hair), but he's fully dressed and off to find the car, which is possibly parked on a bridge... Mitchell is left with the cleaning up – in Bristol they have 'people' who deal with these messes for them, but in London? Herrick has fallen out with the London vampires – he's quite proud that he killed their leader's mother. Mitchell is left to do what he can with the chaos, blood and bodies, and a drop of Fairy Liquid. I bet he wishes he had his Marigolds.

Compared with Herrick's good humour, Mitchell seems dazed and, knowing what we know of his future, regretful. Is this the start of his turning against the blood? Or maybe just a hangover.

Washed and dressed, he clears away the remains of the party and wipes up the blood – his cleaning skills were obviously honed later at the hospital. The flat is tidy and vacuumed, the bodies are wrapped up and in the hall ready for disposal and he's done. In a rather dapper black suit and skinny tie he heads out to meet Herrick, swiping a bottle of milk on his way out of the flats. Unfortunately the police are already there and are knocking at the door of the ground floor flat, so he has to retreat. A young woman unwisely opens her door and Mitchell pushes her back in, hand over her mouth.

Although she's scared, she's not *that* scared and is quite capable of sarcasm when Mitchell is looking for another way out. Under the circumstances, it's not surprising that he has completely lost his sense of humour. She lies to the police when they come to her door – she has seen nothing odd – but they tell her there has been a murder. She knows that Mitchell is a killer.

"It's the library books, isn't it?"

Back in the present and Mitchell has another rude awakening. This time there are flashing blue lights and the police hammering on the door. George sleepily goes down to open the door in his jimjams (yes, I know, why does he have a door in his jimjams) and two policemen force their way in. They run up the stairs, straight through Annie, and into Mitchell's room. He is – understandably – a little concerned; what have they found out? OK – his Jilly Coopers are overdue but he'll pay the fine. He's bundled into a car and driven away, leaving George and Annie worried.

"What's he done?" "How far back do you want to go?"

At the police station, Mitchell is manhandled out of the car and down to the cells. No niceties of charging and booking him in, it's as if they have been told that he doesn't deserve to be treated as human. Still handcuffed and dishevelled, he's faced with Chief Constable Wilson, immaculately and formally uniformed. He tells Mitchell about the man in the cell – he's a paedophile but they can't keep him in prison; he's dangerous and Wilson wants Mitchell to kill him. Problem solved.

He thought Mitchell would be pleased, he thinks he's giving him a rare treat – a captive that he can kill with complete impunity. It will give him a hold over Mitchell as well as being a way of dealing with all those nasty little monsters that the courts never seem to understand. Mitchell tells him he is clean, that none of them kill anymore and Wilson is just as disbelieving as everyone else. He even finds it funny. How could a nest of ruthless killers choose abstinent Mitchell as their leader? That's democracy for you. Mitchell walks away (hopefully someone unlocks his handcuffs at some point), leaving Wilson considering his next move.

Back at the house, George is seeking Annie's advice on impressing Sam's daughter, Molly – he has a choice of magazines for her. Annie hadn't realised that Sam had a child and wonders how George feels about it. It's fine of course, although he is rather defensive. He knows things are moving fast, probably too fast, but he wants his life to change. He is well aware of Annie and Mitchell's concerns. He himself is concerned about Mitchell having been carted off to the cells in the middle of the night, but Mitchell brushes it off. They just had the wrong person, nothing to worry about. He too is concerned about George, who he thinks still loves Nina, and is scathing about Sam being a single mother. The implication that she must be desperate really gets to George and he flounces out. He is determined to prove them wrong.

Excitement for Annie when she gets a letter! Of course it's junk mail; she's been dead for over a year and she is still getting circulars.

"I might be dead, but I'm still on the database"

George is looking for Sam in the large block of flats where she lives with her daughter Molly. Molly very sensibly opens the door on the chain – security conscious and all the better for insulting Mum's new boyfriend. For a seven-year-old she has a great line in insults and her commenting on George's dog-breath does make us wonder if there is more to this little girl than meets the eye. The magazines are not a great success and George continues his initial good impression by assuming that Sam's mum is the cleaner. She looks him up and down and her verdict is clear. Sam has found herself another loser.

Molly continues to undermine George and he cooperates rather nicely. He can't sit down as that's where her dad sits and he can't lean on the counter as that is the cat's space. At her suggestion, he sits on the bin. Oh George, you do know your place!

"You're a ghost. And this is a very small ghost!"

Annie is being shouted at through the letterbox. Used to being invisible again, it takes a moment for her to realise that this person can actually see her. Opening the door, she finds Kathleen and her baby. She professes to be thrilled to meet Annie, she's famous and Sykes has been telling everyone all about her. Annie realises that they are ghosts, they are waiting to pass over, but Kathleen has a ghostly social life that never seems to have found Annie and she is there with her own agenda. She wants Annie to look after the baby – she's got a date with a dead fireman. Annie is very unsure, worried that she'll drop him, but Kathleen reassures her. The baby is already dead, what harm can she do? She turns down the thermostat (ghost babies need to be cold) and she's off. She's less bothered about the famous or infamous Annie than in finding a new and gullible childminder!

At the funeral parlour, Mitchell is going through old paperwork. He tells Campbell he's just familiarising himself with the business, but is he trying to find out what Herrick had been up to, what deals he had made? It's a nice touch to see Herrick's police uniform hanging up at the end of the row of filing cabinets. No doubt it'll come in useful one day. Campbell is concerned and wants to talk to Mitchell. He has started to dream about his ex. He killed her when he wanted to recruit her but he didn't know how and she just died. Now he is off blood, the memories are coming back in detail and are starting to really hurt. Mitchell reassures him that it's normal, it happened to him too and he just has to bear it for a while and it will go away. Trouble is, Mitchell's tortured look is not entirely convincing.

"Tomorrow I won't even remember what they looked like"

Back in 1969, Mitchell is still in the flat and after allowing the girl to use the bathroom he finds she has resourcefully written HELP on the window using lipstick. He ties her hands behind her to a bookcase, but he can't stop her talking to him, challenging him. She wants to know why he killed, what was the motive, but her questions are making him uncomfortable. He still tries to answer her though, tries to put his feelings into words. He is torn between bravado and shame; he just kills, he's killed "more than a hundred, less than a thousand," but he can't admit that he does it because he enjoys it. He looks at her family photos, she's an only child and so was he. There's a sense of some kind of connection being made. She should be terrified and he should have killed her, both are out of their assigned roles and this could go anywhere.

There are no rules anymore.

Back in the present, Mitchell is confirming his dinner date with Lucy; she's downloaded Nigella so this must be serious. He's more interested in seeing her than the food and they finally seem to have come to some sort of relationship, although Lucy still holds the whip hand. Especially when we see Kemp in the distance, listening to their conversation through an earpiece. Not the ideal eavesdropper when you are trying to chat up a vampire. He is scathing about the rituals, how they are dancing around each other and where it will inevitably end. Lucy is determined, this is not about sex, it is about the scientific study of evil, but Kemp has her sussed. She is underestimating the attraction of evil, of Mitchell, and he thinks she is already committed beyond science. She is firm with him: "When did assassinating vampires become part of the brief?" An interesting comment, we haven't heard either of them speak of killing vampires before. Kemp thinks they are lost, irredeemable and maybe this was always in his grand scheme. Or is Lucy thinking ahead, ready to rebuff what she thinks Kemp will want from her. Her doubts about Mitchell's essential evil remain; she still thinks he is different. Kemp is clearer, he knows he has a duty to eradicate evil. It's a promise to those lost before and his face speaks of a story that we have yet to hear.

"At least not as scared as I probably should be"

Mitchell's hostage is still challenging him about why he kills. She's not scared of him, even though he thinks she should be. But then she thinks she should be married to David Bowie and we don't always get what we want...

She can see that Mitchell is playing a role – she has no idea just what that role is yet – but by assuming a mantle he can avoid reality and remorse. She wants to tell him her name but he doesn't want to know. He still thinks he'll have to kill her and she is already a person to him, albeit an irritating one, and a name just makes her even more real. She is genuinely curious and wants him to explain; after all, she's not going anywhere. Eventually she goads Mitchell into furiously admitting he has no choice. She believes him. She believes he thinks he has no choice, but that really he doesn't want to do it, doesn't want to kill. It's too close to what Mitchell is coming to realise for himself and he can't listen anymore. He gags her – no more inconvenient truths.

George and Sam are dropping Molly at school – she favours George with a very hard and thoughtful stare but saves the insults, for the moment anyway. George is dismayed at just how badly he has handled meeting Molly, but actually he's done OK. She bit the last one. Sam tells George that she and Molly live with her mum, rather than her mum living with them – they can't afford a place of their own. She's a great catch – a poverty-stricken single mum – and she suggests that she look away while George escapes. He can't resist it and hides, but her face says she expected him to go and she is hugely relieved when he pops out from behind a tree. She may not be perfect, he tells Sam, but he is – well, far, far worse.

"What are babies usually called? Tim? Brian?"

George gets home to find Annie frantically trying to comfort the baby. A classic double take and he wants to know what is going on. Annie's misleading comment that it is 'one of hers' does make him wonder if he's been away a while or maybe ghost gestation is different. She can't get the baby to stop crying and dumps him on George – immediately the baby gurgles cheerfully, leaving Annie desperate to know how he did it. George seems quite content with the baby and Annie is just relieved to be relieved! Maybe she's different, she tells George when he says that he thought all women got broody. This was what he always wanted, what was on his 'to do' list – the old one, not the one with the cage – but it will never happen now. The wife and houseful of children – they are for other people, not people like them. A truth he says without thinking, that belies his desperate rush to try and have that family with Sam and Molly.

Annie looks as though she suddenly has to confront this children issue. Her relationship with Owen was all-encompassing, obsessive and controlled. Although she mentioned the nursery she planned, it didn't seem to be on Owen's list and so she suppressed her own desires and plans. Anything so as not to upset Owen.

Kemp is watching Lucy prepare a meal for Mitchell – a last supper. A quick diversion into the iniquity of the word 'tea', which is on a par with showbiz news to Kemp, and he gets to the point. He is worried about her and presses a gift on her. It's a stake – every girl's ideal present. It's very old and has saved many people and she takes it. He wants her to be careful. He can see the attraction between Lucy and Mitchell and he thinks it could lead to violence, but Lucy is convinced it makes Mitchell vulnerable. Kemp has deep concerns, but are they for Lucy's safety or is there something else?

Back in the 60s, Mitchell's hostage manages to get out of her bonds – Mitchell obviously didn't get his knots badge at Scouts. He's distracted, looking out for Herrick and she gets out of the front door before he realises she's gone. She's relieved to see a policeman on the stairs and drags him back to her flat, to Mitchell. Unfortunately for her it's Herrick in a stolen uniform, a small trickle of blood on the collar giving away how he got it. He's very pleased with himself, he could go anywhere dressed like that – seeds sown for the future. The girl tries again to get away but, unlike Mitchell, Herrick is not messing about. There's no existential discussion on the motives of guilt for him. He throws her down and even when criticising Mitchell's granny knots he is far more single-minded and frightening than Mitchell. She can have no doubt that this is a cold and remorseless killer showing none of the regrets that Mitchell has.

"I had someone like that. Someone who knew everything about me"

Mitchell gets his turn with the baby, doing his Athena poster impression in the kitchen. He thought about having kids way back when, but he doesn't look as though he feels he missed out. He's had a very long time to come to terms with his condition – a century compared to Annie and George's very few years. What about Annie? She jokes; being dead is not a great start to procreation, but being dead is forever and how does she feel about that forever being without children. She won't answer him and it is clearly something that is starting to bother her. She cheers them up, amusing the baby by doing George impressions, complete with ears, before gathering him up to go out and scare the ducks.

George and Mitchell are left to talk and Mitchell tells George he is having dinner with Lucy that night – finally some progress! His casual remark about patience gets George leaping in defensively. It wasn't what Mitchell meant at all, but OK, he and Sam are moving too fast, he needs to take his time, not rush in. There will be other women, maybe another Nina. But George 'cares for' Sam, not the greatest of romantic declarations, but he is content. He has no intention of telling Sam about the wolf, all relationships have secrets and it isn't natural to know everything about a person. They'll be fine. Mitchell disagrees. He once had a relationship that had no secrets at all – she knew every inch of his soul. But that was forty years ago...

Forty years ago, Mitchell is tying up his hostage again – this time more firmly. Now she is frightened, scared of Herrick and she asks Mitchell that, when it comes to it, will he kill her and not leave her to Herrick?

Would you like to try again?"

She makes a last try to get to him. She can tell he isn't like the immoral Herrick, that he really wants to stop killing but he just can't imagine how. He describes the urge as a monster that has to be fed, that if it isn't then there is horror and panic and the memories overwhelm him. Killing isn't an addiction but cowardice, the fear of what will be remembered. She can see he is hurting and she wants to make it stop, somehow she knows that this is the right time and she can help. She asks him if he wants to try and stop.

Herrick has a plan – he'll put Mitchell in handcuffs and take him out the front door. He is really enjoying the policeman's uniform. He wants to check that the girl has been dealt with and goes to do it himself but Mitchell stops him. It's sorted, she won't say anything. Herrick looks straight into Mitchell's eyes, he knows him too well, and he knows something has changed.

George is still trying to impress Molly. He's made her a packed lunch, crusts cut off and everything, and rushes to the school to give it to her. She calmly informs him that she has school dinners and heads into class. Sam is more impressed and lets slip that she already loves George – as well as cheese and pickle sandwiches!

Annie can't get the baby to settle, it doesn't appear that this is her forte. She tries bribery and stories, and – of course – it's the scary ghost stories that he enjoys the most.

Annie and Mitchell are playing happy families with the baby when George decides it's time for an announcement. He won't prevaricate or beat around the bush or put it off or ... just get on with it George! Eventually he blurts it out. He is going to ask Sam and Molly to move in with him. With them. They are momentarily speechless. Annie is concerned about sleeping arrangements; will Molly sleep in the cage? Although, she is prepared to give up her room; she and baby Tim can make do in the living room. By the way – she's adopting the baby. This is a family home, having a family here will be great for her ghost baby.

"If you guys want to play happy families then go for it, but not under my roof"

Mitchell thinks they have all gone completely mad – what are they thinking of? Sam is all wrong for George, they can't be in love after just two weeks, they just feel sorry for each other. He certainly isn't having them move into his house and neither is the baby staying. Both George and Annie walk out on him, leaving him frustrated that they won't listen to him. Mitchell has lived a long life and, although there are many areas of humanity he has never figured out, he can see that they are rushing into things. After a century of remaining unchanged, George's panic-stricken rush into commitment looks ridiculous to him and he knows that Annie hasn't had time to accept her state. His impatience that they are not like him is clear, but has he said too much this time and pushed them away for good? He at least has thought it through. If Sam and Molly move in, Annie may as well be gone – they won't be able to acknowledge her – and, after having had the house in which to live openly, Mitchell will have to hide what he is again. In his rush for normality, George is ignoring the basic fact that none of them, including him, are normal.

George is packing, the cage making a useful wardrobe. He wants Sam and the life they could have together with Molly, regardless of Mitchell's concerns. If he has to make a choice then he will choose Sam over his friend, even if it means losing Annie too. He goes, leaving his keys behind.

Kathleen arrives to retrieve her baby as Annie is serenading him with La Roux's *Bulletproof* – seems like ghost babies prefer songs a touch more grounded than *Rock-a-Bye Baby*! Annie isn't impressed, even though the date with the dead fireman went well. Very well, considering that Annie has had the baby for a day and a half. She's not keen to hand him back and there's a bit of ghost jumping, appearing and disappearing as she tries to keep him out of Kathleen's reach. Kathleen shows Annie a neat trick – she jumps the baby from Annie's arms to hers. Annie reckons she can do that too and ends up cuddling the toaster; apparently there has to be a family link. It should have been the kettle really. Anyway, Kathleen admits she's not mother-of-the-year material, but Rufus (yes, Rufus, not Tim or Brian) is hers and she's the best for him.

Annie knows she can't keep Rufus (especially now she knows he's called Rufus) and reluctantly hands him over. As Kathleen leaves, Annie can't help asking what it's really like to have a baby of her own. "Exhausting. Terrifying. Expensive." But, Kathleen concedes, it really is all worthwhile. Annie voices what she has come to realise:

"I've left it too late, haven't I?"

Kathleen tries to put it in perspective – after all, Annie wasn't to know, but she leaves Annie in reflective mood. Sitting in the hall, traditional place for their times of contemplation, she accepts that she will never have a baby, a family of her own. She wipes away a tear, exasperated with herself for minding so much.

George is at Sam's door, bag in hand, asking her to get a place with him, somewhere they can be together. With a bakery nearby, of course, a proper bakery. She tries to slow him down, admits they hardly know each other, but George can't or won't see any insurmountable impediment. He gives her a quick FAQ of his life – including his favourite colour, his impossible to guess password and exactly where he lost his virginity. How can she possibly resist? Sam looks very unsure about the unstoppable force that George has become and tries to make him realise it is not that simple. She needs to think, there is Molly to consider, but she doesn't say no and she invites him to stay.

198

"He should be home by now, watching Tracey Beaker with a box of tissues"

At the funeral parlour, Wilson is waiting for Mitchell. The paedophile he wanted Mitchell to kill is out on bail and he wants Mitchell to sort him out. Wilson is in charge of this deal and Mitchell is coming to realise that he is trapped and there is no way out for him. He seems continually at the mercy of power-crazed short men. He doesn't want to be Wilson's assassination squad but if he refuses then Wilson will step away. Eventually, inevitably, the vampires will kill and instead of a cover-up they'll be investigated, rounded up and every last one of them will burn. He will make sure that the world knows they are monsters and that he, Wilson, was the hero who stopped them. He gives Mitchell the address. What can he do? He wants to protect the vampires but can he do that and keep himself safe and clean?

In 1969, Herrick is waxing lyrical about Lewis Carroll, about the strange world he writes of. He sees it as symbolic of the vampires: they too have gone through the looking glass. Herrick believes that vampires are the only free men. They can do anything they want, let free their deepest, darkest desires and they have no time for details like mercy. People tell them they are monsters but they are just jealous, the only limit to a vampire is their own imagination.

Herrick sees that Mitchell is trying to break free of him and he needs to pull him back, rein him in. He asks Mitchell if he ever wondered why he chose him. It was nothing to do with saving his men – Herrick saw something in Mitchell. He saw potential. He's persuasive, almost hypnotic, and when he tells Mitchell to go and kill the girl, Mitchell goes.

"A great man. A terrible man. An orphan maker. A breaker of hearts"

Mitchell is in the paedophile's flat and it's hard to tell who looks the most apprehensive. The man assumes his past has caught up with him and that Mitchell is someone's dad. He's bracing himself for a beating and only asks that Mitchell calls an ambulance when he's done. He talks about fighting his urges, how he can't stop, how he wants to, how he needs help. It's uncomfortably close to what Mitchell feels about blood and he has to shut him up. But he won't kill him. He tells him to hand himself in, tell the police everything, make it up if he needs to but make sure he goes to prison. He'll be safer there that out here with Mitchell.

Back at the funeral parlour, Mitchell is angry with the position Wilson has put him in. Finding him passing the time with a quick BJ from Vicky the vampire behind a coffin does not put him in a better mood. Mitchell tells him again that they will not kill for him, he will not kill; things have changed. It's Wilson's last chance if only he knew it. Wilson has no belief or conviction that the vampires will stay dry, it's not natural and he wants his system back. He wants ruthless killers that run to his command; after all he has a little list. He wants to control Mitchell, patronise him and keep him obedient. Wilson can see the power MItchell could have if he were allowed to go his new, moral way and take the other vampires with him. That cannot be allowed to happen.

Mitchell walks to the door and Wilson relaxes, thinking he is going back to kill the man for him. Mitchell gets to the door, pauses and then locks it. He's made a choice, he knows what he has to do and he turns back to Wilson, eyes black.

In 1969, another choice is made and Mitchell goes back to the girl, still tied to her bed. He closes the door and looks at her, eyes black, face hard and cold and she screams.

Wilson lies dead or dying, pools of blood around him and the artery in his ruined neck still pumping the last of his blood out of his body. Mitchell is standing back from him – horrified, distraught but also somehow triumphant; will the blood always win? Then the horror takes him over and he leaves, running bloodstained though the streets as if all the demons in hell were on his heels.

He reaches Lucy's front door, hammering to get in. She opens the door and as he goes past her there is a look on her face that seems to say "now what?" Was she wrong about him – is Kemp right? What has he done and is this her opportunity to get him to talk, really talk. She's washing the blood off his face as he spins her a line about being attacked, but she stops him. He's devastated, distraught, but she pushes him – whatever it is, however bad, however unbelievable, he has to tell her the truth. So he does. He tells her he's a vampire.

Her reaction is not what he expects and he realises that she already knew. She should be scared, why isn't she scared of him? What she says next changes everything.

"At least, probably not as much as I should be"

It echoes something that he heard once before and his desperation is suddenly tinged with hope. Lucy thought he was safe, clean and abstaining and he tries to say that he still is, but covered in Wilson's blood it is not convincing. He can't hold back the desire for blood, it is part of him, deep in his bones and he needs her help. He has been clean before but he had someone to help him, someone he could change his life for and he wants to know if she can be that person. Lucy is concerned and getting worried. In his desperation and passion Mitchell is close to her, towering over her and she feels threatened, after all he is covered in blood. Her hand is on the stake which is close by with the other kitchen utensils, but as she listens to his words she is drawn into his need. His need for her as the one person who could make him different, make him good. How can Lucy possibly resist the chance to be his salvation, the one who can cure evil? Mitchell has been just as lonely as George and Annie have, but this is the first time we have ever seen the rawness of his solitude.

"Save me"

The 1969 Mitchell is putting flowers outside the flats where he and Herrick killed. As he turns to go, the girl he held hostage is walking towards him. He needs her; he can't help himself or live with how he is any longer. He finally asks her name and she takes his hand and tells him. It's Josie.

"Help me"

We see both Lucy and Josie with Mitchell – cutting backwards and forwards between the 60s and the present. Two similar women in two similar rooms with one immortal man. Is history repeating itself? Now we know this is Josie we remember how that story ended, with a great love and even greater sacrifice. But we already know too much about Lucy. Can she really break free from her beliefs and from Kemp to help Mitchell? There is passion in both encounters but there is a huge difference between "save me" and "help me".

Mitchell is sleeping in Lucy's bed but she is up, restless, and has the stake that Kemp gave her in her hands. She's not sure what to do. How can she tell if Mitchell can really change? Can she change him or is this just evil, pure and simple. She sits astride him holding the stake over his chest, her hands shaking – how can she know what might happen? Can she take the risk? She lifts the stake high ready to plunge it into his chest, to eradicate the devil that is a vampire, but she can't do it. Not after the confidences and the passion they have shared. She drops the stake and lies against him as he sleeps.

"Because I can't help myself"

Musings on episode five...

Does history inevitably repeat itself? If we were to live forever would we all go around in ever decreasing circles? How much can we learn before we forget it all and have to start again? This week we see some more of Mitchell's history and how much it repeats and repeats...

In the swinging 60s, Mitchell and Herrick are, well, swinging. And doing rather well for themselves if the blonde and bloodied bodies are anything to go by. But Mitchell has also found something new – his conscience – and his doubts about his lifestyle are torturing him. It's the perfect time for him to meet Josie, Mitchell's one true love, who we first saw in series one. It's not a great start to a relationship – she talks too much and he gags her and ties her up – but the attraction is there and Mitchell wants something new, something good.

This is the start of the moral vampire – the blood is sickening Mitchell, he wants to stop but he can't see how. The connection and chemistry between Mitchell and Josie is electric – probably helped by the actors being real-life ex-lovers. We know where this ends and that this is the beginning of Mitchell's greatest love. This is when he first went clean, he did it for Josie, and now he thinks Lucy can do the same for him.

The parallels between Josie and Lucy are not entirely subtle, it is hammered home a little that Mitchell is repeating a pattern. However, the scenes where he first beds both Josie and Lucy forty years apart are incredibly clever. The lighting and settings are gorgeous and the cutting between the two eras is so cleverly done that it isn't always clear who we are watching.

At that first meeting, Josie asks Mitchell that when it comes to the time would he kill her and not let Herrick do it? Perfectly in context but a dark foreshadowing of her end that neither of them could possibly predict. Eventually she gives her life, her humanity, to Mitchell to save him instead of to Herrick to save herself. I still want to know more about Josie but maybe that isn't wise – why did she and Mitchell part? Was it just impossible to live forever with a man who never ages, never changes? There must come a point where it is impossible to bear and impossible to explain.

Charlene McKenna could have had a poisoned chalice in taking on the role of the young Josie. Clare Higgins's performance in series one was pitch perfect – a lasting impression in a relatively small role and one that spoke volumes without words. Her love for Mitchell was evident in every look and every gesture and even this hard-hearted cynic snivelled a bit (OK – quite a bit!) at her right and true end. However, Charlene did great – you really could see the attraction and her curiosity about Mitchell, too visceral to be explained. She can see the good in him and he fights that understanding by depersonalising her. It is only when he admits his need and asks for her help that he wants to know her name.

Oh Herrick!! I've missed you; welcome back to the best, the most bonkers megalomaniac, bar none! What can be said about Jason Watkins as Herrick? He is the perfect immoral foil to Mitchell's 'crisis' and he always gets the best lines – loved the fact that he "sort of killed" the London vampire leader's mum! Also very nice to see where the policeman idea started.

Mitchell has decided that Lucy is his new Josie and this need for someone to help him is blinding him to her agenda. His terrible dilemma over Wilson and the paedophile and his protection of the vampires doesn't help. This time he really has no choice and something has to give. He kills Wilson – was that better or worse than killing the criminal? How do we value a life? Either way he has done exactly what he vowed not to and even if he didn't drink he has tasted the forbidden and his body must be howling for blood. Running to Lucy, telling her what he is, is all part of his desperation and why he really doesn't question how she already knows. So much for her denial to Kemp; Lucy is smitten but which way will she go? Is she under Mitchell's defences to kill him or to love him and help him? Who knows...?

George is also ploughing on regardless with an unsuitable relationship – although not quite on Mitchell's scale! He can't help himself; he wants the life he feels he is owed and is determined to get that with Sam and Molly. Right now. Nice to see that the temptation of putting Sam and Molly in a really dodgy block of flats – graffiti, drug users, wrecked cars – was resisted. The block is big and plain but just fine, and perfectly in keeping with Sam's situation. George is as blinkered as Mitchell in his desperation to be in a normal relationship and he is being unusually selfish. He wants to move Molly and Sam into the house but hasn't – and won't – consider what this means for the others. It would kill Annie – she would be really invisible as Mitchell and George would not be able to talk to her when Sam or Molly were there. Mitchell would have to hide his true self in his own home. Maybe Mitchell doesn't want a kid under his feet – I can't really see him and Molly together. Although, actually, maybe it would be a match made in (some sort of) heaven...

Annie doesn't get a good deal in this episode. It's just another item to tick off the list – this time it's babies and family. Sykes has been telling other ghosts about her, and that does raise some questions. Is there a whole community of ghosts somewhere having tea parties, book club, stitch 'n' bitch – and why isn't Annie part of it? Is her connection with George and Mitchell actually keeping her away from the other ghosts?

It's because Annie is famous that Kathleen turns up. She's looking for a babysitter and I suspect she's exhausted all the other ghostly possibilities and so Annie is left – quite literally – holding the baby. There's some nice comedy in the care of ghost babies – they need to be cold, you can drop them (they're already dead...) and scary ghost stories not fairy tales are the way to go. Presumably no nasty nappies either. Having a baby in the house brings the inevitable confidences as George and Mitchell get a turn each. George wanted a houseful and Mitchell hasn't really thought about it for, oh, a hundred years, but Annie has never really put this to rest. When Kathleen retrieves little Rufus, Annie doesn't want to let him go and she is forced to accept that this is never going to be her life. She left it too late. It's a nice story but please give Annie something meaty to do – she's treading water and capable of so much more.

As with the 80s soundtrack to the Gilbert story, the 60s songs that bookend this episode give a very different feel and are perfect with the action. The 60s detail is marvellously observed: not the glossy, perfect 60s from the magazines, but the eclectic mix of real life. The similarities to Lucy's very twenty-first century apartment are subtle, but just to mention a few – the iron bedsteads, the clutter of books and Lucy's oriental kimono that could have come straight from Josie's lacquered armoire.

Best lines? It may not have been laugh out loud but I did love Josie's "You mean like a secret tunnel that connects to the sewage system?" That is true grace under pressure! A close second is the complete, sneering distaste Kemp can put into the word "tea".

Final thought – I can't help wondering if Molly is just a precocious little madam or is there more to her than meets the eye?

Bum notes...

Lucy has a rosary by her bed, a cross on the bedroom wall and leaves her church pew stake on the duvet. And Mitchell, with his finely honed vampire senses, notices *none* of them?!

Between the filming of series one and two, Aidan Turner got a tattoo of Chinese characters on his right arm (does it say serenity, love and light, egg fried rice and a spring roll – who knows?) It was covered for continuity in the episode two flashbacks to 1999 but is visible in the 1969 scenes, although covered in blood.

A couple of issues that were later explained by Toby Whithouse – how does Mitchell get into Josie's and the paedophile's flats without being invited over the threshold? Vampire rules do vary (which is useful) and in this case he would have been invited into the block and then have free reign inside the various flats. Of course other sources vary and in *Buffy*, for example, every flat would have required an invite, while Anne Rice's vampire hoards didn't seem to have to worry about such niceties.

Josie described her first meeting with Mitchell in series one and it was a very long way from 'remember when you tied me to the bookcase?' So, was this is a mistake? On the BBC *Being Human* blog in February 2009, Toby explained it as follows: "Basically you have a choice of two answers. (a) Yes. (b) Relationships don't always follow a linear pattern." The second is, of course, the preferred one and it is a fair point. Meeting Josie was a fresh start for Mitchell and there is logic in seeing their relationship start from there with a proper date and not from the hostage taking. Thanks for that Toby – nice recovery!

... and the bottom line

Sightings of Russell Tovey's bare backside – none, sorry. However, we get a bare-chested Mitchell in Lucy's bed and in those dodgy 60s knickers...

He said, she said...

There are many things I hate in this modern world – secularism, showbiz news... But 'tea'... is barbaric.

......

My mother's maiden name is Herod, my internet password is 'password1', I'm indifferent about all competitive sports, and I prefer lager to beer. I don't understand fishing, what is fishing? I'm scared of cancer, I voice hypocritical objections to drive-through takeaways, and I lost my virginity on a canal boat in Tring.

......

Favourite colour?
That would be gamboge. It's kind of orangey-brown.

......

Do you like cats?
Yeah... I couldn't eat a whole one though. Who am I kidding? Of course I could!

......

I'm not scared of you... at least not as scared as I probably should be.
You should be terrified.
I should be married to David Bowie.

......

You're not scared of me?
No, at least probably not as much as I should be.
What did you say?

Where have I seen... Charlene McKenna (Josie)?

Charlene McKenna became a well-known face on Irish TV after she starred as Jennifer in *Pure Mule* in 2005. She appeared in the leading role of Karen in *Whistleblower* in 2009, winning the Golden Nymph for Best

Actress at the Monte Carlo Television Awards. She also had a leading role as Jojo in *Raw* in 2009-10.

On UK television she has been seen as The Marchioness in *The Old Curiosity Shop* in 2007, as Elish in *Single-Handed: The Stolen Child* in 2008 and as Paula in an episode of *The Fixer* in 2009.

On the big screen, she has appeared in John Boorman's *The Tiger's Tail* (2006) and as Mary in *Dorothy Mills* (2008).

When filming for the (as yet unreleased) independent Irish film *Porcelain* in 2007, she took the lead role of Sarah alongside Aidan Turner as Kevin. The pair dated for some time afterwards, although their relationship had ended before Charlene appeared in *Being Human* as Josie.

Music in episode five

The Velvet Underground	*Venus in Furs*
Herman's Hermits	*I'm Into Something Good*
Charles Gounod	*Funeral March of a Marionette*
Jefferson Airplane	*Somebody to Love*

episode six

Annie helps a fraudulent stage psychic and finds out rather more than she expected.

The repercussions of Mitchell and Lucy's relationship are violent and explosive.

Sam puts George on the spot.

broadcast:	14 FEBRUARY 2010	director:	CHARLES MARTIN
writer:	LISA McGEE	producer:	MATTHEW BOUCH

cast:

Annie	LENORA CRICHLOW	Robin	AIMEE-FFION
Mitchell	AIDAN TURNER		EDWARDS
George	RUSSELL TOVEY	Molly	MOLLY JONES
Kemp	DONALD SUMPTER	Jimmy	MORGAN JONES
Lucy	LYNDSEY MARSHAL	Orla	SALLY-ANN
Ivan	PAUL RHYS		MATTHEWS
Technician	MARK FLEISCHMANN	Carmen	JACQUETTA MAY
Young Kemp	MATT BARBER	Neighbour	JOE HALL
Sam	LUCY GASKELL	Older Woman	MARLENE SIDAWAY
Alan Cortez	SIMON PAISLEY DAY		

"Before he was given up to a death he freely accepted…"

London 1972 and a large church with an evening congregation led by a fresh-faced vicar. Telling the story of the last supper, he is quietly passionate, clear in his belief and the everlasting truth of his words of blood and the new covenant. Of the forgiveness of sins.

Along with his words, we see a young girl, already in her pyjamas and hiding from her mum, a game they obviously play often. As her mum gets ready to search for her and the girl waits in happy anticipation behind the sofa, the doorbell rings.

Reverend Kemp – as we hear him called by his parishioners – is on his way home, placing his leather Bible carefully on the seat beside him in the car.

As her daughter watches, the mother is dragged back into the room, screaming. She's being held by three people and as they lift her up we see her daughter watching her mother's blood pooling under her feet. These are vampires.

Reverend Kemp arrives home, calling for Maria, but he's too late. The vampires are still with his family, he scares them away with his Bible but his wife is dead and his daughter dying. As he holds his daughter, trying to cling to the last of her life, he opens the Bible in the spilled blood. He's weeping.

In the present day, Kemp is kneeling at the altar, holding the same Bible to his lips as he remembers that dreadful day. His face devoid of any life, all he has left now is revenge and he finishes the quotation:

"And whosoever eats my flesh and drinks my blood will live forever"

The morning after. Lucy is dressed, ready for work and wondering just what she has done. Looking in her mirror just reminds her – the bed looks empty but Mitchell speaks and we remember that he does not reflect. He's keen to drag her back to bed but she resists and he thinks he understands. She is going to have problems coming to terms with what he is. Her glance at his discarded bloodstained clothes seems to confirm that. But Lucy knows so much more about him than he realises and she is not at all confused, unless it is about her real feelings for him. Seeing the cross on her wall reminds us of what she is. Another look in the mirror at the seemingly empty bed where the man who thinks she can save him lies and she leaves for work.

But Lucy doesn't go to the hospital – first she needs to ask forgiveness. She's in church, the same church that George went to for advice and strength in series one. She kneels in front of the altar and prays – her stance that of a child, hands held high and palms perfectly together. She asks to be cleansed of her sins – the sin of passion, of caring or of consorting with evil? As she prays we see Mitchell walking home, passing a policeman, wary in case they are looking for him. Have they found Wilson yet or has the well-oiled vampire machine dealt with that? He gets back to his room and can't wait to strip off the clothes that are stained with Wilson's blood, a reminder of his failure.

"Just flinging crockery around like a common poltergeist"

Heading downstairs he hears Annie and George arguing, and the crashing of broken china. This is all he needs – he's made a commitment to Lucy and sorting out the house squabbles is not what he wants to do right now. George is horrified that Annie has thrown something at him but she didn't really, it slipped. Slipped rather violently, judging by the fallout and debris! She is very annoyed with George and wants to get Mitchell on her side. The cause of all this? George and Sam are looking at a house. Mitchell refuses to get drawn in. George has to look at houses, how else can he move out? It appears that George's storming out in the previous episode, bag in hand, has been temporarily retracted for the very practical reason that he needs somewhere to live!

They sit on the sofa together and Annie explains. She never really thought that George would go; she thought it was a whim, a passing fancy. Now he is looking at a real house it has just sunk in, he is really going. She thought it was just like the time he thought he should wear skinny jeans, just a phase. Mitchell is fascinated by the whole idea of George in skinny jeans – that has really made his day and he won't let it rest, to George's discomfort. He told that to Annie in confidence...

Mitchell shyly confesses that he has been with Lucy, he's almost coy. "You had sex!" interrupts an infuriated Annie to the series of er's and um's. We know George is a softy, but this is a new side to Mitchell. He is properly smitten and acting like an adolescent rather than a 116-year-old vampire! Was he like this with Josie? I suspect not, Josie was committed to Mitchell even before she knew what he was. Lucy has her own agenda and she has played him perfectly: he's committed, under her control. He hasn't even questioned how and what she knows about vampires.

Mitchell doesn't want George to leave either, but what can they do? He's a grown man (or wolf) and has to make his own decisions. He promises to visit often, but it really won't be the same. No one can disagree with this and Annie disappears, the ghost equivalent of storming out and just as annoying.

Mitchell reminds George that this is especially hard for Annie because if they are not there the house becomes just another haunted house. It is the vampire and the wolf that give the ghost a life. Anyway, he might have plans in the future too, maybe with Lucy (insert soppy grin) and where will that leave Annie? He leaves, George leaves and the house is empty, just empty tea cups and flattened cushions left behind.

"We can't keep him prisoner" "We do have a cage"

Annie has jumped far from the house and is looking for distraction. She passes a theatre and sees a show advertised: 'Alan Cortez – Psychic Experience'. Right, this should be a laugh and in she goes. The audience is a bit sparse so Annie gets a great seat right in the middle and the show starts. Alan Cortez is a rather cheesy psychic who seems strangely uncertain under the thick coat of stage makeup. He tells the audience that he has the ability to communicate with the afterlife and Annie looks forward to, well, communicating.

George, Sam and Molly are indeed looking at a house, a real house. Sam is so excited, it is perfect, there's a garden and the rent is reasonable. George is agreeing with her – it's great, great, yeah... great. However, when Sam tells him it is available immediately his face changes and suddenly this is actually happening. He tries some excuses – it's a long way from town and he'd like to be closer to his friends. "Mitchell," says Sam contemptuously; it's strange how none of George's girlfriends like Mitchell! She reminds him that his life is changing and as she turns away his face falls. He has gone too far too fast. He won't admit he's wrong though and pastes the mask of excitement back on – they'll take it!

"I wasn't strong enough. I thought I was"

Lucy is with Kemp. Like a little girl who's been caught out, she's sitting in front of him in tears, penitent. She's apologising. She really thought she could kill Mitchell, but she couldn't. She can only see him as a person, not the devil he is to Kemp, and this stopped her. She's scared of her feelings for Mitchell, she is being drawn in despite herself and their physical passion has shifted the balance of power, just a bit. Kemp is disappointed in her but not entirely surprised. The devil can be alluring and so can Mitchell; after all, vampires are made in the image of the devil. Lucy, he reassures her, is a child of God. She is less convinced – sometimes, just sometimes, she wants to give in – but Kemp is adamant and forceful. She must fight or the devil will win, and he has a suitably bloodthirsty bible quote for every occasion. His God is a vengeful one and He will punish them if they do not fight this evil.

Kemp will help Lucy, she wants to fight and he will tell her how to. She is relieved now that the decision has been taken away from her; this confident, educated woman becomes a snivelling child with Kemp and she hugs him, shedding her last tears on his shoulder. There is a very uncomfortable moment when he can't touch her, his face changing. Then, as his hands are on her head, in her hair, her face becomes confused and concerned. His feelings for Lucy are not those of the guide and mentor that he would seem. There is something very dark and complex here and more than a little disturbing.

"For they have sinned against the Lord and their blood will be poured out like dust"

Back with Alan Cortez (psychic experience) and he is floundering. This is the worst kind of stage medium, he is quite obviously making it up as he goes along – and not even making a good job of it. Annie is rolling her eyes energetically, irritated at the fraud. There's a confusing mess about various identities of an audience member's deceased husband and the varying sex and happiness of their equally dead Yorkshire terrier. In frustration Annie shouts out, not really expecting him to hear her but worth a try. An usherette shines a torch at her, furiously hushing her, telling her she is sitting in the wrong seats. Annie is puzzled – she can see her! She follows her up the aisle though, where *should* she be sitting? It is only when another usher walks right through her guide that she realises she's a ghost too. Of course, "What did you think I was?" It always seems to be the last thing on Annie's mind that she'll ever meet another ghost.

"Christmas 1998. Faulty panto pyrotechnic"

Poor Robin, doomed to spend an eternity in an usher's uniform, a one-size-fits-none shirt and eminently sensible shoes. Although she's got it good compared to the ghosts in the cheap seats backstage. She explains to Annie that every time there is a psychic show they all turn up to see if they can be heard. It's a motley crew – a selection of nightwear, an army uniform, a large furry dog costume (luckily the head comes off) and a poor soul doomed to be forever encased in an unfortunately small selection of leather straps and a gag. Makes you want to rethink your hobbies, just in case...

Annie is rather scathing about the gathering. She thinks Alan Cortez and his psychic powers are pretty rubbish, but Robin is quick to defend him. Something has gone wrong, Alan used to be fabulous but for some reason he has started to ignore them. Now Annie is interested and maybe she can help. After all, what else has she got to do?

In his dressing room after the show, Alan is drinking a glass of wine, desperate for a break. Annie starts to berate him. Why has he stopped listening to the ghosts, stopping passing their messages to their loved ones, why is he lying to his audience? He's startled, he can hear her! Although he can't see her and neither can he hear the other ghosts as they shout, vying for his attention. He sees the doors as they swing open though. Suddenly Annie has it figured out – he's not ignoring them, he truly can't hear them.

"Right, so you and Mitchell? You toboggan? In Liverpool?"

George and Sam have the keys to their new house and they are excited. Well, Sam is hopping up and down excited; George is doing a great job of looking thrilled. As they walk away, arm in arm, with Sam holding Molly's hand, she reminds George about the parents' evening at Molly's school. She's very keen for him to go, which is a little odd as they have only known each other a couple of weeks. It's symptomatic of their relationship and there's nothing like ploughing on regardless. George realises that he can't possibly go, it's on the 27th. He has a thing, a planned thing – it's full moon that night, but he can't say that. Sam is so disappointed and he digs himself into a very deep hole by trying to find an explanation. George and Mitchell – champion tobogganists. It's less than convincing and Molly looks sceptical. She seems to have sussed that the more an adult flounders around embroidering a story, the more likely it is that it isn't true. Sam wants to believe it, otherwise it means George is lying to her and she is in too deep now to even consider that.

Alan is talking to Annie, although he still can't see her, and he's telling her about when it all went wrong. He was in Newcastle and an overenthusiastic trainee went mad with the smoke machine. In the gloom, he fell off the stage and when he woke up the ghosts had gone. So far, they haven't come back, not until Annie that is. Yet another indication that she is, as Sykes told her, something else. Alan used to wish he had no sixth sense, that the voices would go away, but now he misses them.

"Back then, I would pray that they would stop. Now that's finally happened and I'm praying they come back"

Lucy and Mitchell are having coffee and the silence is uncomfortable. They both cling to their mugs as if it will stop them from drowning, but for very different reasons. Mitchell is still convinced that Lucy is the one who will save him; he can do anything with her by his side. She is completely, totally fixated on the fact that he has killed people. Not unreasonably. Whatever he says, she can't – or won't – get past this. He tells her outright that she could be his "salvation" and her immediate reply is "don't think so." Yet he still can't see the danger he is in. Mitchell is blind to the undercurrents here and he only sees what he wants to. He's in love with being in love and apparently love changes everything. (Although it would be just too annoying if Andrew Lloyd Webber turned out to have been right all along.)

For Lucy, Mitchell will walk away from his world, from the vampires that are his kin, but she is still unconvinced. Mitchell decides, he will tell the vampires he is done with them, it is all over. Lucy's reaction is odd – all she wants to know is when he'll tell them. He looks puzzled for a moment but... tomorrow, he'll tell them all tomorrow at the funeral parlour. He kisses her cheek and is gone.

She finds her phone and dials, telling Kemp that Mitchell is calling a meeting and when. She cuts him off before he can ask questions – she's done what he wanted. But has she done the right thing? Her feelings for Mitchell are still unclear to her despite Kemp's lecture. She couldn't kill him before, how can she do it now after his pledges to her, however little she wants his trust and devotion?

"It's done"

George is packing, or rather rummaging through boxes of mismatched oddments. He's looking for his phone charger but finds a photo of Nina and his face softens. That is what he has been missing. Annie appears and he tries to explain what he is doing without saying the word 'house'. That is very ridiculous, Annie is hardly going to cry she says scornfully, but when George tells her he and Sam are going to their new house tonight, she sobs. She's distracted by the phone charger issue, it's in the oven. She's been hiding George's things in the hope it will stop him leaving. She is comforted by the three of them in the house, it feels safe and protected, but George cannot stay like that forever. He has reminded Mitchell and Annie in the past that they will stay as they are and he will age, so he has to move on. He can't hide anymore – he has to change, to take chances. He leaves Annie thinking about

210

what he has said. George is moving in with Sam and Molly; Mitchell has Lucy and a whole new life (or thinks he has). What about Annie? What next for her?

"I don't want to be against the world anymore. It gets so tiring"

Annie has found a project – she is going to help Alan Cortez with his psychic blockage, whether he wants her to or not. She has a clipboard and she means business! She is talking to Robin using a headset, being very particular about correct use of call signs and "over", until Robin loses patience. They are not connected and anyway she is standing right next to Annie.

Alan takes to the stage and Annie carefully selects the first ghost to help. Eeny meeny miny mo... and it's Jimmy. Clad in full scuba diving gear, he is looking for Orla, his wife. She's in the audience and Annie translates between Jimmy and Alan. It's not the 'normal' psychic experience as Jimmy is very unhappy. He gets Alan to tell his wife that her new man is an idiot, he doesn't want her to marry again and he knew she was having an affair. Orla is angry and upset, this is not what she wanted. It's a long way from happy, fluffy spirits wishing their loved ones happiness. It's raw and human. Oh, and Jimmy died in a car crash – in a diving suit?

Mitchell is calling Ivan to arrange the meeting at the funeral parlour. He won't explain why, but he'll tell everyone tonight in person. Languid Ivan is not terribly interested but he'll sort it out, make sure everyone is there.

"I've got most of them on my Twitter feed so it'll be all right, OK?"

Ivan hangs up as someone bangs on the door of the funeral parlour. It's Kemp's technician, back in his utility company overalls and guess what, another gas leak has been reported. Ivan isn't worried – they're all dead in there anyway – and lets him in, leaving him to do whatever it is he has to do.

Kemp has his Bible opened to the pages stained with his family's blood. He remembers the night when vampires killed his wife and his daughter died in his arms, remembers the pain and the blood. He will have his vengeance – an eye for an eye, blood for blood.

Jimmy is still on stage, glaring furiously at the wife who cannot see him, who thinks he is lost. He's frustrated, why does it matter so much, he can't work it out, but Annie has it. She tells Alan that Jimmy just needs Orla to admit to her affair and Alan passes the message on. Orla realises that she too needs to say it – Jimmy was right and she is so very sorry. That is all it takes, and there is blue light spilling down the aisle as a door opens. It is for Jimmy. He leaves, pausing only to see Orla realising that she too can move on now and to thank Annie. He is gone, the door shuts. Annie watches him go. Is she happy she has helped him or envious that he has moved on? Does she even know?

"Do you use a katana sleigh or a tanto?"

George is failing to put together a piece of flat-pack furniture – a bloody bollocking piece of flat-pack furniture to be exact. He is giving it a serious swearing at, not realising that Molly is listening. She wants to talk to George, she's been reading up about tobogganing at school and wants to know what sort of sleigh he uses. George flounders as Molly watches and she tells him she

211

has made it up – he has no idea about tobogganing at all. She's concerned about her mum; Sam is so much easier to fool than she is. This is a sharp, switched-on little girl and she's more than a match for George.

Annie is still organising the ghosts for Alan Cortez and she's decided to go on tour with him to do her thing in his other venues. Robin is envious of Annie's confidence; she could go with them but there is no point, Alan can't hear her. This is Annie's idea of how she can move on, of giving her existence some validation. They are sorting out who gets to go on stage when Annie sees a familiar face in the audience. This one is for her.

Annie is back on stage, hesitant, her breezy confidence gone. She tells Alan to call for Carmen. Carmen stands up but she is uncertain about this. "This is insane," she says, and her speech and manner are familiar. She is Annie's mum.

Carmen talks of her pain, the pain of losing a child, a pain that is "spectacular". But despite the agony, she can't bear that pain to ease because it will mean that Annie is gone. She is punishing herself for not helping Annie. Since Owen handed himself in, Carmen knows that her daughter was killed by the man they thought loved her most and she is berating herself. She should have known that Annie was fearful, that she was at risk, and she didn't help her. She let her die and she can't say any more, sitting down before a crying Annie can speak.

"Don't hurt her. Or if you have to hurt her, do it once, do it now. Leave"

Molly and George are talking seriously. Molly knows her dad hurt her mum and she doesn't want George to do the same. She knows he is telling her lies. He should leave; hurt her once now and not over and over again. George tries to explain that he has a problem that he can't talk about. That is why he has to sometimes keep himself away from them. He tells Molly he is scared that Sam won't want him if she knows he is a freak. He is not thinking; despite her seemingly mature attitude Molly is only seven – to her a freak is a boy in her school who has six toes. What will her imagination make of George? And what of George wanting to go out and take risks, to stop hiding? Nothing really changes.

Meanwhile, Mitchell is practising his grand exit speech. Lots of variations and all of them, frankly, pants. The *Dragons' Den* impression at the end isn't going to cut it either.

"I'm out"

Alan has asked Carmen to meet him after the show and when she arrives he tells her that Annie is with them. Seeing Carmen earlier left Annie unable to speak. Carmen can't take that – she wishes she hadn't come. Why can Annie speak to Alan, to other people, but not to her? She's her mum and this silence is devastating, but Alan shows Carmen what Annie is doing. Carmen can't see her, but Annie is making a rose from a tissue and that Carmen can see. Annie learnt how to do it from *Blue Peter* and made hundreds of them all the time. Carmen loved them and she knows that it really is Annie.

She takes the rose and the floodgates open – she has so much to say. She misses Annie all the time, talks about her all the time. She is fixed in her loss and Annie realises that, and knows that her mum has to move on, has to let her go. Annie loves her, loves her so much, but it is time Carmen lived her own life. She can't stay forever mourning the life that Annie lost. Annie wants her mum to do something for her, one last thing.

Carmen is at Annie's grave, it's the first time she has been there. She didn't want that to be her memory of her daughter, but now it is time. She kisses the tissue rose and leaves it on the stone, and she walks away. She is released to go on with her life, knowing that she will always have Annie with her. She doesn't look back and even if she did she wouldn't be able to see that Annie is smiling.

"The time is almost upon us"

Kemp and Lucy are at the Facility, Lucy still looking lost and unsure. Mitchell is leaving for his meeting, the start of his new life with Lucy, his salvation. Walking away from the house, there is a sense of finality – this is it.

Kemp is already on his knees at the altar, candles burning, and Lucy joins him. They pray, giving thanks that what they are doing is God's work. Kemp is sure, he has no doubts at all, and this is right and good and pure.

George and Sam are cuddled on the sofa in front of the TV, a picture of suburban bliss, Molly asleep upstairs. Or at least she was, she's calling for her mum, she's had a nightmare. She dreamt about George but it wasn't George, he was staring at her but looking inside her and she stares hard at George as she tells the story. Is this the overactive imagination of a seven-year-old, working on what George told her – or does she see more than we know?

Annie is with Alan, telling him she can't go on tour with him, but he isn't surprised. Seeing her mum and helping her to move on has made Annie think. She can't run away. Alan asks if Robin would go with him, would she help? He still needs a helper and he has heard her – the ghosts are coming back to him. Annie has helped Robin too, given her confidence. Annie tells Alan that he must continue what he does. He must never underestimate what it means for the ghosts to speak to those they left behind. It has helped her too and she has made a decision.

"I think it's time to go"

Outside the funeral parlour, the technician is watching, counting the vampires in. Inside, Ivan is hosting quite a party. Alcohol flows – just alcohol though, no blood – and candles flicker in those red glass holders that are so beloved of dated Italian bistros.

Kemp and Lucy pray, him leading and her following less certainly. Mitchell arrives at the funeral parlour and the technician calls Kemp to let him know. Mitchell is greeted excitedly by all the vampires but he's distracted, before anything else he needs to speak to Ivan.

"Professor, it's time"

Kemp is ready but Lucy wants to delay – whatever they are planning, Mitchell has got there earlier than they thought. She stalls; there may be more vampires still to arrive.

Mitchell is trying to convince Ivan to take over his role as leader. It's straightforward, everything is set up. The vampires are clean and all that is left to do is for someone to be a caretaker. Ivan is not interested, he's not ready for that sort of grown-up stuff, even though at over 200 years old that time is not likely to come now. Mitchell is frustrated, if Ivan won't do it then who will? He can see all his plans, his future with Lucy, fading away. Ivan's main objection is that this is not a sustainable situation. Mitchell argues that they are all clean, but Ivan knows it won't last. He has no doubts: the vampires will kill again and, after all this restraint, the next time will be extravagantly bloody. He has controlled his wilder urges out of curiosity and because it amuses him, but he is getting desperate.

"I'm just one step away from wiping out an entire branch of Argos"

As a last resort, Mitchell tells Ivan that he has met someone, someone who could be his way out of the life he has been leading. That he can't be with her if he still lives in the world of the vampires. There's a silence and then Ivan relents. Mitchell should have told him it was all about being in love. He knows exactly what it means to Mitchell – they live such long, lonely lives that without Daisy he would not survive. If Mitchell has found his Daisy then he understands and he will do all he can to help.

They go back to the other vampires so that Mitchell can say his farewells and hand the torch to Ivan.

Lucy is still trying to convince Kemp to wait, but he has waited long enough. He knows this is what God wants and he will do what he has been tasked to do. He makes Lucy say it, makes her commit.

"Do it"

The technician's phone rings as Mitchell gathers together the assembled vampires, and Kemp tells him it is time. He gets out another phone and makes a call – the screen of the phone says 'goodbye'. As Mitchell speaks, Ivan's attention is caught by something – a sound, a light? Under the floor he sees a half-buried phone with a screen that is lighting up and saying 'hello'. Ivan's eye follows the wires from the phone to see the explosives and he moves fast, pushing Mitchell clear.

There is a huge explosion, flames and debris bursting out from the funeral parlour, and through those flames we hear screams and see the face of Kemp. Calm and controlled – this is closure. He and Lucy return to their prayers, to their knees, as the flames burn. After a final Amen Lucy crumples, she has done it, she has renounced evil, but at what cost?

In the wreckage, Ivan lies utterly motionless, the blood, the life force of this 237-year-old vampire pooled around him. He has gone, and a bloodied arm beside him shows the ferocity of the blast. There is silence and stillness. Surely no one could have survived that?

"And the deed is done"

Musings on episode six...

All of our trio move on in this episode – George to his new life in semi-detached splendour and Mitchell in his misguided assumption that Lucy is as deeply into their affair as he is and is ready for a whole new life. Annie starts off with what seems like yet another comic aside, but which grows into something very moving and important to her future.

Annie has not had the best of storylines in series two and initially this seems no better – a fake psychic and another way for Annie to be bright and amusing and to help out without George and Mitchell. She's been sidelined by the boys who both have other concerns and she's looking for a purpose. What she sees as a distraction – touring with Alan Cortez, helping people and their ghosts – all crumbles when her mother comes to the show. It's a lovely performance by Jacquetta May, she captures Annie's mannerisms and speech patterns perfectly. It turns out that Annie's mum has been punishing herself for Annie's death, feeling that it was all her fault as she should have known that Owen would hurt her. Her raw description of the "spectacular" pain of losing a child is heart-wrenching. Annie needs Alan's help to tell her mum to move on and live her own life again and this very personal resolution gives her pause for thought.

There is some wonderful comedy in the psychic scenes and it is perfectly underplayed. We don't need to know the stories of the costumed ghosts, just the knowledge that they are stuck in the clothes in which they died is enough. I particularly like the fact that Jimmy's diving suit/car accident confusion is never explained. Having been a theatre usher myself (in another life!) I do love Robin, the headset moment is classic, and when I saw her in an empty theatre with a bin bag I had to wonder if writer Lisa McGee had been there herself – so perfectly observed. Annie helps Robin to find her way, not to pass over but to be heard. Seeing her in the empty theatre sitting beside Alan Cortez, such an essentially lonely man, is the right end for them both.

Alan Cortez – moustache of the year! Played very straight by Simon Paisley Day he could have been a terrible cliché – a fake psychic, tricking his audience in his rather camp costumes and overdose of stage makeup. He actually comes over as an essentially honest but tortured soul. His loneliness without the ghosts he had wanted to be rid of is underlined by his carrying on regardless when they are gone. Starting to hear the voice of Robin again gives him hope.

The comedy also turns to genuine emotion in a matter of seconds – Jimmy's fury turning to forgiveness and Annie joyfully running the show in her headset but falling into tearstained silence at the sight of her mum. Taking her mother to her grave for the first time and then watching her walk away, back to her own life without Annie, was beautiful and right. It was good that Annie stayed invisible, that the resolution came without a miracle, without Carmen seeing or holding Annie again and with just a tissue rose to smooth the way.

It leads to a big decision for Annie. She sees the ghosts moving on with her help, her friends finding new lives and what does she have to look forward to? Going on tour was a pipe dream, just a way of getting away from the house which had been her refuge and would be nothing without Mitchell and George. She has decided – it is time for her to go.

George knows he has to move on too – despite Annie's tears, protestations and hiding his possessions around the house. He's painted himself into a corner, he does care for Sam but not with the passion he had for Nina, a passion that scared him and led to him giving her his curse. Caring is enough, it is fine and it's safe; he even gets a readymade family. He's in too deep now to admit that Mitchell and Annie were right. He and Sam get a house, a flat-pack table and the start of George's compromises. In an attempt to excuse himself for the full moon, he manages to dig a very big hole, quite big enough for a toboggan! Molly knows he is lying, this is a smart kid and there is a temptation to wonder if she is all she seems. Could she be a supernatural being herself? The power of the writing of *Being Human* makes this something you consider without even thinking about it! I actually think that Molly is just a clever little girl, pushed into the adult role by her mother's dippiness. (Although she bears a scary resemblance to the very old vampire child in Ivan and Daisy's prequel on the BBC *Being Human* blog, of which more later...)

Why does George – brain the size of a planet – get himself into such a mess? He may not want to lie to Sam and Molly, but couldn't he have come up with something better than tobogganing? Of all the sports he and Mitchell might take part in is there anything less likely? OK – maybe ice dancing... Even an evening class might have been more believable, but then maybe he subconsciously wants them to know the truth. He knows now that he can't drug and cage the wolf – the wolf will revenge itself on human George, making him violent and scary. It seems that the savage attack on the school principal was enough to pacify the wolf; it had its chance to rage that was denied at full moon. It can leave George be – until next time.

Mitchell is doing just the opposite to George and is being far too open. He's told Lucy everything, convinced she is his saviour even though she tells him quite plainly that she is not. He doesn't want to hear it. In his mind she is another Josie, just through an accident of words, because she wasn't as scared as she should be. He sees it as fate and he won't see any obstacles. When he told her he was a vampire, she was not surprised and she is clearly familiar with his kind, but has he questioned this? No, of course he hasn't. He has misjudged Lucy very badly and there can be no happy ending for either of them.

Having played Mitchell, teased him and then hooked him, now Lucy is panicking. She thinks that maybe she could love Mitchell, but Kemp's influence is too strong and her faith can't allow her to excuse what he is. Her horror at her own weakness and the power of Kemp's vision causes her to overreact in the biggest possible way, to collude in Kemp's plan. It's a powerful scene when Kemp makes her say it, makes her give the command to kill, especially after her being totally unable to accept the deaths on Mitchell's conscience.

Mitchell is prepared to give up everything for Lucy and has asked her for nothing in return. Oh yes, except for saving him and changing his general blood lust and essential nature that is! He asks Ivan to convene a meeting. In Ivan-speak this means a party and Ivan will use his Twitter feed to make sure it is done! Somehow, the thought of Ivan on Twitter is just perfect.

So tell me something, when did vampires get so damn soppy? Mitchell is flouncing around like a teenage girl about Lucy, all coy smiles and happy ever afters, and now Ivan is at it as well. Without Daisy his long, long life would be unbearable, and this immoral, inhuman immortal will put himself out for Mitchell, not because it amuses him but because of love.

We know more about Kemp now. His tragic tale means he has a very strong reason to hate vampires and his journey of revenge has led him into wider supernatural pursuits. Quite how he has ended up at this point we don't know, but we can see why he hates Mitchell so much. There are also some disturbing undertones to his interaction with Lucy after she has slept with Mitchell. Could he be jealous? Is that fatherly role hiding something very dark indeed?

How do vampires die? It rather depends on whose mythology you use. The classic stake in the heart is an obvious method and one we saw in series one with Seth and Lauren. Mitchell told us vampire bodies cannot make new blood, but what happens then – do they fade away? The ferocity of the explosion is presumably enough to destroy the vital essence of the vampires and annihilate the bodies of the younger ones. Ivan, at 237, is still physically present but his life force has gone – his blood spilled from what looks to be catastrophic damage to his head. Has anyone survived? The next episode preview cleverly leaves out Mitchell, so we just don't know.

We are left set up beautifully for the final two parts of the series. George is in his house with Sam and Molly but with a full moon bearing down on him. The full moon is on a day Sam wants him with her – how can he reconcile the family man and the wolf? Annie has made the biggest decision she could ever make. What is she going to do – will she tell anyone or just slip away? And Mitchell? Has he survived? If he has, what will he do when he finds out the role Lucy has played in the explosion. Lucy has committed murder too, except she thinks she has killed in the name of God. So that's all right then.

Serendipity is when a favourite show confirms all your favourite prejudices, and this episode did it for me: religion is madness; children are evil; and love makes your brains fall out...

Bum notes...

Annie's gravestone is different to when she first visited it with Gilbert. In series one it said 'ANNA CLARE SAWYER BELOVED FIANCÉE OF OWEN 1985-2007' and was close to a path and a very distinctive wind-shaped tree. In this episode it just says 'ANNA CLARE SAWYER 1985-2007' and is set in a grassy area among rows of graves, and the stone has a design at the top which wasn't on the first one. It's quite possible that the family may have changed the words after Owen's confession – but moving it? Less likely.

I know it's a story (honestly), but viewing a house and moving in that night? What about references, deposits, packing? Too literal? And just how quickly did they unpack and make it look like home?!

... and the bottom line

Sightings of Russell Tovey's bare backside – none (again) and just a couple of quick views of a topless Mitchell. Let's agree to not go anywhere near the theatre ghost rather sparsely clad in his bondage gear (with white socks, which is even more disturbing!).

He said, she said...

I love mum... but if she were in my class I have a feeling she'd be on the yellow table.

And the yellow table is...?

It's not good, George. It's not good at all.

······

You should've said it was about love. Get in there. We all lead long and appalling lives. I have my Daisy. Everyone deserves a Daisy.

······

Where the hell were you last night?

I was with Lucy. We, er... we finally, um... You know. Decided to, erm...

Oh, this is like the problem pages of Just 17. You had sex, Mitchell. Sex.

Yeah.

Where have I seen... Jacquetta May (Carmen)?

Jacquetta May is best remembered for her role as Rachel Kominski in *EastEnders* from 1991-3 and as regular character Liz Moss in *Dangerfield* in 1996. She has also appeared in *Crocodile Shoes* (1994), *Cardiac Arrest* (in 1996), *I'm Alan Partridge* (in 2002), *Holby City* (in 2003), *Silent Witness* (in 2005) and *The Bill* (in 2006).

Jacquetta has had an extensive stage career, including performing at the National Theatre, Manchester Royal Exchange and the Liverpool Everyman, with roles ranging from Lady Chatterley in *Lady Chatterley's Lover* to Rita in *Educating Rita*, from Adriana in *The Comedy of Errors* to Beverly in *Abigail's Party*. Jacquetta co-founded Plain Clothes Productions, commissioning and developing new scripts for small-scale national touring. In 1997 she directed *Her Sister's Tongue* at The Lyric Theatre.

She has been a well-respected TV writer since 1999 and is a mentor to aspiring writers. She has written episodes of *Where the Heart Is* (in 2000), *New Tricks* (in 2006) and *No Angels* (in 2006), as well as writing the episode *Random Shoes* for *Torchwood* (in 2006). In 2008, she wrote the BBC Four TV film *In Love With Barbara* about the life of Barbara Cartland, and appeared in the film as Polly Cartland, Barbara's mother.

Music in episode six

Rebekka Karijord	*The Noble Art of Letting Go*
The Unwinding Hours	*Peaceful*
Genaro	*Anyone Home*
The Voodoo	
Trombone Quartet	*Your Pleasure is Our Pleasure*
Fever Ray	*Now is the Only Time*
Amon Tobin	*Foley Room*
Felix Mendelssohn	*Song Without Words*
Sigur Ros	*Heysatan*
Hope Sandovai	*Trouble*

episode seven

Mitchell and Daisy seek vengeance after the massacre, and we finally see the Mitchell with 'the darkest heart of all.'

Nina presents George with the biggest decision he has ever had to make.

Annie considers her situation and asks Kemp for help.

broadcast:	21 FEBRUARY 2010	director:	CHARLES MARTIN
writer:	TOBY WHITHOUSE	producer:	MATTHEW BOUCH

cast:

Annie	LENORA CRICHLOW	Molly	MOLLY JONES
Mitchell	AIDAN TURNER	Sam	LUCY GASKELL
George	RUSSELL TOVEY	Hennessey	ADRIAN SCHILLER
Kemp	DONALD SUMPTER	Daisy	AMY MANSON
Lucy	LYNDSEY MARSHAL	Train Worker	DAVID WEBBER
Ivan	PAUL RHYS	Chaplain	MICHAEL BEGLEY
Nina	SINEAD KEENAN	Werewolf	PAUL KASEY
Technician	MARK FLEISCHMANN		

"Every human life is just another story by the same author"

This week's tale of the past takes us back to London in 1941 and an air-raid shelter during a bombing raid. The flame of a cigarette lighter shows us Ivan with a rather suave moustache and elegant silk scarf. He holds the flame across to Daisy – she's slightly less elegant but we recognise that same confrontational stare. He's asking about her daughter, Pearl, his curiosity intense. Her father died and Daisy doesn't really know what to do with her baby anymore – it doesn't seem real, she doesn't feel like hers. Ivan asks if Pearl is her jewel, but is he assessing Daisy's pain or her need?

They hear a voice calling for help and Ivan listens, eyes closed, savouring the despair. Daisy is mesmerised by him and – just for a moment – it seems that she knows exactly what he is doing.

He almost dances in front of Daisy, the hypnotic movements of a cobra – drawing her in, fixing her with that compelling stare. He paints a picture of the misery of her life to come; she'll suffer because she dares to have dreams. She'll settle for a man who'll do, she'll become pinched and provincial and ruined. A life amounting to nothing and not even her child will mourn her. She can't see how he can possibly know that – it is everything she fears.

He strokes her cheek and goes to leave, but then turns back and holds out his hand. "Come with me." The appropriate response is that she doesn't know him, how could she, but she wants to go, wants to be with him. It's beyond want. Daisy *needs* to follow Ivan, they are a pair, they fit. He opens the door to the bombs, the fires and the destruction and leads her into a new life. Well, what would you do?

"But I'll make you indestructible"

A conventional street, normal little houses side by side, wheelie bins and recycling boxes, scruffy lawns; this is George's new life. George is asleep, snoring as Molly watches him. He wakes up with a start and she tells him Sam wants to ask him something – it's 08.08 on the bedside clock. For once Molly looks just like any other seven-year-old as she teases George about his snoring and runs away laughing.

Nina is walking towards George's old house – down the middle of the road. Strange how supernaturals have no need of pavements, Mitchell is just the same. Annie is thrilled to see her and they hug, but Nina can't wait to ask how George is. Annie sits her down and tells her that George has moved in with someone new. Nina looks surprised, that's fast, even though she told him to get on with life. She can only ask what his new girlfriend is like.

What Sam is like is frantic. As George shambles into the kitchen in his pyjamas she's busy clearing up breakfast things, obviously trying to get to work and Molly to school on time. Nice of George to help. She still wants George to go to the parents' evening with her, even though he has already told her it's toboggan night with Mitchell. Sam really feels his heart is back in his old house, with Mitchell and *The Real Hustle*, and she's right. She wants George to commit; after all it was him that moved their relationship on so fast. Nevertheless, it is unreasonable of her to expect him to drop his whole life for her, even though George isn't really sure he's done the right thing. He's very keen to know the time for some reason – checking that the clocks are right. Sam has to go and leaves George half-watching a news report about the fire in the funeral parlour. The bodies recovered had not died in the fire and the Powers That Be have concluded that dead bodies were being stored there – not that far from the truth! George doesn't seem to be paying much attention – he must already know about the fire and know what happened...

"After the fire was extinguished thirty-one corpses were removed"

Nina is upset to hear about George, although she tells herself that he is only doing what she told him to. What did she expect? She really needs to talk to him before the full moon when he is expected at the house to use his cage, but Annie tells her it's no problem. He'll be around earlier. It turns out that George hasn't really moved out, he's left half of his things behind in the house and he's there a lot. Sam has got it spot on – he really is hedging his bets.

"It's like we've become his shed"

Nina asks about Annie and how she is, and she's unsure of what to say. She ends up saying that she's tired, and there are many, many meanings in those few words. It's all been a bit odd recently, even by their supernatural standards. She goes to make Nina tea as she asks about Mitchell. Annie's face and her pause make us wonder – what about Mitchell?

Mitchell has survived. He's heading for the boarded-up funeral parlour, scruffy as ever and not even the slightest bit singed. He gets into the building, it's black, destroyed, but he can hear someone crying. It's Daisy, sitting where Ivan died, flowers in her hands. She throws herself into Mitchell's arms and he tells her that Ivan saved him. He was the only one who escaped.

Daisy has salvaged Ivan's lighter and watches the flame as they talk. Mitchell is convinced the police set the explosives, retribution for him killing Wilson and the coroner has covered it all up as agreed. Daisy is less sure. The police haven't been looking for Mitchell at work or at the house, and although the explosion was brutal it was not professional. She is quite sure, this was not the police. They leave together, Daisy's flowers the only spot of colour in the debris and destruction.

Nina is looking at George's cage in the soundproofed room, her face sad at what he (and she) have come to. She hears the front door close and takes a deep breath, preparing herself for a difficult conversation. George has bags of shopping and is cleaning the counters – not the actions of a man who has moved out. He sees Nina and his face lights up but then changes as he is forced to remember what she did, how she pushed him away. She witters on as his face becomes hard, he won't admit he is happy when she asks him, he's even surprised she wrote a letter and didn't chuck him with a text. Feisty Nina leaps in – he made her a werewolf, no one gets the moral high ground here. Head in hands, she wants to start again, she has to tell him something important.

"Right, so we've a defrocked priest and a mad scientist. Nope, no alarm bells ringing so far"

She tries to explain about Kemp and the Facility but George doesn't want to hear. To him it's all about religion and even hearing about the presence of science in the form of Professor Jaggat won't make him listen. There is no cure, there can't be, he can't even begin to consider that such a thing exists. That kind of hope is far too cruel for George and he can see how much Nina wants to believe and how hard she will fall when it doesn't happen.

He will meet them and hear what they have to say though. He's only doing it for Nina and for that very faint chance that maybe, just maybe they can help. As she says, if it doesn't work they can walk away. Only it isn't that simple, as we have already seen.

As George leaves, Nina tells him that it is nice to see him and his face is a mixture of pain and pleasure. She has discarded him, pushed him into Sam's arms and now she's back and it's nice to see him? How is he supposed to react to that?

Mitchell and Daisy are in a cafe and she is expounding her theory of the explosion. All over the world are groups of vampires, some hide but others have systems with the authorities like the one in Bristol. But recently there have been 'accidents', vampires are dying, they are being hunted. Mitchell wants to wait and see, but Daisy is adamant – she will retaliate. Her husband died in the fire as he saved Mitchell, someone he considered a friend – and he is going to *wait*?

"I'm going to track down everyone who knew. I'm going to torture them. And when I find out who did this, I'm going to kill them"

Mitchell is still convinced it was the police, there are no other possible options in his mind – if he dug a little deeper he could work it out but he won't go there. He will take Daisy to talk to someone who can clear this up.

Back at the house, Mitchell gets ready to go out. Although cleanish clothes off the floor and rubbing yourself with an aftershave sample from a magazine don't exactly make the top tips in the 'personal hygiene for boys' handbook. He's pleased for George that Nina is back, but equally scathing about the 'priest/professor with a cure' situation. Annie appears from nowhere and is equally annoyed – she even made Nina toast and she didn't tell her. She's keen to hear all about it and plans to hide in the kitchen and eavesdrop when they meet. Especially as George intends to speak his mind! Mitchell can't be around, but he does want to know that George is going to be OK. It seems he is asking if he is OK with the meeting with the mad priest, but maybe he means more. Mitchell is getting deeper into a world that doesn't include George and Annie, but he's still worried about them. George thinks it'll be fine and he asks about Lucy. Mitchell looks rueful but not entirely surprised – he can't find her.

"Remember when you said I'd be an idiot if I told her what I was?"

Lucy is in the Facility – a large, imposing building but with no outward clues that this is a place where the impossible is rationalised. Trevor the goldfish is on her desk – he now has a nice bowl rather than a jar with a string handle, but does look a touch sluggish. Although, given the normal life span of a goldfish, maybe this is already Trevor Mark 2, Trevor the First having made that great journey down the loo. There's also a worn and faded Garfield mug with 'Lucy' on it. This is somewhere Lucy plans to stay and she has brought her treasures with her.

Kemp is off to see George. Lucy offers to go with him, after all she met George at the hospital and he may be happier to talk to someone he recognises, but Kemp declines. He plans to be vivacious and engaging – and that is a scarier thought than all the werewolves and vampires in the world!

"I shall be nothing short of bubbly"

Kemp needs to keep Lucy away from Mitchell's house, it is too soon and he has her under his control now. He can't risk her pulling away again. They believe Mitchell is dead and Lucy wants to know how George reacted. Kemp accepts he was probably devastated, as they had what appeared to humans to be a friendship, but it was just that the vampire seduced George too. A pointed look at Lucy to remind her of her weakness. She turns away, looking at Trevor, a tangible reminder that Mitchell seemed to care for her – is she having doubts, more doubts?

George and Annie are already in fits of giggles about Kemp's visit, which get worse when he knocks on the door. Annie is banished to the kitchen so she can't make George laugh (and make Nina get ratty with him). Initially Kemp riles George by telling him he is possessed by Satan, but he continues and his matter-of-fact explanations start to pull George in. This stern man, a man of faith, is credible because he truly believes he is right. He explains their theory to George, that every full moon makes the wolf stronger and that eventually it will bleed into the rest of his life. This resonates with George after the time he drugged the wolf and then became vicious and angry as the wolf retaliated.

"The wolf is not allowed to manifest. It becomes weaker. It dies"

He admits that George will be the first to be cured. That's true but not the whole story, it takes no account of the werewolves that have already died in the chamber and neither George nor Nina asks that question. George still isn't convinced, he doesn't believe in Satan, but Kemp becomes more forceful. He must believe, after all they know better than most what monsters really exist.

223

This seems to be the final clincher for George – what Kemp is calling monsters includes his closest friend. He knows there isn't a cure, that religion certainly isn't the answer. George is Jewish, he has said that that is important to him and he took great comfort from the chaplain in series one, so this is not a blinkered refusal. He can't explain werewolves but that doesn't have to mean they come from God or Satan. Unlike Kemp, George can see the shades of grey in both the human and the supernatural worlds. He leaves, Nina following to try and convince him to return.

"So it's less of an exorcism. It's more like a... vivisection"

Nina is angry with George – she can't understand why he won't listen, won't even consider the fact that maybe they could be helped. In turn, he can't believe that she has been taken in by it all, can believe in such obvious religious mumbo-jumbo. Impasse. Someone has to give and neither is prepared to budge an inch, that is unless something changes their minds.

Annie has been listening and her interest was caught when Kemp explained that he has done exorcisms, has helped souls to pass over. She isn't giggling anymore. As Kemp sits alone on the sofa, looking so very out of place in the house, she puts a note down beside him. "Could you help me?" He can't see Annie, but he knows about her and he answers her. "Yes."

George already has his cure, his life is under control; even if the cage is just a precaution that is not such a bad thing. Nina wants her life back – this is new to her, but George has had longer to accept the wolf and he insists that he has a life now. He has a girlfriend who won't leave him. This hurts Nina as it was meant to and she strikes back. George should do this for Sam; after all, he thought he had the wolf under control when he was with her and look how that turned out. Nina apologises to Kemp about the wasted trip, but he smiles. Annie has made contact – it wasn't wasted at all.

"They're offering back our lives"

Back with Sam, and forceful George is still in evidence. He tells her that he will go to the parents' evening with her but he must leave in good time. Mitchell is OK about missing toboggan practice but he will go over and see him anyway. (Just give up with the tobogganing, please!) It's important he shows his commitment and that is why they are going to get married. Sam isn't entirely sure she heard that right but she did – they are getting married. Nothing like a bit of well-meant criticism to send George heading along the path of self-destruction. She's shrieking in excitement, amused that George can propose to her when she's wearing rubber gloves. What is he thinking – wouldn't that squealing get on your nerves after a while (about half an hour, I should think).

"Stephen, this is Daisy. Daisy, Stephen, the coroner"

At the hospital, Quinn the coroner wearily comes into his office to find Mitchell behind his desk going through his paperwork. As he looks startled, Daisy jumps him from behind and pins him down with a knife to his throat. Mitchell explains that her husband died in the funeral parlour fire. They'd been together for 69 years so she's understandably a little annoyed. He wants to know why and who. Quinn is insistent that it wasn't them who organised it.

The bodies came in with no warning – of course he knew what they were, but all he could do was cover it up, they had no plan.

Despite the knife that Daisy is holding and Mitchell's anger, Quinn laughs. He knows this is the end and he just doesn't care any more. He realises that the vampires are being hunted and he is pleased. He wishes he had been involved in the fire so he could have watched and gloated, so that the families of their victims could have the closure that Daisy wants. Even Mitchell's violence doesn't make him say anything different and Mitchell has to accept that he is telling the truth. It was someone else. Mitchell is walking away but Quinn cannot resist telling him more. He knew something was happening, a woman spoke to him, told him she knew what he was doing and that he was unhappy about it. Everything was in hand, she reassured him, and it would be fixed, there would be a fire. Now that woman has disappeared. Mitchell is starting to realise how all the pieces fit together – he doesn't want to hear it but he has to. He has to know her name and Quinn tells him. Lucy.

Mitchell snatches the knife and plunges it into Quinn's chest. We hear him stabbing him again and again but only see Daisy's face and the horror of the violence in her eyes. Is she shocked or just re-evaluating the Mitchell she sees and remembering the Mitchell she used to know?

He leaves Quinn's bloodied body on the floor and destroys the office. Mitchell is beyond any restraint, he has tried to protect humanity and it is humanity that has carried out this destruction, this murder. Not only that, but the woman he thought could save him, could be his future, was the one who killed them all and intended that he should die too.

"You want retaliation? I'll show you retaliation"

George and Sam are dropping Molly off with her friends in the playground as they head for parents' evening. George is playing his part to perfection: attentive to Sam, fetching tea and earnestly comparing the relative merits of private schooling and extra tuition. They are waiting for their turn with Molly's teacher when he yelps – he can't help it, the change is coming. Outside, Molly is looking up, it's not quite dark but she can see the full moon in the sky. George yelps again and flinches as the wolf flashes into his mind.

Meanwhile, Annie is alone in the house (again) and she's making a recording on the old-fashioned answerphone. She is trying to explain what she wants to do, that it is time for her to go. She can see eternity stretching out in front of her and the truth of this never-ending life is scaring her. She's finished by the time the doorbell rings, but her tearstained face tells us this is not easy.

Kemp is at the door and he is accompanied by the psychic he used in the house before: Hennessey. Presumably he is out of prison now and working for Kemp, at least he is slightly better dressed! Annie can't speak when Kemp asks her if she is sure, and although Hennessey can sense where she is, she still can't reply. Kemp can't force her and he's about to leave when she speaks, almost deafening Hennessey.

"Jesus, she's powerful!"

At the school, it is time for George and Sam to see Molly's teacher. George is sweating and shaking, convulsing and he can't stop it. He can't understand, his watch says it is not much past seven, this is too early.

Kemp scatters holy water around Annie and prays. As he gets to the part about casting out spirits, things crash down from the shelves and the curtains flap about, but Annie stays still – she is waiting for her door. As the prayer ends, she is getting less concerned and confused and rather more impatient. She isn't alone, Hennessey is discretely yawning and looking at his watch and Annie asks him the time. She really thought they'd be done by now and he nods in agreement – all this unseen by Kemp. Annie realises that George should be there by now, where can he be?

George is still at the school and he is starting to transform. He asks Sam the time and she starts talking about the clocks going back. He's holding her arm, hurting her and she's getting scared. She changed his watch when she changed all the clocks, it is seven but yesterday it would have been eight. She doesn't understand – everyone gets a bit put out when the clocks change but George is really overreacting.

George has to get away, he's transforming right now in a primary school, his worst nightmare. He collapses on the floor screaming, in front of the other parents. Desperate to get out, he pushes Sam away. He runs through the school and we see this through George's eyes, the child-sized furniture and rows of child-height hooks and coats just emphasising the danger he could pose. He keeps falling and a mother bundles her children away from him, but Molly has realised that something is wrong and she is looking for him. She finds him on the floor and when he turns to her she sees the wolf. His eyes have changed, he has the wolf's teeth and all he can do is scream at her:

"Run. Run!"

George runs through the streets – we see his face changing, the agony and confusion and the terror that he is out in the street. He's surrounded by people. There are the confused flashes of what George and the wolf are seeing – blurred street scenes, the colours somehow dulled but vivid and we see the fear in the faces of those who try to help or just get away. His claws have erupted and he is desperate to get to safety. What can he do? What might he do? How can he not hurt someone?

In complete contrast, we see a busy train carriage and the usual assortment of people – reading, listening to music, eating crisps. The usual annoyed but accepting faces when the announcer tells them of a signal failure. They are going to be stuck for a while. As he finishes the announcement there is a strange noise – a tearing, crunching sound. A few puzzled faces, but then who can ever hear these things properly anyway? Then there are screams and the lights flicker – now people are looking up, confused and curious.

The lights come back on and at one end of the carriage is Daisy – balanced across the seats, eyes black and fangs bared. There's no escape – at the other end is Mitchell, already stained with blood and equally ready for retaliation. He too shows his bloodstained fangs and there are screams and darkness and blood.

"We need a door. Did we bring a door?"

Back at the house, Kemp is still exorcising away, but Annie and Hennessey are getting really bored and are not paying him any attention. Annie has had enough. She attracts Hennessey's attention and tells him there has to be a door for her to move on. This is news to them and guess what – they didn't bring one with them.

Before they can get too deeply into the availability of a door and propose a trip to B&Q, George arrives, running up the street part-transformed and hammering at the door. Annie drags him in, horrified at what she sees, telling Kemp and Hennessey to stay back. Kemp automatically brandishes his bible but that is going to have no effect on George, except that the movement catches the wolf's eye. The wolf sees Kemp and Hennessey, it snarls at them, moving as if to go for them, but Annie stops him. Taking George's face in her hands, she manages to get through to him and helps him upstairs to the cage. He understands her but he's beyond speech. Annie gets him there just in time and as she locks the padlock the wolf is fully there – pulling at the bars and raging for freedom. All Annie can do is watch and wait.

"Has someone been playing silly buggers with this?"

Back at the stranded train and the cavalry has arrived. Well, a cheery maintenance engineer anyway. He'll have the lights on in a jiffy. The carriage is pitch black and he only has a torch but he is starting to feel something's badly wrong. We see splashes and smears of blood in the flashes of torchlight. In the middle of the carriage he manages to fix the light and the full horror is revealed. Everyone is dead, torn apart and abandoned where they died. The inside of the carriage is covered in blood. It's total and utter carnage.

Annie can't continue with Kemp, she needs to be with George and although Hennessey is still translating he is petrified. What was that?! He has never seen a werewolf, never knew they existed. Kemp can't be bothered with his supernatural education right now; he reminds Annie that she asked for his help and leaves her his card. He hopes that she will come and see him – and maybe bring George too.

Next morning, George is desperate to see Sam. He can't remember what happened, but Annie is still angry that he was transforming in the street. George was aware she was with someone when he got home, but she just says she had friends over, other ghosts. She can't tell him she met Kemp or she will have to tell him why.

"So this is... the thing"

Sam is not happy with George, although she appears to be in a better temper than he anticipated. She is horrified at the embarrassment and concerned that he may be a risk, but is busy rationalising his behaviour. It is part of his anger management, and he assures her that it is a condition that he can usually manage. Sam startles George when she asks if this is "the thing" – this is what George has always called the wolf. What she means is that no one she ever dates is perfect – they are mean or cruel and in contrast she thinks George is still a decent choice. At no point do either of them mention that he never wanted to be at that parents' evening at all. As long as he apologises to Molly, they can move on.

Calling Molly downstairs, Sam is keen to reassure George. She sent people to look for him she was so worried, and he wonders if buying a gift for the school might help. Molly comes in, but as soon as she sees George she screams and screams. She can't look at him, she is terrified and inconsolable. Sam takes her away and George knows that that is it, there's no way back, and his eyes are full of tears.

"There's someone else"

Mitchell and Daisy are in his bed, the physical sensuality of the vampires evident as they revel in blood and passion and death. They are plotting what to do about Lucy, and Mitchell knows he can find her. The hospital chaplain will tell him how, if he scares him enough. If not then they'll kill everyone until they find her and that prospect seems the perfect answer to them both. Mitchell tells Daisy that they are not alone – there is someone else to help them.

George knows he has to leave Sam, he will never be able to live with Molly and eventually the secrets will destroy them. Better what Molly said all along – hurt her now and be done with it. He tells Sam he was fooling himself, he cannot have this life. He has realised what he should have known all along, that he cannot keep the wolf away from a family and he can't pretend it doesn't exist. Whether or not Kemp was right about it bleeding through into his life, he cannot ignore the wolf and box it away between full moons. Sam has no idea what he is talking about, no idea why Molly is so scared, but George can't explain. He kisses her – although she tries to pull away – tells her she is wonderful and leaves.

"We were so eager to be normal and needed, we filled in the rest"

Mitchell has washed off the gore and Annie finds him in the kitchen, but this isn't Mitchell – not the Mitchell she knows. It's as if he is drunk, intoxicated with blood and he comes on to Annie. He wonders about her body, her skin under her clothes and he looks at her with such casual lechery that she is uncomfortable, and as he moves towards her she is scared.

George is back and Annie goes to him for help but he is busy packing, not forgetting his vitamins. He is going to the Facility. He is still horrified that he transformed in the street and that he could have hurt Molly and he wants to take himself away from people. If there is a cure, however small the hope, then he has a duty to try it. Annie makes her decision – she'll go with him, keep an eye on him. But first she wants him to talk to Mitchell, something isn't right.

George thinks he's drunk, but there is more to this. In the very first episode, George told Annie about the rage and fury of the vampires and how much effort it must take Mitchell not to be like that. Now the restraint has gone – this is Mitchell the vampire, the one with the darkest heart of them all. He's glad to see the back of George, can't wait for him to go. He sneers and scorns, he doesn't care and the irises of his eyes are black.

With a visible effort his eyes clear to their normal brown and the Mitchell we know breaks through the vampire, and he warns George to get away, gives him his car keys. But he must go now, get away from here. George doesn't understand, but as the vampire takes over again and those black eyes bore into his soul he realises that something is terribly wrong. He takes the keys and drags Annie out but Mitchell calls him back. With a huge effort of will he warns George – he wants him to stay out of the cities, they won't be safe. He asks George if he is his friend and George replies immediately: "Always."

"We're not coming back here again, are we?"

Annie and George leave, to what they have no idea but Annie knows this is final. They have left the house forever. George denies it but with no real conviction. She looks back for a last glance and sees Mitchell, predatory dark Mitchell, watching them leave.

Mitchell is at the chapel, looking for the chaplain. His determination gets him so far but he can't enter and just being there is painful to him. The chaplain knows who and what he is and Mitchell tells him he is looking for Lucy. He claims he just wants to speak to her but this is less than persuasive, he looks hungry for revenge.

Annie and George arrive at the Facility and a young man makes the sign of the cross as they drive in. They look slightly perturbed at this, but there is no turning back now.

The chaplain thinks he can save Mitchell; that there is still something left to save. He saw Mitchell and George at the hospital when Mitchell was stabbed and he knows that George risked his life for him. He knew there was someone there worth saving. Mitchell can still be that man, he is still there inside the vampire and he needs to reach deep to find him.

Mitchell is past caring – all he wants is Lucy. He would kill the chaplain for the information he needs, but he cannot enter the church. The chaplain tells him to stay away and, in an echo of when he and George repelled the vampires looking for Mitchell, he goes. As Mitchell stumbles away, the chaplain continues to call after him:

"Whoever you are, you stay away from here! Whoever you are, you stay away from Lucy Jaggat!"

It's all Mitchell needed to hear – now he knows where she is, what she is. He already knew she betrayed him, tried to kill him, but the devastating depth of that betrayal is suddenly clear. He realises the danger that George and Annie are in. The human Mitchell is visible again and the hurt and pain are clear.

At the Facility, Nina is introducing Professor Jaggat and George realises who she is. Does he know what she has done to Mitchell? Kemp and Hennessey are there too and they know Annie is with them. They welcome them in and the doors – two massive sets of metal shutters – close.

"Welcome to freedom"

Musings on episode seven...

The flashback of Ivan meeting Daisy is a lovely treat after seeing Ivan's death in the previous episode. Watching them meet shows us the depth of their attraction and connection and just how devastated Daisy will be at losing him after 69 years. Ivan is such a fantastic character, wonderfully played by Paul Rhys – hypnotic, compelling, devoted and yet totally amoral. He leaves us wanting more – much, much more!

This episode is all about moving on – or so it seems. The house sharers are all planning to change their lives – George to marry Sam, Mitchell to re-create his 60s blood-free haven with Lucy, and Annie – well, Annie thinks it's

229

time to go. Of course, these are only their plans and what life actually has in store for them is something else entirely.

As if in reflection of all this movement, the house seems different – it's still cluttered and busy but somehow emptier, less lived in. Mitchell's room is messier than ever as his life unravels, and even though George is still popping in to clean the kitchen there is a feeling of something ending, of preparation for departure.

George's new life is about to self-destruct in grand style. He's settled with Sam and Molly – or so he thinks – but seeing Nina for the first time since she left knocks him sideways. Russell Tovey's face shows all the emotions that George runs through – joy at seeing Nina, pain from remembering how she left, through to resentment and coldness as he hardens his heart against her. He meets Kemp as a favour to her but remains unconvinced and can't understand how Nina – a switched-on, intelligent woman – can believe all this pseudo-scientific religious clap-trap. He has never really come to terms with how Nina feels – she has only had one or two months to come to terms with what she is, not the years that it has taken George. He cannot think himself back to how he felt at that stage. For all his empathy with others, especially with Annie and Mitchell, George is blind to Nina's situation and true feelings. Perhaps it is just too raw – after all, this is all down to what he did to her and he knows what she has to come.

As always, a bit of well-meaning advice (or gentle criticism) sends George flying off to overreact. In this case proposing to Sam. Great plan – he hasn't even figured out how to get out of a parents' evening yet, how is he going to avoid her every month at full moon. Tobogganing is not going to cut it. Perhaps he could try ice sculpture or luge? (And yes, he can take Mitchell – there are two-person luges. Very cosy!)

The terror of George's transformation – to him a whole hour early – in the middle of a primary school is painful. It's hard to see how he is going to get out without the messy prospect of a wholesale massacre of the reception class. He does get away – just – but at what cost after Molly goes looking for him.

The sequence of George transforming as he runs through the streets is amazing. Filmed by a camera harness attached to Russell, it remains resolutely, unflinchingly focused on George's face. Intercut with some shots from the point of view of the part-transformed George, it plunges us deep into the horror, agony and terror of what is happening.

Sam would probably have let George rationalise away what happened. She didn't see any sign of the wolf and she is much more embarrassed at just how much George showed her up at the school. But Molly saw him and he can't get over that. Far from the precocious little madam or the supernatural being Molly might have been, she's just a terrified, inconsolable little girl. That is the end for George and whatever he can say to Sam to distract her, convince her that all is normal, he can't do that to Molly. She saw the wolf and she'll never forget that.

He can see no choices left – he has tried life with Nina and that didn't work; he tried hiding away and that didn't work either. Normal life, family life – also no good. If there is any chance of a cure, however ridiculous it sounds, however slight that chance, he has to take it. There's nothing else left for him.

Annie made her choice in the last episode – sitting with Alan Cortez

(Psychic Experience) she finally admitted to herself that it is time to move on. She can't tell Mitchell and George as she knows that they will try and convince her she is wrong, but she is lonely. George is with Sam, Mitchell has plans with Lucy and Annie is left alone again. After Kemp speaks to George, Annie thinks that maybe he can help her, he talked about exorcism and perhaps that is what she needs. She records a final message for the boys and Kemp arrives for the ritual. It's all completely ridiculous despite sounding very right and proper – proper Hammer House of Horror, that is. Kemp prays away with never-ending energy and enthusiasm as the contents of the shelves fly about, but to no real effect. Annie and the psychic Hennessy sitting there looking bored, hair-twiddling and clock-watching in the middle of the mayhem is a lovely image! In a fatal mistake, Annie tells them that there needs to be a door for her to pass – they don't have one with them, but now Kemp knows how she must go and he stores up the information for the future.

When George admits defeat and heads to the Facility, Annie goes too. Her claim that she wants to watch over him is partly true, but she can see no place for herself in the house with dark-eyed, dark-hearted Mitchell. A Mitchell who is scaring her with his predatory lust. There has always been a connection between Annie and Mitchell and this lechery is uncomfortable. His previous attitude was more fatherly, the wisdom of his century of living, and this is just wrong. Although, in a question on the BBC blog about whether Annie and Mitchell should get together, the responses were split about 50/50. Personally I think it'd be too easy. Genuine friendship between men and women (however supernatural), uncomplicated by sex, is so rarely portrayed on TV with any truth that it seems a waste of an opportunity to pair them up. Also there is the squishy ghost thing – without getting into too much prurient detail, how would that work?!

And what of Mitchell? All through the series we have been told that Mitchell was the darkest vampire of them all, the most evil, the one with all the best stories. Herrick was quietly in awe of what he could be, and old, amoral Ivan counted him as a friend. If we never get to see that dark heart then this is all pointless blather, window dressing, and his history becomes meaningless. In finding out that Lucy was behind the massacre, and with the support of Daisy, we finally see that darkness. There's a build-up to the eventual explosion – Mitchell has to find out the worst, the depths of Lucy's involvement and her betrayal. He has to know that the woman he loved and wanted to be his saviour was to have been his killer. All the little details are trickled in and finally the control and restraint are gone. When an alcoholic falls off the wagon it is rarely with a small sweet sherry, and Mitchell's bloodlust is realised in the most almighty binge.

Along with Daisy and her desire for bloody retribution for her husband's murder, they rage as their kind were always intended to do. The commuters trapped on a train with two vampires is a horrific image – the boredom, the claustrophobia and then the terror. It's perfect that we don't actually see the rage and the destruction, just the bloody aftermath and then Mitchell and Daisy in bed, drenched in blood and satiated with sex and death. Is it realistic that Daisy screws Mitchell so soon after losing Ivan? Well, we already know that she was with George while her husband watched. Vampires live such long lives, they cannot be judged by human morality, they are sensual beings and their entire existence is bound up in the physical, so this is their normal response to the blood and death, possibly even a celebration.

The train scene shows the touches of black humour that *Being Human* does so well – along with the (very realistic) wounds and intestines and the gallons of blood there are some lovely touches. The woman with *Heat* magazine shoved down her throat (I feel like that when I read it – not often, I hasten to add!) and the unfortunate, disembowelled young man with his still-playing iPod in his mouth. Despite these it is chilling, there is no dignity left to these poor humans, sacrifices to Mitchell and Daisy's revenge. We don't need to see Mitchell do this to know how far he has descended into his dark soul.

There was some concern about how to pull Mitchell back from such an uncompromisingly evil massacre. Tony Whithouse told *SFX* magazine's Vampire Special in May 2010: "We were very worried about the audience's sympathy for Mitchell after we had done episode seven. But the reaction was 'God, he's so sexy when he's killed 20 people.' Of course, what we weren't factoring in was the Aidan factor." Beyond the squee factor, it's also a tribute to the writing and portrayal of Mitchell that there is a way back at all. We understand – or think we understand – this dark being, this man who wants to be different, to change his nature. We've seen how Lucy betrayed him and the knife-edge balance between the humanity and vampirism inside him. It shouldn't be a surprise when his true nature shows, we have been warned about it often enough. What is important for the character is what happens next.

The scenes with Mitchell when George and Annie leave are both clever and disturbing. Aidan Turner plays the switch between dark and human Mitchell beautifully, aided by the CGI black irises, a subtle touch of evil. His attitude towards his friends is cruel and derisive, but when the Mitchell they know struggles to be heard he still manages to warn them – after all, George is still his friend. Always. He warns them to stay away from the cities. Exactly what mischief and evil have he and Daisy cooked up? They clearly have a cunning plan.

Lucy has moved into the Facility – this may always have been on the cards but it also gets her away from Mitchell. He initially thought she was scared off by him being a vampire and he still hasn't thought that deeply about her – beyond the obvious. The relationship between Kemp and Lucy is still shifting, but since she slept with Mitchell it is Kemp who is in control. Even seeing Lucy with Trevor the goldfish (who can't be great company or a great conversationalist) is enough to prompt some rather barbed remarks from him about the seduction of evil. They think that Mitchell is dead; they don't know he escaped from the explosion.

Kemp's air of righteous conviction is never stronger than when he tries to convince George about his work. Even George's rejection of it all wavers. Kemp is so stern and controlled – maybe there is something in this? This man is so sure he is right. Although, that dour control cracks when Kemp speaks and warns of the powers of evil. It gives us a glimpse of what is lurking behind that upright façade.

The BBC *Being Human* blog published the original pre-title sequence Toby Whithouse wrote for this episode. It wasn't made – it was too long and would have been too expensive. It does, however, shed light on the origins of

Lucy and Kemp's odd partnership and yet again we wonder who is actually in control, in charge?

The story is intercut throughout with scenes of George's life – his transformations, meeting Nina and killing Herrick. It tells of how Kemp is called in to help a family with their son Craig, a son who is a werewolf. They have him shut up, hidden, a sad secret until Kemp takes him away. He has already contacted Lucy after her work on intelligent design was published, despite her scepticism of what he tells her. She has already been pushed aside and ridiculed by her research colleagues, the last thing she needs is more weird research. Kemp shows her Craig transforming and she's hooked. She starts to see how she can set up what will be a world-changing research project, but is stopped in her tracks when Kemp tells her there are also vampires.

The Facility is set up and Lucy and Kemp watch Craig die in the chamber. The first one. Lucy is uncaring, almost callous about his death. She knows that she just had the settings a bit wrong. It will work next time, she's sure, but Kemp is more sceptical.

Tully and Amy arrive at the Facility, they want to be cured. Amy was Craig's lover and he made her a werewolf too. Somehow she's hooked up with Tully who has been looking after her, but she has always known they had Craig and that he died. Lucy has convinced her that this time it will work.

Amy dies – and that is two. Tully could leave, but to what? He is sick of his life, he told George as much, and he hates the wolf too. He does tempt Kemp and Lucy though – still playing games, that's the Tully we know. He tells them about our trio, that a vampire, a werewolf and a ghost are living together. But he won't tell them where they are – he'll only take them there once he is cured. If he dies then George is protected. If he is cured then he can take this gift to George himself, the opposite of the gift he gave him that was so unwelcome. But Tully knows he won't be cured and before he goes to the chamber he writes something on the wall of his room. He dies – and that is three.

Kemp tracks down Owen with the help of a psychiatric nursing message board; after all, Owen and his fantastical claims were never going to be a secret for long. The sequence ends: "Professor Jaggat. We've found them."

It would have been wonderful to see how Kemp and Lucy started their crusade against evil. It would have been even better to have seen Tully again! But to do that would have been at the expense of knowing how Daisy and Ivan met, and Daisy's loss, her rage and desire for revenge would have been less effective. She lost more than the love of her life – she lost the man who offered her the world and forever.

The episode runs at a frantic pace and packs in a huge amount. We see the plans and dreams of our trio torn apart and trampled, leaving them facing uncertain futures. We see death and destruction and the depths of Mitchell's dark heart. We see George narrowly avert tragedy, his dreams of normality crushed. And Annie? The loneliness is too much to bear – but maybe the boredom of exorcism is almost as tough!

An episode with George's beautifully filmed transformation or Mitchell's rampage or Annie's exorcism on their own would be fantastic, but to put all three in leaves us wondering what on earth could be left to do? There is despair and darkness but also humour as always, and we are perfectly set up for the finale. Can there be redemption for Mitchell? Cures or at least safety for George and Nina? Peace for Annie?

Bum notes...

Annie and George make no mention of the funeral parlour explosion to Mitchell, not a single solitary word. They must know about it and even if they think he wasn't there why wouldn't they ask? Are they not even a touch curious?

Aidan/Mitchell's peek-a-boo tattoo has gone again this episode (although possibly covered in makeup). Maybe the Chinese characters actually translate as 'now you see me, now you don't'?

George refers to Kemp as a Catholic priest – in the flashback he was married, although I suppose he could have changed denomination since. No robes though and I can't see him missing out on a sumptuous set of those...

George may not have known Lucy well from the hospital, but Mitchell did (or thought he did), and as everyone wears a name badge why did neither of them know her surname? I wouldn't expect Mitchell to know her middle name, dress size or if she takes sugar, but how could he not know her name?

Surely George would have realised when the clocks went back – a bit crucial for werewolf timings. And how many schools have parents' evenings on a Sunday?

... and the bottom line

Sightings of Russell Tovey's bare backside – one. Plus some topless Mitchell both clean(ish) and rubbed down with a magazine fragrance sample, and an extremely blood-drenched version in bed with Daisy.

He said, she said...

I've met some people. They might have a cure.

For what?

Cystitis. What do you think?!

······

You know, it's like you're still there. Sat in that house with Mitchell, watching The Real Hustle, surrounded by cups of cold tea.

······

Thing is, like I said, tonight's my practice session with Mitchell.

Your toboggan practice.

Oh, sorry my being a tobogganist was such a surprise. I really should have thought that through...

······

234

It's been a bit weird since you left.

Well, isn't it always?

Even by our standards.

......

Well, then, one by one, we'll kill everyone in the world until we find her.

Sounds fun. But just the two of us? That could take a while.

No. There's someone else...

Where have I seen... Lucy Gaskell (Sam)?

Lucy studied at the Welsh College of Music & Drama and got her first TV break playing Ruby Ferris in *Cutting It* from 2002-3. She was nominated for the Best Newcomer award from the Royal Television Society for this role in 2003.

She has also appeared in *Waking the Dead* (in 2004), *Vincent* (in 2006) and *Paradox* (in 2009) and has been in both *Holby City* (in 2002) and *Holby Blue* (in 2008). In 2007 she featured as Kathy Nightingale in *Doctor Who: Blink*.

In 2010 Lucy joined long-running series *Casualty*, playing Senior Staff Nurse Kirsty Clements.

Film roles include Judy in *Lesbian Vampire Killers* (2009), Benitta in *The Last Drop* (2005) and Ormaline in *Dungeons and Dragons 2: Wrath of the Dragon God* (2005).

Lucy made her professional stage debut in the Oxford Stage Company's production of Chekhov's *The Cherry Orchard* in 2003.

Music in episode seven

Peters and Lee	*Welcome Home*
The Oak Ridge Boys	*I Wish You Could Have Turned My Head*
Colourmusic	*Yes*
Jeremy Summerly, Oxford Camerata & Schola Canorum of Oxford	*Miserere*

episode eight

George and Nina want to believe that Kemp and Lucy can cure them, but there is a grim warning from an old friend.

What are Kemp's plans for Annie once George and Nina are cured?

Driven to despair and fury by Lucy's betrayal, Mitchell can still see the danger and vows to rescue his friends.

Is there a way back from the darkness for Mitchell?

| broadcast: | 28 FEBRUARY 2010 | director: | CHARLES MARTIN |
| writer: | TOBY WHITHOUSE | producer: | MATTHEW BOUCH |

cast:

Annie	LENORA CRICHLOW	Herrick	JASON WATKINS
Mitchell	AIDAN TURNER	Hennessey	ADRIAN SCHILLER
George	RUSSELL TOVEY	Daisy	AMY MANSON
Kemp	DONALD SUMPTER	Technician	MARK FLEISCHMANN
Lucy	LYNDSEY MARSHAL	Daniel	EDWARD FRANKLIN
Nina	SINEAD KEENAN	Amy MacBride	SARA
Cara	REBECCA COOPER		LLOYD-GREGORY

"I'm with the soul-saving army, beating on a big bass drum"

A group of clean-cut young men in a plain, almost monastic dormitory. They are identically dressed and immaculately tidy. It's five in the morning and one by one they leave the room, each collecting a Bible from a rack outside the door as they go. They process through endless corridors and up stairs. There's been no date or location for the first time this series – is this a flashback? It could be any time from the 1950s on, and the bluegrass gospel *Saved* on the soundtrack gives us no clues at all.

The boys arrive at their destination. It's Kemp's altar and Kemp is already there on his knees. So this is here and now.

Later on, Lucy's alarm clock wakes her – it's now eight-thirty but at least she saved some time by sleeping fully dressed. She seems to have been living at the Facility for some time. Looking across to her desk she sees a terrible sight. It's a young woman but barely recognisable as such. She's gowned, covered in blood and deformed, almost as if her flesh has exploded. She looks straight at Lucy and giggles.

"It's coming"

Lucy is frozen in horror, but not just horror – there's also the shock of recognition. She manages to tear her eyes away and takes a deep breath, willing the apparition to go away. When she looks around again she has gone.

Where did Kemp's mysterious disciples spring from? Have they been there all along? Daniel, who seems to be Kemp's favourite, collects a placard from a storeroom – it reads: *In my name they shall cast out devils; they shall speak with new tongues.* He carries it out, pausing in an adjoining room where four coffins stand, perfectly aligned, candles burning at head and foot.

The lids are secured – were these the unfortunate werewolves? The boys, the disciples, leave the Facility with the placard, their pamphlets and Kemp following with his trusty Bible. Kemp is preaching on the street about evil to disinterested commuters and cyclists stopped at the lights. It gives a whole new side to Kemp – the rational man of faith aligned with science is becoming less rational by the minute. Is this the action of a man of science? Is this what we suspected all along and were seduced away from? Either way, it doesn't bode well for George and Nina.

They return and Daniel stays close to Kemp. As they walk through the Facility they pass George. He is sitting on a hospital bed, hooked up to machines, being tested. Daniel pauses to look at him – is it curiosity, fear or is he concerned that this is not what they preach?

"Annie says 'Do you know what the weird thing is?'"

Daniel is making tea and has a tray of mugs to distribute. Firstly to George, Annie and Hennessey in a large room that seems to be some sort of canteen. Daniel seems very uncomfortable with George, he can't meet his eye. Hennessey is automatically repeating Annie's words, to George's annoyance; he has to keep reminding him that he can actually hear her. Annie finds it very odd that no one can see her – not the Bible-boys, no one except for George and Nina. Hennessey can hear her and Kemp and Lucy know she's there, but that's it.

Annie and George have realised that Lucy is Mitchell's mystery girlfriend, what a small world. As if. They seem genuinely puzzled about why she hadn't told him about the Facility, but I suppose they haven't found the stock of stakes and Semtex yet. Knowing that Kemp and Lucy have just chalked up the deaths of thirty-one vampires might dent their self-consciously breezy show of confidence. George is still completely disbelieving that a cure is possible – they are testing him and have even stopped him eating meat, in case it strengthens the wolf. He'll put up with it for Nina because, since she became a werewolf, this is the only thing she has ever asked of him. Good old George and his selective memory.

Annie is worried about Mitchell and how he was behaving when they left the house. George wants to believe he was just drunk but they both know that isn't true. Annie knows something has happened and George does too. He suspects but doesn't want to think about just how bad it must have been to have left Mitchell in such a state of blood-drenched decadence.

"What's he done?"

The lights flicker on and off and the power buzzes. Daniel's next tea stop is with Lucy. She's irritated, where's her special Garfield mug? Daniel is concerned about her, obviously being snappy is out of character, but she assures him she is OK. But she is not, and as he leaves she sighs.

Kemp is recording his observations; we have to assume they are about our trio, about what he calls the "façade of friendship." He can see no other explanation. These beings are not human and so they cannot possibly have genuine emotions and affection. He labels the tape – 3 – and puts it away in a drawer full of miscellaneous items: a hairbrush, a mug. It's only on closer inspection that we see it is Lucy's missing Garfield mug, still stained with her lipstick. The hairbrush and hairclip are hers and there is a box of her belongings that Kemp must have purloined. He strokes the hairbrush and then caresses the lipstick imprint of her mouth, bringing his finger up to his own mouth. He is obsessed – or maybe, we finally realise, insane.

A knock and Lucy comes in, and Kemp smiles as he closes the drawer. She wants to tell him she saw Amy MacBride that morning. She's dead, Kemp points out quite reasonably. He can't imagine why Lucy would see Amy or, if she did, why she is so concerned. After all, Amy went to the chamber willingly, even though she knew that her lover had died in there before her. These must be the werewolves who have been there before. So that's three we know about – Amy, her lover and Galvin; who is in the fourth coffin? Lucy remembers it differently, Amy changed her mind but they were so sure that the chamber would work that they convinced her, possibly forced her. Kemp doesn't care. The werewolves die or are cured but either way it stops the possession spreading, and it looks as though their death is what he really craves. Lucy is losing faith, starting to doubt – is this faith or science or something else entirely?

"I'm saying we're doing good work"

Annie is sitting with Hennessey – she seems lonely, George has Nina and Mitchell, well Mitchell is gone. At least Hennessey can hear her and he knows what she means to do. She still can't tell George that she plans to leave and she's finding the waiting hard.

Daniel's last tea is for Lloyd, the technician. It's clear to see just where he is in the pecking order – he gets the one where the milk ran out. Daniel can't get any more as 'they' – presumably Kemp's Bible-boys – don't carry money. He finds some bags in the control room where Lloyd is watching a bank of CCTV screens. They are body bags, ready for the type threes, Lloyd confirms. Daniel is horrified, if they are supposed to be curing them then how do they know they'll need the bags? It confirms Kemp's plans – death has been the cure all along.

Lloyd has spotted Nina on screen; she's heading for the bathroom in her dressing gown and he is desperate to get Daniel out of the room. He sends him off to see Thomas at the main entrance – he can give him some cash for milk. He leaves as the technician reaches for a tissue, watching Nina take off her robe for a shower.

In the room where the coffins stand waiting, a shadow plays across the wall. We hear footsteps heading away and the candles all extinguish together.

Lloyd is far too busy indulging in his... 'hobby' to notice Daniel waving to him on camera – there is no one at the main door. Neither does he notice doors opening on the screens entirely on their own, at least not by anything that can be seen on film. What Daniel can't see is Thomas's body in the entrance, sprawled dead and drenched in blood.

"They hid all my stuff and drew a cock on the back of my lab coat"

George is looking at the chamber as the lights go out. Again. Lucy joins him – the wiring is the problem with this old building but she likes it, it used to be a bank. To her, commerce and banks are the churches of the modern world and she feels she is claiming them back for her much older faith. As a scientist, it was always her secret that she has a faith. It was her published work on intelligent design that ostracised her from the scientific community and exposed her to ridicule. It also brought Kemp to her – or her to Kemp.

George tells her he knows about her relationship with Mitchell and she tells him that she only used Mitchell to get close to George. It was always all about George, but she messed it up and got in too deep. It's part truth – the evil of vampires and her part in the deaths, she still can't admit to. She does manage to confess that she loved Mitchell – who knows what she'd have done if she'd just fancied him a bit! He's gone, says George, and she nods, they both know that. But while Lucy thinks he's dead, destroyed in the explosion, George is mourning his friend, the Mitchell who has disappeared into the dark-hearted vampire.

George admits to Lucy that he is unsure around her; all his senses are telling him to get away. She calmly replies that it is the beast inside him that is scared, scared of her and what she is going to do to it. George doesn't accept this, he's learnt to trust his senses. He is wary of Lucy – apart from the whole possession/cock on the lab coat/religious madness stuff, he suspects that this woman had something to do with what happened to Mitchell. It is just too neat and pat that she only wanted to get to George, and there's no way she'd have given Mitchell a peck on the check and walked away.

"He's a 116-year-old mass murderer, not a fucking gerbil!"

George is worried about Mitchell, especially now his doubts about Lucy are growing – what has happened, exactly what did he do? He spins Nina a line about Annie being concerned about what has happened to Mitchell to excuse him leaving the Facility, but she is utterly unsympathetic. George really should have gone for the 'but he's *MY* 116-year-old mass murderer' line at this point!

Nina is really unhappy with George. Status normal. She can't understand why he wants to find Mitchell, he made a commitment to her, to the Facility, to the possibility of a cure and already he's leaving. Nina has never thought much of Mitchell; she seems to blame him for everything. George isn't giving up on the cure but he finally has to say it – he's scared. He doesn't think there is any chance of it working, but actually, what if it does? The wolf is George's cage, the mask he wears. It is the perfect excuse to fade into the background, work as a porter, not have to do anything, not get involved. Without the wolf he will have no excuses and it's utterly, totally terrifying. What if he can't do it? Nina is also scared – she admits she has never been "lucky in love," the tears breaking through and the Nina behind the stroppy mask showing at last. She realises that if she and George are cured then they are just left with themselves. She's never known that before – the scars that George gave her run deep but she has other scars, and that story hasn't been told yet. Desperation and need can hide under a 'don't touch me', prickly exterior.

George will stay – he can't leave her now that they have both bared their souls and shared their fear and longing.

"My God. George, you think *you're* scared?"

George won't leave to find Mitchell but he does want to try and call him, asking at the desk to use the phone. He calls Mitchell's mobile – is that a phone he can hear ringing somewhere in the building? Surely it can't be. The phone rings and rings, we see empty corridors and hear the same footsteps, steady and determined. One of the Bible-boys is there cleaning and suddenly there is a scream and a spray of blood over the window and a glimpse of a familiar silhouette.

Voicemail. George tells Mitchell to leave them alone. He can't keep helping him back from the vampires' world and this time he knows that Mitchell has gone too far, too deep. If George is cured then he and Mitchell are finished, what would be the point anymore, what would they have in common? He hangs up, has he done the right thing? It feels like betrayal.

George calls home to see if there are any messages and he hears Annie's voice. The message she recorded before she let Kemp try and exorcise her – she expected to have gone by the time anyone heard it. She tries to explain: she has realised that any hell, any torture that is through the door, can't be worse than the life, the existence she sees for herself. Never aging, never having a family, never being human – that is truly hell. But she loves George and Mitchell and it was having them with her in the house that meant she has lived, even though it took until she was dead to realise that this is what life means. George is upset and can't understand why he doesn't know Annie felt like this – why did he not notice or why didn't she tell him? It is also a timely reminder to him of what Mitchell can be – the caring friend who protected Annie, protected both of them, and helped them face their new worlds.

"Primarily, I suspect he's looking for you"

Lloyd is in the loo – and frankly we need to know no more about his personal habits. Luckily he's distracted by blood dripping into the hand basin. Looking up, there is a body jammed in the ceiling, the blood dripping from the lifeless staring eyes down onto him. Shrieking like a girl ensues...

Finally they spot the mysterious opening and closing of doors on a clear route around the Facility. Lucy is sure it is Mitchell, but Kemp knows he was destroyed. But the boundaries are blurring and how can they be sure what is real anymore? Lucy knows that Amy MacBride died but she still popped by to see her this morning. They realise that Mitchell has been in the control room where they are standing as the body bags have gone. Who is he looking for? Well, for all of them, but mainly, inevitably for Lucy. Kemp could look a little more concerned – he sees it as predictable and he still hasn't forgiven Lucy for her weakness in being seduced by Mitchell, but he does tell her to lock herself away somewhere safe. Daniel is to collect George and Nina, but Kemp will only call them "the type threes" – he's depersonalised them, ready for what he has to do. He tells Daniel to move them, lock them up somewhere, spin them a story. When they have finished with Mitchell he will need Daniel's help to dispose of them – they can't let them go, let them infect others. Daniel looks upset, this wasn't what he signed up for, but Kemp's influence is strong and he goes to carry out his orders. Kemp and Lloyd wait; Kemp has his Bible and his stake ready. He relishes the thought of confronting Mitchell – he is invulnerable because he is right, God says so...

"You want Father Lurch to exorcise you?"

As they are whisked through the corridors, the lights flickering constantly now, George insists on speaking to Annie. He leaves Nina and Daniel to wait in the corridor, one bored and one desperate to be out of the way. George confronts Annie about her 'suicide note'. He is angry with her but in an oddly calm way. Hennessey knows her plan, so why didn't she tell him? Annie knows he would try to stop her and she's right. George has lost Mitchell and he can't bear to lose Annie as well. It's selfish of George, he is hoping for a cure, why can't Annie look for her own answers? George has never realised what his cure will mean to Annie. When he is human he will never be able to see her again – she'll be invisible, gone, so why stay? He offers to give up the cure that he doesn't believe in, to stay a werewolf for Annie but she won't hear of it, he has Nina to think of. I'd love to hear how he would have explained that one to Nina! He makes Annie agree to wait, just a day, so that they can talk, and they tell each other "I love you." It feels like a real farewell somehow and everyone is tearful; even Hennessey has a lump in his throat.

"It's weird. But I feel very frightened"

Nina is still waiting, kicking her heels, bored, but Daniel is reduced to whimpering quietly and paging through his Bible. They really have to go. Now!

In the control room, Kemp and Lloyd hear the lift start to move. They know where everyone is, they are all accounted for and there is no one left to be in the lift. They wait for it to arrive, Kemp rather more keenly than Lloyd, but he does cooperatively hold the stake poised and ready.

Lucy has made it to the observation room and she slams the door, locks it and then puts a chair under the handle. Someone's scared. She crouches by the wall, hands clasped, but it is too late for prayers.

The lift arrives and the door opens; Kemp and Lloyd are poised to deal with whatever hell and devil emerges. It's a dead man in a body bag, but Lloyd descends into hysteria, to Kemp's impatient disgust.

Back in the observation room Lucy can hear tapping, and she looks around. The lights are still flickering and they go out for a few short seconds. When they come on again she is faced with Mitchell – blood-soaked, fangs bared, looming over her. Not the Mitchell she claimed to love, but the Mitchell of her nightmares, the Mitchell she created.

George and Nina have been shut in a plain room, empty of any furniture. Nina is waiting patiently but George is convinced something is going on. He could smell the adrenaline on Daniel, but Nina's wolf sense isn't sorted out yet and she just thinks everyone reeks. So, what do you do when you're shut in a bare room in a religious/science facility with mayhem and vampires outside? Obvious really – I Spy. Nina gives George a W and he gives in – it's 'writing'. Something is written on the skirting board and George goes over to investigate.

"George. All the werewolves die. Tully"

Now we know who is in the fourth coffin.

Mitchell and Lucy confront each other in the observation room with Kemp watching through the window. Watching his two obsessions – a vampire and the woman he – well, actually, just what is Lucy to him? A replacement daughter, a disciple, the object of his misshapen desire? Somehow I doubt even he knows.

First Mitchell needs to know about George and Annie, and Lucy reassures him that they are still alive. Could have chosen her words better there – "still alive" doesn't suggest that her plans for his friends included a long and happy life. He also wants to know what Lucy did to him, she betrayed him and lied to him. Was any of it true? She tries to rationalise it all away, she wanted to study the three of them – a ghost, a vampire and a werewolf. To her they negate every scientific discovery, every tenet of her faith and she needed to know more; she needed to get closer. There is none of the admission of love that she made to George, however reluctantly. As Mitchell asks her – is anything she says true?

"So you took it upon yourselves to do a bit of ethnic cleansing"

She admits they blew up the funeral parlour; they got sidetracked into dealing with the vampires. She gets angry, very angry with him, he has killed her people. Just because she pissed him off a bit? But he won't let her get away with that – they have both killed, not just him. She tells him of the evil in the werewolves, insisting they are sick, and this is not the hope of a cure she has been selling before. Mitchell knows the truth; he knows George and knows he is not evil. He is well aware that the body bags were ready before any attempt at a cure was made and that they were meant for George and Nina. She is staring at him, defiant, prepared to defend what she is against him, maybe to the death.

George meanwhile is desperate to get out of the room. Banging on the door, he attracts Daniel's attention by shouting that Nina is ill. Trusting, innocent Daniel opens the door and gets locked inside in place of the werewolves.

"You don't get a life and lovers and hope"

Lucy's anger is fuelled by terror and righteous indignation and she is pushing herself away from Mitchell. She wanted to study the trio in the house, they were something new, both fascinating and worrying. A ghost, a vampire and a werewolf together, but all that Lucy could see was that they had to be planning something. It would never have occurred to her to actually talk to them, it might have ruined her preconceptions. All they wanted was to be left alone, but Lucy refuses to accept that and Mitchell isn't exactly looking like the human he wanted to be. He's starting to find her amusing, scorning her "reductive view of the world." The Mitchell that cared for her has gone and her insistence that he is evil isn't in dispute right now. He smiles at her through the blood, maybe vampires aren't what she thinks they are. If humans are made in God's image then why not him? Maybe vampires are God's anger and bitterness and malice, perhaps they too are a part of God's divine plan.

"But God's a bit of a bastard"

Kemp can't bear to listen anymore, these are the ravings of real evil, how can vampires be a part of God? It runs counter to everything he believes – he picks up his stake and leaves, abandoning Lucy to Mitchell. Mitchell has her by the throat, his face up against hers, whispering these unpalatable truths to her, forcing her to listen. They may both have killed but she was the one who made the deliberate and conscious choice.

242

But where is Kemp going in such a hurry? What is so important he'll leave Lucy at Mitchell's mercy? He throws open the door to Annie's room and, ignoring her and Hennessey, clears the table with a sweep of his case. He starts to lay out his cross and the stake and the other holy items he needs – he intends that Annie will cross over. Right now. Annie is scared, she had decided to stay, had promised George she would wait for him. She keeps saying she isn't ready, Hennessey translating for her to Kemp, but he doesn't want to hear it. They both start to get frantic – she needs to stay, she needs to talk to her friends, say goodbye at least. The word 'friend' is the final straw for Kemp, he won't have it. How can she have friends? She isn't human; they aren't human. He will listen to no one. She is going, he will send her away.

George and Nina have found the control room – they can see Lucy (but not Mitchell standing over her) and Hennessey arguing with Kemp, but there's no sound. They can see Annie faintly and they watch as Kemp carries out his plan.

"Annie's different. She won't budge"

Hennessey is insistent that Kemp must let Annie be; he doesn't want her to go either and is sure that Kemp cannot do this by force. Anyway, they have established that they need a door, a death before she can go anywhere. Kemp has thought about this and how to make sure there is a door, and before anyone can react he forces his stake deep into Hennessey's chest and watches him fall.

Annie is completely horrified – she laughed at Kemp before but this madman, this maniac, is terrifying. George and Nina are also watching open-mouthed as Kemp smoothes back his hair and calmly wipes the blood from his hands.

Hennessey is dead and his ghost is looking at Annie; it's the first time he has seen her. He realises what has happened and the danger they are both in. Kemp begins the exorcism and a door appears. It's metal, rusty and battered and it is rattling, and there is knocking and banging from the other side. It is suddenly thrown open and the inside is pitch black – no blue light, no corridor, just impenetrable darkness. Hennessey is pulled across the floor with no chance to fight and no choice. This is not a door that he can walk through or can choose; this is compulsion. He disappears into the darkness and Kemp's prayers grow in intensity. The door is still open and he turns on Annie, commanding her to go.

George is transfixed by the screens, begging Annie not to go. In the observation room Mitchell still has Lucy by the throat and tells her to close her eyes. As she does he changes – black eyes and fangs – a sight he is still protecting Lucy from even though he intends to kill her.

"No, please! No, I'm not ready!"

Kemp's prayers are getting more and more frantic and Annie cowers away. She's as far away from the door as she can get but it's no good. She is dragged across the room by an unseen force – she can't fight, can't stop and she is calling for George, for help, screaming that she is not ready. All George can do is watch helplessly as she goes. She manages to hang onto the edge of the door for a moment but to no avail. Annie disappears into the darkness and the door slams shut.

George and Nina watch the door crash shut, hardly able to believe what they have seen. George is motionless, unable to speak or move, but Nina knows they have to get away. They are still in danger, even more so now they know what Kemp is capable of. She drags George away.

Mitchell is about to kill Lucy, but at the moment Annie crosses over he collapses in agony. He has no idea why but the pain is unbearable. The pain of Annie being wrenched from the world – what is the connection they have that hurts Mitchell so much? He can't face Lucy anymore, he has to get away and he stumbles out, leaving her relieved, confused and concerned but still alive.

Kemp retrieves his stake from Hennessey's body and leaves the room. He has dealt with Annie, cured her, now who is next?

Lloyd is making his escape, running through the facility with a box full of... what? Research papers, evidence, CCTV tapes or his collection of specialist magazines and some clean pants? He uses his code to open the main doors but before he can get out he hears someone coming. He needs to hide.

George and Nina are also heading out and luckily they find the door open, but before they hit the pavement George stops. Nina is desperate to go, they can't help Annie anymore and they need to get away, to save themselves, but George is determined. Somehow he knows Mitchell is inside and he has to go back and find him. He may not be the Mitchell that George knows, but he has to see if he can be saved. Nina is really not impressed. She can see daylight and people and shops but George is heading back for his mass-murdering dead best buddy who she was never all that keen on anyway. Perfect.

Lloyd has hidden in the chamber – the brightly lit, glass-fronted chamber. Great plan. He is still panicking and terrified but is trying to calm himself; he is nearly out, nearly safe from the monsters. Or is he? As he turns, Amy MacBride is there, looking at him through the one eye left in her ruined face. She's smiling; she licks her lips and Lloyd screams and screams.

Kemp is calling to Mitchell, taunting him about how he killed Annie, forced her out of the world. Mitchell runs at him and although Kemp is ready with the stake Mitchell is too fast for him and too strong and he has hold of Kemp. He's past caring, still goading Mitchell – does he want to die? Somehow he knows that Mitchell felt Annie pass, but how can he possibly know that? It seemed that Mitchell didn't know what the agony meant, only now does he know that Kemp killed Annie – or is there much more to this? Kemp is happy that Mitchell feels pain, this is his reward. It's revenge for all of Mitchell's victims and their loved ones who felt that same tearing pain. The pain that Kemp's family felt and he wants Mitchell to experience the same savage mourning that he did. All Mitchell wants is to kill him, to tear him apart and Kemp is ready.

"I'm ready to meet my maker. Are you ready to meet yours?"

Who can Kemp mean? Who is Mitchell's maker – is it Lucy's God of love, Kemp's seductive, tempting Satan or Mitchell's bastard God of spite and rage. Could it even be Herrick, Mitchell's vampire creator?

As he lifts Kemp, ready to destroy him, George runs towards him, calling for him to stop. Mitchell is desperate, this is for Annie. Kemp killed her and it is right he should die in his turn, but George can't accept that. If Mitchell has to kill then so be it, but George refuses to let him kill in Annie's name – despite everything that Kemp has done it is the very last thing she would want. He knows that his friend Mitchell is still there somewhere even though Mitchell himself doubts it. His humanity still lingers in his awareness of what he has done and his knowledge that George can never accept it, but George needs him back. He has lost Annie and he can't bear to lose Mitchell too. Mitchell is fighting himself – the humanity nurtured by George and Annie trying to get through the darkness of the vampire soul. The conflict is hard and the darkness may be winning, but George reaches out and Mitchell takes his hand. George literally pulls him back. They stagger away, holding each other for support, leaving Kemp slumped on the ground.

"*They're* monsters. Not us"

A quiet country lane, there are fields, trees, an isolated cottage and the Royal Mail van. It could almost be *Postman Pat* (except for the lack of a monochrome feline) and the caption tells us that three weeks have passed. The postman knocks on the door and we see Nina hide until he puts a package through the letterbox. When he's safely away she picks it up. It's a book, Lucy's book – *God's Blueprint* – and Nina harrumphs as she reads the blurb. In the kitchen, Mitchell is sitting, motionless, listening to the radio. The announcer is talking about the memorial service for the Box Tunnel 20 – the twenty people mysteriously killed on a stranded train. Nina goes to switch it off, asking if he's listening, but he stares at her with a frightening intensity and just nods. She's uncomfortable; whether or not she knows what he did, she's not keen to be around him. Mitchell's eyes are dark; the battle is still raging inside him.

In the bedroom, Nina has been busy. She has a table covered in research about Lucy; she has Post-it notes and a mug full of pens. She's looking for Lucy, trying to get inside her head. She is making progress though and has identified the technician. George is patient with her – she really doesn't have to do this, it wasn't her fault. He is unhappy about all this work as it's verging on obsession and look where that took Kemp and Lucy.

But Nina has to carry on as she knows it was all her fault. She got them involved with Kemp, he 'met' Annie at the house and she convinced George to go to the Facility against his better judgement. She has to atone somehow.

"It's other people's grief. It's pornographic"

Mitchell is still listening to the radio; the police are now being quoted. They have many lines of enquiry but rumours are circulating. Was it a turf war or some kind of bizarre ritual? One thing is for sure – it hasn't been covered up and tidied away. George switches off the radio. Mitchell shouldn't be listening to this.

Mitchell is still, he seems withdrawn and introspective but he is far from calm. He can't understand why George doesn't want to know what he did, just how bad it was. After all, it's clear George knows that something pretty extreme happened. Does Mitchell want to unburden himself; does he see it as a catharsis? Whatever, George really can't know just now – he needs Mitchell too much to hear it. He couldn't bear it.

Mitchell is walking down the lane in the rain when he stops. He's seen something that he can't quite believe. There's the back of a familiar blue coat – it's Lucy, wet, nervous and waiting. Mitchell is furious. How did she find them? Nina's research has left a trail that was quite easy to follow and Lucy was looking for them too. She tried their old house but they can't go back there. She doesn't understand why, there is no threat now; she doesn't even know where Kemp is or what happened to him. Mitchell has to remind her that the house was Annie's and now they have lost her they can't be in her house.

Lucy finally admits that she designed the chamber and that four werewolves died in it. She names them – Craig Ford, Amy MacBride, Lee Tully, Richard Galvin. She sees their faces every day but Mitchell is totally unsympathetic – he too has to live with what he did, what she reduced him to. He takes hold of her; he should tear her apart and he has to struggle to resist the dark urges that want to do that. This is how he is now – this is what she did.

"It was Inch High Private Eye that led her here"

He wants to walk away but she begs him, she needs to see George and Nina. Nina is cold and angry and she grabs Lucy by the throat, pushing her up against the wall, wondering why she's there. Lucy finds that odd as Nina has tried so hard to find her. She even manages to offer her a refund on the book she bought and is so disparaging about. Nina's instinctive reaction is to wonder why Mitchell didn't kill her, but he and George just look at her. No more killing; that is what the monsters do.

Lucy really wants to say sorry, to explain, to offer some restitution, but Nina is dismissive. How can she just say sorry? Actually it is brave of Lucy to even try. She knows what she unleashed in Mitchell, and Nina and George are under no illusions about what was planned for them, but still she came. Maybe Nina could just bite Lucy, she'd enjoy that. Just a little tiny bite, see how she likes it, but Nina's reaction is fuelled by her feelings of being to blame.

The trio head for the kitchen to talk before Nina does something that George will regret. Mitchell really believes that Lucy is sorry, that she has come with good intentions, but Nina is dubious. She thinks Mitchell is deluded, that Lucy really must have been quite something in bed! He's trying to convince them that this isn't what it is about, but Nina is not going to listen. To the boys this is all about Annie and – after all – it wasn't Lucy that killed Annie. But they're forgetting about what happened to Nina. She was in the Facility for two months, was even in the chamber, and Lucy was part of the reason she convinced George to go with her. There's guilt and horror, resentment and revenge all mixed up in Nina and she can't match the resignation of the others. She hasn't got their disgust and rejection of any more death; she'd like to see Lucy bleed and squirm. She hates it that they – the victims – are supposed to walk away, that they are weaker, but George reminds her that they cannot be the monsters anymore, that it will not gain them anything. She can't talk to them anymore, she has to walk away.

George follows her – he can't forgive Lucy either but he doesn't want her dead. That would make them as bad as her and Kemp. He can't help Mitchell protect Lucy. It was Mitchell that Lucy used to get to them all and there is still some sort of connection between them. To George that still makes her dangerous.

"Oh, now you're getting squeamish"

Somehow Mitchell has persuaded the others to let Lucy stay – at least for tonight. Or maybe he didn't ask. He takes her a cushion and a coat so she can sleep on the sofa, although I suspect she wouldn't turn down an invitation to his bed. His coat is the one he wore in the Facility and it still has blood on it. Neither can figure out why the other is being so understanding – Lucy knows exactly what she did to Mitchell, the deaths of the vampires and his descent into evil, and she doesn't understand why he didn't kill her. He couldn't, he needs forgiveness too and if he can't forgive Lucy he can't see how he could ever begin to forgive himself. Lucy is floundering, she's lost. She betrayed everything she held to be true and right – her faith, her science, even Mitchell, and she no longer recognises herself. What can she be now?

"I guess you're a monster now. Just like us"

Nina is brooding, wide awake alongside a snoring George. It's no good – she needs to have it out with Lucy. Again. She heads downstairs and the sofa is empty but Lucy's coat is still there. A door bangs. Outside Lucy is standing stock still, but Nina is determined to sort this all out and then she wants her gone. Lucy's face is frozen with terror but she manages to warn Nina, telling her to run. Nina doesn't understand but Lucy howls in pain and a bloodstained stake appears through her chest, and as she falls we see Kemp standing behind her. He looks unkempt (no pun intended) but he still manages to give Nina that insane smile as he moves towards her.

George wakes as Nina screams and he and Mitchell run outside. Mitchell is initially repelled by Kemp's cross but manages to get to Lucy and kneels beside her. There's so much blood and she's dying, but she's calm. She looks at Mitchell and tells him she wants to go, it's right and it's time. She says his name – there's more she needs to say but she can't, it's too late.

Kemp has the stake to Nina's throat and George begs him not to hurt her, tries to get Kemp to take him instead and let Nina go, but there's no point. Kemp fully intends to kill them both. Suddenly George is distracted, looking over Kemp's shoulder at the door that has just appeared. Kemp's attention is taken away just long enough for Nina to ply a vicious and well-placed elbow to break his grip and run to George.

They all look at the door, it must be for Lucy but her ghost has not appeared. It flies open revealing darkness inside and as they watch a vision of Annie appears. She grabs Kemp and pulls him through the door with her and the door instantly slams shut.

"Oh my God, that was Annie"

They hear a sound. The TV in the kitchen is flickering, the screen fuzzy. It isn't switched on; it can't even be plugged in. As they watch, Annie appears and she needs to know that they are safe. They are – she saved them from Kemp.

They miss her and she misses them. She is tearful and frightened and is stuck in an endless bureaucratic limbo. She tries to explain – there are forms to fill in, they have numbers and there are buzzers and bells. They have no idea what is supposed to happen but she is scared and the endless anticipation is terrifying. She wants it to be over. The people behind the doors are angry with her for going after Kemp, after all she didn't have the right paperwork, and there isn't even a form for that. She's scared that Mitchell and George will forget her, but how could they? She puts her hands to her side of the screen and they put their hands to hers, Mitchell's still stained with Lucy's blood and Nina watching them. Annie has to go and she fades away as they watch, tearstained and bereft.

"What happens now Mitchell? What do we do?" "We're going to get her back"

Can that be all? No. In an isolated snow-covered field, two women crouch, arms outspread and blood running from their wrists. They are surrounded by pools of red blood staining the white snow. We come closer – it is Daisy and Cara. Cara is determined, she's changed, become stronger and is definitely the leader of the two, while Daisy is weaker. Daisy rescued Cara from the caves; she is the other vampire that Mitchell said had survived. Mitchell told them that this is where the bones lie, insists Cara. They cannot give up.

Suddenly the ground shakes, an arm appears and then a body, rising from the earth. Standing over the weakened vampires, he howls at the sky.

It's Herrick.

"We can't stop. Not now"

Musings on episode eight...

A very different episode in that it is almost entirely set in the claustrophobic, flickering caverns of the Facility. A setting that just helps rack up the tension, as if we need any more!

It starts with a weird scene – Kemp's Bible-boys are preparing for the day. After the tradition of flashbacks this could be another one, but it turns out that this is not some austere 1950s boarding school but right here, right now. We have to presume these boys have been groomed for some time by Kemp. It is a clever turnaround for Kemp. His first appearances made us think 'OK, standard issue religious nutter' but then he belied that impression. He was rational, reasonable, a man of unwavering faith aligned with science and he was convincing, almost compelling – although very far from bubbly! In this new version he is preaching in the street to bored cyclists about evil and has a cellar full of young men. Does he see himself as a Messiah and them as his disciples? He is certainly using them to help spread his warnings about possession, to show people the path. So, that takes us right back to the religious maniac idea...

His interactions with Lucy also change. It has always been unclear as to who was in charge; Lucy certainly isn't an innocent in any of this but we can see that Kemp is clearly in control now. The turning point was when Lucy slept with Mitchell, which changed everything for Kemp. He thought she was incorruptible but his protégée, his substitute daughter, and the woman that he can't admit he desires, turns out to have feet of clay. She can be seduced by

248

evil. We see his hidden store of her personal items and when he tastes her lipstick from her mug with that unchanging, stern face it is extremely disturbing. The fatherly mien turns to something less sane.

What is also disturbing is that the assorted human baddies don't really have much of a plan. They rely on the werewolves walking meekly into the chamber but George is different. He may not like what he is but he accepts it in his way, and with Nina by his side he can question their motives in their search for the werewolves' cure. Then there is Annie, who the humans can't see and therefore can't control, and all this takes them out of their comfort zone. And this is before Mitchell starts his invisible rampage, snacking randomly on the Bible-boys. And how cheeky is it that Mitchell doesn't actually appear for so long?! Mind you he certainly makes up for it when he does.

The time in the Facility starts with tedium and treading water – George and Nina, Lucy and Kemp have to wait for the full moon, there is nothing they can do until then and it's still weeks away. They drink tea and watch the lights flicker. Annie has company in psychic Hennessey, a sweet portrayal by Adrian Schiller. It seems that Hennessey has always been considered a freak and Annie is his first real friend. The look in his eyes when his ghost sees her for the first time is lovely.

Of course the tea drinking and time wasting can't last and there is a vampire on the loose. After Mitchell's train carriage rampage can he redeem himself? Well, no. He prowls the Facility, invisible to the cameras, murdering and looking for Lucy. He finds her and their two-hander about who has the most reason to feel guilty is powerful but inconclusive. His theory of a spiteful, malicious God backfires in its effect on Kemp, and he still feels Lucy's betrayal keenly. If only she could have told him what she admitted to George – that she loved him. What would he have done then? Maybe exactly the same, but then we don't even know if it was true. In fact by this time it seems that everything that Lucy says is in doubt, tailored to her own agenda and to her audience. Mitchell is going to kill her – the remnants of his humanity warning her to close her eyes so she doesn't see the face of the vampire.

Kemp can't listen to Mitchell talking about vampires being part of God and he still can't accept that Lucy chose Mitchell over him, even if it wasn't forever. He needs to revenge himself on Mitchell and the best way to do this is through his friends. He is determined to make Annie cross over and by killing Hennessey he creates a door. This is a new type of door. Gilbert and Jimmy had doors with a bright light – they each had their resolution and went willingly. Saul's doorway was red-carpeted and wood-panelled and was to drag Annie to hell, to the men with sticks and ropes and black-feathered wings. This door just opens onto deep, black darkness. A door of compulsion – Hennessey is dragged through and so is Annie. Is it Kemp's prayers that push her from this world or does the blackness, the limbo, drag her there despite him.

The loss of Annie pains Mitchell; he collapses in agony when she leaves the world. In this she saves Mitchell, as the pain stops him from killing Lucy. What is this connection? George didn't feel it but then he is still alive – is it the separation that hurt or conversely the connection now that Annie is gone? She – with help from George – saves him again when Mitchell is going to kill

249

Kemp. Despite all that Mitchell has done, the depths of his darkness, George can still get Mitchell to hear him "in Annie's name." Annie and George have nurtured Mitchell's humanity and it is the pain of losing Annie that lets George pull him back. Mitchell can leave with George but what and who is he now? His friends have seen the darkness inside him for the first time; can they ever come back together from that?

There is no redemption for Mitchell, no act of bravery or sacrifice, no great resolution to bring him back to humanity. As we all do, he has to find some way of dealing with what he has done (although few of us have quite such a terrible back catalogue). It would have been easy to give him a great act, to make him a hero or even to destroy him, but making him go on despite all is the hardest route.

The only person with any resolution is Tully and he is sadly long gone. Reading Tully's message clears George's head of all the claims of cures, and by getting out of the room to escape with Nina he can also try to pull Mitchell back to humanity. He sees Annie's end but couldn't save her and it makes him all the more determined to take Mitchell with him. Tully has done what he can to repay George and hopefully he has found peace from his torment.

The trio have escaped Bristol and found an isolated bolt hole. Mitchell is withdrawn, George is quiet but has a job, and they are both dealing with losing Annie. Nina is manic, angry and wants revenge on Lucy – but strangely not so much on Kemp. For all Nina's anger and need for revenge, it is hard to see who has lost the most. Yes, Nina was almost killed and fooled into taking George into danger. They all lost Annie, although her connection to Mitchell seems to have caused him immense physical pain. Mitchell lost his family, his kin – the vampires were destroyed and he was meant to be among them. The woman he thought he could love, who could save him, was a liar and betrayed him. He descended into the darkness of his soul and killed with abandon, losing the last of his hard-won humanity. As he said to Lucy on their very first meeting – if we're having a 'crap life' competition, "I think I win."

So Nina looked for Lucy, Lucy followed that trail back to Nina to find Mitchell, and Kemp followed Lucy. Lucy's brave attempt to make amends ends badly, but her death was calm and looked welcome. She had no idea what she was anymore and maybe this was what she wanted from Mitchell all along, something that she was too scared to do herself.

The door that appears for Lucy gives us an interesting prospect. No sign of Lucy's ghost – or doesn't it work like that if she had already found her resolution? Whatever, she didn't go through her door so will her spirit linger? As Kemp was pulled through her door by Annie what does that make him? He has passed over but is not dead. It's all getting exceedingly complicated.

The scene of Annie in the TV making sure the boys don't forget her is so touching – how could they forget her? Mitchell is convinced they can get her back. Her descriptions of the Kafkaesque bureaucracy of the limbo she is stuck in are wonderful – somewhere between the DWP and Argos. It is also good to see that some of Annie's powers survive – the skills that Sykes taught her in controlling the TV are going to be very handy.

It would have been the perfect place to stop, but wait, look, there's more. Cara, but it's not mad Cara anymore. She's frighteningly sane and along with a rather ditsy Daisy is resurrecting Herrick. In episode one, Annie realised that the bits of his body had gone from the isolation room, and it turns out that Mitchell knew where they were all along. He also told Daisy where Cara was. Is this the beginning of the plan that Mitchell and Daisy put together after their killing spree and blood-drenched passion, a plan that made Mitchell warn George to stay clear of the cities. Just what are they going to do?

Is Mitchell really ready to meet his maker?

Bum notes...

The Bible-boys – a neat addition as an insight into the psyche of Kemp, but where, what, how...? Really would have liked to know more!

George and Annie work out that Lucy, Professor Jaggat is Mitchell's mystery girlfriend, the one who tempted, bedded and dumped him. Isn't it all a bit *too* connected? Do they not wonder if there might be a touch more to this than meets the eye? Where are all the questions? Is neither of them even just a bit nosy?

All of Annie's powers, all she has learnt, seem to have been forgotten. Aura reading, door closing and jumping great distances – all this could have saved her but she stayed and was vanquished by Kemp. Did he have more power than we yet know?

... and the bottom line

Sightings of Russell Tovey's bare backside – none, all fully clad and actually, isn't this terribly shallow?! Not that I'm saying that's a bad thing...

(On a similarly shallow note, I must say that I am very annoyed that Mitchell didn't leave those damned awful tracky bottoms in Bristol... can we hope he's at least lost the tartan hat in the move?)

He said, she said...

She said "It's coming."

What is?

Retribution, my stuff from Amazon...

•••••

We could play I Spy.

Oh, no.

I spy, with my little eye...

Please. Please don't do this!

Live with it. It's happening.

•••••

God made man in His own image. But what if that included His rage, and His spite, and His indifference, and His cruelty? God created all of us; we are all God's children but... God's a bit of a bastard... isn't he?

......

I've got one of your books. Six hundred pages of utter bullshit!
Did you keep the receipt?

Where have I seen... Adrian Schiller (Hennessey)?

Adrian Schiller's TV roles include Gold in *Prime Suspect 2* (1992) and *Prime Suspect 3* (1993), Dominic Collins in *Judge John Deed* (in 2002), Judge in *The IT Crowd* (in 2007), John Thurloe in *The Devil's Whore* (2008) and John Davies in *New Tricks* (in 2010).

He has appeared in films including *Brighton Rock* (2010), *The Infidel* (2010), *Bright Star* (2009) and *Good* (2008).

Adrian played the lead role of Ian Dury in the 2008 West End run of the musical *Hit Me! The Life & Rhymes of Ian Dury*. He has worked extensively on stage, including playing Alexander in *Every Good Boy Deserves Favour* by Tom Stoppard and André Previn for the National Theatre, as well as many roles with the RSC. In 2006 he played the title role in Ranjit Bolt's translation and adaptation of Molière's *Tartuffe*.

Adrian appeared in an anti-drink driving advert, *Frozen in Doubt*, as the barman with many voices who warns of all the likely consequences of drink driving, finishing with "So, what'll it be?" The advert won the Best Casting award in the British Television Advertising Craft Awards in 2008.

Music in episode eight

John Herald	*Saved*
David Holmes	*No Man's Land*

7

... and the future?

The success of *Being Human* just keeps on growing. *Being Human*'s official website – bbc.co.uk/beinghuman – is BBC Three's best performing site ever and has built a dedicated fanbase through regularly updated posts from cast and crew throughout the show's two series.

The online community that was so very vocal about the show right from the beginning, from the broadcast of the pilot, is also constantly expanding. For example, at the time of writing (Autumn 2010), there are over 115,000 people on the *Being Human* Facebook page and @BBCBeingHuman on Twitter has over 6,000 followers. And that's not even looking at the BBC *Being Human* blog, the forums, message boards and various other fan sites!

The opening episode of series two was watched by an audience of 1.6 million and the final showdown of the series by one million people. On top of these figures, the series received 1.7 million viewing requests on the BBC iPlayer.

What the papers said about series two...

"Fantastic" *****

Heat

"Warm, witty, sexy, and... very human"

The Guardian

"British genre telly has seldom looked in such fine fettle"

Time Out

"One of the best new British series of last year returns"

The Independent

"Funny, moving, unmissable and the highlight of my weekend"
Lorraine Kelly, *The Sun*

"A series that's as much about human nature as it is about spookiness and bloodsucking – and that's why it works"

The Daily Telegraph

"The best vampire series on TV (yes, we think little old BBC Three's *Being Human* is better than mega US hit True Blood)"

TV Times

"Smart and cultish comedy horror... excellent"

Total TV Guide

A London Werewolf in America...?

Series one and two of *Being Human* have been shown on BBC America and got great audience reactions, some cracking reviews and some of BBC America's highest ratings. Despite that – or maybe because of it – it has been picked up for an American remake, what they are calling a reimagining, by Syfy.

"*Being Human* is a smart, contemporary, young and imaginative series that reflects Syfy's new brand positioning. We are very excited to adapt this for an American audience and bring it into Syfy's family of programming," said

Dave Howe, President of Syfy.

The series will star Sam Witwer (*Smallville, Battlestar Galactica*) as vampire Aidan, Meaghan Rath (*The Assistants*) as ghost Sally, Sam Huntington (*Cavemen, Superman Returns*) as werewolf Josh and Mark Pellegrino (*Lost, Supernatural*) as Aidan's vampire mentor Bishop. This recurring character could be a brand new addition to the US version, or perhaps a different take on vampire leader Herrick?

And yes – you did read that right, the vampire is called Aidan!

Completing the creative team is: Adam Kane (*The Mentalist, Heroes*) as director and co-executive producer, with executive producer Michael Prupas (*The Kennedys, Pillars of the Earth*), alongside husband-and-wife executive producers/writers Jeremy Carver (*Supernatural*) and Anna Fricke (*Men in Trees, Everwood*).

Muse Entertainment will be producing thirteen (yes – thirteen!) one-hour episodes. "We're incredibly proud of our British series and had a tremendous amount of interest in adapting the project for the States. With Syfy's unwavering passion and dedication for the show, we're confident it can be as successful here as it is in the UK," said Chris Coelen, CEO of RDF Media USA (the US arm of RDF Media Group, which incorporates Touchpaper Television).

Of course the idea of a remake – sorry, reimagining – hasn't met with universal approval in either America or the UK, especially when early reports suggested that vampire Mitchell and ghost Annie would swap sex – or maybe I should more correctly say gender.

The success of the show did really make this inevitable and it will be interesting to watch – as I write, only a teaser trailer and a few photos have been released and it looks... very American. I'll reserve judgement until I see it, but when I say American I mean rather neat and clean-cut and without the quirky oddness that British shows can (but don't always) do so well.

I am determined to stay optimistic though as *Being Human* creator Toby Whithouse's comments are reassuring. He told Daniel Martin of *The Guardian* in January 2010: "They will have a very specific take on the American version and they understand that marketplace much better than I do so I'm happy to help out and advise as much as I can. It's fantastic. I'm fully aware that the transition of British shows into American have met with mixed success, to put it mildly. So I haven't bought the yacht yet, but I'm really, really pleased that it's happening."

Series Three

At time of writing (autumn 2010), series three has just finished filming and is due to be screened in early 2011. So – what can we expect?

Ben Stephenson, BBC Controller of Drama Commissioning, says: "BBC Three drama is all about allowing the singular imagination of a writer the room to flourish, and Toby's extraordinary creation of an emotionally rooted yet mythic world personifies this completely. I can't wait to see where Toby and Touchpaper Television's imaginations will take the story over another eight episodes."

The following isn't really intended to be spoilers. There's nothing here that isn't easily available or widely reported, but if you are reading before you've seen series three and want to avoid hints of any kind at all, then –

*** STOP RIGHT HERE! ***

Of course, I may be about to make myself look very silly if any of this turns out to be wrong, but while I may speculate I don't have a crystal ball. These are just my thoughts and views – unless a publication is credited (in which case it is they who are right or wrong, not me!). Only time will tell!

Moving to Wales

Russell Tovey, Lenora Crichlow and Aidan Turner are all returning for series three. The new series will see the housemates move from their pink corner house in Bristol to Wales – a move brought about by events in the dramatic finale of the second series. They are not, however, going to be in the house we saw them hide out in for that final showdown with Kemp and Lucy.

Rob Pursey of Touchpaper Television says: "BBC Three continues to provide us with a great opportunity to make unusual, ambitious drama, and we are very excited to be able to take the new series of *Being Human* into fresh territory. With the new location in mind, we've already established some startling new storylines and characters. We'll also aim to deliver plenty more exclusive online content in the gaps between series."

New Producer Phil Trethowan told *SFX Magazine* that: "The new house was a real dilemma because obviously the pink house has become iconic. What we arrived at is an old bed and breakfast called Honolulu Heights, that was decorated at the height of '70s kitsch, and hasn't been touched since. So what was once this really trendy place is now somewhere between an eyesore and really f**king cool."

Unofficial photos of filming in Barry promise another great house and that Mitchell has retrieved his 1963 Volvo from Bristol – presumably with Ivan's immortal motoring advice in mind!

From the horse's mouth...

Toby says...

> In series one the threat was supernatural.
> In series two the threat was human.
> In series three the threat is from within...

In February 2010, Toby put a tantalising line at the foot of a post for the BBC *Being Human* blog: "Hey, I've nearly finished the first draft of episode 1, series 3. Blimey. It's bonkers."

So, the threat is from within? Hmmmmm... That could mean almost anything! Mitchell's darkness could remain, or his recent killings could come back and haunt them. Speaking of haunting, what about Lucy – did she cross over? – and Kemp – he really shouldn't have! Nina's Inch High Private Eye impression could land them in all sorts of hot water. What might she find or what might find her? What about two werewolves in the same house?

Concurrent PMT is bad enough – what on earth could this bring? Puppies? Annie is in purgatory and Mitchell plans to pop over and fetch her back – now, that cannot possibly be that simple! Is this how he will redeem himself? Or might they open the doors to the human world? Remember the Gatekeepers' warning: "You don't want our rascals coming out there." If Annie returns, how will that enhance her skill set? Herrick is back – but as what, and what of Daisy and Cara? Daisy's probably bored and wandered off by now, but is Herrick still Cara's Dark Lord? And what of an immortal, undead vampire in purgatory – there surely isn't a form for that!

Toby always felt that Herrick wasn't really done, and after having him back for the 1969 flashback he decided that he had to return. However he does caution us – is he the Herrick that we knew?

Aidan Turner let slip in an audio interview with *earthsmightiest.com* in September 2010 that Herrick returns in series three with no memory at all of what he was. An interesting prospect – no memories of carousing or fighting with Mitchell, no memory of George's wolf and how he was dismembered, and a blank slate for any less than scrupulous vampire. Enter Cara?

New Producer Phil Trethowan takes over from Matthew Bouch for series three. He was formerly the Script Editor for the pilot and series one and two, and so is thoroughly steeped the world of *Being Human*. He told the BBC *Being Human* blog that the new series will look at more of the world of the werewolves. They have already fairly thoroughly explored the vampire community, but this time they will focus more on the werewolf hinterland. Hinterland? Just a nice posh word, or does this mean something more precise?

There is – apparently – something decidedly awful that vampires do to werewolves, which they have always done. This is something that we have never seen before, that has never been alluded to. Frankly, in the world of *Being Human* I'm not sure I have any chance at all of guessing what that might be, but we'll find out in series three.

Lacey Turner as Lia

The BBC Press Office announced in June 2010 that award-winning actor Lacey Turner, *EastEnders*'s Stacey Slater, will guest star in episode one. Speaking about her first TV role outside of *EastEnders*, she says: "It was fantastic working on *Being Human*. I had some great scenes with Aidan Turner, especially when his character Mitchell is facing up to some of the things he has done in the past. The cast and crew were really welcoming and I can't wait to watch how the story comes together on screen when the series airs.". After losing Annie at the end of series two, Mitchell misses his friend and is anxious to try and save her, and so he enters purgatory and it is here he meets Lia (Lacey Turner), who steers him on his journey.

Robson Green as McNair

Phil Trethowan gave a sneak preview to *SFX Magazine* in September 2010 of a new werewolf on the block – McNair. "We felt that we'd really explored the broader vampire world pretty extensively so with Robson we wanted to explore the broader world of werewolves a bit more and so he brings all that world into the show with him." Of course the perennial question about werewolves was asked – will he be stripped off at any point at all? "I can tell you exclusively that you will not be disappointed. And I can also tell you Robson's in good shape. He definitely works out."

The previous werewolf costume had to perform double duty between George and Nina, but McNair has a different look: "Now we've got a whole new werewolf. We had the idea that each werewolf lineage as it were, had a slightly different look about them. McNair looks a bit more grizzly."

Actress Nicola Walker told Ian Wylie (see below) that Robson's role was not a humorous one: "I can't wait to see him in it. I know a little bit about the part he is playing and it's going to be brilliant. He's not playing a comedy role at all..."

Robson also tweeted photos of his werewolf transformations on his Twitter account: @extreme_fishing.

Nicola Walker as Wendy

Spooks star Nicola Walker was interviewed by Ian Wylie in October 2010 on *lifeofwylie.com*, and confirmed that she had filmed a guest role in series three of *Being Human*. "The cast were telling me things about the show. And I was going, 'No, no, no, you don't understand. I know everything about it. I'm a fan.' I had the best time." She plays health visitor Wendy who stumbles into the house occupied by our supernatural trio. "She thinks she's having a bad day. But because she doesn't know anything about the people in the house, she doesn't realise just how bad a day she could be having."

Other snippets and nuggets...

Nina is back, Sinead Keenan was filming series three. However she did Tweet in the last week of filming: "The Final. Ever. Week!!" Interpret that how you will...

Also on Twitter, Russell Tovey said he had been filming with Scott Arthur who had a role in the final episode of series three. Kai Owen (Rhys in *Torchwood*) is appearing in episode one as Bob. While Rebecca Cooper (Cara) was spotted filming in Wales.

Is there anything we won't see? Well, the *Miami Herald* asked Lenora about series three in July 2010 and the phone line went ominously silent. She was perfectly willing, though, to talk about what she *doesn't* want to see: an all-musical episode, a popular suggestion on *Being Human* message boards in the UK. "Listen, there's a *reason* that not everybody is writing series for television," she snorted. "The idea of putting a musical together is the most terrifying thing I can imagine. The support for that has just been ridiculous. I can't imagine a TV show doing that." Lenora lapsed into silence when a reporter told her that *Buffy the Vampire Slayer* did just that in a 2002 episode. "Good God," she murmured. "Don't breathe a word of that to anyone here."

So what can we really expect? The sky's the limit. Aidan Turner was asked what he thought could happen next by *Digital Spy* in May 2010: "I have no idea what could happen. That's why I'm not a writer! Toby's imagination is off the wall, so it could go anywhere."

I rather like the summary by Dan Martin in *The Guardian* in June 2010:

"As unsolvable cliffhangers go, the end of *Being Human 2* might claim to approach the heights of *Doctor Who*'s *The Pandorica Opens*. Annie was left trapped in a bureaucratic purgatory. Her monstery BFFs were left emoting glumly without her, in Wales. They'd even had to leave the cool pink house. And the deliciously sarky vampire leader Herrick had been reanimated through a bizarre bloodletting ceremony. I'm getting the sense that series three is going to turn the outrageousness up to 11. With no need to set the programme in the real world any longer, it's going all-out bonkers, horrific and heartbreaking. Could this world be approaching a big, end-of-days climax to take the series out on a high?"

Couldn't have put it better myself!

8

I'm ready for
my close-up,
Mr Whithouse...

Costume and Makeup

Annie

Annie stays forever in the clothes in which she died, as do all ghosts. They are fixed in a moment in time, their last moment. However... there is always an angle! Annie's outfit is incredibly flexible – her grey cardigan can be wrapped around her, pulled up as a hood and even worn back to front. She always has her Ugg boots and legwarmers but sometimes she is all covered up and sometimes there is a gap to her leggings – after a couple of years in those boots any fresh air must be welcome! Her clothes also reflect her state of mind and her self-esteem – more confidence equals less wrapped up, and at the height of her visibility and solidity at the start of series two she has some different pieces to wear. In fact, after her cinema date with Saul, she even removes enough layers to bare her arms! It quite obviously makes her irresistible to poor Saul, especially with Terry Wogan and the newsreader egging him on from his TV. After Saul fails to take her through his door and the Gatekeepers make her invisible again as a punishment, Annie is back to her original grey layered set.

In a post about acting in September 2010 on the BBC *Being Human* blog, Lenora said something I think we can all sympathise with: "Girls, you know what I'm talking about. When you're having a day... one of them days and they dangle leggings in front of you, and you're like 'Today? Leggings? Really? I just want to be in a sack!'"

Annie's makeup is very natural – lucky Lenora doesn't really need it, being very lovely. It is somehow weirdly comforting to see that a ghost can still smear her mascara when she cries. It would just be too cold and emotionless if everything stayed put regardless.

Annie wears her engagement ring until she finds out the truth about Owen and what he did to her. It has gone in episode five – does she take it off or does it disappear? It is never mentioned, maybe it just no longer belongs with her and it is as if it had never been there at all. I would be curious as to whether a ghost can add to their attire – put on a coat or jewellery – or if their ghostly body would somehow reject it, if whatever they tried would just go straight through them? Or maybe it just would never occur to them that it could be an option.

George

George looks like a perfectly normal although rather buttoned-up young man, but his outfits are very carefully put together. He is rather more tucked in and tidy than Mitchell, and he obviously has a relationship with an iron – unlike Mitchell. He has neat jeans and nice white trainers and sensible warm fleeces. He always has two pens in the top pocket of his work scrubs – one red, one black – and they are always neatly spaced and clipped in place.

He plays safe, he isn't confident about his wardrobe so takes few chances – after all, he doesn't really want to be noticed. His 'not-a-date' (in a gastro pub) with Nina gives him a sartorial crisis and he parades a selection of outfits for Annie and Mitchell to consider. None get unanimous approval – or actually any approval at all! I really hope he took the orange flowered item back – let's never see that again.

George always wears his Star of David, except when he transforms. Although he pretty much lost his faith when he became a werewolf, when he was cursed, the idea of belief and faith is still comforting to him and he takes strength from the hospital chaplain. Maybe that hope for something to believe in has been rocked by Kemp and Lucy but, then again, what they did doesn't deserve to be seen as being in the name of faith, so perhaps he'll see beyond it.

The scars from the werewolf attack that made George what he is now are always there. The three deep scratches across his shoulder have healed but the scars are raised, savage and unchangeable. A permanent brand and a constant reminder of what he is. Presumably Nina's arm will always show the same vicious marks, and Tully went to the chamber with the tracks of George's claws across his face.

Mitchell

At the start of episode four, Mitchell muses about tribes and where we belong, and we see him walking through the dark city in a variety of outfits from his 116 years. His WW1 army uniform, a rather suave dinner suit, a punk, a new romantic and then the Mitchell we know. The implication is that he finally knows who he is. Mitchell's clothes are contemporary; they don't look out of place for the age he appears and the life he lives. He seems unconcerned about the impression he gives, his dates with Becca and Lucy don't really see any change in his style, there's no sign that he feels the need to dress to impress. With his age he has the confidence to say take it or leave it. Whatever.

Mitchell can carry off the less than mixed and matched ensembles that probably come straight from his bedroom floor-drobe, but the one constant item of clothing is the fingerless gloves. Mostly in sludge green. Hopefully he does have several pairs – I hate to think what is getting ingrained in the wool otherwise... Also constant are the Celtic silver rings, which seem to date back quite some time as he was already wearing them in the 1969 flashback.

When Mitchell gets drawn back to the vampires and the darker side of his nature starts to show, his clothes also get darker. The reds and yellows disappear in favour of a more sombre pallet of greys, blues and black. There is a lot more sweeping about in leather coats. He never quite gets to the suited and booted look of the funeral parlour vampires though.

Mitchell is seen in two of the flashbacks. In the 1999 scenes with Carl as Mitchell goes cold turkey there isn't a lot to go on costume-wise, but in 1969 the details are perfect. A rather more bouffant 'do' – not great on the hair products front were the 60s – a pair of run-of-the-mill white knickers, but a very dapper black suit and Chelsea boots. Rather reminiscent of a young Brian Jones of the Rolling Stones, even though David Bowie was Josie's preference. Never mind – she managed to get over that quite successfully!

The Vampires

Being Human avoids the usual gothic vampire clichés and the assorted vampire hoards are not dressed in standard issue black draperies, or lace and floppy cuffs. They are what they are. When necessary they have fangs – the old-fashioned way with added teeth (that can't be easy to talk in). The black eyes are CGI-generated, and just these two effects, a dab or two of blood and some cracking writing and acting are all it takes to keep them scary and unpredictable. Who needs all that daft twinkly sparkly stuff?!

Herrick has his police uniform and when he is at the funeral parlour they all wear the suits that would be expected in that environment. Gloves are still a feature though – black leather for the funeral parlour vampires such as Herrick and Seth. Of course they may just feel the cold, but there is something appropriately sinister about pulling on the black leather gloves before a confrontation.

Lauren looks like any young woman of her age and era, but as she becomes more integrated into the darker side her looks get a little glossier, harder but more glamorous.

Ivan is perennially sharp-suited – a perfect expression of his elegantly wasted attitude – while Daisy is in the modern equivalent of a 1940s tea dress, although hers is rather more flimsy and considerably shorter than the originals! She wears ornate rings and, given the travels of this immortal couple, the story behind them may be fascinating. Or maybe they just came from Accessorize – with the atypical vampires of *Being Human* we just don't know!

Cara is transformed by the end of series two. Her madness has gone, replaced by a cold determination and a much sharper look that is a far cry from her nylon canteen overall and dodgy hot chocolate.

265

Other outfits...

While firmly grounded and set in the present day and in very everyday and normal lives, there are opportunities for the costumes to really make a character work. The ghosts of Gilbert and Sykes are immaculately costumed in their respective periods. Sykes's uniform is faultless and Gilbert's 80s garb is perfect down to – we are assured – the Y-fronts! It's the little details that make it work – the fag behind the ear, the digital watch and the quiff.

The humans all have touches that make them very real and recognisable. Janey has her vivid orange salon tan and the perfect matching outfits that probably have designer labels but actually look a touch Matalan. Nina – out of scrubs – wears the basic casual attire that helps her disappear; she seems to be hiding just as much as George is and the horribly realistic scars she shows him makes us realise she doesn't want to be noticed. She is always covered up, even before George scratches her.

The two versions of Josie work equally well. We first see the older Josie and she is perfectly dressed to make her slightly bohemian background clear. The rings and earrings, her bag and her layered look – she looks so much younger than we know she must be but she is clearly very comfortable in her skin, a little like Mitchell. Young Josie is the perfect flashback – her bright mini dress and extravagant eyelashes put her firmly into the 60s, but this is no *Austin Powers*-styled outfit. It's practical, affordable and she would have looked smartly fashionable while still being able to work as a teacher in a much more conventional time.

Kemp is a perfect product of his time as well – always in a jacket and tie but with the sensible addition of a warm jumper. He doesn't look out of place anywhere. This is just another upright, elderly gentleman – probably ex-army, certainly a professional and that is what makes him so convincing. The mere hint of a robe, a dog collar or a sash and it would have been far too obvious. Such a normal man with such obdurate beliefs – exorcism in tweed and cavalry twill.

Lucy appears to be exactly what a young successful doctor should be and she wears what looks like a uniform of her own devising. Practical shirt-dresses and extremely sensible shoes, they are all perfectly presentable but just a little old for her. When she finally hooks Mitchell and sets the scene for seduction, she blossoms into a sleeveless black dress with dangly earrings and lets her hair down. There is even a pair of very high-heeled shoes in the picture! Another part of the role maybe?

It is interesting that Lucy wears a turquoise ring. Turquoise is one of the oldest protection amulets, and was also known as a symbol of wealth in many ancient cultures. It also bestows strength, protection from harm, psychic sensitivity and connection to the spirit world. Interesting. Coincidence?

Werewolves and transformations

One of the early decisions to be made about the pilot episode of *Being Human* was about how to show the transformation from George to the werewolf. CGI effects were ruled out immediately as it would have cost pretty much the whole budget for the show! So it had to be done the classic way with animatronics and prosthetics.

Toby Whithouse thinks that this is the right way. He has written for *Doctor Who* and when filming the monsters on that much bigger budget show he saw David Tennant and Billie Piper being chased down a corridor by a person with a long pole with a tennis ball on the top! Transformation the *Being Human* way is very real – it actually happens and when filming in the woods the light falls on the wolf and on George in the way that it really should.

There are several posts on the BBC *Being Human* blog about the various stages of the transformation and about how it is for Russell Tovey and Sinead Keenan, plus an extra feature on the series two DVD – and quite frankly they explain the detail way better than I can!

The process was developed further for series two, with more prosthetics and the need to portray Nina's transformation as well as George's. The werewolf, the outcome of the transformation, is also different to that of series one. The series two werewolf is much more powerful, more muscular and considerably scarier than the much slighter series one wolf.

The stage one makeup for the actors takes around two and a half hours to put on and is the early stages of the transformation, including the contact lenses to alter the eyes, werewolf teeth and the claws. Conversely this is filmed second and the heavier, more detailed stage two effects are filmed first to make the best use of the time available. Stage two takes about four and a half hours to put on but does give much improved effects compared to series one, where the transformation as seen on screen went straight from something similar to the stage one makeup to the animatronic heads. The prosthetics used for stage two include chest pieces for the actors which more effectively bridge the gap between the actor and the animatronics. The face pieces totally change their looks – the werewolf teeth, the shape of the brow and the (rather cute) pointed ears make the transformations even more effective than in series one. With so many hours in makeup added to all the screaming and the physicality of the transformation scenes, it must be utterly exhausting for Sinead and Russell.

The actors wear contact lenses and teeth, false claws that protrude from the ends of their fingers and there are various other prosthetic pieces, some of which inflate and move, before the filming swaps to the animatronics to show the jaw extending and the final stages of becoming the wolf. The very final stage – the full werewolf – is played by Paul Kasey, an experienced actor who has played pretty much all of the monsters in the new *Doctor Who* series.

We get fairly used to seeing George transform in series one and the shock value of Nina becoming a wolf is enhanced by that familiarity. Sinead is tiny and the transformation of this small, delicate woman to the wolf is somehow disturbing as well as terrifying. It was also good to see that Nina's scars hadn't been forgotten and were worked into the prosthetic pieces made for her.

Kensington Gore

The accepted name for theatrical blood, which comes in a variety of colours and consistencies – not to mention different flavours!

If you are going to have a story about vampires then there is bound to be blood. Despite Mitchell being on the wagon in series one, it doesn't stop anyone else and as early as episode one we have Becca with her throat torn out on the ground and George and Mitchell covered in her blood. Mitchell gets stabbed by Herrick – yet more blood – but all of this is nothing compared to what we get in series two!

The gore quotient in series two is considerably higher. We have blown up werewolves in Lucy's chamber who need prosthetics to make them look as though their flesh has exploded as the blood pumps out. There are dead, bloodied bodies in the 1969 flashback and Chief Constable Wilson comes to a gory and very sticky end at Mitchell's hands (or fangs).

All of this is before we get to the carnage after the explosion that kills Ivan and the vampires, leaving Mitchell and Daisy to rampage in revenge. The scene on the train after they have left and when the light comes on to the mess of blood and bodies is incredible – gory, scary, but still humorous in places. The effects are fantastic – not that I know what a train full of vampire-ravaged humans would actually look like, but I expect it would be pretty much like this! There is no dignity left to any of the victims and the wounds and the blood are realistically done. There is a great extra on the DVDs which shows how it was all done and just how excited Aidan Turner got about all that blood!

The blood always stays shocking, it's used well and the effects are so good that the horror remains. If the wounds look real and the hospital scenes with the vampire victims look right then we can see the story beyond the gore – it's not that clichéd splattering of ketchup that always looks so corny. It could be very stomach churning to have all this blood, but the strength of the writing and acting takes us beyond it. It is always right there with the storytelling and never seems to be gratuitous, even though in a supernatural drama that must be a temptation.

While the train carriage is grotesque and shocking, some of the other bloody scenes linger more in the mind. For me, the most effective include the death of Galvin in the chamber, sliding in his own blood as he tries to escape while his body tears itself apart, the shock of the stake appearing through Lucy's body as Kemp kills her, and that tiny trace of blood on Mitchell's mouth as he weeps for Josie.

9

location, location, location...

Totterdown, Bristol

Bristol was chosen as the location of *Being Human* for a number of reasons. Firstly the show is made by BBC Wales, which necessarily limited the choice to cities in a particular geographical area. Secondly, Bristol has the wealth of architecture and settings that fitted the feel of the show perfectly, with the slave trade angle being picked up by Declan O'Dwyer, the director of the pilot. It seemed a sensible assumption that vampires could have used the slave trade to get into the country and to establish a significant base in Bristol, which continued until Herrick and Mitchell's day. Mitchell tells Seth about the first vampire to live openly in Bristol – Richard Turner in 1630: "The first to have a double life. He ran for Parliament, was a slave trader, killed maybe, I don't know, a thousand people."

Totterdown, a suburb of Bristol, is where you can find the *Being Human* house and many of the exterior locations used in series one and two. It's a distinctive area of tightly packed steep roads with classic Victorian terraces, rather less classically painted in an array of colours, giving a slightly seaside air. Vale Street is reputed to be the steepest residential street in England.

Totterdown grew rapidly in the late nineteenth century and was mainly built to house the workers from the nearby Temple Meads railway station and other central Bristol industries. It was mainly a working-class area serving local industry, but is now a popular choice for younger people working in the city centre. It is perfectly in context as the place where George and Mitchell would take up residence.

1 Windsor Terrace

The house where our supernatural trio take up residence is easy to recognise. It's a corner house at the apex of two Victorian terraces, it's pink and the name of the road is clearly visible high on the wall. The house began life with another identity – it started out as retail premises, like many other corner houses in the area. Visible and easy to find – they are their own perfect advertising. Also very appropriate for our trio, none of whom are living out the identities they were born with. It is thought that the house was a pub due to the engraved window to the side of the front door advertising wines and spirits (George and Annie?!), but it would probably have been a general store – grocery, maybe a butcher's and, of course, an off-licence. In the opaque glass over the front door is etched 'Corner House' – nothing like pointing out the obvious!

The houses of Totterdown, like our trio's house, show signs of decay, of water damage and staining. Some have already been beautifully refurbished and some are yet to be loved. If you want to hide but still participate, keep separate but blend in, then what better place than a pink house on a corner – neither flashy nor derelict, and just quirky enough.

In her article *Ghostly Architecture* on BDOnline.co.uk in March 2009, Denna Jones considered the colour of the house: "The precise shade of pink is unknown, but 'P-618' aka 'Baker-Miller Pink' is a suitable candidate. Used in correctional facilities and drunk tanks, it works physiologically to reduce aggression. Think of it as Totterdown's passive community assistance to rein in the anti-social proclivities of the dead, the undead and hirsute half-

271

humans." Although, judging from Mitchell's behaviour at the end of series two, he seems to have managed to override all the soothing effects of that very special pink. It didn't do much to calm the wolf at the start of series one either... Maybe they should have painted the inside completely pink too.

Come inside luv...

The interiors of the house are filmed in specially built sets, designed to resemble the actual interior of the house. It's not an exact copy – HD cameras need space and the crews need room to move around. It's also far more controllable and adaptable an environment to work in. The interiors are put together with incredible attention to detail and it feels as if it really was furnished and lived in by George, Mitchell and Annie and their very different personalities.

In the pilot, the estate agent tells Mitchell that the house had been a sculptor's studio before being bought by Annie and Owen to refurbish. Inevitably it didn't ever get finished as Owen murdered Annie and then rented out the scene of the crime...

The house has clearly evolved – design is not how this interior came together! There is 1970s wallpaper in the kitchen and I bet it is that plastic-y stuff that was just so cool and trendy back then. There are changes of colour and pattern and the classic black and white tiles of the hall floor bisect the wooden floorboards of the downstairs rooms. Plus, of course, the cracked tile – an ever-present reminder of where Annie fell and died.

After the first episode, when George transformed in the house, there are deep werewolf scratches visible on the walls and the rooms are left empty. The werewolf shredded the furniture and destroyed everything else and they are left with the need for a trip to IKEA – Mitchell's all-time favourite. After that the downstairs rooms gradually develop and fill up with the eclectic clutter than makes it all feel very real (and I doubt any of it is from that well-known Swedish emporium!). There are books, magazines, videos, tapes and an increasing collage of flyers on the wall by the door. The kitchen is full of crockery, cereal and even a pair of fighting grannies! There are lamps everywhere and plenty of comfy seating, although every time there is a crisis they all revert to sitting on the floor. There are also stacks of board games, and in the *Being Human* book *The Road* we are told that these are mostly Mitchell's and that Waddington's *The Vampire Game* is a particular favourite!

Mitchell's room

Andrew Purcell, the Set Designer, pointed out that Mitchell's room is coffin shaped – a lovely touch and I'm sure it helps him sleep much more soundly. There are decent-sized windows, but whenever Mitchell is there the blinds are always down; a sunny aspect is not a vampire's favourite. It has to be said though that the main factor defining Mitchell's space is mess! It looks rather like the habitation of a teenage boy or domestically challenged student. Is this really Mitchell or just the role he is playing at the moment? Looking closer there are clues that this is probably not just any 20-something's lair. It is full of odd vintage items – vinyl singles and albums and an old record player (yes, that's what we had before HiFi, CDs and MP3); there are old film posters and quite an array of musical instruments. Amongst the encroaching tide of clothes, odd shoes (very odd shoes) and old singles are a guitar, a saxophone and a squeezebox... and can he play any of them we wonder?! Presumably 116 years give you plenty of time to take lessons and fit in some practice...

Annie's Room

Annie doesn't have a bed – ghosts don't sleep – or much in the way of storage – ghosts cannot change their clothes. There is so little in her room it seems to emphasise just how thoroughly Owen excised her from his life – no sign of her is left in their home. She has an oversized comfy armchair and on the mantelpiece is a picture of Loveheart sweets – an image that somehow seems to sum up Annie's sunny, affectionate personality. Annie's room is an old-fashioned pink, a dusty greyish pink, a lovely contrast to her grey layers and a colour that is soft and gentle – much like Annie.

In series two, George swaps rooms with Annie so he can fit in his cage. He moves in his bed and soundproofs the walls. We never see what Annie does to George's old room though. I hope she kept the gnomes.

George's Room

I suspect that when they first moved in, George and Mitchell tossed a coin and Mitchell won, whether by fair means or foul. That left George with the smallest room. It was a child's room at some point in the past and has wonderful vintage wallpaper featuring cute happy gnomes. The whimsical pictures couldn't be a better contrast with the savagery of the werewolf. Putting George in the smallest space seems appropriate – while he is the tallest of the trio he compresses his essential self to avoid attention and it is only the wolf that gets the freedom that George has lost. The restrictions of the space seem somehow very apt.

He is considerably tidier than Mitchell (not difficult) and I can imagine he probably has a colour-coordinated sock drawer. There are some other neat contrasts – George's sleek DAB radio versus Mitchell's rather chunkier transistor radio.

The Funeral Parlour

B. Edwards, Funeral Directors. The Bristol base for vampires for the last twenty-seven years and, as Kemp reminds us, a very convenient way to dispose of dead bodies.

The building used for this location (1-3 Alma Vale Road, BS8 2HL) was a car showroom and a vast empty white space which had to be fitted out to look like a funeral directors. The showroom was dressed to give all the rooms required by the story, including the pantry/human blood bank. There had to be a front office – appropriate and dignified, where Nanna can sit to give a little extra atmosphere. Herrick also needed an office and that was a space that was mostly left alone. A cavernous empty area with a very large table – what more does a potential world leader actually need? Oh, except for a hearse or two and a happy band of willing and able acolytes.

There's a nice contrast in series two in the Funeral Parlour – the coffins

273

and the gathered vampires baying for Cara's blood, juxtaposed with delicate china cups and saucers for 'Nanna's special tea' and there's even a proper cake stand. I would expect fondant fancies to be offered at the very least!

When Mitchell becomes 'King of the Vampires' he reopens the Funeral Parlour, which had presumably been abandoned after Herrick's dismemberment by George as the wolf. He takes over an office – more of a proper office than Herrick's vast open space. He has a desk, phones, mug of pens and a big throne-like chair. Maybe Mitchell needed a little extra help to look the part of a world-conquering megalomaniac – Herrick, of course, found it natural and effortless. Judging by the rows of filing cabinets and boxes, vampires aren't great declutterers – even Herrick's old police uniform still hangs on a coat stand. Wouldn't you like the chance to browse through some of the files?

Homes from Home

Josie's flat when Mitchell first meets her in 1969 is a beautiful homage to the 1960s. There is an immense level of detail in the dressing of Josie's home, as well as the flat of the bloodied, blonde and very dead girls who had the misfortune to party with Mitchell and Herrick.

Josie's flat isn't glossy, shiny, magazine-styled 1960s but a proper home, a mix of 60s kitsch (or so it seems to us now) alongside older furniture, and that combination gives a great sense of time and place. In the party flat there are the wonderful details of the cocktail glasses, cigarette cases and the state-of-the-art vacuum cleaner, and then we see Josie's flat – less debauched, less blood for a start, but still all that fascinating detail. Of course we don't know for sure that this is Josie until the very end of the episode, but the clues are there if you look and particularly if you listen. In series one, Mitchell remembers that Josie was a dance teacher, and there are dance posters and ballet manuals in the flat.

Lucy's apartment – somehow it isn't a flat – is a much more twenty-first-century affair. We see her kitchen and her bedroom – she seems to bypass a lounge entirely. Despite a clutter of recipe books and plenty of kitchen paraphernalia as well as more books in the bedroom, Lucy's place seems somehow sterile, there is nothing there to tell us anything about her. She does have a cross on the wall and a rosary by the bed – is this the real Lucy? Where are her treasures, where is Trevor the goldfish? Josie's flat was full of her personality, while Lucy's is just part of the role she is playing. As with her whole persona, can we believe anything that her home is telling us? Although, all homes should come with that one very important accessory – the essential thirteenth-century stake! Personally, I keep mine with the TV remote, nice and handy...

Owen and Janey's house couldn't be more different to the pink house he bought with Annie. It is far more conventional, perfectly normal and much more what you would expect from an up-and-coming young professional – although professional what? Do we actually know what Owen does for a living? We know Janey works in a tanning salon – hence the chic Tango-orange tan – but Owen? No idea, he was studying computing when he and

Annie met... of course it becomes slightly irrelevant once Annie takes her revenge and drives him totally mad!

Nina's place could be a house or a flat – we only see the living room briefly on two occasions: once when George is collecting her in his bar staff outfit and again when he runs to her after Bernie is knocked down. It's a perfectly cosy home, full of the usual ornaments, clutter and cushions of a normal life. There are thriving plants, flowers in vases, pictures and wall hangings – it's a rather lovely room in truth. So what happened to it all when she moved into George's small and bijou room in the house? She had a few clothes and some tampons and that was it... Not even a favourite mug and some photos? Surely she didn't abandon everything – that doesn't seem like Nina, although after finding that George had scratched her maybe she felt that she had to shake off her old skin and start anew.

The Facility

The location used for Kemp and Lucy's Facility is in the centre of Bristol, on Wine Street, and is actually the old Bank of England building. The distinctive Grade 1 listed Brutalist architecture makes the building both forbidding and somehow anonymous – the perfect location for some science/religion fusion and a sideline in exploding supernaturals!

It was built in 1844-7 by Charles Robert Cockerell with a Doric pseudo-portico of three bays recessed between low pavilions: the attic storey is arcaded with a triangular pediment. OK, I looked that up, but just imagine that sentence read aloud in Kemp's sonorous tones and you can see why I can't resist including it!

Unusually, compared to most other locations, the interior scenes were also filmed in the same building – it is incredibly distinctive and the claustrophobic corridors and lack of natural light add to the tension. You can feel the weight of the building, the security and the feeling of being utterly, totally trapped. The clang of the closing doors seems to echo endlessly through the corridors.

There is a great tour of the Facility by Lloyd the Technician on the series two DVDs (but you have to find it first!). He shows us all round, including a peek at Kemp's altar, and lets us into the deep dark secrets of Kemp's love of candles and Coco Pops.

The hospital

In *Being Human*, the hospital where George and Mitchell work is called St Jude's, but it is really Bristol General Hospital. Of course Nina, Lauren and Lucy also work there, as does Becca who has a fatally unsuccessful date with Mitchell.

There are scenes which clearly show the real name of the hospital as well as the temporary St Jude's set dressing, but it doesn't look at all odd. Most old hospital sites have a plethora of extremely confusing signage! It's a classic old hospital building with bits added on, developed, altered – and not altered – over the years since it was opened in 1832. Despite the name it is actually a rehabilitation hospital for the elderly and stroke patients rather than a general facility. Some interior scenes are also filmed there.

Pubs and Clubs

The New Found Out (60 Green Street, BS3 4UB) was where Annie got a job after declaring her great ambition was to work in a pub. "Jesus! Aim for the stars," as Mitchell exclaims in delight! She gets a job in The New Found Out just down the road from the house and George pays a few visits to meet landlord Hugh and slightly odd new regular Saul – wonder what would come of that...?

The Shakespeare (1 Henry Street, BS3 4UD) seems much more like suitable George and Mitchell territory than the rather nautical New Found Out, and they visit with Annie at the end of the pilot episode.

The King's Head (60 Victoria Street, BS1 6DE) is where George and Mitchell have their uncomfortable heart-to-heart at the start of series two. Nice wood panelling but George declares he hates it, although, frankly, at that point would you believe anything he says, given he's still in his utter idiot phase? A nice touch contrasts George's straight pint glass with Mitchell's old-fashioned, dimpled-glass beer mug.

The Rummer Hotel Bar (All Saints Lane, BS1 1JH) is Mitchell's 'dress to impress' venue and where he takes Becca and then later Lucy after their night together.

The Fleece (12 St Thomas Street, BS1 6JJ) was what Lucy got on their first 'date' – mainly due to the 'two for one' offer on pints of scrumpy. Mitchell misjudged that one pretty badly and if it hadn't been for Lucy's special secret-squirrel agenda he was unlikely to have ever got a second chance!

Chesters (Frogmore Street, BS1 5UX) closed down in 2009 but was the club where Annie was introduced to Gilbert on 80s night. The scenes were filmed with the help of a group of 80s -enthusiasts – who all had their own outfits...

Other Random and Recognisable Places...

The **War Memorial** that Mitchell is looking at in the introductory sequence to series one is on Rupert Street in Bristol and commemorates the fallen from both World Wars.

The labyrinthine **Redcliffe Caves** in the Redcliffe area of Bristol are where Cara is imprisoned by Mitchell and the setting for the sixteenth-century flashback. Originally old mine workings, the caves were used for many purposes including storage of goods. There is a barred section in the caves where it is rumoured that slaves were kept.

Alan Cortez – Psychic Experience is appearing in the **Curzon Cinema** in Clevedon, just outside Bristol. It is reputed to be the oldest purpose-built, continuously operated cinema in the world.

There is an amazing view of **Clifton Suspension Bridge** in the pilot when George awakes the morning after the full moon clutching the remains of a deer with the bridge dominating the scene behind him.

George takes Kirsty to **The Watershed** (1 Cannon Street, BS1 5TX) cinema to see the very, very (very) long German subtitled film with so very, very (very) many clowns.

Kirsty's market stall where she aims to be an artist with flowers is in **St Nicholas Market** (Corn Street, BS1 1JG), part of Bristol's finest independent shopping area.

The Mercure Hotel (Redcliffe Hill, BS1 6SQ) is where Mitchell meets Lauren for some bloody – very bloody – sex. Hope they left a good tip for the chambermaid who had to clean up after them!

Bristol Temple Meads Station (Henry Street, BS3 4UD) is seen twice – Nina is outside, presumably contemplating a proper escape when she is approached by Kemp. Bernie and Fleur leave from platform 8 – although quite whether Bernie's hunger will be satisfied by a butty from the buffet is a whole different matter!

10

read all about it
– the books

In 2010, BBC Books published three novels featuring the characters and settings from *Being Human*. Each book stands alone, but they do follow on in sequence if you want to read all three right through in one go. They are well worth a read if you love the series, and I will try and review them without giving away too many vital bits of the plot in case you haven't read them yet.

If you want to read them first completely unspoilered (is that even a word?!) – then you might like to come back to this bit!

The books are set somewhere alongside the early episodes of series two. Annie has left the pub, Saul is in the past and she is invisible. Nina has left George, but he is still working at the hospital and is in his pre-cage period. Mitchell hasn't yet become fixated on Lucy (or at least doesn't mention her) and the vampires are without a leader now that Herrick has gone.

Book one – *The Road* by Simon Guerrier

Annie has learned quite a lot about her new friend Gemma: she's from Bristol, she used to work in a pharmacy, and she's never forgiven herself for the suicide of her teenage son. She also died ten years ago and doesn't know why she's come back through that door...

The main story of *The Road* is about Gemma, a ghost who appears from a door and has no idea what she is doing there. It turns out that this motherly figure, still mourning her teenage son who killed himself, is actually manipulating the household. She tries to take on Annie's role in looking after the boys and the house, but why is she really there? And what is that odd chemical smell?

Also unbalancing the house is the whiff of redundancies at the hospital. There is a new Administrator – Doctor McGough – and he is forcing change, peeking into corners, installing CCTV and a sense of fear. He also seems to have an unhealthy interest in our boys and his is a story that continues through the three books.

The mystery of Gemma seems to be connected with a road-building plan which gives George the idea of organising a protest. It's a nice idea that could have been developed further and, while it moves the story on as it is intended to, we could have had a lot more fun with George carrying the banner. The protest is all over and done in a flash except for the mild diversion of retrieving the film from reporter Gavin's camera as it contains a photo of the space where Mitchell should be standing.

Gemma is a dark and mysterious character and we are never quite sure what she is doing or what she can remember or, more likely, what she claims to remember. We sympathise with her predicament and her uncertainty until we discover more about her and realise that we too are being manipulated. We realise she was not what we thought she was and her story – and that of her son – becomes horribly clear.

It's a new way of seeing ghosts. For a start, Gemma returns through a door – this is new and is frightening to Annie in a way she can't really understand. Gemma is manipulative; she seems to have an agenda way beyond the yearning for life and resolution of the ghosts we've met so far. She saps the energy of those around her, feeding off their strength – especially

Annie who becomes increasingly wary… and weary. In *The Road*, Annie sleeps for the first time since she died.

There are some introductions to people we'll see again – Kaz and Gail, Trevor Moss – Mossy – of the bowling club, Gavin Foot, intrepid investigative reporter and last, but very definitely not least, the effective, efficient Doctor McGough.

Book two – *Chasers* by Mark Michalowski

George's friend, Kaz, arrives at the flat with a staggering request: she and her partner Gail want to have a child, and they'd like George to be the father. George is warming to the idea – he's always wanted kids, and he can be as involved in the baby's life as he wishes – but he is wary: what if his condition is genetic?

Ostensibly all about George and his innocent plan to father a child for Kaz and Gail, *Chasers* also gives us an outwardly simple tale of Mitchell befriending a patient which meanders into rather darker territory.

A vampire diary is dotted through the book – exploits of blood and death in Paris, Las Vegas and Ibiza. Are we finding out more about Mitchell's dangerous past? Keep reading – it may not be all that it seems.

Unfortunately Kaz and Gail are not terribly well fleshed out and Kaz in particular suffers from being a New Age stereotype. Yes, we get she's meant to be a bit ditzy and annoying – no need to overdo it! It's a useful plot that lets George consider babies without Nina being involved – he's always wanted a family and this would give him a child while keeping it safely a step removed from the wolf and so it seems the perfect solution. Mitchell and Annie are less than sure and George's annoyance with them is done beautifully – it feels just as Russell Tovey would play it.

There is a very touching section where George and Mitchell discuss the prospect of children – it's spiky and caring and exactly catches the relationship between them. Mitchell is concerned that there may be a genetic component to George's lycanthropy, but George tells him how he just wants to be normal and that to have a child is as normal as can be – and is his own form of immortality.

Mitchell meanwhile is spending time with Leo, a patient at the hospital, and they bond over 80s music. But why is Leo quite so keen to spend time with Mitchell? And why can he see Annie? Leo has secrets too and there is way more to him than you will guess. And just what are all those bruises…

Annie doesn't get a great deal to do in this book, but she gets a night out with Mitchell and Leo. She also saves Mitchell from himself (again – no change there then) with the neat assistance of Google Streetview.

Chasers also introduces us to some new vampires. They are mostly pale, drifting figures with little to distinguish them, but watch out for Olive King. Sleek, sexy and sarcastic – might this be the new Herrick? What does she have to tell Mitchell about Leo? She seems to know all about him.

George eventually, regretfully, declines the date with the turkey baster; it just isn't the right thing to do. Gail and Kaz have also decided they are not ready, well Gail has. Kaz is being distracted rather neatly by Moonpaw, an elderly hippy but much sharper than she looks! We'll see more of Moonpaw…

Book three – *Bad Blood* by James Goss

One of Annie's oldest friends has come looking for her – and what's more amazing is that she's found her. Denise is the ultimate party girl, and she's determined to bring Annie out of her shell. Mitchell is delighted, but George thinks the last thing they need is to go out and meet new people.

Annie's old friend Denise turns up at the house, looking for her and Owen. She's been away, she's a holiday rep and doesn't know that Owen is mad and that Annie died or more exactly that Owen killed her – the only explanation is that they must have split up. Oddly she can see Annie and hug her and Annie hasn't the heart to tell her the truth.

Having been spun a line about Owen leaving her and Annie retreating into the house to recover, Denise decides that she needs bringing out of her shell. It's a process that involves her taking them all out drinking. A lot. To the point that even Mitchell's legendary vampire alcohol tolerance is reduced and Denise's very presence seems to render him tipsy.

There is something very odd going on all around. It's not just Mitchell that can sense something in the air. There are vampires everywhere, absolutely everywhere – and to them the very air smells like heaven. There is even a lovable pair of old age pensioner vampires with a few wild animal snacks in their shopping bag on wheels. (Lovable pensioner vamps? I need to get out more!)

One very different aspect from the other books is a series of internal monologues from the characters about a variety of questions, like age, holidays and death. A brave move when writing for characters created by someone else – and it works beautifully. There are also lots of messages slipped into the text for Annie. The men with sticks and ropes are reminding her that they are still there. They are still waiting for her and they'll get her. Soon. Don't miss the demonic bingo calling...

Denise's plans for Annie involve a bingo night in a local hall run by Moonpaw and her pal Rainbow. Now Moonpaw can see Annie although Rainbow can't – just what is going on there? There has to be some connection. Annie flings herself body and soul (or spirit and soul) into the organisation – doing the cooking and decorating the hall. It seems as though Denise's plan might work – she even has Mitchell distributing flyers.

But Denise has another reason for being in Bristol – she wasn't just there to see Annie. She is attending the hospital, where her physician is none other than Doctor McGough. Just what is this mysterious and ancient virus she has contracted and why is he the very best person in the world to treat her? Could there be a connection between Denise arriving and the vampires appearing? And how does this link with Leo?

The bingo night ends in disaster as the vampires gather. Something is calling them and they will not be thwarted. They have a new leader – well, she thinks she is anyway. Not the sleek Olive but the hospital's HR Manager Janice. She's finding that change management course really useful in helping her in the transition to the undead, although the lack of PowerPoint is holding her back.

Somewhere between Denise and Leo and Doctor McGough, the stage is set out ready for another tale. *Bad Blood* ends with a woman knocking at the door of the house. There's no one in and she walks away...

Storytime

If you're a fan of the series (and if you're not why would you read the books?) it is very easy to slip into Mitchell, George and Annie's world. We already know what the house looks like, how they speak and how they dress, and it all helps plunge us straight into the stories.

There are some nice references to the TV shows, and places where I went "Oh yeah! That's just how it is!" In *The Road*, the piles of old board games that litter the house are mentioned and we find out that some are new but most are second hand and bought as they made Mitchell smile. They include the classic 'Ghost Castle' from MB Games and 'The Vampire Game' from Waddington! There are jigsaws too but all with a couple of bits missing.

There's a nice section in *The Road* where Annie and Mitchell go to the shop and are laughing and bantering together. Mitchell can't understand why the shopkeeper assumes he is drunk. He has completely forgotten that Annie is invisible and he must have looked like a loon talking and laughing to himself!

Mitchell's photo ID is explained – Herrick had a useful sideline in look-a-likes, a very important tool for non-photogenic vampires in this ID-driven age. Mitchell has to keep his hair and stubble just like his photo and needs Annie's help to do so. This just emphasises the inconvenience of life without a reflection – and explains a lot about some of Mitchell's outfits!

In *Chasers*, George's drink is spiked and his resulting manic loved-up behaviour is perfectly in character. The idea of George being made to sit down but still dancing from the waist up while doing ridiculous arms did make me smile.

As did the whole idea of George at the doctors trying to ask about the genetic implications of being a werewolf via the medium of a nonexistent Welsh great-grandmother called Bertha who had 'mood swings'.

Mitchell is obsessed with old black-and-white films and there are the occasional times when he forgets that he is rather older than the 20-something he appears. It's a new view of Mitchell to be able to see this internal self-editing.

The idea that Annie can jump to places she's seen on Google Streetview is wonderful! Wouldn't we all like to be able to do that...?

In *Bad Blood*, the descriptions that Denise comes up with for George and Mitchell are just spot on. Mitchell is "a proper 'meet you in the bar on the first night, bang you senseless and then smirk at you as he neatly avoids you for the rest of the holiday' bastard." Maybe a touch unfair but I do know exactly what she means! George, in contrast, very much in contrast, is "nervous, very nervous – and the panic suits him. He's got a face made for worrying." Admittedly George is fending off the vampire hoards at this point with his bum wedged against the letterbox, but she's caught him perfectly.

Niggles and Quibbles

Although the books are enjoyable and an easy read, they don't have the multilayered depth of the series. This is probably as they appear to be aimed at a younger market. They are occasionally a touch hit-and-miss in catching the 'voices' of the characters we know and love, but not often. On the whole, it's easy to hear the familiar voices in your head as you read.

If you are a proper *Being Human* addict there are a few glaring inconsistencies.

In *The Road* Annie has bare feet and in *Bad Blood* she is wearing pyjamas, when we know she is stuck in her grey leggings ensemble with Ugg boots. In the books, Mitchell is a porter or orderly (the same as George) but in the series he is a cleaner. Mitchell is surviving on donated blood stolen from the hospital – this is something he doesn't do in the series, telling Lauren that it won't work and the only way to stop is to go completely clean.

We never get George on a full moon which is real shame and leaves his stories feeling rather lacking. It may be that as series two was very bound up in the cycle of change for George – and for the Facility – that using it in the books as well would have felt out of kilter. They also seem to take place in quite a short space of time.

Quibbles aside, the books are an entertaining read. Sharply plotted, they rattle on at a good pace – I read each one in a single sitting! They are also different enough in style to each other to feel distinct while keeping the overall 'feel' of the series. There is a book each for the main trio, but Mitchell's story always seems to be the strongest and his character is at the centre of events throughout – rather as it is in the house. It makes a change to see him rendered, well not helpless but certainly rather silly in *Bad Blood* – an amusing contrast to his usual strong, calm, centred presence.

I hope there are more to come – there are certainly enough loose ends left to be tied up. What happened to the blood samples and Doctor McGough's research? Who was knocking at the door at the end of *Bad Blood*? What about Gavin's investigations into the altered hospital records to cover up an unusually high rate of suspicious deaths? And just who did join Mossy's bowling team in the end?

I suppose the main difficulty with the books is placing them within the timeline of the TV series without having to replicate what happens on screen. Although I'm sure that could be managed. Of course there are always flashbacks, stories from the past – there you go, endless plots and opportunities!

I'd be curious about how the books would work for someone who hasn't seen the TV shows, but even then I think they would hold up well. After all, they have some very good characters to build on.

11

the BBC
being human
blog

The BBC *Being Human* website is the best performing BBC Three website and was launched alongside series one of *Being Human*. The BBC Press Office said at the time:

> "A *Being Human* blog will update regularly before and during transmission of the drama for fans to engage with the mythology, story and characters.
>
> "In addition, exclusive online-only prequel films will tell the story of how each of the characters came to be.
>
> "The blog will be written by those closest to the show and fans will be able to talk to them through it. There will also be regular exclusive video packages posted, which will let fans into some of the secrets and challenges faced by the *Being Human* team."

Between December 2008 and September 2010, the BBC *Being Human* blog posted 173 items ranging from deleted and extended scenes to Russell Tovey's very own George Sands action figure to video diaries by the cast and Q&A interviews with Toby Whithouse. It proved an essential means of keeping in touch with the show, finding out about the way it was put together and whiling away the long months between series. During series two, the blog announced that for each episode there would be the opportunity to comment online during the showing of each episode. The 'As it happens' post for Episode Two garnered 468 comments and the final episode 579. Given the number of people who were also watching and commenting on Twitter and other forums, that is pretty impressive!

I'll look at just a few of the highlights – especially at the character prequels and CenSSA (The Centre for the Study of Supernatural Activity) – and pick out a few other favourite bits. I find it all fascinating and love to hear how the show came together, and if you haven't seen the blog it is well worth a visit – put aside quite some time though, there's a lot to see...

The Actors

There are lots of interviews with the main actors as well as with several of the guest stars. During and just after series one was being broadcast on BBC Three (February – March 2009), there were video diaries posted on the blog made by Lenora, Russell and Aidan about their time filming, as well as interviews where they each answered questions submitted by readers of the blog. Aidan did his interview while filming *Desperate Romantics* and is seen complete with hair extensions and in Rossetti's costume!

It is always fascinating to hear an actor's take on the character they are playing but one message comes through loud and clear from almost everyone – it's the writing that makes *Being Human* what it is and makes their job just that bit easier and more satisfying.

Particularly worth a look are the interviews with Alex Price (June 2009) who played Gilbert in series one, and Paul Rhys (February 2010) who played Ivan in series two. Both have clearly thought deeply about their characters and in a very short time give a lot of depth and background.

It's a huge shame that there are not similar interviews with Amy Manson (Daisy), Lyndsey Marshal (Lucy) and Donald Sumpter (Kemp) – but then, you can't have everything...

Behind the scenes

There's a huge variety of behind-the-scenes footage and information on production details. If you want to see some of the stunts and how they were put together look for Bernie and Mitchell's car crash and Annie's death at the foot of the stairs (both posted in February 2009) and the series two explosion in the funeral parlour (February 2010). There are behind-the-scenes looks at makeup and costume, how the werewolf transformations are done, storyboards, original and unseen scripts and film of the read-throughs. There are even step-by-step instructions on how to make a *Being Human* Halloween pumpkin!

Deleted and Extended Scenes and Director's Commentary

There are a series of scenes from series one posted in July 2009 with commentary by the directors – yet another insight into the workings of the show and some of the thought processes behind it. There are also some deleted and extended scenes, all posted in March 2010, including a remake – word for word, gesture for gesture – of the scene from the pilot when George and Mitchell first find Annie in the house, but with Lenora and Aidan instead of Andrea Riseborough and Guy Flanagan.

The Prequels

Before the start of series one, three prequels introducing the characters were posted on the blog, also usefully showing us the new faces of Annie and Mitchell. There was another prequel for series two, introducing Daisy and Ivan.

George

George's prequel takes us to Scotland in the company of a VERY annoying American tourist, Andy, who is filming every scrap of scenery and every blade of grass. George is off out for a walk and reluctantly he lets Andy tag along, although in all fairness he didn't get much choice in the matter. Of course they get lost just as it is getting dark. The full moon rises and they find a butchered – or rather a savaged – sheep. Its exposed innards are filmed in every detail, despite Andy having to pause for a quick vomit. Give him his due, he didn't miss a drop!

There's the sound of a wolf howling. A wolf? In Scotland? Surely not. Nevertheless there's some running and some whimpering and then, finally, the very bright idea of phoning for help. Not to mention a quick row about whether the light on the camera or George shrieking like a baby is more likely to attract the 'something out there'.

More howling – now much, much closer and some more running and then George realises he knows where they are! Such a relief – they're OK. But suddenly the howling is really close and Andy drops the camera as they run. The howling gets closer and louder and now there is screaming as well.

Someone picks up the camera. The rescue team are here and they use the light on the camera to see what they are dealing with. Andy is on the ground, ripped apart, a mess of blood and entrails, and as they keep looking they find George is beside him. He's on the ground, still conscious but bleeding from his shoulder.

"It got me."

Mitchell

London 1964, and Mitchell and Herrick are in Mitchell's shiny new Volvo as 'She's Not There' by The Zombies plays.

Herrick is in the back of the car with Shirley while Mitchell drives, looking detached, hair slicked back, avoiding getting involved. Shirley is cheerfully flirting but Mitchell really doesn't want to play. Herrick apologises for him, normally he's very keen and it was him that fancied Shirley when they saw her in the pub.

Herrick makes his excuses and leaves Mitchell to start without him, and Shirley coaxes him until his eyes are black. He clears his head with an effort and reluctantly gets in the back seat with her. He really doesn't want to do this and somehow he has to put her off. He comments that she's small. He doesn't really like small women, but "afterwards they fit in the boot of the car." She's getting worried now – Herrick was all easy charm, but Mitchell's dark menace is something else. Didn't her mother warn her about strange men? He tells her exactly what is in store – they will kill her and drink her blood and his eyes go black. He's revolted by the need to drink, especially as he knows that so many do not even fight, and he pushes her away. She takes her chance and runs.

Herrick returns and notices that Shirley has escaped. Nothing gets past Herrick. Mitchell's claim that he tried to drink but she fought and got away doesn't really seem all that believable and Herrick knows that there is something wrong. He's concerned about Mitchell – why didn't he do what he was supposed to? Why wouldn't he kill? From now on he will have to keep him close, be attentive to his every need. Mitchell seems to be trying to distance himself from Herrick and that just won't do.

"From now on I'm going to keep a very close eye on you."

Annie

This prequel focuses on a couple, Lucy and Mal. They've just moved into their new house – which looks strangely familiar. Mal thinks it's haunted and is keen to capture the ghost on film. He spots the cracked tile at the bottom of the stairs, he is fascinated by it, and he thinks it must be where the last owner died. Lucy is less understanding and isn't keen on the constant filming; she's more concerned that the house is absolutely freezing and some of her things have disappeared.

Right on cue odd things start to happen, initially to Mal's excitement but then it all starts to get a bit too real. The chairs piled up in an artistic heap and the crashing and banging – well that's all OK I suppose, but the ghostly figure he hears crying in the night is a step too far. And who is the girl in grey he sees crossing the landing at night, going downstairs – was it her that wrote 'GET OUT' on their wall?

It all gets too much for them. Mal is determined not to be intimidated (he's paid a deposit) although he's shaking like a leaf, but the sound of Lucy sobbing is the last straw. Or was that last straw the glimpse he got of Annie in the mirror? It's only a fleeting glance but it's a vision of someone who just isn't there.

They've had enough and they move out. Annie has the house to herself again and she's pleased. We see her smiling as she watches them leave from the empty rooms. But now she's alone again, just waiting and watching, wondering who will move in next?

"Happy now?"

Ivan and Daisy

Singapore, and a young woman in a short tight dress has her feet propped up on a bar. She is talking to the barman about family although he isn't hearing the words. Someone she should forget about, someone who may even be dead by now, but who she thinks of every Mother's Day. The barman follows her high heels and long bare legs, her unspoken invitation, to the Ladies and he runs his hands over her body. He's not the best judge of character, she acknowledges, as she knocks him senseless with one neat, effortless blow.

Her eyes go black and her fangs are bared – a vampire – but she's distracted by a voice from the bar. It's a little girl, maybe seven or eight in an old-fashioned school uniform, followed by an elegantly languid, sharp-suited man.

Ivan introduces Daisy to Hettie – the little girl is actually one of the old ones: "462 and still got my own fangs." Daisy in contrast is a newbie, having only become a vampire about 69 years ago and she almost curtseys to Hettie.

They talk about Bristol. Hettie is going to Bolivia where most of the old ones are; since Herrick was killed, Bristol is far too messy for her. She knows about Mitchell being clean and that the werewolf that killed Herrick lives with him and a ghost. Daisy is excited, she really wants to see this werewolf – she's imagining rippling muscles and teeth and sweat. Ivan intended to go to Cambodia but you just know that he'll always let Daisy have her way. She wants to add the werewolf to her collection and Ivan is intrigued...

These immortal vampires declare their love, they call each other by their pet names – Pooh and Piglet – and then Ivan kneels to drink the barman's blood as Daisy watches devotedly, listening to the screams.

"I have such a good feeling about this trip. I think great things are going to happen."

The prequels are a useful addition to our knowledge about the main characters. From the pilot we already know how George became a werewolf, so this is added detail and a touch reminiscent of *An American Werewolf in London* although not set on the Yorkshire moors, or with two Americans, or... enough!

Annie's tale, however, is less straightforward. It is easy to forget that smiling sunny Annie haunted all the past tenants out of her house. Seeing her in series one and two, cheerfully making tea and coffee... and more tea and coffee... it is hard to reconcile the Annie we know with the terrifying presence in the prequel. A combination of loneliness and confusion gives the haunting of Mal and Lucy a real sense of cold terror and it is all the more effective that we hardly see Annie at all.

Mitchell's prequel links better to series two – especially with the flashback to 1969, five years after the prequel was set. It seems that he got disillusioned by the vampire world long before he met Josie. Although we must remind ourselves that five years to a vampire is just the blink of an eye. Herrick could already see the writing on the wall and was keen to keep Mitchell close. He can sense his disillusionment but Herrick needs Mitchell and in his own weird way he loves him.

By the way, I think we all know about the dangers of talking to strange men, but – well, what would you do?!

It must have been hard to choose who to feature for series two – well, actually maybe it was easier that it seems on first glance. Toby Whithouse told the blog in November 2009: "We considered doing prequels to introduce Mr Kemp (who you saw at the very end of series 1) and the mysterious Professor Jaggat – but there wasn't really a way to introduce them in the prequels without giving away all the juicy stuff we were gradually unpacking in the series proper."

There would have been logic in showing Lucy or Kemp's past, but to do that so early would have spoiled the reveals of both Professor Jaggat and of the fate of Kemp's family. In any case, the pre-title flashbacks of series two covered Kemp's past without using a prequel, although there is still much about Lucy we can only guess at.

Ivan and Daisy are captured very neatly in just five minutes – we see Daisy as impetuous and rapacious, tempered with the musings on her lost family. Ivan – immortal and amoral – but uxoriously besotted with his wife. Despite the devouring of the barman, the Pooh Bear/Piglet stuff was all a touch 'Valentine's Day in *The Guardian* personals' – extraordinarily odd but somehow in keeping.

And Hettie – we really should see more of Hettie! Is this the same actress who plays Molly? They look and sound very alike and that was a very clever way to get us all thinking that little Molly could not possibly be just an innocent little girl. It turned out in the end that she was exactly that – a little girl – but the world of a child vampire could bear some exploration.

The Centre for the Study of Supernatural Activity

Before series two, the blog introduced us to CenSSA – the Centre for the Study of Supernatural Activity – and founder (and possibly sole member) Lloyd, a technician researching into vampires, werewolves and ghosts. There were videos and a website teasing us with what was to come in series two, and five CenSSA updates were posted on the blog before the series started. Once the series was underway, we discovered that Lloyd was actually working with Professor Jaggat and Kemp, and he used his own films to try and justify what they were doing. It was a very successful addition to the blog and a whole new dimension to the story.

The videos are all hidden on the DVD of series two along with a tour of the Facility by Lloyd himself. If you haven't found them yet just leave the main menu for disc one on screen long enough and you will! Take a good look at the image of the house behind the menu while you are waiting – I'll come back to it in a couple of pages...

The story of CenSSA

Initially Lloyd seems eccentric and enthusiastic but rather harmless. He has *evidence* – film of a vampire, or where a vampire might be, and he even thinks he's identified the (in)famous Highgate Vampire! Could it be Mitchell? After all, he was in London in 1969 with Josie and maybe he was existing on the blood of local wild animals rather than the local party girls. Lloyd has also managed to track down Lauren and her two best friends – all vampires.

This is all getting a bit close to home...

Lloyd keeps digging and manages to link Lauren to George and Mitchell through the hospital and then discover where they live – in a haunted house. Everyone else has been scared away, so why have George and Mitchell stayed? What is so different about them? Maybe an insurance claim might give us a clue; it is dated the night after a full moon. Some lovely detail here – among the items claimed for are 46 vintage LPs, a 1972 replica Laurel and Hardy collector's edition statue and a sideboard with wood-effect plastic finish. Lloyd knows what he's found – George and Mitchell are werewolves.

But he was wrong – Lloyd did some surveillance and his photos have proved it. Mitchell is a vampire; his image did not appear on the photos. He needs to know more, he needs to go back and keep watching, but tomorrow night is the experiment... What can he possibly mean? He does manage to do some surveillance of the house, but it doesn't quite go to plan when someone taps on his car window and sends him into total, gibbering panic!

The next broadcast from CenSSA is after we've seen the chamber and Galvin and the blood... Lloyd doesn't look so harmless now. He's trying to convince us (and himself) that they are doing good work. He is a scientist, after all, and he is working from the inside to try and help. They have never tried to cure a werewolf before, he claims, and it was a horrible mistake. There is clearly more to Lloyd than he is letting on...

CenSSA is helping Nina and they are going to cure her – Lloyd seems completely convinced despite the death of Galvin. They will look after her. Lloyd is still playing the innocent – nothing is his fault – but the mask is slipping. He now admits that a couple of werewolves have died rather than just the one mistake that was Galvin, and the anger is directed at us for doubting his wonderful, pure intentions! Evolution has a cost, he tells us, and somehow that makes me think of Herrick...

Lloyd does let us into some interesting background information on Lucy and Kemp, possibly as a way of avoiding telling us exactly what he is up to.

Patrick Kemp came from a Northern Irish Protestant family, his father an old-fashioned 'fire and brimstone' vicar. He has a shocking, dark secret in his past. He – in time – became a Catholic priest and specialised in exorcism, had an 'interest' in the supernatural. He scares Lloyd...

Lucy Jaggat – super intelligent, a proper boffin with a huge scientific future ahead of her. She had a serious car accident, and when emerging from her coma she had a vision and suddenly all her abilities were focused on her religious awakening. She is doing God's work. She started writing about a gene, the source of all human evil and was soundly ridiculed – except by Kemp. But why is Lloyd there with these kooks, as he calls them? He can't help wondering if they might be right, although there is rather a sense of hedging of bets.

After the explosion at the funeral parlour, Lloyd is explaining his actions to his followers yet again. A pattern is emerging. He seems increasingly drawn in with Kemp and maybe, just maybe, he admits, he did want to destroy the vampires, the evil. Maybe it was the right thing to do.

Lloyd has got reports of the attack on the train and he is worried – actually he's scared, really scared. It looks like the work of vampires, type ones, but if there are survivors of the bomb out there then they will be coming for Kemp. And if they come for Kemp then they'll come for him too. He needs to speed things up; he can't risk a vampire getting to him.

There's one last pre-recorded CenSSA film from Lloyd, prepared 'just in case' and it means he is probably dead. He finally seems contrite. He thought he was doing the right thing but maybe he was wrong. Maybe the supernatural cannot be controlled as they thought. He admits he lied, Galvin was the fourth werewolf they killed, that he killed. He really believed he did what he did for the best, but he wasn't brave enough in the end.

So did Lloyd die? We may never know... but I'd like to think that Amy MacBride took revenge for the werewolves and that they can now rest easy. Although what if someone has got hold of Lloyd's files of evidence about the supernatural? Especially the facts about *our* supernaturals...

The hints in the photograph...

There are photos in the Gallery section of the BBC *Being Human* pages with George, Mitchell and Annie stood in the house and there are lots of clues to their secret lives in the room behind them. These are very similar to the background picture to the main menu of the series two DVDs.

So how many clues did you spot? This is what I can see and I don't doubt there are a lot more that I've missed!

If you are looking at the photos with the actors in place, then check out...

- Annie's ghostly aura
- Mitchell's blood bag
- George's ripped shirt

In the room, you can see...

- The paper lampshade in the centre of the room is the full moon
- A sheepskin – or a savaged (toy) sheep on the floor
- An urn
- A toy *Ghostbusters* car on the mantelpiece
- A Ouija board
- A tombstone in the goldfish bowl and the shadow it casts on the floor (is it Trevor's bowl and Lucy's plans ...?)
- A string of garlic
- Funeral lilies
- A raven, or maybe it's a crow (as in a murder of crows?)
- On the coat stand is Michael Jackson's red jacket from the 'Thriller' video, and Dracula's cloak

Also available from Classic TV Press...

DOCTOR WHO: THE PANDORICA OPENS

Exploring the worlds of the Eleventh Doctor

Frank Collins

"I remember you! I brought the others back, I can bring you back too! I remember you, Raggedy Man, and you are late for my wedding!"

Amy Pond, *The Big Bang*

Since its revival in 2005, *Doctor Who* has been transformed from cult franchise into an award-winning, multi-platform, flagship BBC One drama watched by millions each week. In 2010, the regeneration of Tenth Doctor David Tennant into Eleventh Doctor Matt Smith saw the keys to the *Doctor Who* kingdom handed over from Russell T. Davies to new showrunner Steven Moffat. His first series was a highly anticipated moment of change in the production regime of this long-running show.

Cult television and film blogger Frank Collins has significantly expanded upon the original reviews from his popular *Cathode Ray Tube* website to examine this latest series of adventures. He provides an in-depth analysis of episodes, characters, themes and ideas, and places *Doctor Who* within the wider cultural context of contemporary social, political, historical and psychological debates. A unique view of a television icon, providing much food for thought, this book is essential reading for fans of the new series.

This book is illustrated with many exclusive behind-the-scenes production shots and includes a colour plates section.

Format: Paperback (280 pages approx.)
Published: December 2010
Recommended Retail Price: £14.99

Available from Classic TV Press at a discounted price of £12.49 (plus P&P)
www.classictvpress.co.uk

THE COMPLETE SECRET ARMY
the unofficial and unauthorised guide to the classic TV series
Andy Priestner

This comprehensive book, an essential read for any fan of the series, seeks to uncover how *Secret Army* was conceived and details its journey to our television screens. Each episode is reviewed in depth and accompanied by information on the actual historical events which inspired the series's gripping storylines. The book also includes many exclusive behind-the-scenes and location photos, cast and crew interview material, a comprehensive section on spin-off series *Kessler*, and much, much more.

"You need to see *Secret Army* and you need to read this book." Gareth Roberts, writer - *Doctor Who*

Format: Paperback (672 pages)
Published: December 2008
Recommended Retail Price: £30.00

Available from Classic TV Press at a discounted price of £22.50 (plus P&P)

WORLDS APART
the unofficial and unauthorised guide to the BBC's remake of Survivors
Rich Cross

An examination of Adrian Hodges's re-imagining of Terry Nation's cult drama series *Survivors*, exploring its plots, themes and characters. As well as a detailed look at the making of the new series, Cross reviews the episodes in depth, recounts previous attempts to revive *Survivors* and describes the similarities and differences between the new *Survivors* and the original series. The book also includes cast and crew interview material, plus many exclusive behind-the-scenes and location photos.

Format: Paperback (310 pages)
Published: April 2010
Recommended Retail Price: £14.99

Available from Classic TV Press at a discounted price of £12.99 (plus P&P)

About the author

Joanne Black lives near Cambridge in an extraordinarily untidy house with a well-trained herd of shoes. An unashamed TV addict, if she isn't to be found on the sofa then she may be making jewellery or scribbling (and occasionally she may even be at her proper job...).

She never entirely grew out of punk and has promised to stop wearing black as soon as someone invents a darker colour.

This is her first book but she rambles randomly on her blog *Not Just About Shoes...* at http://aquamarinejo.wordpress.com/

About the illustrator

Chris is a freelance illustrator, storyboard artist and designer based in London. He has over ten years of commercial experience in broadcast media, film, advertising, music and stage. Website: www.chriswreford.co.uk